G000097773

The Melton Centre for Jewish Education at the Hebrew University

THE MELTON CENTRE is a centre of learning open to the rich diversity of contemporary Jewish life. Situated in Jerusalem, the heart of the Jewish world, the Melton Centre aspires to create a supportive community where education professionals from both Israel and the diaspora can grow and work together. The Centre makes full use of the unique resources of Jewish scholarship that the Hebrew University offers, with over a hundred faculty members specializing in fields covering the entire spectrum of Jewish culture, from ancient literary texts, through medieval Jewish poetry, to Yiddish, the cinema, and the fine arts.

The Melton Centre is the largest academic centre in the world engaged in teaching and research in the field of Jewish education. The Centre also has a long record of service in the field of Jewish education in many different countries; this includes projects in curriculum development and adult education, as well as consultations on institutional philosophies and vision. The Centre is involved in three major arenas of activity: *academic*—MA and Ph.D. programmes, annual international research conferences, and a range of academic publications; *professional development*—short- and long-term programmes for senior educational personnel the world over; and *educational projects in the field*—including curricular development programmes, in-service training programmes, adult education, and computer-supported collaborative learning.

THE LITTMAN LIBRARY OF
JEWISH CIVILIZATION

Dedicated to the memory of
LOUIS THOMAS SIDNEY LITTMAN
*who founded the Littman Library for the love of God
and as an act of charity in memory of his father*
JOSEPH AARON LITTMAN
יהא זכרם ברוך

*Get wisdom, get understanding:
Forsake her not and she shall preserve thee*
PROV. 4:5

*The Littman Library of Jewish Civilization is a registered UK charity
Registered charity no.* 1000784

Jewish Day Schools
Jewish Communities

A Reconsideration

EDITED BY

ALEX POMSON AND **HOWARD DEITCHER**

Oxford · Portland, Oregon
The Littman Library of Jewish Civilization
2009

The Littman Library of Jewish Civilization

Chief Executive Officer: Ludo Craddock
Managing Editor: Connie Webber

PO Box 645, Oxford OX2 0UJ, UK
www.littman.co.uk

———

Published in the United States and Canada by
The Littman Library of Jewish Civilization
c/o ISBS, 920 NE 58th Avenue, Suite 300
Portland, Oregon 97213-3786

A catalogue record for this book is available from the British Library

Library of Congress cataloging-in-publication data

Jewish day schools, Jewish communities : a reconsideration /
edited by Alex Pomson and Howard Deitcher
p. cm.
Includes bibliographical references and index.
1. Jewish day schools—Cross-cultural studies.
2. Jews—Education—Cross-cultural studies.
3. Community and school—Cross-cultural studies.
I. Pomson , Alex.   II. Deitcher, Howard, 1955–
LC723.J49 2008
371.076—dc22   2008033449

ISBN 978–1–904113–74–4

Publishing co-ordinator: Janet Moth
Copy-editing: Gillian Somerscales
Proof-reading: Mark Newby
Index: Sarah Ereira
Production: John Saunders
Designed and typeset by Pete Russell, Faringdon, Oxon.
Printed in Great Britain on acid-free paper by
the MPG Books Group

In memory of

DAVID POMSON
דוד שמואל בן יצחק
an advocate for Jewish education
and Jewish community in equal
unselfish measure

Publication of this book has been
facilitated by a donation in memory of

ESTHER ROSA WILSACK
(1913–1967)

Esther Wilsack dedicated her life to Jewish education in London. She was headmistress of the Yesodey Hatorah School during the Second World War and of the Mathilda Marks-Kennedy School at Barclay House from 1962 till her sudden death in 1967 at the age of 53.

In a career that spanned thirty years she also taught at the Norwood Jewish Orphanage, the Solomon Wolfson School, the Menorah Primary School, and the North West London Jewish Day School, and was the much-loved matron of the Menorah Kindergarten. Many also remember her as the organizer, from 1954 to 1966, of the Happy Holiday Camp for Jewish children, principally at Hastings on the English south coast, and for playing the violin.

A gifted and inspiring educator, she touched the lives of several thousand children and their parents.

Acknowledgements

All books tell a story; even works of non-fiction. This book's story begins with our shared interest in Jewish day school education. We both graduated from Jewish day schools, of different varieties and in different parts of the British Commonwealth. We both taught in diaspora day schools; we even helped create some of those schools from scratch. Today, although our homes are in Israel, we continue to study and teach about such schools. Our experiences and our research lead us to believe that while the capacity of day schools to nurture Jewish identification and practice has been appropriately recognized and fostered, the community-building potential in schools, for students, their families, and their societies, has been both overlooked and underdeveloped.

Our convictions encouraged us to convene a conference in June 2006 at the Melton Centre for Jewish Education at the Hebrew University. The conference brought together an international coalition of sponsors and researchers interested in exploring the relationships between Jewish community and Jewish schools. This volume is testament to the interest and support of those who made that conference possible: Asher Ostrin at the Joint Distribution Committee, Josh Elkin at the Partnership for Excellence in Jewish Education, and Ami Bouganim in the Education Department of the Jewish Agency for Israel, as well as numerous colleagues of theirs and also of ours at the Melton Centre.

That some of the outstanding papers from the conference came together in this volume is in large measure due to the special interest of Connie Webber at the Littman Library of Jewish Civilization. Connie has been a deeply interested interlocutor from the time of our first contact. Her positive influence on this volume's final shape is greater, we believe, than most authors have a right to expect.

The volume's contents have been prepared—actually improved—for publication by Vivienne Burstein, at the Melton Centre, and by the dedicated team at Littman, including Gillian Somerscales, Janet Moth, and Ludo Craddock. We thank them, recognizing that whatever is deficient here is of our own making, and what is worthy is the shared fruit of many contributors.

ALEX POMSON AND HOWARD DEITCHER
Jerusalem, Adar Rishon 5768 / February 2008

Contents

PART III
Insights through the Prism of Community

Note on Transliteration

The transliteration of Hebrew in this book reflects consideration of the type of book it is, in terms of its content, purpose, and readership. The system adopted therefore reflects a broad approach to transcription, rather than the narrower approaches found in the *Encyclopaedia Judaica* or other systems developed for text-based or linguistic studies. The aim has been to reflect the pronunciation prescribed for modern Hebrew, rather than the spelling or Hebrew word structure, and to do so using conventions that are generally familiar to the English-speaking reader.

In accordance with this approach, no attempt is made to indicate the distinctions between *alef* and *ayin*, *tet* and *taf*, *kaf* and *kuf*, *sin* and *samekh*, since these are not relevant to pronunciation; likewise, the *dagesh* is not indicated except where it affects pronunciation. Following the principle of using conventions familiar to the majority of readers, however, transcriptions that are well established have been retained even when they are not fully consistent with the transliteration system adopted. On similar grounds, the *tsadi* is rendered by 'tz' in such familiar words as barmitzvah. Likewise, the distinction between *ḥet* and *khaf* has been retained, using *ḥ* for the former and *kh* for the latter; the associated forms are generally familiar to readers, even if the distinction is not actually borne out in pronunciation, and for the same reason the final *heh* is indicated too. As in Hebrew, no capital letters are used, except that an initial capital has been retained in transliterating titles of published works (for example, *Shulḥan arukh*).

Since no distinction is made between *alef* and *ayin*, they are indicated by an apostrophe only in intervocalic positions where a failure to do so could lead an English-speaking reader to pronounce the vowel-cluster as a diphthong—as, for example, in *ha'ir*—or otherwise mispronounce the word.

The *sheva na* is indicated by an *e*—*perikat ol*, *reshut*—except, again, when established convention dictates otherwise.

The *yod* is represented by *i* when it occurs as a vowel (*bereshit*), by *y* when it occurs as a consonant (*yesodot*), and by *yi* when it occurs as both (*yisra'el*).

Names have generally been left in their familiar forms, even when this is inconsistent with the overall system.

Jewish Schools, Jewish Communities

A Reconsideration

ALEX POMSON

The Raised Stakes of Day School Education

Towards the end of the first decade of the twenty-first century, more Jewish children attend all-day Jewish schools than at any other time in history. Nobody knows for sure, but it is likely that there are just over 1,400,000 Jewish children enrolled in Jewish day schools worldwide. The great majority of these children, three-quarters of them, are in Israel,[1] but in the diaspora too—the primary focus of this book—an unprecedented number of Jewish children attend Jewish day schools. In 2004 there were about 225,000 children in North American day schools, and approximately 125,000 more scattered across the globe in every continent other than Antarctica.[2] These numbers represented an increase of slightly under 120,000 students (or just over 50 per cent) since Sergio DellaPergola and Uziel Schmelz calculated worldwide day school enrolment as 232,000 in 1982–3.[3]

Growth has been evident not only in the number of children in diaspora Jewish schools but also in the religious diversity of the student population and its size in proportion to the number of Jewish children educated in non-Jewish private and public or state schools. For most of the twentieth century, the overwhelming majority of students served by all-day Jewish schools came from Orthodox homes; by the start of the twenty-first a significant

---

[1] State of Israel, Ministry of Education, *Internet vemeida ḥinukhi*.

[2] The enrolment numbers for diaspora schools are extrapolated from Schick, *A Census of Jewish Day Schools*; Pomson, 'Jewish Day School Growth'; Miller, 'Meeting the Challenge'; Cohen, *Heureux comme Juifs en France?*; and Chs. 6 and 9 in this volume by Gitelman and Goldstein.

[3] DellaPergola and Schmelz, 'Demography and Jewish Education in the Diaspora', 54. Few data sources provide a breakdown between elementary and high schools, but it is generally recognized that enrolment after bar or bat mitzvah (grades 6 and 7) is significantly lower than before that age.

proportion of the growth in enrolment consisted of non-Orthodox students.[4] The changing profile of day school enrolment prompted Walter Ackerman to refer to this development as one of the most remarkable social facts of Jewish life since the Second World War. It indicated, he argued, a veritable transformation 'in the image Jews have of themselves and of their relationship to the wider society'.[5]

A further change concerns the north–south balance. For most of the twentieth century the proportion of Jewish children attending Jewish day schools in the northern hemisphere lagged far behind the corresponding proportion in the southern hemisphere. In Australia, South Africa, and Latin America, more than 70 per cent of Jewish children attended Jewish day schools. In the northern hemisphere the level was everywhere below 50 per cent, barring only a handful of exceptional cases such as that of Montreal, where all public education was organized along religious denominational lines. For the most part—in the United States, the United Kingdom, and France, for example—fewer than a quarter of Jewish children attended all-day Jewish schools. At the start of the twenty-first century, the situation is much altered. While enrolment in the southern hemisphere has eroded by a few percentage points, in the northern hemisphere it has dramatically increased. In Britain, by 2007, a majority of all Jewish children aged 4 to 18 attended Jewish day schools, up from 20 per cent in 1975; in the United States more than a quarter of Jewish children attended day schools compared with 10 per cent in 1975; and in France close to 40 per cent attended day schools compared with 16 per cent in 1986.[6]

As enrolments in diaspora day schools have steadily increased in both number and proportion, Jewish educators and Jewish community professionals have started to think about these schools as places that serve a population more diverse and more numerous than that of the students who sit in their classrooms. They have started to pay attention to aspects of the larger social significance of day school growth. To express this development more succinctly: as the number of children enrolled in day schools has increased,

---

[4] The significance of this phenomenon is discussed in particular by Schick, *A Census of Jewish Day Schools*.   [5] Ackerman, 'Strangers to Tradition', 87.

[6] Enrolment percentages for 2007 are taken from Conference on the Future of the Jewish People, *Background Policy Documents*, 14–15. Data for earlier years come from sources cited in n. 2 above. The reasons for changes in day school enrolment have been much debated, and can be reviewed in Pomson, 'Jewish Day School Growth' and Miller, 'Meeting the Challenge'.

so there has been a growing appreciation that what is at stake in day school education is more than just what those children learn.[7]

This developing perception of the social significance of day school education is not driven solely by an increase in the number of day school students; it is also fuelled by three further forces, elements of which originate beyond the Jewish community, that have inspired a general reassessment of the role of schools in societies.

1. *The evolving role of schools.* For most of the last 150 years, and at least since the introduction of free compulsory education by modern nation-states in the nineteenth century, the primary function of schools was to prepare children for life as productive workers in a post-agricultural industrialized society.[8] Today, schools are asked to do much more. No longer the exclusive preserve of religious and economic elites, they are called on by governments to take up roles once performed by families, religious institutions, and workplaces. In recent times schools have been asked to instruct their pupils in, among other things, how to drink sensibly, eat healthily, vote conscientiously, and take a responsible attitude towards sex.

Jewish schools have not been free from this accumulating burden of social tasks. Jewish children were once expected to acquire knowledge of Judaism, develop attitudes about the Jewish world, and learn Jewish behaviours from people and places in their immediate surroundings—in the family, at the synagogue, even on the street.[9] Today, responsibility for the emotional, moral, and interpersonal development of Jewish children has been increasingly devolved to schools, and day school educators find themselves no less challenged by these changes than their peers in other school systems.[10] In one unexpected development, for example, Jewish day schools have become some of the major providers of informal Jewish education, a field once considered the preserve of youth movements and summer camps. Faculty trained to teach academic subjects in classroom

[7] Wertheimer (ed.), *Family Matters*; Berrin (ed.), *Ten Years of Believing.*

[8] Egan, 'The Role of Schools', 641–55.

[9] Marcus, *Rituals of Childhood*; Kanarfogel, *Jewish Education and Society*; Moore, 'The Construction of Community'.

[10] Evidence of this sense of challenge is seen in professional journals for Jewish teachers that discuss, for example, how to nurture spirituality in day schools (*Jewish Educational Leadership*, 5/2 (2007)); how to make the most of 'educational travel and student exchange' (*Hayediyon* (Passover 2006)); and how to respond to the demands of 'The Evolving Day School' (*Jewish Education News*, 24/ 2 (Spring 2003)).

settings are now asked to provide Jewish experiences such as religious holi-day celebrations, residential sabbath retreats, and trips to Israel that were once the responsibility of synagogues, families, or youth groups.

2. *Financial investment in day schools.* In recent years, private foundations have invested unprecedented sums in the creation and development of Jew-ish day schools. It is estimated that since 2001 'mega-gifts' totalling more than $105 million have been made by private foundations and families to Jewish day schools in the United States.[11] Substantial funding also comes from the Jewish community federations that exist in most large American cities for the provision of welfare and education to the local Jewish commu-nity. In Britain, a mix of private and public funding has underwritten the creation of more than twenty new schools in less than ten years. In eastern Europe and the former Soviet Union, in communities where it was once imagined that Jewish life had little future, tens of new schools have been launched over the past two decades, at the cost of hundreds of millions of dollars, provided for the most part by the Lauder Foundation and by donors affiliated with various hasidic groups.[12]

With so much money being invested in day schools, the benefactors who are providing it—whether private individuals, charitable foundations, or federated communities—are increasingly concerned to get greater returns on their investment, that is, to find out how day schools can serve as resources for the majority of Jewish families whose children still do not attend these institutions. The leaders of Jewish communities have also become more vocal about the profound 'opportunity costs' of investing in day schools: that is, the drain of resources away from other communal and educational institutions. To address these concerns, the advocates of day schools are looking for ways to develop the potential of these schools to serve a broader swathe of families than was once thought possible.

3. *A diversifying day school population.* For most of the twentieth century, until as recently as the 1980s, parents whose children attended day school were, typically, synagogue members and residents of Jewish neigh-bourhoods who had themselves received a relatively intensive Jewish

[11] Tigay, 'As Day Schools Rake in Mega-Gifts'.
[12] Lefkovits, 'Lauder Foundation Marks 20th Anniversary'. The Lauder Foundation provides details of the more than twenty schools launched with its support at <http://www.rslfoundation.org/html/ourwork/ourwork.htm>.

education.[13] With few exceptions, these parents were Jewish from birth, Orthodox in denominational orientation, and married to other Jews: people for whom paying for all-day Jewish schooling for their children constituted the ultimate expression of an already intensely engaged Jewish identity. Today, in many countries, Jewish day schools have successfully recruited increasing numbers of families with diverse religious commitments. Many of the newer families being drawn to these schools lack an intensive Jewish education of their own and depend on the schools to teach their families Jewish practices and ideas.[14] Advocates of day schools argue, meanwhile, that those who are still suspicious of schooling that is faith-based or parochial (in the sense of being affiliated to a religious denomination) will be recruited only if schools can develop new partnerships with a greater diversity of Jewish associations, networks, and social groups beyond their walls; that is, if they demonstrate their lack of parochialism. Both in dealing with an existing broader constituency and in attempting to attract one, there is an onus on the lay and professional leadership of schools to work out how to serve multiple (adult) communities and not just the students in their classrooms. For many parents of day school pupils today, Jewish education was something received after 'normal' school hours, a few afternoons a week, and was intended to do little more than prepare them for a bar or bat mitzvah ceremony, or to say the mourners' Kaddish and marry another Jew.[15]

*

These developments provided the context and motivation for an international conference held in June 2006 at the Melton Centre for Jewish Education at the Hebrew University, organized with the support of the Jewish Agency for Israel, the Joint Distribution Committee, and the Partnership for Excellence in Jewish Education.[16] This event was convened with the specific intention of encouraging researchers to think in new ways about the sociological functions of Jewish day schools.

---

[13] Ackerman, 'Strangers to Tradition'; Beinart, 'The Rise of the Jewish School', 21–3; Murphy, 'Longing to Deepen Identity'.   [14] Pomson and Schnoor, *Back to School*.

[15] For a rich but damning research portrait of the outcomes of after-school supplementary Jewish education, see Schoem, *Ethnic Survival in America*.

[16] For more on the Melton Centre, see <http://www.melton.huji.ac.il>; on the Jewish Agency, see <http://www.JAFI.org.il>; on the Joint Distribution Committee, see <http://www.JDC.org>; and on the Partnership for Excellence in Jewish Education, see <http://www.PEJE.org>.

Entitled 'Reframing Jewish Day School Education Worldwide: The School in the Community—the Community in the School', the conference set out to reframe day school research in three ways. First, by inviting keynote presentations from leading practitioners and researchers in state/public schooling, we sought to view day school education afresh in relation to insights derived from the study and practice of non-parochial education. Second, by bringing a truly international perspective to the study of day schools, we sought to understand schools in relation to the socio-cultural contexts from which they emerge and in which they have impact. Finally, by taking a focus wider than the learner—the child—in the day school classroom, we aimed to see schools as agents both *of* and *for* the community.

This volume presents some highlights from work shared at the conference, redrafted from oral presentations for the purposes of publication. Taken together, this work indicates that the time has come to think anew about the relationships between Jewish day schools, Jewish communities, and the wider contexts in which Jewish schools exist. Following Thomas Sergiovanni, *communities* are defined here as associations, webs, or networks of people 'socially organized around relationships and the felt interdependencies that nurture them'.[17] Two particular varieties or conceptions of community are at the heart of this volume: first, the community found *outside* schools, comprising the overlapping groups connected by place, religion, ethnicity, language, work, recreation, and kinship; and second, the community found *inside* schools and cultivated by them, as a quality of their environment, comprising teachers, students, and others who come together for shared purposes. In the remainder of this introduction I review the grounds for reconsidering the relationships between Jewish day schools and the communities that exist beyond their walls, and for reassessing the practices employed by schools to nurture the quality of community as part of the educational environment. I consider the empirical and educational implications of this conceptual reorientation; I propose future foci for research in the light of the findings presented here; and I explore how attention to the relationship between Jewish schools and Jewish community can bring coherence and clarity to discussion about the purposes of Jewish day school education worldwide.

[17] Sergiovanni, *Building Community in Schools*, 4.

Of course, a focus on the community dimensions of day school education consigns to the periphery important questions relating to the development of day schools themselves. Such questions, which have been richly explored elsewhere, include, for example: What are the distinctive goals and outcomes of day school education and how might these be extended or transformed?[18] What is the place of the different disciplines of Jewish studies in the day school curriculum, and what are the relationships of these disciplines to one another and to the general studies curriculum?[19] What particular pedagogical and professional qualities are demanded of those who head day schools and those who teach in them, and how and why are these qualities different from those required in other school settings?[20]

This volume concentrates attention on the relationship between schools and communities, first because of a sense that the implications for Jewish day schools of significant changes in the sociology of schooling in relation to community have not yet been considered, and second, as I show at the end of this introduction, because an examination of the role of community in Jewish day schools can bring into focus the fundamental educational and social purposes of day school education.

A Conventional View of Day Schools and Community: Integration or Isolation

The first modern all-day Jewish schools were opened under the influence of Jewish Enlightenment thinkers in the late eighteenth century, in Berlin and then in other German cities.[21] These schools differed from previously existing institutions for the provision of Jewish education in their delivery of a curriculum that included not just study of traditional Jewish texts but both Jewish and secular studies, and by their being open not just to the offspring of the wealthy or the learned but to all Jewish children. The intent of such schools was, in the words of Naphtali Herz Wessely, one of their earliest ideologues, to ensure that 'the Children of Israel will also be men who

[18] See e.g. Pekarsky, *Vision at Work*; Wertheimer, 'Who's Afraid of Jewish Day Schools?'; Marom, 'Before the Gates of the School'.
[19] See e.g. Margolis and Schoenberg, *Curriculum, Community, Commitment*; Zeldin, 'Integration and Interaction'; Malkus, 'The Curricular Symphony', 47–57.
[20] See e.g. Ingall, *Down the Up Staircase*; Goldring et al., *The Leaders Report*; Pomson, 'The Rebbe Reworked', 23–34.　　[21] Katz, *Out of the Ghetto*, 126–7.

accomplish worthy things, assisting the king's country in their actions, labour and wisdom'.[22]

The most fully realized institutional expression of this educational vision was seen at the end of the nineteenth century in England, where by 1899 the Jews' Free School (JFS), with more than 4,000 students, had become the largest school in Europe. According to one historian of the school, the aim of the JFS as conceived by its founders was 'to refashion the young by taking them off the streets and putting them in a modern Jewish school where they would learn artisan skills and English manners'.[23] The student body was almost entirely made up of the children of poor immigrants, and the school was widely admired for gathering 'within its walls . . . the children of those who are driven here by persecution, making of them good and desirable citizens of our beloved England'.[24] In the words of Louis Abrahams, headmaster at the start of the twentieth century, the school sought to 'wipe away all evidences of foreign birth and foreign proclivities, so that children shall be so identified with everything that is English in thought and deed, that no shadow of anti-Semitism might exist . . . [and] they may take a worthy part in the growth of this great Empire'.[25] This outcome—known by admirers and critics alike as 'Anglicization'—was forged, it was claimed, on a bedrock of Jewish religious values, but it is notable that rarely more than one hour a day was devoted to instruction in those values and their associated texts. The remaining five or six hours of daily instruction were devoted to a broad curriculum of general studies and to preparation for various artisan trades.[26]

When all-day Jewish schools were established in the United States in the years between the First and Second World Wars, following a short-lived experiment in day school education by Reform Jewish educators in the nineteenth century, they were animated by a different impulse.[27] While

[22] Wessely, 'Words of Peace and Truth', 74.   [23] Black, *JFS*, 33.
[24] Quoted by Black, *JFS*, 149, from an article in *The Sphere* in 1907 subtitled 'Where Russian Jews are Made into Good British Subjects'.   [25] Black, *The Social Politics of Anglo-Jewry*, 110–11.
[26] Not surprisingly, the extreme commitment to Anglicization at the JFS at the end of the nineteenth century prompted more traditionally minded Jewish immigrants to England to establish alternative institutions—ḥeders and Talmud Torah schools—in order to provide their children with a deeper basic training in Judaism. The JFS of the twenty-first century has also abandoned such an extreme integrationist orientation, although its curriculum continues to devote not much more than an hour a day to Judaic studies.
[27] On the Reform day schools of the nineteenth century, see Zeldin, 'The Promise of Historical Inquiry', 438–52.

Jewish immigrants widely regarded the nation's public schools as gate-ways to the opportunities promised by America, Jewish day schools were regarded by their founders as 'fortresses' or 'bulwarks' to protect Judaism from being overwhelmed in America. While public schools were, in the words of one Cincinnati leader, 'temples of liberty [where] children of the high and low, rich and poor, Protestants, Catholics and Jews mingle to-gether, play together and are taught that we are a free people',[28] day schools were seen as training grounds for the future leadership of the Jewish community; its priesthood, as Alexander Dushkin put it.[29] In the words of one prominent school leader writing at midcentury, these schools, with a curriculum that devoted at least the first half of every day to the study of traditional Jewish texts, provided 'the safest assurance for the continuation of Jewish life and the survival of Jewish culture'.[30] From the perspective of their critics, however, this undoubted promise of 'Jewish group survival' came at too high a price—what one opponent called 'the price of segrega-tion'. The establishment of day schools pointed towards 'narrow intellectual and social horizons, to a sect-divided society, and to an isolated Jewish group'.[31]

These two conceptions of the day school—one integrationist, the other isolationist (one designed to facilitate the integration of young Jews into non-Jewish society, the other intended to shield them from it)—although profoundly different from each other, nevertheless shared some common sociological assumptions. First, they viewed the world outside the school door as monolithic: the values and norms of that world were assumed to be uniform and consistent, and were to be either embraced or resisted. Sec-ond, the relationship of the school to that world was highly fragmented, even atomized: the school was seen as constituting a discrete or self-con-tained social entity that was to be either opened up to the world beyond or deliberately closed against it. From this perspective, schools were 'worlds apart', to adopt a term employed by Lawrence-Lightfoot in a related context.[32] They existed as enclaves whose members—their student mem-bers, at least—were assumed to come from communities whose customs

28 Lloyd Gartner, 'Temples of Liberty', 180, quoted in Sarna, 'American Jewish Education', 12.
29 Dushkin, 'Jewish Education in New York City', 15.
30 Lookstein, 'The Modern American Yeshivah', 12.
31 Grossman, 'Parochial Schools for Jewish Children', 24–5.
32 Lawrence-Lightfoot, *Worlds Apart*.

and habits differed from those of the larger society from which they needed to be protected or for participation in which they needed to be readied.

A New View of Day Schools and Community: Reciprocity and Multiplicity

Today, even in the Haredi (strictly Orthodox) world, Jewish day schools rarely serve such polarized ends.[33] Nor are they any longer located at an artificial remove from the communities beyond their doors. With Jews more or less integrated into most liberal democratic societies, Jewish day schools from Moscow and Manchester to Manhattan and Melbourne can promise aspiring graduates access to the best institutions of higher education, whether Ivy League colleges in the United States or the premier state universities in Russia. And schools can fulfil this promise without having to compromise (too much) on the grounding they give their students in Jewish culture and values. Today, moreover, even those Jewish schools that are independently constituted or privately funded (and are not public institutions) exist within a web of regulations and relationships that connect them to an array of communities, interest groups, and authorities.

Research into day school education has not kept pace with this changed world. Until now, and as indicated above, scholarship on day school education has focused on internal matters—on the integration or compartmentalization of the day school curriculum, on what it's like to teach or lead schools, and on their values and vision.[34] This volume, in probing the interrelationships between Jewish schools and Jewish communities, takes up both a less atomized and a less inward-looking view of day school education. In these respects, it reflects the ways in which day schools have changed; but also—and perhaps more profoundly—it reflects a broader change in the sociology of schooling.

Ellen Goldring, in Chapter 1 of this volume, depicts this change as a move towards a more reciprocal view of the relationships between schools and communities: a move from seeing the role of school leadership as that of 'bridge and buffer' between the school and the resources and forces beyond its walls to seeing it as that of building civic capacity inside and out-

---

[33] Krakowski has conducted pioneering work that reveals the interrelationships within the context of curriculum and school procedures between Haredi schools and the broader society. See his 'Isolation and Integration'.   [34] See nn. 18–20 above.

side the school, enhancing the quality of social, economic, and cultural life in school neighbourhoods. In these terms, school and community are not separate entities; their insides and outsides are not disconnected or distinct. Gail Furman, in a much-cited volume, *School as Community*, employs a different image to make a similar point. She depicts the emergence of a conceptual model which sees schools as 'inextricably embedded in the "microecology" of the local community [such that] . . . the relationship between school and community is so organically intertwined and reciprocal that it is specious to consider "school community" without also considering these linkages'.[35]

How the reciprocity identified by both Furman and Goldring takes shape in practice is richly portrayed in a number of the chapters that follow here: in Yoel Finkelman's examination of inspirational literature that depicts the relationships between strictly Orthodox parents and their children's schools; in Elana Maryles Sztokman's account of a religious Israeli girls' school that challenges a social order on whose ideological ground it is built; in Alex Pomson and Randal Schnoor's ethnography of parents' Jewish lives being changed by and changing their children's pluralistic day school; and in Yossi Goldstein's account of the evolving almost dialectical relationship between a school and a synagogue in Buenos Aires. These chapters reveal Jewish schools as arenas for the negotiation and determination of communal values and norms; as hubs of communal life. To use Furman's organic imagery, schools are integral to the ecology of collective Jewish life.

Even more explicitly, many chapters in this book make evident the diversity of the communities that interact and intersect with day schools. Conventionally, the predominant community context for parochial or denominational schools is assumed to be that of a sponsoring religious community; by definition, parochial schools 'belong or pertain' to the parish.[36] This is still the case. Most Jewish day schools in North America, Europe, and the former Soviet Union are sponsored—privately funded, governed, or guided—by a single denominational religious group or body (in many countries, for example, by one of several particular hasidic sects), by a collective of synagogues (such as England's Orthodox United Synagogue), or by a denominational movement (as in the case of the Conservative Solomon Schechter day schools in the United States). Yet even

---

[35] Furman, introduction to ead. (ed.), *School as Community*, 10.
[36] *The Shorter Oxford English Dictionary*.

denominational schools must interact with a bewildering array of communities inside and outside their 'parishes', as is evident from the chapters by Helena Miller (on the impact of government legislation), Scott Goldberg and colleagues (on the influence of communal behavioural norms), and Jay Dewey (on the intergenerational negotiation of authority within a school). Even more starkly, in those Jewish schools that are sponsored not by single denominations but by coalitions of community groups—variously called community, non-denominational, or pluralistic day schools—it sometimes seems as if there is no coherent guiding authority, so diverse are the communities inside and outside the schools that determine their policy and practice. This phenomenon emerges strongly in the chapters by Christine Müller (about student attitudes in the Berlin community school), by Eli Kohn (on curriculum development in a Montreal day school), and by Susan Shevitz and Rahel Wasserfall (on nurturing pluralism in an American community high school).

However originally conceived—whether as denominational or 'community' institutions—in practice Jewish day schools interact with a variety of communities and social forces located at varying proximity to their day-to-day operation. Even the most isolationist schools are far from being fortresses when it comes to their relationship with the external social context.

In the chapters that follow, these multiple social forces are depicted in different ways. Goldberg and his collaborators portray their operation by reference to Urie Bronfenbrenner's ecological systems theory, with its notion of the child embedded within 'nested contexts of influence'—family, neighbourhood(s), and society/societies. Goldring and Smrekar draw instead on sociological theory in attributing the existence of these forces to the multiple social structures and networks within which people live their lives. As Smrekar writes, her starting point is 'a concept [of community] grounded in social structures and social relations' rather than one 'associated with physical or geographical boundaries'.[37] Conceptually and empirically, this book confirms that Jewish day schools are today and perhaps always were woven into social networks that stretch from the most parochial to the national, whatever their founders may once have imagined.

---

[37] See pp. 52–3 below.

The Day School Entangled in a Web of Communities

What, then, are the specific communities or networks of social relations within which Jewish day schools are embedded? Despite popular stereotypes of pushy private school parents and some quantity of research that supports this notion,[38] parents do not loom especially large in this book, even though conventionally they are viewed by teachers and scholars as the most visible representatives of the external social setting that surrounds schools. The only chapter that focuses on day school parents is that by Pomson and Schnoor. Other contributors, taking up an invitation to explore the intersections of school and community, locate the webs of influence—the social and societal relationships within which Jewish schools are woven—in strikingly diverse places. One of the main empirical findings of this volume is just how disparate these communities, or webs of interdependence, are, and how far they extend beyond the parent body of the school.

Most predictably, there are the synagogues that sponsor, fund, and govern some schools. These institutions are in the background of Dewey's and Goldberg's chapters but firmly in the foreground of Goldstein's, where school and *shul* shape each other's development. A less formal but no less powerful role is played by those rabbis (and, occasionally, intellectuals) who may not even have an explicit relationship with a particular school but whose pronouncements and writings both give expression to and guide the values and priorities of influential social groups located inside and outside schools, as seen in the chapters by Finkelman and Kohn.[39] The same social groups—what might be called community elites—are seen in other chapters to exercise more direct influence, even when their members do not themselves belong to a school's parent body. Bouganim, for instance, depicts the sometimes perverse role played in the development of Jewish schooling in France by what he calls the 'Israelites': members of the Alliance Israélite Universelle, a group of wealthy Jewish philanthropists

---

[38] Hoover-Dempsey and Sandler, 'Why Do Parents Become Involved?'; Lareau, *Home Advantage*; Peshkin, *Permissible Advantage?*

[39] The influence of these individuals on Orthodox day schools has been the focus of some controversy among sociologists in recent years, with Heilman attributing what he calls 'a slide to the right' within modern Orthodox institutions to the influence of yeshiva 'personalities' on institutions (such as centrist Orthodox day schools) to which they have no formal connection. See Heilman, *Sliding to the Right*. More unusually, Kohn depicts, in his chapter in this volume, the influence exercised by a local Jewish academic on the direction taken by a school with regard to Hebrew instruction.

and personalities who never considered sending their own children to Jewish schools, but supported Jewish schooling for impoverished Jewish children, especially in foreign lands. Sztokman, in a similar vein, recounts the uncomfortable history of elite Ashkenazi influence on religious schooling in Israel, with particular attention to its negative effect on the educational opportunities of Sephardi girls.

A different set of stakeholders (or interest groups) whose power derives from institutions geographically more distant from the school, but no less intrusive, are brought into view in the chapters by Muszkat-Barkan and Shkedi, on the relationships between ministry of education teacher supervisors and classroom teachers in Israel, and by Dashevsky and Ta'ir, on the relationships between local Jewish teachers in Russia and their Israeli *sheliḥim* colleagues—teachers who come on limited-term contracts to work in Jewish schools all over the world as emissaries of international organizations. Evidently, the agents of different (occasionally transnational) communities meet and work together in Jewish schools, often pulling them in competing directions; but, as Muszkat-Barkan and Shkedi observe, it is sometimes hard to know which interest groups and bodies these agents represent by the time they have spent a great deal of time in a school. Teacher supervisors, for example, although appointed to serve as representatives of the ministry of education, seem torn between their loyalties to the ministry, to ideas about teaching they developed during their own training, and to the local neighbourhood of the school. Miller's chapter on Jewish day schools in Britain explores similar territory. Underlining the extent to which day schools are shaped by the culture of educational bureaucracies, she shows how those bureaucracies exert influence through the agency of curriculum advisers and inspectors but also, less visibly, through government legislation and public funding arrangements.

Jewish day schools, as a number of authors make clear, are participants in a larger public community within which are embedded long-standing assumptions about the relationship of Jews to the state and to state schools, and about the function of schools more generally: for example, concerning whether schools have a responsibility to challenge and transform society or whether they are better suited to preserving and conserving existing social relations. National and communal values figure prominently in the chapters that examine the development and impact of Jewish day schools in France: as Cohen shows, in this country, where a national discourse about the relationship between minority and majority communities is conducted with intensity and occasional violence, the grounds for Jewish schooling are defined in relation to national values such as republicanism, secularism, and non-denominationalism. In other cultural contexts, such as England or countries of the British Commonwealth, public funding for faith schools is so long-established a practice that the general social value of parochial Jewish schooling seems obvious to the point of banality, despite recent controversies surrounding Muslim faith schools. One special advantage of a volume such as this, then, where studies from different cultural contexts rub shoulders, is its capacity for showing that what is taken for granted in one setting carries special significance in another. Thus broad national concerns such as Catholicism in Argentina, bilingualism in Quebec, and post-Communism in the new Germany emerge as distinctive reference points in the development of Jewish day schools in these contexts, reflecting the investment of multiple public communities in determining what Jewish day schools do with regard, for example, to which students they admit and how they allocate curriculum time.

One cultural context in which the web of communities enmeshed with the practices and policies of day school education can be seen particularly vividly is the former Soviet Union (FSU). As Gitelman shows in his ground-breaking chapter, Jewish schools here have emerged more or less from nothing following seventy years of Communist rule, and have come into being as the offspring of numerous competing and occasionally co-operating communities—denominational, sectarian, local, national, and international—among which looms the emergent post-Communist state.[40] It is no wonder, under such circumstances, that Jewish day schools in the FSU can seem such paradoxical places—fiercely ethnic yet open to non-Jews, Zionist but loyal to local Jewish folkways and traditions, at times pedagogically innovative but often stunted in their educational vision. Their foreign benefactors view them as the engines of communal revival, expecting not only that they will produce future generations of committed, knowledgeable Jews but that their 'students will influence their parents to

---

[40] An example of this confusion is seen when attempting to classify schools by affiliation. How, for example, does one classify a school such as Moscow Public School no. 1311, variously known as the ORT Moscow Centre of Education—'Techiya'; a 'Heftzibah'—Jewish Agency/Lishkat Haskesher school; and, most generally, as the Lipman School, after its founding and current head teacher, Gregory Lipman? Each of these characterizations reflects a different community invested in the school's well-being.

become more involved in Jewish affairs and practices'.[41] And yet, as Gitelman makes plain, they are 'lonely' institutions, funded by foreign money, frequently led and staffed by foreigners, and directed towards educational goals—in relation to Zionism and religious observance, for example—that are alien to most local Jews. From a sociological perspective these schools provide a window on to the great diversity of Jewish and non-Jewish communities that can come together in and around the diaspora Jewish day school. More vividly than anywhere else, it is clear in the FSU that if Jewish schools are expected to transform the local community, they are also very much a part of that same community, as well as of many others, both near and far.

Learning Community

While the major part of this volume is moved by a sociological impulse to make visible the relations and structures—the identifiable constituent groups—in the external Jewish and non-Jewish society that shape Jewish day schools, a significant though smaller part of the book is driven by more explicitly educational concerns that relate to a second aspect of the term 'community', referred to earlier as a quality of schools themselves. These concerns relate to what Levisohn calls in his chapter 'community as a means and an end in Jewish education',[42] referring to community as a quality of the learning environment as well as a quality of what is produced by that environment as an outcome of day school education. These 'educational' chapters, like those that are more sociological in orientation, build on a proliferating body of literature on schools and community, and specifically on that part of the literature that focuses on what theorists call the situated quality of learning. Educational theorists argue that learning is fundamentally situated: that is, that it is embedded in particular social and physical environments and is not necessarily portable to other settings.[43] Community, then, viewed from the perspective of contemporary learning theory, not only provides the backdrop for learning—the context of learning, as sociologists of schooling might conventionally have put it; its presence (or absence) transforms in more fundamental ways how and what

---

[41] See p. 125 below.   [42] See p. 90 below.

[43] See e.g. Lave and Wenger, *Situated Learning*; Anderson et al., 'Situated Learning and Education'; Vera and Simon, 'Situated Action'; Brown et al., 'Situated Cognition and the Culture of Learning'.

children learn, and it is itself an integral part of the content of what is learned. Thus it is to be expected that Torah learned in community is as different in content and experience from Torah learned in private study as language learned in the context of ordinary conversation is from language learned from a dictionary.

When we conceived the idea of a conference on Jewish schools and community, we turned to some pre-eminent scholars and practitioners of education who could draw on contemporary educational scholarship to help Jewish educators develop models for how teaching and learning in Jewish schools might be transformed by taking into account the role of community in the learning environment. These models constitute an important component of Part I of this volume, 'Insights from Public and General Education'. In her chapter, for example, Smrekar draws on research from a variety of public and private school settings in the United States to develop a conceptual map of different kinds of family–school–community relationships and their implications for learning. She then invites the reader to consider how this conceptual map can guide the development of teaching and learning in Jewish schools. Goldring takes a different approach, drawing on insights from contemporary cognitive theory regarding the contribution of community to learning in order to suggest how day schools might be organized and operated to maximize their educational effect. Meier draws on more than forty years of experience as a classroom teacher and head of school to describe some of the most profound outcomes made possible by 'learning in community'. Schools and their classrooms, she argues, when organized as intergenerational communities that cultivate the twin capacities of open-minded intelligence and empathy, can serve as the seedbeds of democracy for America and for all democratic societies.

It is worth quoting directly from Meier's chapter, for in one short paragraph she enumerates four qualities that schools should possess in order to produce such desirable outcomes. She writes:

Young people, first of all, need to belong to communities that have standards. Second, the young must also witness adults taking responsibility for their decisions and standing by them, exercising that fundamental capacity of citizenship: human judgement. Third, they need schools that provide safe opportunities to explore their own life-sustaining and joyous powers under the guidance of adults the world respects. Fourth, they need schools that belong to their communities and families, and know them well. They must, in short, be surrounded by grown-ups they can imagine becoming and would like to become.[44]

Meier's chapter, like Goldring's and Smrekar's, is grounded in an assumption that communities make a necessary (even unique) contribution to the capacities that are essential to individual human flourishing. Meier argues that schools are impoverished places when they are not infused by the idea and practice of community. This is an important case to make in a volume on Jewish schooling, for, as Elkin argues in his response to Meier's chapter, Jewish day schools, although often conceived as the agents of particular communities, frequently do not make the best use of the resources community can offer to achieve their ends, particularly when such resources, in the form of personnel and institutions, are located beyond their walls.[45] Elkin argues compellingly that day schools in fact have the potential to mobilize Jewish habits of mind and heart that recognize the contribution of a life lived in community to the flourishing of Jews and Judaism. These habits are directly equivalent to Meier's capacities of open-minded intelligence and empathy. For example, Elkin argues that day schools, when grounded in Jewish values such as *maḥaloket leshem shamayim* (argument for the sake of heaven) and *kavod haberiyot* (respect for others), are unusually well placed to mobilize community as a resource for learning. Schools animated by these values can provide opportunities for their students to interact with Jews and non-Jews, from their own community and from other communities, with whom they can engage and from whom they can learn in a spirit of criticism and respect.

Another group of chapters in this volume, while similarly focused on the educational dimensions of community, are grounded in a different assumption that is rarely explored: that community—Jewish community—is not valuable only as a resource or a means to the flourishing of Jewish life and Judaism, but is an educational end in itself. To express this more fully: community is not only a quality of schools that can transform what children learn, as seen above; it is also an outcome of schooling, a quality of commitment to a life lived together with others and with others' interests and needs—their dignity—in mind. Levisohn draws on the ideas of Yitzchak 'Yitz' Greenberg to argue that this quality gives expression to an existential

---

[44] See p. 80 below.
[45] Elkin's is the one chapter in this volume that originates as a direct response to one of the conference presentations that spawned this collection.

dimension in Jewish day school education that goes beyond the intellectual and emotional development of Jewish children. This existential dimension sees the nurture of community as one of the ultimate purposes of Jewish schooling. To make this point, Levisohn quotes Greenberg's claim that 'day schools give educators the opportunity to create a world which can embody the holistic holy community which is our dream for the world'. What Greenberg means—as he elaborates in the source from which Levisohn quotes—is that day schools can become models (powerful examples and inspirations) of 'how Judaism has an important and dignified role to play in the vision of and process of perfecting the larger world'.[46] Far from being segregated enclaves, schools can be what he calls 'covenantal communities . . . marked by commitments of love to each other'. In schools, these commitments are expressed 'in the way the adults listen to a child, in the way students are respected, in the way each person is helped to develop his/her *tselem elokim*, image of God'.[47] Students can thus internalize a sense of community in the day school that can enable them 'to help forge an ideal society for the Jewish people and for humanity'.[48]

Of course, Greenberg's language is intensely theological. One wonders if even a majority of day school educators would conceive of their work as 'holy'. But, as Levisohn argues, Greenberg communicates an image of community that captures well what for many is an ultimate purpose of day school education: a Jewish community that can make a positive difference to the world.

The final three chapters of the volume—those by Kress and Reimer, Dewey, and Shevitz and Wasserfall—describe something of how holistic holy community is created in schools. The shared starting point for these chapters is an assumption, like that of Greenberg, that community is a good in and of itself. These chapters therefore focus on questions of *how* rather than *why* community can be built in schools, or at least how the precursors of community—the dispositions and habits that make possible its cultivation—can be nurtured. Strikingly, each of these three chapters devotes attention to an educational setting that might have been expected to divide students from one another and even be destructive of community: a Shabbaton (a residential sabbath retreat) for students of diverse religious backgrounds; prayer services in a multidenominational school; and what one

---

[46] Greenberg, 'Judaism and Modernity', 36.   [47] Ibid. 34–5.   [48] Ibid. 36.

author calls 'Town Meeting', a forum for school government by students in which 'each member has a single vote and equal freedom to discuss community issues'.[49] These chapters develop a case about what allows qualities of community to take root and flourish in schools at moments when some of the most personally important differences between students are exposed, such as when students with diverse religious commitments come together to pray.

According to Dewey, the key is for adults (specifically, educators) to have faith in the wisdom of young people to act responsibly when necessary. This does not mean that educators can abdicate responsibility for educational and organizational decisions, but rather that while 'adults serve as guides, adolescents bear the burden of real practice'. For Shevitz and Wasserfall, the cultivation of community in schools depends on finding a balance between risk and safety so as to create what they call (adapting Winnicott) a 'safe enough' environment; safe enough to 'stimulate differentiation and debate while providing support and acceptance'. From their perspective, community depends on people accepting their differences while remaining committed to what they share, even if what they most deeply share is a commitment to the legitimacy of difference. For Kress and Reimer, quality school Shabbatonim—informal (that is, loosely structured, non-hierarchical, and highly experiential) religious settings that embody community—incorporate five guiding ideas: they provide safe environments for students and teachers even when both have left behind the set structures in which they usually interact; they include caring relationships among all participants, students and teachers alike; they provide meaningful roles for students; they offer multiple entry points into ritual practice in ways that recognize the diversity of the participants; and they include the deep integration of learning and feeling.

Intriguingly, without referencing one another's work the authors of these three chapters make use of a set of shared concepts that highlight the balance between risk and safety, and between the group and the individual. In addition, they underline the vital role played by educators in facilitating the creation and maintenance of educational settings that cultivate an acceptance of otherness and co-operation within difference, qualities that themselves are precursors of community.

[49] See p. 363 below.

What Community-in-School Looks Like

A problem for all who are interested in community, whether as a sociological context or as an educational means or end, is that few scholarly accounts exist of what community looks like in Jewish schools and of how it is experienced. As suggested above, this is probably because research into all-day Jewish schooling has tended to focus on inputs and outputs, on those who teach in schools and those who graduate from them.[50] Thus, while it is generally agreed that all-day Jewish schooling has a positive effect on measures of Jewish identification and practice that no other educational vehicle can match, little is known about why Jewish day schools produce the effects they do or, in particular, how qualities of community contribute to these outcomes. The Jewish school still remains very much a black box, what happens inside hidden from view.

Literature of this kind on school and community exists in abundance in the field of general education, where it is equally likely to be produced by sociologists, ethnographers, historians, or practitioners writing in an autobiographical or confessional vein.[51] There is no shortage of evocative accounts of community in schools that in turn both shape and are shaped by theories of schooling and community. Such literature is rare, however, when it comes to Jewish day schools.

In this volume only a small number of contributors attempt to capture or reconstruct the inner life of Jewish schools with descriptive detail. Dewey, writing as a head of school, Shevitz and Wasserfall, writing as practised ethnographers, and Gitelman, writing as a sociologist relaying the account of a graduate of a Ukrainian Jewish day school, provide some intimation of how community is learned and lived in settings where students possess diverse Jewish commitments. But theirs are empirically fragile accounts based on very small samples of data. The significance of their writing therefore lies not in the size of the sample they study but in the richness of the detail they provide, and in what Connelly and Clandinin would call the 'verisimilitude', the life-likeness, of their accounts.[52] It is no coincidence that their descriptions of the relationships that constitute community in

---

[50] See e.g. Gamoran et al., *The Teachers Report*; Cohen, 'The Differential Impact of Jewish Education'; Chertok et al., *What Difference Does Day School Make?*

[51] Bryk et al., *Catholic Schools and the Common Good*; Smrekar, *The Impact of School Choice and Community*; Calderwood, *Learning Community*; Meier, *The Power of their Ideas*.

[52] Connelly and Clandinin, 'Stories of Experience and Narrative Inquiry'.

Jewish schools resonate with Meier's account, drawn from her own experience as a practitioner, of how communal sensibilities and values emerge from relationships between young people, and between young people and adults. In their fragility and in their detail, these chapters indicate how much our understanding of the inner workings of Jewish day schools would benefit from a systematic and co-ordinated effort to describe life in Jewish schools in all of its rich international variety.

An Enduring Question: One Jewish Day School or Many?

These comments regarding the anticipated benefits of rich descriptive research into the inner life of Jewish schools can easily be misunderstood. They might be taken to imply that Jewish day schools constitute a singular object for examination; that schools separated by thousands of miles and by even greater gaps in culture nevertheless share more than divides them.

In fact, the tapestry of accounts brought together in this volume indicates that, when one adopts a cross-cultural view, Jewish day schools differ sharply from one another. They are differentiated in terms of how they are funded (publicly or privately) and how they are governed (by a denominational body, communal representatives, or parents); in terms of what are envisaged as the alternatives to Jewish schools (whether private schools, public or state schools, or other Jewish schools); and ultimately in terms of their core purposes (whether religious, academic, or associationist—that is, as spaces for young Jews to be schooled together). These differences bear heavily on the balance of the curriculum, for example in the relative weight given to Judaic and general studies, and in the relative emphasis on the academic and the non-academic, what is commonly called the experiential.

As we have seen, these differences can readily be attributed to the relative influence of the various Jewish and non-Jewish communities invested in Jewish schools. Jewish day schools in different contexts are the products of different communal coalitions, and their organizational, educational, and philosophical diversity reflects this variety.

Under these circumstances, it is worth asking what, if anything, these widely varying Jewish day schools do actually share. Put differently, one might wonder if this volume indicates whether it is meaningful to talk about the Jewish day school as a singular or distinct international phenomenon. To take one comparative example: the Berlin Jewish High School, described by Müller in her chapter, differs in such profound ways from 'Tikhon', the pseudonymous American Jewish high school portrayed by Shevitz and Wasserfall in their chapter, that it seems misleading to refer to them both as community Jewish high schools, as the authors of each of these chapters do. The two schools exhibit little similarity in their student demographics, their Jewish curriculum, their relationship to the outside community, or the profile of their teaching staff. Thus, although both schools wrestle with diversity, Tikhon wrestles with the diversity of Jewish religious commitments held by students, while the Jewish High School in Berlin wrestles with a diversity of religions and nationalities among the student body—a majority of which is not even Jewish. What is it, then, that makes it intellectually meaningful to compare the experiences of these schools? What aspects of their experience do they share?

To find the answer to these questions, and to the larger one about whether it is reasonable to talk in international terms about 'the Jewish day school', it is helpful to take up a distinction between *Gemeinschaft* (community) and *Gesellschaft* (society) developed in the nineteenth century by Ferdinand Toennies, one of the pioneers of modern sociology.[53] Toennies employed these terms to describe the shift from a hunter–gatherer society to an agricultural society and thereafter to an industrial society. Since the early 1990s, following the groundbreaking work of Thomas Sergiovanni, these terms have been widely used to make sense of the quality of life in schools, as will be seen below.[54]

Sergiovanni argued that contemporary schools have unhealthily tilted away from *Gemeinschaft* towards *Gesellschaft*, especially in public, bureaucratically managed education systems.[55] Students, their families, and even teachers generally come together in schools, he implies, not as an expression of communal belonging, but to gain some personal benefit. Their relationships are focused on the exchange of wants and needs. According to Sergiovanni, life in schools frequently resembles Toennies' description of a *Gesellschaft* milieu: 'Every person strives for that which is to his own advantage as he affirms the actions of others only insofar as and as long as they

---

[53] Toennies, *Community and Society*.
[54] Sergiovanni, *Building Community in Schools*, and subsequently e.g. Boscardin and Jacobson, 'The Inclusive School'; Furman (ed.), *School as Community*.
[55] Sergiovanni, *Building Community in Schools*, 13.

can further his interests . . . all agreements of the will stand out as so many treaties and peace pacts.'[56]

Undoubtedly, there are significant elements of *Gesellschaft* to all Jewish day schools. When these schools send out tuition contracts, they enter into a compact with parents to deliver academic and personal outcomes in exchange for parents' trust and money. In these terms Jewish schools differ little from most other schools. This is hardly surprising given that the societies in which Jewish day schools exist are characterized by what Sergiovanni calls 'technical rationality', where consumers expect institutions to function efficiently, effectively, and responsively. If day schools do not satisfy these expectations, many parents will enrol their children elsewhere.

And yet, even in those Jewish schools that are little more than private schools for Jewish children and have a minimalist Jewish mission or vision, there invariably exists some trace of what Toennies identified as the elements of *Gemeinschaft*: shared kinship, place, and mind. These elements—primarily kinship (membership of the same ethnic community) and mind (some shared values, culture, or religion)—undergird Jewish day schools worldwide, but are not often present in state or non-sectarian schools. This is because (much as Coleman and Hoffer showed in their large-scale comparison of American public, Catholic, and private schools) Jewish day schools, like other private and religious schools, exist by definition within functional and value communities.[57] Functional communities are communities in which 'social norms and sanctions . . . arise out of the social structure itself, and both reinforce and perpetuate that structure'. Value communities are communities where people are united around similar values and educational philosophies even if they do not possess the shared neighbourhood, backgrounds, or occupations characteristic of functional communities. These functional and value communities provide Jewish schools with a *raison d'être* they would otherwise lack if they operated exclusively in *Gesellschaft* terms as economically efficient purveyors of academic services, as non-sectarian and/or public schools do. This is why many day school parents, with apparent irrationality, do not withdraw their children from these schools even when they are deeply dissatisfied with the academic quality of the education their children are receiving. Day schools not only provide them with a service; they are part of their functional and/or

[56] Toennies, *Community and Society*, 77.
[57] Coleman and Hoffer, *Public and Private High Schools*.

value community. Put differently, day schools are not only vehicles for the intellectual or emotional development of the individual student; they are the creations of (and for) Jewish communities, even if, as is often the case in eastern Europe, they are created by outside agencies.

Jewish day schools are inherently *Gemeinschaft* institutions, even when they downplay such 'parochial' characteristics in their self-presentation and their practices. They are grounded in some mixture of shared kinship, place, and/or mind. Absent *all* of these qualities—the presence of a Jewish student body (kinship), location in a Jewish locale (place), and the inculcation of Jewish values, culture, or religion (mind)—it would be sociologically meaningless to regard a day school as being Jewish.

It is, by the same token, the presence of these qualities, in different combinations and expressed with different cultural emphases, that makes it possible to talk about and study the Jewish day school as a distinctive international phenomenon, whatever the circumstantial or organizational differences that distinguish one school from another. The diverse schools described in this volume—in Boston, Buenos Aires, Berlin, Britain, France, the former Soviet Union, and places in between—are constructed from some combination of the components of *Gemeinschaft*. The components of community are what unites them.

Community, then, does not just provide the context and content for the Jewish day school; its constituent components ultimately provide the *raison d'être* for Jewish day school education. Without community in the multiple senses explored here, the Jewish day school has no meaning or purpose. If this sounds like a normative statement, I am suggesting that it is also a sociological fact. This fact suggests, as the title of this volume also indicates, that the time is long overdue to think again about both Jewish schools and Jewish communities, and about the relationship between them.

Bibliography

Ackerman, W., 'Strangers to Tradition: Idea and Constraint in American Jewish Education', in H. Himmelfarb and S. DellaPergola (eds.), *Jewish Education Worldwide: Cross-Cultural Perspectives* (Lanham, Md., 1989), 71–116.

Anderson, J. R., L. M. Reider, and H. A. Simon, 'Situated Learning and Education', *Educational Researcher*, 25/4 (1996), 5–11.

Beinart, P., 'The Rise of the Jewish School', *Atlantic Monthly*, 284/4 (Oct. 1999), 21–3.

Berrin, S. (ed.), *Ten Years of Believing in Jewish Day School Education* (Boston, 2007), <http://peje.org/publications/books_and_articles/200710_PEJE_10Yr_Report.pdf>.

Black, E., *The Social Politics of Anglo-Jewry* (Oxford, 1988).

Black, G., *JFS: The History of the Jews' Free School, London, since 1732* (London, 1998).

Boscardin, M. L., and S. Jacobson, 'The Inclusive School: Integrating Diversity and Solidarity through Community-Based Management', *Journal of Educational Administration*, 35/5 (1997), 466–76.

Brown, J. S., A. Collins, and P. Duguid, 'Situated Cognition and the Culture of Learning', *Educational Researcher*, 18 (1989), 32–41.

Bryk, A., V. Lee, and P. B. Holland, *Catholic Schools and the Common Good* (Cambridge, Mass.: 1993).

Calderwood, P., *Learning Community: Finding Common Ground in Difference* (New York, 2000).

Chertok, F., L. Saxe, C. Kadushin, G. Wright, A. Klein, and A. Korin, *What Difference Does Day School Make? The Impact of Day School: A Comparative Analysis of Jewish College Students* (Boston, 2007).

Cohen, E. H., *Heureux comme Juifs en France? Étude sociologique* (Paris and Jerusalem, 2007).

Cohen, S. M., 'The Differential Impact of Jewish Education on Adult Jewish Identity', in J. Wertheimer (ed.), *Family Matters: Jewish Education in an Age of Choice* (Hanover, NH, 2007), 34–56.

Coleman, J., and T. Hoffer, *Public and Private High Schools: The Impact of Communities* (New York, 1987).

Conference on the Future of the Jewish People, *Background Policy Documents* (Jerusalem, 2007).

Connelly, F. M., and D. J. Clandinin, 'Stories of Experience and Narrative Inquiry', *Educational Researcher*, 19/5 (1990), 2–14.

DellaPergola, S., and U. O. Schmelz, 'Demography and Jewish Education in the Diaspora: Trends in Jewish School-Age Population and School Enrolment', in H. Himmelfarb and S. DellaPergola (eds.), *Jewish Education Worldwide: Cross-Cultural Perspectives* (Lanham, Md., 1989).

Dushkin, A., 'Jewish Education in New York City, 1918', extract republished in *Journal of Jewish Education*, 20/1 (1948), 15.

Egan, K., 'The Role of Schools, The Place of Education', *Teachers College Record*, 93/4 (1992), 641–55.

Furman, G. C. (ed.), *School as Community: From Promise to Practice* (Albany, NY, 2002), 1–19.

Gamoran, A., E. Goldring, B. Robinson, J. Tammivaara, and R. Goodman, *The Teachers Report: A Portrait of Teachers in Jewish Schools* (New York, 1998).

Goldring, E., A. Gamoran, and B. Robinson, *The Leaders Report: A Portrait of Educational Leaders in Jewish Schools* (New York, n.d.).

Greenberg, Y., 'Judaism and Modernity: Realigning the Two Worlds. An Edited Transcript of an Address by Rabbi Dr. Yitzchak Greenberg', in Zvi Grumet (ed.), *Perspectives on Jewish Education* (Ramat Gan, 2006).

Grossman, M., 'Parochial Schools for Jewish Children: An Adverse View', *Jewish Education*, 16/3 (1945), 20–5.

Heilman, S., *Sliding to the Right: The Contest for the Future of American Jewish Orthodoxy* (Berkeley, 2006).

Hoover-Dempsey, K. V., and H. M. Sandler, 'Why Do Parents Become Involved in their Children's Education?', *Review of Educational Research*, 67/1 (1997), 3–42.

Ingall, C., *Down the Up Staircase: Tales of Teaching in Jewish Day Schools* (New York, 2006).

Kanarfogel, E., *Jewish Education and Society in the High Middle Ages* (Detroit, 1992).

Katz, J., *Out of the Ghetto: The Social Background of Jewish Emancipation, 1770–1870* (New York, 1978).

Krakowski, M., 'Isolation and Integration: Education and Worldview Formation in Ultra-Orthodox Jewish Schools', Ph.D. diss., Learning Sciences program of Northwestern University, Chicago, School of Education and Social Policy, 2008.

Lareau, A., *Home Advantage: Social Class and Parental Intervention in Elementary Education* (Lanham, Md., 2000).

Lave, J., and E. Wenger, *Situated Learning: Legitimate Peripheral Participation* (Cambridge, 1991).

Lawrence-Lightfoot, S., *Worlds Apart: Relationships between Families and Schools* (New York, 1978).

Lefkovits, E., 'Lauder Foundation Marks 20th Anniversary', *Jerusalem Post*, 26 Oct. 2007, <http://www.jpost.com/servlet/Satellite?pagename=JPost/JPArticle/ShowFull&cid=11923 80659366>.

Lookstein, J. H., 'The Modern American Yeshivah', *Jewish Education*, 16/3 (1945), 12–16.

Malkus, M., 'The Curricular Symphony: How One Jewish Day School Integrates its Curriculum', *Journal of Jewish Education*, 68/1 (2002), 47–57.

Marcus, I. G., *Rituals of Childhood: Jewish Acculturation in Medieval Europe* (New Haven, 1996).

Margolis, D., and E. S. Schoenberg, *Curriculum, Community, Commitment: Views on the American Jewish Day School in Memory of Bennett I. Solomon* (West Orange, NJ, 1992).

Marom, D., 'Before the Gates of the School: An Experiment in Developing Educational Vision from Practice', in S. Fox, I. Scheffler, and D. Marom (eds.), *Visions of Jewish Education* (Cambridge, 2003), 296–331.

Meier, D., *The Power of their Ideas: Lessons for America from a Small School in Harlem* (Boston, 1995).

Miller, H., 'Meeting the Challenge: The Jewish Schooling Phenomenon in the UK', *Oxford Review of Education*, 27/4 (2001), 501–13.

Moore, D. D., 'The Construction of Community: Jewish Migration and Ethnicity in the United States', in M. Rischin (ed.), *The Jews of North America* (Detroit, 1987), 105–17.

Murphy, C., 'Longing to Deepen Identity, More Families Turn to Jewish Day School', *Washington Post*, 7 Apr. 2001, B1.

Pekarsky, D., *Vision at Work: The Theory and Practice of Beit Rabban* (New York, 2006).

Peshkin, A., *Permissible Advantage? The Moral Consequences of Elite Schooling* (Mahwah, NJ, 2001).

Pomson, A., 'Jewish Day School Growth in Toronto: Freeing Policy and Research from the Constraints of Conventional Sociological Wisdom', *Canadian Journal of Education*, 27/3 (2004), 321–40.

—— 'The *Rebbe* Reworked: An Inquiry into the Persistence of Inherited Traditions of Teaching', *Teaching and Teacher Education*, 18/1 (2002), 23–34.

—— and R. F. Schnoor, *Back to School: Jewish Day School in the Lives of Adult Jews* (Detroit, 2008).

Sarna, J., 'American Jewish Education in Historical Perspective', *Journal of Jewish Education*, 61/1–2 (1998), 8–21.

Schick, M., *A Census of Jewish Day Schools in the United States, 2003–2004* (New York, 2005).

Schoem, D., *Ethnic Survival in America: An Ethnography of a Jewish Afternoon School* (Atlanta, Ga., 1989).

Sergiovanni, T. J., *Building Community in Schools* (San Francisco, 1994).

Smrekar, C., *The Impact of School Choice and Community: In the Interest of Families and Schools* (Albany, NY, 1996).

State of Israel, Ministry of Education, *Internet vemeida ḥinukhi*, 2007, <http://cms.education.gov.il/EducationCMS/Units/Owl/Hebrew/UvdotNetunim/netunim/Stat.htm>.

Tigay, Chanan, 'As Day Schools Rake in Mega-Gifts, Some See a Trend in Jewish Giving', Institute for Jewish and Community Research, 2006, <http://www.jewishresearch.org/v2/2006/articles/philanthropy/5_9_06.htm>.

Toennies, F., *Community and Society*, ed. and trans. C. P. Loomis (New York, 1957); first published as *Gemeinschaft und Gesellschaft* (1887).

Vera, A. H., and H. A. Simon, 'Situated Action: A Symbolic Interpretation', *Cognitive Science*, 17 (1993), 7–48.

Wertheimer, J. 'Who's Afraid of Jewish Day Schools?', *Commentary*, 108 (1999), 49–54.

—— (ed.), *Family Matters: Jewish Education in an Age of Choice* (Hanover, NH, 2007).

Wessely, N. H., 'Words of Peace and Truth', in P. R. Mendes-Flohr and J. Reinharz (eds.), *The Jew in the Modern World* (New York, 1995), 70–4.

Zeldin, M., 'The Promise of Historical Inquiry: Nineteenth-Century Jewish Day Schools and Twentieth-Century Policy', *Religious Education*, 83/3 (1988), 438–52.

—— 'Integration and Interaction in the Jewish Day School', in R. Tornberg (ed.) *The Jewish Educational Leader's Handbook* (San Francisco, 1998), 579–90.

PART I

Insights from Public and General Education

ONE

Building Community Within and Around Schools

Can Jewish Day Schools Measure Up?

ELLEN B. GOLDRING

IN 1990 the Commission on Jewish Education in North America con-
cluded that 'the system of Jewish education is plagued by many problems,
and because of its inadequacies it is failing to engage the minds of a critical
segment of the Jewish population who have no other way of experiencing
the beauty and richness of Jewish life'.[1] The Commission then went on to
suggest that strategies to address 'this crisis of major proportions' should
rest on two building blocks, one of which is mobilizing community support
to meet the needs and goals of Jewish education. In specifying what 'community support' or 'community mobilization' might involve, the Commission recommended 'recruiting top community leaders to the cause of
Jewish education, raising Jewish education to the top of the communal
agenda, creating a positive environment for Jewish education and providing substantially increased funding from federation, private family foundations and other sources'.[2]

However, the Commission viewed the community not only as a key part
of the solution to the crisis in Jewish education, but also as part of the problem. The Jewish community, it remarked, 'has not yet recognized the indis-
pensable role it must play, . . . it lacks understanding . . . and it is not
sufficiently supportive of the massive investment required to bring about
systemic change'.[3]

What strikes me when rereading this assessment from over a decade ago
is the prominence given to the need for the community to support the
school, while there is the absence of any substantial role for the school in

---

This chapter is based on M. Driscoll and E. Goldring, 'How Can Educational Leaders Incorporate Communities as Context for Student Learning?', in W. Firestone and Carolyn Riehl (eds.),
A New Agenda for Research in Educational Leadership (New York, 2005).

[1] Commission on Jewish Education in North America, *A Time to Act*, 16.
[2] Ibid. 63.   [3] Ibid. 40–1.

redefining the nature of collaboration between itself and the community it serves.

In this chapter I focus on the role of the school in redefining that collaboration. I argue that it is important to explore the purposes and mechanisms of school–community collaboration. Why should a school pursue collaboration with the community, and what are the mechanisms by which schools and communities can interact with and mutually support one another? I focus on three purposes, on the corresponding perspectives on why and how school–community relations can 'work', and on appropriate mechanisms for bringing this about.

Background

Clearly, addressing the topic of community in general, and as it relates to Jewish day schools in particular, is very complex. What do we mean by 'community'? What did the Commission on Jewish Education in North America mean by 'community'? Who makes up the 'community' of a Jewish day school? Those parents who send their children to the school? The larger Jewish community of the locale where the school is situated? Those who are associated with the day school but have no other association with the Jewish community or the formal Jewish institutions of the school's locale?

I take up Amitai Etzioni's definition of community as my starting point. Etzioni proposes that 'communities are webs of social relations that encompass shared meanings and above all shared values'.[4] This definition helpfully serves an examination of Jewish day schools, for Jewish communities tend to be bound not by geography, as physical neighbourhoods, but rather by institutional affiliations that help maintain social norms. From this definition, it is clear that individuals are likely to be members of a 'pluralist web of communities', belonging, at one and the same time, to work, professional, residential, religious, and other communities. In this sense, communities are nested, although the extent of this nesting or overlap will vary greatly according to context: in a small Jewish locale, for example, these different communities may overlap to a very great degree, while in a larger population they may be more distinct.

As will become increasingly evident in this chapter, I view the relationships between school and communities as reciprocal: schools have an

---

[4] Etzioni, *Essential Communitarian Reader*, p. xiii.

impact on communities and communities have an impact on schools. My observations suggest that many of those involved in Jewish education take a 'school-centric' view of the relationships between schools and communities, in which communities are required to support schools. However, as I argue below, schools have a central role to play in developing communities as well.

In this chapter I focus specifically on three strands of school–community relationships. The first strand concerns school–community collaboration for the purpose of enhancing learning. Drawing on current learning theory, I claim that linking schools to communities is important because it will enhance learning—learning that includes the development of Jewish identity. Second, I discuss school–community collaboration for the purpose of developing social capital: that is, how school–community collaboration develops shared norms and relationships of social trust that enhance the development of learning and Jewish identity. Third, I present the notion of school–community collaboration for the purpose of building and developing the wider Jewish community. Here I claim that Jewish day schools should be engines for the development and support of the entire community.

These three perspectives, I suggest, are needed to refocus school–community collaboration on the core mission of Jewish education: namely, teaching and learning, rather than the structural arrangements and supports that Jewish schools need from the larger community. In overarching terms, following the lead of Jonathan Woocher in his paper 'Toward a Unified Field Theory of Jewish Continuity', my goal is to think about Jewish day schools as a way to 'make our Jewish community more community-like, more effective in providing a social/experiential/cognitive reality that will attract engagement and build commitment'.[5]

It is widely believed by both educators and others that school improvement and student learning must include parent and community involvement. Educators have long argued that schools on their own lack the capacity to address the multiple goals of education as well as the social problems facing students in today's schools. However, recent theories of social cognition and situated instruction further suggest that communities can be much more integrally linked to the core mission of schooling, namely

---

[5] Woocher, 'Toward a Unified Field Theory', 24–5.

teaching and learning. Parents and communities are central to supporting the development of human, social, and financial capital in schools and their students. Simultaneously, newer perspectives suggest that schools could be and should be engines for social change *in and of* communities: in other words, schools and their leaders can be central to community development and building community capacity. Thus the links between schools and their communities form a two-way path.

Typically, conceptions of the links between schools and communities situate schools as receivers of resources in a 'school-centric' view or notion of learning. 'Such a school-centric frame assumes that schools are the primary influences for learning in the lives of children and youth rather than one part of students' broader developmental contexts.'[6] Thus, despite decades of reform, much research and development around school–family–community relations is still narrowly focused on parents' roles in supporting schools' work, such as helping with homework, coming to parent–teacher meetings, or volunteering in the library or office.[7]

Accompanying this line of enquiry, a body of research on school leadership examines how principals facilitate home–school relationships, negotiate the politics of parent and community involvement with the school, and act as a buffer between teachers and the academic core on the one hand, and the wider community on the other. In these instances 'the focus remains "inward," on the school rather than "outward," toward change in the surrounding community'.[8] From this perspective, principals are seen as garnering resources from the community or managing a delicate balancing act of buffering and bridging through parents and the board.[9]

Contemporary research suggests fresh perspectives that radically realign our views of schools and communities and carry with them new imperatives for understanding effective leadership. I turn now to a discussion of each of three perspectives or strands that contribute to this alternative view: situated cognition, social capital, and community development. For each of the three strands I will first provide a brief example; then I will present more information about the perspective or strand. I will end discussion of each strand by asking emerging questions that have implications for

[6] Honig et al., 'School–Community Connections', 1001.
[7] e.g. Epstein et al., 'Involving Parents in Homework'.
[8] Crowson and Boyd, 'The New Role of Community Development', 15.
[9] Goldring and Hausman, 'Civic Capacity and School Principals'; Ogawa and Studer, 'Bridging and Buffering Parent Involvement'.

understanding ways in which Jewish day schools can both develop and inhibit community. Ultimately, I seek to ask: Can Jewish day schools meet the challenges raised by these conceptions of school–community collaboration? I take an optimistic view and believe that matters of territory, politics, and money should not stand in the way of reaping the benefits of school–community collaboration.

The 'New Science' of Learning and School–Community Connections

One clear purpose or goal in school–community co-operation is to support and enhance learning, including the development of Jewish identity.

Example 1

High school students are doing a project on Jewish medical ethics. Rather than having students do research, use texts, and write a paper, the project design includes specifications that require students to engage with the community outside the school. The goal of the project is to help students understand how questions of Jewish medical ethics play out in practice in that wider community. The teacher invites Jewish physicians into the class and asks them to put to the students real ethical dilemmas they face, such as: What is the status of the family of a deceased person with respect to consenting to or refusing organ donation? Or: In a multiple pregnancy, in which the chances of all the foetuses surviving are extremely small, is it permissible to decrease their number in order to increase the chances of survival for the remaining foetuses? The students then do research in the conventional way, but also, as part of this research, confer with Jewish community leaders—for example, rabbis from various denominations; they talk or correspond with individuals who have confronted questions of medical ethics as members of the Jewish community; and they discuss these issues with practising physicians, both Jewish and non-Jewish, to gain a comparative perspective. They then make a presentation of their findings to an authentic audience, that is, one consisting not only of teachers and students from their classes, but including physicians and community members, whom they invite to hear their conclusions and offer feedback. Then the students teach others in the community about ways of confronting dilemmas involving Jewish medical ethics. Sharing in the process of learning together creates a sense of community.

This example highlights the connections between school and community as joint contexts for learning: students are provided with real, authentic problems that are linked to expertise in the community, and the community learns along with the students. These images of learning are not new. In many respects, they echo the work of John Dewey over a century ago, which connected learning with the social and physical environment of the child.[10] But while Dewey's views on learning rested on a philosophical conception of understanding and experience, this recent work has developed from empirical enquiry. A report by the US National Research Council, *How People Learn*, provides a concise overview of this 'new science'.[11] The 'new science' itself presents a vivid portrait of the ways in which schools might be envisioned. Below I summarize three of the issues that, I believe, have particular salience with respect to making the connection between schools and communities.

The Importance of Pre-existing Knowledge for Understanding New Learning

Perhaps the most central tenet of the new science of learning is that all new knowledge is scaffolded on to pre-existing knowledge. Building on the earlier work of cognitive scientists Piaget and Vygotsky, Bransford and his colleagues note that 'the contemporary view of learning is that people construct new knowledge and understandings based on what they already know and believe'.[12] This means that 'teachers need to pay attention to the incomplete understandings, the false beliefs, and the naïve renditions of concepts that learners bring with them to a given subject'.[13]

The lion's share of pre-existing knowledge that learners bring to school is likely to be shaped by the home and community contexts in which they spend most of their time. Active enquiry on the part of teachers is one way of making the connection between what students already know and what they need to know. Even more important is encouraging students to develop the kind of metacognitive skills—that is, the ability to think about their thinking—that permit them to articulate points of confusion. Making connections between school and these other learning contexts is vital if learners are to sort out what they already know, what they think they know, and what they need to know.

Understanding that Learning is Transferred from One Context to Another

A second critical premise is that learning can be transferred from the context in which it is learned to other relevant settings. Context helps to provide both the conceptual framework and the organizing structures that enable

[10] Dewey, 'My Pedagogic Creed', 77–80. [11] Bransford et al. (eds.), *How People Learn*.
[12] Ibid. 10. [13] Ibid.

the learner to take the understandings and competences gained into a new cognitive venue.[14] Learning may be organized around general principles: for example, how geographical features of a river affect the development of cities, of trade, and of political borders. Such a conceptual framework makes it likely that learners will be able to transfer these implicit theories to any study of any river in a different setting, rather than applying them only to a detailed study of, say, the Mississippi River alone. It is particularly important, then, that subjects be taught across multiple contexts, with the kind of examples that demonstrate 'wide application' and encourage a 'flexible representation of knowledge'.[15]

School and community connections that support transfer of learning must link that learning to the real world contexts in which such knowledge must be used.[16] Understanding some of the key differences between school and non-school settings is important in constructing optimum learning environments which are likely to encourage transfer, especially those that emphasize 'problem-based' learning. This means understanding the non-school environments in which children learn.

Dewey's insight that 'the school must represent life, life as real and vital to the child as that which he carries on in the home, in the neighborhood, or on the playground' captures the critical nature of this connection.[17] Such 'real-world' contexts are vital because they permit learners to develop the kind of robust conceptual knowledge that transfers across a broad array of contexts.

Communities as Contexts for Learning

Another element of the new science of learning with significant implications for our understandings of schools and communities is the importance of community itself in this literature. Bransford and colleagues argue for a 'community-centered approach' to learning, where both the classroom and the outside world support core learning values.[18] Teachers must help students to form the kinds of learning communities in which they can both give and receive assistance in solving problems. Similarly, teachers themselves must be connected to one another in learning communities that

---

[14] Brown et al., 'Situated Cognition and the Culture of Learning', 32–41.
[15] Bransford et al. (eds.), *How People Learn*, 62.
[16] Wehlage et al., 'Standards of Authentic Achievement and Pedagogy', 21–48.
[17] Dewey, 'My Pedagogic Creed'.   [18] Bransford et al. (eds.), *How People Learn*, 25.

focus on developing expertise in pedagogy and curriculum. Equally critical is the imperative to use the broader community as a source of context and experience in learning. Communities not only provide the structures that facilitate learning; they also shape and determine what learning is valued. Thus it is critical to recognize that these out-of-school contexts include non-school learning communities that shape students' understandings. 'Effective learning occurs when schools, after school programs, and other organizations use the resources and challenges of the community as a living textbook for learning.'[19]

Questions Provoked by the New Science of Learning

Taken together, these precepts from the new science of learning press us to examine new questions about the connections between communities and schools, and to imagine the actual and potential effects of such relationships on student learning. For Jewish day schools, these questions include the following:

- How can Jewish day schools gain a better understanding of the out-of-school contexts of their students and families and thereby genuinely enhance learning?

- If real-world contexts are critical to learning, how can schools and school leaders extend the context for learning to include the community and vice versa?

School and community connections must be constructed in terms of their capacity to provide both opportunities to learn and opportunities to teach.[20] In the public (state) school sector, school and community connections, such as integrated services programmes or inter-agency services, have often been constructed as ways of removing barriers to learning, so that, for example, students are more likely to have adequate nutrition and rest, or to be absent from school less often. But only rarely have these connections been considered in terms of their ability to 'reinforce and extend youth's opportunity to learn'. Much traditional thinking underestimates the importance of the structures and activities outside schools among the peer groups that provide learning communities of support for students. There is

[19] Melaville et al., *Making the Difference*, 22.
[20] Cahill, *A Documentation Report*; Pitman and Cahill, 'Pushing the Boundaries', cited by Honig et al., 'School–Community Connections'.

insufficient appreciation for 'community classrooms' that 'are often more meaningful and motivating than those found in school', especially given that 'the engagement with learning that is generated in community classrooms often carries back to school'.[21] In a Jewish context, formal and informal Jewish educational experiences and settings are invariably divorced from one another. Little connection exists, for example, between Jewish summer camps and Jewish day schools. Jewish youth groups and their activities are not considered as offering opportunities to learn that support, and intertwine with, Jewish day school education. It is worth considering what might happen if teachers thought about these connections in terms of opportunities to teach.

Currently it seems that these ties between schools and communities are, at best, ad hoc and haphazard, based on peer networks of individuals or groups of individuals. In order to institutionalize the funds of knowledge and experience on which students and their families draw and to which they contribute, we should consider how these ties get formed; this is the kind of systematic thinking for which Jack Wertheimer calls in his recent AVI CHAI report, *Linking the Silos: How to Accelerate the Momentum in Jewish Education Today*. The key here, I suggest, is to keep the focus on teaching and learning. Teachers can extend the space and time for teaching into the community, using the 'access to funds of knowledge about their students provided by connections with communities and families, the involvement of community partners in teaching who also provide resources connected to real world contexts, and the opportunities for teachers as well as students to create expanded professional networks and supports'.[22]

If we believe that communities of learners are vital contexts for learning, how broadly do we envision the community that defines and values that learning? Schools frequently discount the out-of-school peer and organizational communities that shape students' understandings and provide skills useful in school.[23] We must first ask: What are the external communities that help students in Jewish day schools to learn? What should or could their role be in supporting students' learning? Relationships between these multiple communities and day schools are often increasingly remote. How, then, do day school leaders develop knowledge about these different communities and foster interaction in pursuit of common purposes and with

---

[21] Honig et al., 'School–Community Connections', 1016–17.
[22] Ibid. 1017.   [23] McLaughlin, *Community Counts.*

shared resources to create the best possible conditions for student learning?

I suggest that in the Jewish day school context there may be some clear advantages in looking to synagogue settings and synagogue leadership, even though this route relies perhaps too heavily on formal organizational structures and families who are already members of other community organizations. Schools must also consider those students and teachers who are not affiliated with other communal institutions. They must ask how they can form bridges linking them with other out-of-school learning contexts whose values, practices, and observances may be different from those sanctioned by the school itself.

Thinking back to the example of the student projects on medical ethics, we see that its promise derives from the engagement of students with others in the community, and of the community with the school, around real, authentic problems; thus the students are linked to expertise in the community and to learning in the community.

Social Capital and Schools

The development of social capital, a concept rooted in the importance of relationships, is a second important goal of school–community collaboration.

Example 2

Service learning, which integrates community service into class learning, is a mechanism to develop social capital. A class on Jewish *mitsvot* contains a compulsory civic engagement component. Students commit to a year of service. One such project involves teenagers working with Jewish senior citizens resident in assisted-living facilities in the same community, many of whom are lonely. During their visits, as well as the typical volunteer activities (playing games, making Hanukah cards) the day school students conduct oral history interviews with the residents as part of their history study, which requires them to learn about the Holocaust. The grown-up children of the senior citizens who are visited often send the school thank-you notes and become new members of the school's community.

Teachers strive to construct service projects that involve students in the planning, that involve face-to-face service with beneficiaries, that allow for repeated interactions with those served over time, and that allow servers and those served to discuss and reflect on their experience afterwards.[24] These types of project are the basis for developing relationships—social capital.

[24] Sander and Putnam, 'Rebuilding the Stock of Social Capital'.

Convincing evidence shows that school students who engage in community service and service learning are more likely to sustain civic engagement in the longer term. Community service in schools is already widespread. Five recent surveys suggest that between 25 and 35 per cent of US high schools already require students to engage in community service, and some 42 per cent of high school seniors in 1998 performed community service either within or outside their schools. National surveys in the United States show a significant increase in youth volunteering, and follow-up studies have shown that community service has a long-term effect on civic engagement. Nevertheless, much could be done to deepen the impact of this work.[25]

The example given above is rooted in the notion that learning can develop social capital. In simple terms, the concept of social capital can be summed up in two words: 'relationships matter'.[26] Social capital refers to 'the set of resources that inhere in relationships of trust and cooperation between and among people',[27] or, in the words of Robert Putnam, 'the features of social organization, such as networks, norms and social trust, that facilitate coordination and cooperation for mutual benefit'.[28] The formation of social capital both within school communities and between schools and the communities in which they are situated should be a very explicit and important goal.

Social capital is a popular term. In fact there is an organization that sums up the essence of its meaning: <bettertogether.org>. This organization's website, whose strapline summarizes its principles in the words: 'Connect with others. Build trust. Get involved', suggests 150 things anyone can do to build social capital. One of the items on the list is: 'collect oral histories from older town residents'.

Social capital has become an important concept in explaining the mechanisms by which communities and schools interact. The essential characteristic of social capital is the fact that it resides in the relationships among individuals within a social organization. The educational benefits accrue when the community as a whole values education and shares some degree of oversight for all its children.

---

[25] Ibid.
[27] Warren, 'Communities and Schools', 136.
[26] Field, *Social Capital*.
[28] Putnam, *Making Democracy Work*, 67.

Much of the research on social capital dates from Coleman and Hoffer's seminal study of academic outcomes in public and in Catholic high schools in the United States.[29] The positive effects they found in the Catholic sector were linked, they believed, to the social structures that supported Catholic schools. They posited a set of overlapping norms and relationships that supported educational achievement and greatly enriched the resources available to any individual student. This 'social capital', as Coleman termed it, was as vital to student success as the physical, human, and financial capital that supports learning.

The idea of social capital has been extended to include the political and civic networks in communities. Overlapping webs of relationships—what Putnam terms 'networks of civic engagement'—enrich the quality of life of any individual residing in the society.[30] Such networks foster robust norms of reciprocity, facilitate communication and the development of trust, and 'embody past success at collaboration, which can serve as a culturally-defined template for future collaboration'.[31] Although dense social networks may not be focused on the exchange of educational information, they still provide a rich context to sustain and support schooling.

Overall, social capital is formed when there are opportunities for students to build social trust and norms of mutual understanding through bonding with adults, sharing information, and forming links with other individuals in various institutions. Evidence for its positive effect is overwhelming: 'Statistically, the correlation between high social capital and positive child development is as close to perfect as social scientists ever find.'[32]

Emerging Questions about Schools and Social Capital

What does social capital mean for the Jewish community? Clearly, there are different levels of analysis: there is social capital for individual students, and there is social capital for the school, at an institutional level. At the school level, rich social networks may help to create some of the structures that better connect learning in school with real-world contexts, or improve the degree to which teachers are aware of the knowledge students bring to school. As schools actively seek to use communities as contexts for learning and to acknowledge the cognitive structures that students have already

---

[29] Coleman and Hoffer, *Public and Private High Schools*.
[30] Putnam, *Making Democracy Work*, 173.
[31] Ibid. 173–4.   [32] Putnam et al., *Better Together*.

formed, social capital may be an important element in developing the trust and information needed to create opportunities for teaching and learning. Two questions in particular present themselves:

- How can school leaders—both head teachers and administrators—maximize the social capital already available in the community and contribute to creating the kinds of network that support educational success with the community?

- What can school leaders do—either by themselves or in concert with teachers—to learn about and develop the connections that exist between community networks and contexts for learning?[33]

It is particularly critical that school leaders attend to the different kinds of network that are created and assess the many aspects of these connections between schools and communities. Putnam describes both 'vertical' and 'horizontal' networks among individuals and institutions.[34] The relationships between schools and their communities have most often been constructed vertically, reflecting an imbalance of power.

Further questions arise. What opportunity costs are associated with a renewed focus by school leaders on the creation of social capital? At the school level, there are multiple demands on principals' time and efforts. Paying significant attention to social capital will require a substantial investment of time and effort on the part of school leaders that may represent a displacement of focus from other critical factors affecting the school. What are the choices and priorities principals face, and how can leadership of the school be distributed in a way conducive to maximizing social capital, both by lightening the load on those at the top and giving more scope to others to develop significant relationships?

In sum, the service learning example shows that social capital can be developed through civic engagement, perhaps involving cross-generational relationships, but that these relationships are rooted in and connected to classroom activity over time.

Community Development

Schools as the focus of Jewish community development are a third goal of school–community collaboration.

[33] Sanders and Harvey, 'Beyond the School Walls', 1345–68.
[34] Putnam, *Making Democracy Work*.

Example 3

The local Jewish day school, after conducting a needs assessment in the community, decided to embark on a community outreach project to focus on learning Hebrew. It then embarked on the process of engaging with the other organizations, institutions, and synagogues in the same district to provide Hebrew instruction to adults, high school students (for credit towards qualifications), local college students (also for credit), and school parents. The Jewish day school students offered one-to-one tutoring, in addition to the classes taught by teachers. The process was not an easy one; co-operation between institutions does not always come readily, and change meets resistance. However, in this way the school became an invaluable resource to the community and over time developed extensive expertise in providing Hebrew language instruction. This was a good use of the school's resources, since a year earlier the Jewish Federation had provided grant funding for the day school to purchase curricular materials and train its own teachers in teaching Hebrew. Thus the Federation's grant helped the entire community, not just the Jewish day school. Some of the Hebrew classes met at the day school, while other classes met at the Jewish Community Centre, a senior citizens' centre, and a synagogue. During the process, negotiations among various interests were handled through a set of agreed principles that now serve as a foundation for future collaborations.

In this example the Jewish day school is the centre of Jewish education in the community, functioning as the axle of the wheel; the school is construed as the agent of community development. This perspective posits schools as proactive institutions that are integral to the overall development and growth of the community. Schools are seen as both the most universal and the most stable entities in communities that often face multiple challenges. From my experience this is an underdeveloped avenue of school–community collaboration for Jewish day schools. It is unusual for Jewish communities to think about their Jewish day schools as engines or agents of support and change for the community. In other words, the school could more productively be seen as being in the service of the community, rather than the other way around.

This view of the school as a vital and central force in supporting the community is not new. It emerges from a notion that public (state) schools can be tools for community and economic development. A report by the Harvard University Joint Center on Housing Studies stated: 'As major place-based infrastructure and an integral part of the community fabric, public schools can have a profound impact on the social, economic and psychological character of a neighborhood. Addressing public schools, therefore, is a good point of entry for community based developers to place their work in a comprehensive community development context.'[35]

Integrating school reform and neighbourhood revitalization has been central to some community development initiatives. For example, this perspective was behind school reform programmes in three of some of the most challenged schools and communities in Baltimore, St Louis, and Atlanta.[36] In the public school arena, community development with schools often involves projects such as providing better school-to-work transitions, by developing better relationships with local employers, or creating schools that are joint-use facilities, offering for example job training for adults in the evenings.

Two elements distinguish this perspective from earlier efforts at school–community collaboration. One is the degree to which schools are integrated with other, non-educational, institutions as part of a comprehensive community development strategy in what has been termed the 'holistic' perspective.[37] Timpane and Reich call this 'an ecosystem—a total environment supporting the healthy growth and development of America's youth'.[38]

A second element is the degree to which collaborative structures across multiple institutions—in the Jewish community, for example, local foundations, synagogues, Jewish community centres, and so on—work together with schools as the collective agents of community development. In this framework, often referred to as the 'alliance' model, existing institutions within a community—of which schools are often the most prominent—work together to build the resources available to the community at large.[39] Informal networks and arrangements together with formal structures help to provide support for the development of institutions within a community.

It is important to construct a role of community development for Jewish schools. This process can result in greater attention to the ways in which communities and schools define the boundaries between them and expand the areas where they overlap; greater consideration of the multiple cultures and histories that characterize both schools and their communities; and sustained engagement that permits students to gain the kind of deep

---

[35] Chung, *Using Public Schools*, p. iii.
[36] Proscio, *Schools, Community and Development*.
[37] McGaughey, 'The Role of Education in Community Development', 125.
[38] Timpane and Reich, 'Revitalizing the Ecosystem for Youth', 465–6.
[39] Crowson, 'Empowerment Models'.

knowledge that will inform their understandings in other locations. Schools, for example, may play a particularly crucial role in creating and maintaining public spaces that permit communities to enact and integrate their values.[40] As Timpane and Reich indicate:

At its heart, community development constitutes a philosophical change in the way schooling is conceived. Community development changes the core identity of schools from isolated, independent agencies to institutions enmeshed with other community agencies in an interconnected landscape of support for the well-being of students and learners . . . It beckons schools to consider and respond to learning needs throughout the community, not just to those of children within the school building.[41]

With greater emphasis on community development comes a necessary redefinition of the place and roles of schools in the larger revitalization of communities, and a reassessment of the role of communities in supporting the revitalization of schools. Recently the concept of 'civic capacity' has been applied to the notion of community development and school reform.[42] Civic capacity is defined as the 'degree to which a cross-sector coalition comes together in support of a task of community wide importance'.[43] The concept refers to the ability to build and maintain effective alliances for collective problem-solving.[44] Civic capacity emphasizes the collective role of community stakeholders, going beyond the view that any one single institution, such as a school, can address the needs of its constituency. 'In the education arena, the capacity of any set of stakeholders is limited, and so long as various players think and act in terms of a narrow view of their duty, they miss the full scope of the problem they face and the response to which they could contribute.'[45] Civic capacity is the cornerstone of community-building, itself defined as 'continuous, self-renewing efforts by residents and professionals to engage in collective action aimed at problem solving and enrichment that creates new or strengthened social networks, new capacities for group action and support and new standards and expec-

40 Driscoll, 'The Sense of Place'.
41 Timpane and Reich, 'Revitalizing the Ecosystem for Youth', 466.
42 Orr, 'Urban Politics and School Reform'.
43 Stone, 'Civic Capacity and Urban School Reform', 234.
44 Orr, 'Urban Politics and School Reform'.
45 Stone, 'Civic Capacity and Urban School Reform', 254.

tations for life in the community'.[46] This process can thrive when key professional and lay leaders embrace widespread civic capacity in place of narrow institutional interests.

Community development will not happen spontaneously; people from various agencies, institutions, and groups do not naturally come together to solve mutual problems and develop initiatives. Civic capacity denotes the motivation, community-mindedness, and activities necessary to address community-wide problems that are central to schools.

Civic capacity goes far beyond notions of social capital.[47] Social capital relies on the development of reciprocity and trust. However, it may not transfer easily from one context to another or from one situation to another. 'Social capital also rests, in significant part, on a basis of *shared loyalty and duty*. Reciprocity and trust are thus circumscribed; they may apply within some circles but not in others.'[48] Community development must engage individuals in an intergroup, rather than an interpersonal, context; hence the idea of civic capacity.

Social capital, or interpersonal trust, can be a starting point for developing civic capacity; civic capacity itself involves the need for communal groups to put aside competitive impulses and focus on community-wide alliances. In fact, co-operative relationships and mutual problem-solving between institutions and organizations can actually contribute to the development of social capital.[49] 'If social capital grows out of experiences of successful cooperation across differences in sector and power, agencies that can successfully bridge those gaps in order to promote cooperation can play an extraordinarily important role.'[50]

What about the political and financial issues involved in this approach? It is not unusual for institutions to compete for the hearts and minds, and monies, of the same community members; it is not unusual for institutions to think of their members as 'their own' and thus be concerned that other institutions in the community may lure them away. For example, in one community the day school could not overtly publicize its adult education programme for fear of angering some of the other Jewish agencies offering adult education in the community. Obviously, a community development perspective is quite contrary to this view of conducting the community's business.

[46] Walsh, *Stories of Renewal*, 5.
[47] Stone, 'Civic Capacity and Urban School Reform'.
[48] Ibid. 268 (emphasis in original).
[49] Brown, 'Creating Social Capital'.
[50] Ibid. 240.

Jack Wertheimer, in the AVI CHAI report mentioned above, addresses the question of community development by using a bus metaphor.

Imagine a bus is driving from the pre-school to the day school or supplementary school and then to the summer camps, teen programs and Israel trips. Who is working to get parents and children to board the bus, rather than remain fixed in only one institution? Few communities offer such a bus service and few education professionals think it is their responsibility to play the role of bus driver, announcing the stops and encouraging riders to get on and off the bus at as many stops as possible.[51]

Perhaps the community can be reshaped in such a way as to offer incentives for institutions to collaborate and co-operate. It might, for example, introduce a community-wide membership fee that afforded community members affiliation with a range of institutions in the community, rather than a separate membership fee for each and every organization to which one belongs. Thus a person could pay, say, X amount and then be a member of the Jewish Community Centre, a synagogue, and one other Jewish institution of their choice.

Questions Considering the Community Development Aspect of School–Community Collaboration

What school leadership arrangements facilitate the school's ability to undertake its core educational mission hand in hand with community outreach? It is evident that involvement in community development may require professional skills and knowledge to be distributed within the schools and their communities in a manner that is not presently the norm. A further challenge lies in discovering how these outreach activities—normally not the province of school leaders—can be integrated with the kinds of educational activities likely to have effects on learning.

We also need to know about the pitfalls of this approach for school leaders. Little of the research explores the 'downside' of connecting schools and communities, especially around development initiatives that locate schools more firmly in a sense of place and local culture.

We need to understand how principals who invest substantial time in developing community relationships integrate these demands with the

---

[51] Wertheimer, *Linking the Silos*, 31.

work of leading instruction in the school, and which activities yield the greatest rewards for student learning. Unless connections are made between this community work and the teaching and learning activities in the school, such investment may turn attention away from the important work of creating meaningful contexts for learning.

Implications for Leadership

New directions are required in leading schools and communities to become joint contexts for teaching and learning. I believe a focus on student learning in the community, developing social capital, and embarking on community development are good starting points for the endeavour to establish true school–community collaboration. I know this is an ambitious agenda. Thus, I end with the question: Can Jewish day schools meet the challenges raised by these conceptions of school–community collaboration?

Bibliography

Bransford, J., A. Brown, and R. Cocking (eds.), *How People Learn: Brain, Mind, Experience and School*, Commission on Behavioral and Social Sciences and Education, National Research Council (Washington, DC, 2000).

Bronfenbrenner, U., *The Ecology of Human Development* (Cambridge, Mass., 1979).

Brown, J., A. Collins, and P. Durgid, 'Situated Cognition and the Culture of Learning', *Educational Researcher*, 18/1 (1989), 32–41.

Brown, L. D., 'Creating Social Capital: Nongovernmental Development Organizations and Intersectoral Problem Solving', in W. W. Powell and E. S. Clemens (eds.), *Private Action and the Public Good* (New Haven, Conn., 1998), 228–41.

Bryke, A., and B. Schneider, *Trust in Schools: A Core Resource for Improvement* (New York, 2001).

Cahill, M., *A Documentation Report on the New York City Beacons Initiative* (New York, 1993).

Chung, C., *Using Public Schools as Community-Development Tools: Strategies for Community-Based Developers* (Boston, 2002).

Coleman, J. S., and T. Hoffer, *Public and Private High Schools: The Impact of Communities* (New York, 1987).

Commission on Jewish Education in North America, *A Time to Act* (New York, 1990).

Crowson, R., 'Empowerment Models for Interprofessional Collaboration', in M. Brabeck, M. Walsh, and R. E. Latta (eds.), *Meeting at the Hyphen: Schools—Universities—Communities: Professions in Collaboration for Student Achievement and Well-Being*, 102nd Yearbook of the National Society for the Study of Education, Part II (Chicago, 2003), 74–93.

—— and W. Boyd, 'Coordinated Services for Children: Designing Arks for Storms and Seas Unknown', *American Journal of Education*, 101/2 (1993), 140–79.

—— ——'The New Role of Community Development in Education Reform', *Peabody Journal of Education*, 76/2 (2001), 9–29.

Dewey, J., 'My Pedagogic Creed', *School Journal*, 54/3 (1897), 77–80.

Dika, S., and K. Singh, 'Applications of Social Capital in Educational Literature: A Critical Analysis', *Review of Educational Research*, 72/1 (2002), 31–60.

Driscoll, M. E., 'The Sense of Place and Conant's Legacy: Connecting Schools and their Communities', in F. Hammack (ed.), *The Comprehensive High School Today* (New York, 2004), 114–28.

—— 'The Sense of Place and the Neighborhood School: Implications for Building Social Capital and for Community Development', in R. Crowson (ed.), *Community Development and School Reform* (New York, 2001), 19–41.

Epstein, J., B. Simon, and K. Salinas, 'Involving Parents in Homework in the Middle Grades', *Phi Delta Kappa Research Bulletin*, 18 (Sept. 1997), <http//:www.pdkintl.org/research/rbulletins/resbul18.htm>.

Etzioni, A., *The Essential Communitarian Reader* (New York, 1998).

Field, J., *Social Capital* (London, 2003).

Goldring, E., 'Elementary School Principals as Boundary Spanners: Their Engagement with Parents', *Journal of Educational Administration*, 28/1 (1990), 53–62.

—— and C. Hausman, 'Civic Capacity and School Principals: The Missing Link for Community Development', in R. Crowson (ed.), *Community Development and School Reform* (New York, 2001), 193–210.

—— and A. Sullivan, 'Beyond the Boundaries: Principals, Parents and Communities Shaping the School Environment', in K. Leithwood, J. Chapman, D. Corson, P. Hallinger, and A. Hart (eds.), *International Handbook of Educational Leadership and Administration* (Boston, 1996), 195–222.

Granovetter, M., 'Economic Action, Social Structure, and Embeddedness', *American Journal of Sociology*, 91/3 (1985), 481–510.

Honig, M. I., J. Kahne, and M. W. McLaughlin, 'School–Community Connections: Strengthening Opportunity to Learn and Opportunity to Teach', in V. Richardson (ed.), *Handbook of Research on Teaching*, 4th edn. (Washington, DC, 2001), 998–1028.

Kerchner, C., 'Education as a City's Basic Industry', *Education and Urban Society*, 29/4 (1997), 424–41.

—— and G. McMurran, 'Leadership Outside the Triangle: The Challenges of School Administration in Highly Porous Systems', in R. Crowson (ed.), *Community Development and School Reform* (New York, 2001), 43–64.

McGaughey, C., 'The Role of Education in Community Development: The Akron Enterprise Community Initiative', in R. Crowson (ed.), *Community Development and School Reform* (New York, 2001), 121–38.

McKnight, J., and J. Kretzmann, *Building Communities from the Inside Out* (Evanston, Ill., 1993).

McLaughlin, M. W., *Community Counts: How Community Organizations Matter for Youth Development* (Washington, DC, 2000).

Mawhinney, H., 'Schools in the Bowling League of the New American Economy: Theorizing on Social/Economic Integration in School-to-Work Opportunity Systems', in R. Crowson (ed.), *Community Development and School Reform* (New York, 2001), 211–44.

Melaville, A., B. Shah, and M. Blank, *Making the Difference: Research and Practice in Community Schools* (Washington, DC, 2003).

Ogawa, R., and S. Studer, 'Bridging and Buffering Parent Involvement in Schools: Managing Exchanges of Social and Cultural Resources', in W. Hoy and C. Miskel (eds.), *Theory and Research in Educational Administration* (Greenwich, Conn., 2002), i. 97–128.

Orr, M., *Black Social Capital: The Politics of School Reform in Baltimore, 1986–1998* (Lawrence, Kan., 1999).

—— 'Urban Politics and School Reform: The Case of Baltimore', *Urban Affairs Review*, 31/ 3 (1996), 314–45.

Pena, R., C. McGill, and R. Stout, 'Community Based Organizations, Title 1. Schools and Youth Opportunity: Challenges and Contradictions', in R. Crowson (ed.), *Community Development and School Reform* (New York, 2001), 65–91.

Pitman, K., and M. Cahill, 'Pushing the Boundaries of Education: The Implications of a Youth Development Approach to Education, Policies, Structures and Collaborations', in Council of Chief State School Officers (ed.), *Ensuring Student Success through Collaboration: Summer Institute Papers and Recommendations of the Council of Chief State School Officers* (Washington, DC, 1992).

Pribesh, S., and D. Downey, 'Why Are Residential and School Moves Associated with Poor School Performance?', *Demography*, 36/4 (1999), 521–34.

Proefriedt, W., 'Education and Moral Purpose: The Dream Recovered', *Teachers College Record*, 86/3 (1985), 399–410.

Proscio, T., *Schools, Community and Development* (Washington, DC, 2004).

Putnam, R., *Making Democracy Work: Civic Traditions in Modern Italy* (Princeton, NJ, 1993).

—— L. M. Feldstein, and D. Cohen, *Better Together: Restoring the American Community* (New York, 2003).

Sander, T. H., and R. D. Putnam, 'Rebuilding the Stock of Social Capital', *The School Administrator*, 56/8 (1999), 28–33.

Sanders, M., and A. Harvey, 'Beyond the School Walls: A Case Study of Principal Leadership for School–Community Collaboration', *Teachers College Record*, 104/7 (2002), 1345–68.

Shirley, D., *Community Organizing or Urban School Reform* (Austin, Tex., 1997).

Stone, C. N., 'Civic Capacity and Urban School Reform', in C. N. Stone (ed.), *Changing Urban Education* (Lawrence, Kan., 1998), 250–74.

Timpane, M., and B. Reich, 'Revitalizing the Ecosystem for Youth', *Phi Delta Kappan*, 78/6 (1997), 464–70.

Walsh, J., *Stories of Renewal: Community Building and the Future of Urban America* (New York, 1997).

Warren, M. R., 'Communities and Schools: A New View of Urban Education Reform', *Harvard Educational Review*, 75/2 (2005), 133–74.

Wehlage, G., F. Neumann, and W. Secada, 'Standards of Authentic Achievement and Pedagogy', in Fred Neumann et al. (eds.), *Authentic Achievement: Restructuring Schools for Intellectual Quality* (San Francisco, 1996), 21–48.

Wertheimer, J., *Linking the Silos: How to Accelerate the Momentum in Jewish Education Today* (New York, 2005).

Woocher, J., 'Toward a Unified Field Theory of Jewish Continuity', in I. Aron, S. Lee, and S. Rossel (eds.), *A Congregation of Learners* (New York, 1995), 14–55.

From Control to Collaboration

Mapping School Communities across Diverse Contexts

CLAIRE SMREKAR

Introduction

How do schools' cultures and organizational priorities coalesce to produce particular models of school–community relations? How are these models mapped on to different kinds of schools, including choice ('charter' and 'magnet'), public or state, and private (independent and religious) schools? What are the implications of the types of relationship formed between families and schools for Jewish day school education worldwide?

This chapter addresses these questions by exploring four different models of school–community relations: co-optation, management, engagement, and coalition. These models are derived from qualitative case studies of public and private schools, including magnet schools,[1] Catholic schools,[2] workplace schools,[3] and neighbourhood schools,[4] located in urban and suburban contexts in the United States. Each model includes four elements that define the nature, quality, and intensity of association between schools and their communities—its goals, functions, relationships, and outcomes —and are reflected in the organizational practices and priorities of the schools.

The Concept of Community

According to contemporary notions of community, the community of residence does not reflect the community of psychological meaning for most families in today's society.[5] Observers distinguish between a concept associ-

---

[1] Smrekar and Goldring, *School Choice in Urban America*.
[2] Smrekar, *The Impact of School Choice and Community*.
[3] Smrekar, 'Lessons (and Questions) from Workplace Schools'.
[4] Smrekar and Cohen-Vogel, 'The Voices of Parents'.
[5] Bronfenbrenner et al., 'Child, Family, and Community', 103; Coleman and Hoffer, *Public and Private High Schools*; Newmann and Oliver, 'Education and Community', 61.

ated with physical or geographical boundaries and a concept grounded in social structures and social relations. For example, Newmann and Oliver include in their definition the following criteria, each of which is viewed as a continuum and indicative of greater or lesser degrees of community: (1) membership is valued as an end in itself, not merely as a means to other ends; (2) members share commitment to a common purpose; and (3) members have enduring and extensive personal contact with each other.[6] The sense of solidarity, membership, and mutual support that results from community is thought to impact both on the individual, in terms of personal development and social integration, and on the larger society, in terms of social cohesion and stability.[7]

The notion of a school as a community embraces both the communal associations and personal relationships sustained by a school's symbolic and personal dimensions and the more associative relationships driven by the need to accomplish structured activities and maintain particular work relations.[8] The vision of the school as a community portrays adults and students linked to one another by a common mission and by a network of supportive personal relationships that strengthen their commitment to the organization.[9]

The impact of community on the degree of social integration between families and schools is examined by Coleman and Hoffer in a study of private and public schools.[10] The researchers argue that both the type and strength of community in schools have varying effects on the critical social connections that bond families and schools in the joint enterprise of education. This concept of community refers to two types: functional and value. In functional communities, which are characterized by structural consistency between generations, social norms and sanctions arise out of the social structure itself, and both reinforce and perpetuate that structure. Functional communities exhibit a high degree of uniformity and cohesion within geographical, social, economic, and ideological boundaries. Value communities describe a collection of people who share similar values about education and childrearing but who do not constitute a functional community; they are strangers from various neighbourhoods, back-

---

[6] Newmann and Oliver, 'Education and Community', 6.
[7] Raywid, 'Community and Schools', 197.
[8] Bryk and Driscoll, *The High School as Community*, 5.
[9] Ibid. 18.   [10] Coleman and Hoffer, *Public and Private High Schools*.

grounds, and occupations united around an educational organization—their children's school.

Catholic Schools

Families of Catholic school students may constitute both value and functional communities. Besides having values in common, these families may attend the same religious services and know one another. These functional communities, however, are more circumscribed than the prototypical one described above: they encompass only a religious institution and do not apply across other social or economic institutions.

Magnet Schools

Parents of children who attend a magnet school may constitute a value community if they exhibit a high degree of value consistency—for example, commitment to a particular educational philosophy—but for the most part are strangers drawn from a wide collection of city neighbourhoods who they have little contact with one another outside school corridors.

Neighbourhood Schools

Many public, neighbourhood elementary schools reflect geographical communities but lack the value consistency or interinstitutional linkages of either the value or the functional community. In the early twentieth century neighbourhood schools served residential areas that were functional communities; more recently, social and technological changes have transformed many of these communities from enclaves of shared values and daily face-to-face talk into somewhat disparate sets of interests and weak affiliations.

*

The research on organizational features that promote community in schools points to an array of structural and compositional factors, including school size, sector, diversity of student body, and student selectivity.[11] The empirical research in this area has focused primarily on the characteristics of 'effective' schools in the Catholic and private sectors.[12] The explicit mission or ethos of Catholic and private schools, and their comparatively

---

[11] Bryk and Driscoll, *The High School as Community*, 30.
[12] Bryk et al., *Catholic Schools and the Common Good*; Cookson and Persell, *Preparing for Power*; Peshkin, *God's Choice*.

smaller and more homogeneous student bodies, have been considered of key importance in creating the foundational elements of community (for example, shared goals, personal ties) within these schools. Questions remain as to how organizational practices and priorities that specify particular goals, functional arrangements, relationships, and outcomes related to school–community connections are mapped on to particular school types, including both public (choice and non-choice) and private (independent and religious) schools. How do these elements coalesce to shape various models of school community across different school types? The next section unpacks each model to examine the implications of various organizational priorities for new conceptions of community in Jewish day schools.

Models: Practices and Priorities

The Co-optation Model

The co-optation model is derived from studies of public schools located in urban contexts characterized by high levels of poverty and social isolation. In these settings, schools often establish control as a goal in their association with families and community members, pre-empting other more collaborative and reciprocal approaches. The relationship is defined by a provider–receiver arrangement in which a school assumes the role of provider (of educational services) and families are assigned the role of receiver.[13] The essential outcome of the family–school relationship in this context resembles a contract. This contract may take the form of a school-wide, codified discipline policy and/or other formal agreements between school and parents, including the Individualized Education Plans required for the (often high) percentage of students in these contexts who receive services under the US special education law. This outcome tends to restrict the nature of family–school relations to the legal–instrumental functions specified in a set of requirements and obligations that exist between parents and school officials.

In case studies of urban elementary schools many of whose students are poor and many of whom belong to ethnic minorities, researchers in the United States have found a persistent pattern of school communities suggestive of a co-optation model.[14] Harvard researcher Sarah Lightfoot argues

---

[13] Smrekar and Cohen-Vogel, 'The Voices of Parents', 85.
[14] See Delgado-Gaitan, 'School Matters in the Mexican-American Home', 495; Goldenberg,

that the lives of families and schools are 'worlds apart'.[15] This pattern, it appears, has endured for decades. Willard Waller, author of the classic work *The Sociology of Teaching*, published in 1932, called parents and teachers 'natural enemies'. Our qualitative study of a public elementary school located in an ethnically diverse community in northern California provides an illustrative example of the social distance, gaps in communication, and legal controls characteristic of the co-optation model.

Structured interactions delimit communication between families and schools to formal, abrupt, and incomplete exchanges. Time and space are highly regulated within this domain. Unannounced visits to the classroom are discouraged; parents are expected to check-in at the front office or to make pre-arrangements with a school official. Parents are seen as intruders . . . Evening meetings are convened on school grounds rather than in community centers or parents' homes. Meeting agendas are set internally and reflect school officials' registered concerns and priorities. Letters go home to inform, rarely to solicit input or to generate sustained dialogue. Telephone calls from school officials signal a serious problem, not a friendly inquiry.[16]

This study was based upon extensive interviews with parents, teachers, and non-teaching staff. The interview data suggest that school–community relations in this case were defined primarily by a pattern of unilateral decision-making and limited social interactions. As one parent observed: 'We only talk when the teacher feels it is important and we only talk about what the teacher feels is important, not what I feel is important.'[17] A father of four children who was active in the school's parent–teacher association noted: 'A lot of people don't think that the parents are related to the school, but they are. In order to get this relationship stronger, they must build a fellowship—academic, social, whatever.'[18]

Other parents pointed to the formal, often legalistic, conditions established by the school through the set of parental agreements it creates, including school-wide discipline policies, school visiting policies, homework policies, and special education programmes. These policies tend to imply an asymmetry of power, knowledge, and control and the appropria-

'Accommodating Cultural Differences', 16; Harry, 'An Ethnographic Study', 66; Henry, *Parent–School Collaboration*; Mapp, 'Having their Say', 35.

[15] Lightfoot, *Worlds Apart*.   [16] Smrekar and Cohen-Vogel, 'The Voices of Parents', 92.
[17] Ibid. 94.   [18] Ibid. 95.

tion of these attributes by school officials. Rather than fostering a sense of community grounded in mutual respect, shared commitment, and sustained co-operation, these one-way binding agreements—much like a contract—establish an oppositional and litigious culture that pits parents against school officials.

How do classic or contemporary conceptions of community inform the co-optation model? The historical distinctions made by Tönnies between *Gemeinschaft* (community) and *Gesellschaft* (society) provide point and direction to this discussion.[19] These differences relate to the nature of relationships within, respectively, communities and societies, which range from more natural and organic in communities to more mechanical and rational in societies. Thus, relationships within an authentic community (*Gemeinschaft*) are rooted in familiarity and interdependence, whereas societal relationships (in a *Gesellschaft*) reflect formal, contractual relations of the kind found in legal and commercial institutions and bureaucratic organizations. *Gesellschaft* provides the conceptual scaffolding for the co-optation model. The co-optation model—which, as noted above, persists especially in school–community contexts characterized by high levels of poverty and high numbers of ethnic minority students—stands bolted to the formal, bureaucratic, and contractual relations found in the broader society. In these school contexts, the social relations between families and schools are codified in the legalistic relationships and prescribed functions outlined in disciplinary codes and Individualized Education Plans. These relations fall far short of the notion of a school as a community, embracing neither the communal associations and personal relationships described by Bryk and colleagues in their study of Catholic communities, nor the familiarity and continuity that characterize Coleman and Hoffer's value and functional communities respectively.

Arguments and evidence linked to the role of schooling in social reproduction within American society and the social stratification effects of education in these contexts stretch beyond the scope of this chapter. For Jewish day schools, it may be more instructive and more productive to consider alternative models that move schools from co-optation to collaboration. Henry suggests replacing the contemporary or 'corporate' model, in which 'autonomy, separation, and distance' are valued, with a more 'democratic' one.[20] The new model would encourage school communities to develop

---

[19] Tönnies, *Community and Society.*   [20] Henry, *Parent–School Collaboration*, 39.

new priorities and processes that diminish conflict and distance between families and schools. This fresh concept might render the term 'parent involvement' insufficient and parent report cards illegitimate, allowing an alternative to emerge whose language embodies a mutual, communal, and equitable exchange between families and schools.

The Management Model

The extant research on school–community relations suggests that a management model predominates in public schools across the United States. Schools run in this way emphasize certainty and structure as essential goals in their associations with families and members of the community outside school. The relationship is defined by a co-production orientation. Schools produce particular educational services; parents produce parallel but distinguishable services in predictable and reliable ways. These institutionalized functions are both taken for granted and explicated in a set of outcomes— categories of family participation that describe (and, to some degree, prescribe) a set of school–community interactions.

Although the nature of family–school relations could be construed as both broad and complex, the management model reflects efforts by advocates and policy-makers—and even some education researchers—to provide specific categories of parent involvement. In training manuals assembled by school districts for teachers and parents, charts describe parents acting in roles ranging from 'advisers' and 'advocates' to 'home-based tutors' and 'traditional audience'.[21] Other researchers map the locations of potential parent input and action to include the home and the school; within those broad categories, activities are identified as either advisory or collaborative.[22] Perhaps no other model has emerged to dominate research, policy, and practice more than the 'partnership' model developed by Johns Hopkins University researcher Joyce Epstein.[23] The Epstein framework is designed as a template for school administrators; in effect, the types of interaction and involvement identified by Epstein become the predictable categories of interaction with families and external community members

[21] See Burch, 'Circles of Change', 12; Chrispeels, 'Effective Schools', 8; Comer, *School Power*, 23; Davies, 'Schools Reaching Out', 379; National Education Goals Panel, 'Executive Summary', 32; Swap, *Developing Home–School Partnerships*, 22; US Department of Education, *Strong Families, Strong Schools*, 8.   [22] Shields and McLaughlin, *Parent Involvement*, 13.
[23] See Epstein, *School, Family, and Community Partnerships*, 42.

that are (or should be) managed by school officials. The model includes six distinct strands or types of involvement:

1. *Parenting*, which includes the basic obligations of families to create healthy and nurturing home conditions.

2. *Communicating*, which includes the basic obligations of schools to communicate with families about school practices and programmes.

3. *Volunteering*, which involves roles for parents that assist teachers and administrators in supporting academic, sporting, and other activities.

4. *Learning at home*, which involves family involvement in skill-building and educational enrichment activities at home that support classroom learning.

5. *Decision-making*, which involves parent participation in school decision-making and governance through school site councils and other organized policy-making and advocacy groups.

6. *Collaborating with community*, which includes the obligation of schools to identify and integrate community resources and services in order to enhance school and family practices and promote student achievement.

Epstein argues that 'the term "school, family and community partnerships" is a better, broader term than "parent involvement" to express the shared interests, responsibilities, investments, and the overlapping influences of family, school, and community for the education and development of the children they share across the school years'.[24] Unlike the co-optation model, the management model—with the Epstein template embedded as a blueprint for family–school relations—presumes two-way communication across a more robust array of differentiated tasks, scripted well beyond the legal and formal arrangements prescribed in the former, more asymmetrical, model. At the same time, this 'partnership' emphasizes the separable and identifiable activities that comprise school, community, and parent activities.

Over time, these distinct categories or roles have become institutionalized in many US public schools, producing common understandings about what is appropriate and fundamentally meaningful behaviour for,

---

[24] Id., 'School and Family Partnerships', 39.

respectively, parents, teachers, and external school communities. Manuals and reports issued by the US Department of Education embrace these categories as appropriate, research-based activities for parents, teachers, and community members that lead to highly effective, high-performing schools. Institutional theory helps explain how school-based activities (such as fundraising functions and parent–teacher meetings) and home-based activities (such as helping with homework) become ritualized events, further legitimating the roles defined for school community members.[25] The institutional environment then sanctions similar organizations—schools —on the basis of these established norms. Parents learn over time the circumscribed roles that they are expected to assume. They learn to think of themselves as 'supporters', 'helpers', and 'fundraisers'. Our studies of elementary schools—both public and private—suggest that parents' involvement in schools beyond these functions, as 'decision-makers' and 'partners', may be compromised by the press of other obligations, including work and family responsibilities.[26] In an illustrative case study of an elementary school community located in a middle-class neighbourhood in northern California, parents regularly and predictably recited an inventory of activities they assumed in a co-production relationship with the school.[27] Most identified their primary role by context: that is, they expressed an overwhelming willingness to assume the role of teacher or monitor (of homework) in their home. This relational perspective—definition of the parent's role in relation to the role of the teacher or the arrangement of school activities—was taken for granted, unquestioned. As one mother of three observed, 'She teaches; I reinforce it, go over it, whatever it needs, at home, to back up that teacher.' Homework provided the institutionalized niche for parents to engage in their children's schooling, along with school meetings and teacher conferences, fundraisers, and occasional 'reading nights'.

The experiences and explanations of parents in this case study suggest that the organization of parents' working lives critically influences their patterns of participation in *school-based* events. Parents are involved *at home*; family rhythms and routines reflect rather insular patterns of social interaction within families and at work in the absence of social networks with other school families or interactions with school officials. In the end, parent involvement of this limited but predictable nature may be managed easily

---

[25] Meyer and Rowan, 'Institutionalized Organizations', 350.
[26] Smrekar, *The Impact of School Choice and Community*, 4–5.   [27] Ibid. 141.

and effectively, for both parents and teachers. Homework completion rates may be high; school meetings may draw acceptable numbers; fundraising goals may be met. But in the absence of a robust community characterized by a sense of social cohesion, commitment, communication, shared values, familiarity, membership, and ownership, these are tenuous connections among school families, and between parents and the school. What are the consequences of this situation?

The management model provides an instructive note for Jewish day schools by underscoring the value of school communities and the importance of 'bringing community back' to the discussion and research surrounding families and schools. How are the concept and reality of the robust school community different from categorized parental involvement? Why does community matter? (For general support and fundraising? For help with homework?) Why is community valuable to parents? Our studies point to the importance of building networks of trust and respect, and a sense of ownership and familiarity, in the construction of school communities.

The next section explores the engagement model, in which a robust school community is fully realized in the context of public choice and Catholic schools.

The Engagement Model

Evidence suggests that public (choice) schools and many private (religious) schools, including Catholic schools, develop an engagement model with parents and members of the external community.[28] The relationship between families and schools embedded in this model portrays parents as constituents or clients and school officials as professionals, suggesting distinct roles coupled with mutual respect and shared values. In functional relationships defined more as social than legal/instrumental or institutional, public choice and private schools often seek a product-oriented goal of consensus. The material outcome of this association resembles a co-constructed compact, rather than a restrictive contract. The process of building consensus rests on relationships built upon shared commitment and sustained co-operation—across school families and between families and school officials. Thus the elements of the engagement model are

[28] See Bryk and Driscoll, *The High School as Community*, 21; Smrekar, *The Impact of School Choice and Community*, 141; Smrekar and Goldring, *School Choice in Urban America*, 98.

mutually reinforcing. The compact is co-constructed by both families and schools, and may reflect a set of 'vision statements' related to the educational goals for children. These statements establish a set of strategies for achieving the goals—ideas that can evolve only through meaningful and sustained interactions between each student/family and the school. The compact reflects parallel convictions, intentions, and obligations on the part of parents and school officials. Since parents have voluntarily selected the choice school or private school, there is little sense of institutional control or power play.

In our study of magnet and non-magnet schools in two large urban districts in the United States—St Louis, Missouri, and Cincinnati, Ohio—we found in both survey data and qualitative case studies that parents who selected a magnet school attended more school activities, volunteered more frequently, and visited the school more often.[29] This heightened level of commitment among magnet school families reflects the constituent elements of value communities described by Coleman and Hoffer. As one father in our study framed it: 'There is something that unites people. Maybe it is because they feel like they strive for the same goal and that everyone has their kids there for a particular purpose.'[30] Parents in magnet schools construe a deeper level of commitment, caring, and responsiveness in their school environment as compared to non-choice school settings. They report a consensus view with other parents who have chosen alternatives to the neighbourhood schools. As another parent observed: 'Everybody has a common goal, a common mission.'[31]

The nature of magnet schools and private schools means that families whose children are enrolled in these schools live scattered across geographical space; these social spaces differ from the geographical or functional communities outlined by Coleman and Hoffer, which exhibit a high degree of uniformity and cohesion within geographical, social, economic, and ideological boundaries. Magnet school parents in St Louis and Cincinnati agree that scarce discretionary time, long distances, and multiple work and family obligations inhibit involvement in school-based activities beyond the occasional fundraiser or social event. These conditions were reported in

[29] Smrekar and Goldring, *School Choice in Urban America*, 79. Magnet schools in the United States, which offer a distinctive curriculum or instructional programme, are designed to attract students of different racial backgrounds from across a school district. They were introduced in the 1970s as a tool for voluntary racial desegregation.   [30] Ibid. 89.   [31] Ibid. 92.

earlier multi-case studies of a neighbourhood school, a magnet school, and a Catholic school:

Across social class and school setting . . . for many parents, the exigencies of work and family lives demand deliberate rationing of their limited time and energy. School-based activities such as PTA meetings, spaghetti dinner fundraisers, and parenting workshops are considered extras that they cannot afford. Unless their children are involved in an event or activity, there is little interest in making the effort. Even then, many parents find it difficult to adjust their work schedules to fit school hours.[32]

Parents' exchanges regarding common values and shared beliefs are tethered to rather brief, abbreviated, and anonymous parent-to-parent interactions. These parents report that they 'do not know many other parents' in their choice school, but most maintain an unwavering belief that other magnet parents or Catholic school parents are like-minded in terms of educational values and commitment. To be sure, these are communities formed around commitment to an organization, not grafted on to an elevated sense of familiarity (or functional community) with other members.

For school officials, particular challenges are provoked by the problems of parents' distance, distraction, and disconnection. To the extent that the school community is viewed as a crucial aspect of a school's capacity to promote student learning, these findings are important. Schools organized as communities that support and develop robust, reliable, and sustained family–school interactions both in the home and at the school create conditions for increased collegiality, improved problem-solving, and enhanced capacity-building.[33] We argue that authentic school communities embrace both value and geography. Driscoll observes that 'the concept of school community reflects the needs that are derived from shared activities and territory but also embodies the culture of sentiments, traditions, and practices that link its members and from which they take meaning'.[34]

It is with this principle of shared space and shared meaning clearly in view that Jewish day school educators need to consider the distractions within everyday working and family lives that prevent the actual patterns of involvement and sense of community in choice schools—public as well as

[32] Smrekar, The Impact of School Choice and Community, 143.
[33] Bryk and Driscoll, The High School as Community, 16.
[34] Driscoll, 'Thinking Like a Fish', 120.

private—reaching promised (and optimal) levels in terms of magnitude and quality. These challenges represent the lessons learned from our study of public choice (magnet) and private (Catholic) schools, and provide the point of departure for Jewish day school leaders who emphasize the importance of both value and functional communities simultaneously. Still, the questions remain: How can schools organize themselves to be better prepared to confront the exigencies of hectic working lives and chaotic family lives? With policy-makers in both public choice schools and private schools predicting new and expanded pathways for parental involvement, innovative strategies are required to form new communities within this pattern of geographical dispersion and social disconnection. How can (or do) Jewish day schools move beyond the institutionalized information and communication channels (newsletters, emails) and traditional avenues for participation and performance (PTA meetings, fundraisers, science fairs)? How can Jewish day schools knit together the elements of community fractured by the constraints of competing work, school, and family demands? What new social scaffolding may be bolted to the infrastructures of working families? The next model provides a blueprint for considering new social structures that promote authentic *Gemeinschaft* communities.

The Coalition Model

Coalition models, though rare, may be found in the relationships defined as partnerships between public choice schools and their corporate sponsors.[35] Embedded in a school culture framed by focused instructional designs and sustained by a goal of collaboration with members of their corporate community, workplace schools highlight the orientation to familial functions among public school teachers, private corporate employers, and those companies' employees. These schools produce an outcome closely approximating *Gemeinschaft* community.

In the early 1990s corporate-sponsored elementary schools were established in dozens of workplaces across the United States, including the corporate headquarters of Target Stores, Bank of America, Hewlett-Packard, and Mt Sinai Medical Center. These arrangements typically require corporate sponsors to provide the facility and assume full responsibility for maintaining it; school districts provide the staff and assume full responsibility

---

[35] Smrekar, 'Lessons (and Questions) from Workplace Schools', 174.

for instruction. These public schools of choice give parents who are employed by the corporate sponsor the option of selecting the workplace for their 'neighbourhood' school. By bridging the geographical gap between work and school, the concept of workplace schools confronts the tension between a socially sanctioned pattern of increased time spent at work—the 'culture called to work'—and the increased demand for parental involvement in the educational lives of schoolchildren.[36]

Among the case studies of family–school–work integration, the Midwestern Downtown School provides one of the most vivid illustrations of the value of locating a school close to where parents *work* rather than to where they *live*.[37] The Downtown School reflects a partnership among a group of businesses that share a physical (downtown or business park) address and a school with whom all partners share an educational philosophy anchored to the value of *Gemeinschaft* communities.

In the first year, forty-five children enrolled in the tiny elementary school. The Downtown School was highlighted in a local newspaper article in the summer of 1993 but was not advertised by the school district in any way; information regarding the 'experiment' spread by word of mouth among the employees of American Equities, Digital TelComm, Danforth Agricultural Research, and other downtown businesses. One parent interviewed for this study recalled the first year as one 'based upon a blind faith in a school that felt like a big family and like a small business'.[38]

In the autumn of 2003 the Midwestern Downtown School enrolled 160 pupils aged between 5 and 11 in a non-graded, year-round instruction programme directed by a faculty comprising ten full-time teachers. No transport is provided for students; parents simply walk their children to school on their way to work. Over 90 per cent of the parents are employed, most of them in downtown Midwestern City, where they work in occupations that range from attorney and financial analyst to waitress and data entry clerk. The school has grown from the original 5,000 square feet of office space on

[36] See Hochschild, *The Time Bind*, 16. Almost half of the American workforce is composed of parents whose spouses or partners also work outside the home (US Bureau of Labor Statistics, *Handbook on Labor Statistics*; Galinsky et al., *The Changing Workforce*). These parent employees are part of a workforce that is spending more and more hours each month at work, taking less unpaid leave and enjoying shorter vacations each year (US Bureau of Labor Statistics, *Handbook on Labor Statistics*; Schor, *The Overworked American*). In an American 'culture called to work', married couples today spend 185 hours more per year at work than couples spent just ten years ago.

[37] All school and business names listed here are pseudonyms.

[38] Smrekar, 'Lessons (and Questions) from Workplace Schools', 173

the second floor of 501 Hill Street to include two additional nearby office suites.

The Downtown School embraces its urban geography. The teachers and students incorporate the city neighbourhood as their school without walls. This 'sense of place' pays rich dividends to teachers, parents, and community members who nurture the notion that the school's location is much more than an address.[39] For teachers, this translates into an integrated, seamless connection to the physical and cultural landscape enveloping the school. For a study of physics, teachers 'borrowed' the skating rink at the Veterans' Auditorium two blocks away. Lessons were followed by demonstrations of ice-making and melting, and, of course, ice-skating. Nearby, the highly regarded Midwestern City Art Museum, where a few parents of Downtown School children work, provides a free and readily accessible material lesson in art history, architecture, and sculpture. The school's library is the City Library—and the collection is impressive. The students' artwork is regularly displayed on the walls of the skywalk, in the corridors of American Equities Group, and in the windows of the Convention Center. Each year, students from the Downtown School make the five-minute skywalk trip to the Bank of the Midwest, where bank officials (some of whom are parents of Downtown students) relate the concepts of mathematics, currency, and basic investment strategies to the children. For teachers, these events are considered 'field work' (not an isolated 'trip') and are wrapped around the curriculum in fundamental ways that are designed to capture the downtown neighbourhood as canvas for students' learning and expression.

These case study findings suggest that robust and reliable parent involvement occurs naturally under these conditions of convenience, bringing teachers and parents together in the morning rituals of dropping off children at the school, just a minute's walk from the downtown office door. Parents are welcome any time to call in and observe class instruction, take their children to lunch (or eat with them at the school), or read to a small group of students. As the Downtown School principal observed: 'We've changed what parent involvement means. We're re-connecting with families, making it easier for parents to stop by for 10 minutes in a day. It's perfect for teachers, employees, and employers.'[40]

[39] Driscoll, 'The Sense of Place and the Neighborhood School'.
[40] Smrekar, 'Lessons (and Questions) from Workplace Schools', 182.

When the workplace and the neighbourhood are fused, as in the Midwestern Downtown School, the 'coalition' is fully formed, and the concepts of functional and value communities (and new geographical communities) merge. The coalition model explicated in the workplace school community creates new collaborative agreements between schools, employers, and employees characterized by more fluid communication, more natural and organic interaction, and greater financial and cultural interdependence between schools and workplaces. To be sure, these structural and social arrangements between corporate/workplace sponsors and public school districts are unusual: there are fewer than fifty such partnerships across the United States.[41] The rarity and distinctiveness of this model render it somewhat more remote in both concept and practice from the current realities of Jewish day schools. Nevertheless, the intent here is to identify mutually adaptive strategies and concepts designed to link families, schools, and communities within the realities and practicalities of families' working lives.

The social scaffolding, rooted in conceptions of *Gemeinschaft* community, helps to form relationships of a deliberately more familial and interdependent kind than those that make up the social fabric woven in the engagement model. These relationships among parents and between the workplace partners and school officials promote the shared expectations that form the uniformity and interconnectedness of functional communities.

Inevitably, questions arise. What are the implications of such seamless coalitions for issues of authority and control? Whose values and what priorities are privileged in these new workplace schools? Indeed, how far can the 'corporate community' (or government-sponsored organization) move into the discrete sphere of Jewish day schooling without violating cultural norms and sensibilities? Is this coalition model—conceptually and practically—a smart move for Jewish day school leaders? Who benefits? Who loses?

---

[41] The public schools sponsored by the US Department of Defense (DoD Education Activity), which are located on military posts and serve only the dependants of US military personnel, reflect the structurally and socially integrative attributes of workplace schools. The DoDEA operates 206 schools worldwide, serving over 103,000 students in grades K–12 (Smrekar et al., *The March toward Excellence*).

Table 2.1

Family–school relationships

Element	Model			
	Co-optation	Management	Engagement	Coalition
Goal	Control	Certainty and structure	Consensus	Collaboration
Relationship	Producer–receiver	Professional–constituent	Co-producers	Partners
Function	Legal–instrumental	Institutional	Social	Familial
Outcome	Contracts	Categories	Compacts	*Gemeinschaft* (Community)

Summary

With the reality of the new 'culture called to work' moving to the foreground in American life, the 'shared space and shared meaning' of traditional residential communities is shifting to a new address.[42] Consonant norms and shared trust are evidenced in the relations between parents and teachers in workplace schools and are made manifest in the exercise of school choice. This affirmative decision among people who share similar values about education and childrearing, but who are strangers from various neighbourhoods (in fact, are often strangers to one another in their workplaces), creates the conditions for value communities in the context of workplace schools.

The school community models explicated in this chapter—co-optation, management, engagement, coalition (see Table 2.1)—have been examined against the backdrop of contemporary definitions, including communal associations, communities of shared meaning and space, geographical communities, and value communities. The findings provide a framework for considering how these comparative contexts—exemplified by traditional public schools, Catholic schools, workplace schools, and magnet schools—increase our understanding of community building in Jewish schools. What models (or hybrids) best 'fit' within the cultural priorities and organizational constraints of Jewish day schools? To what degree do (or should) Jewish day schools reflect movement across the continuum towards greater social integration and interdependence of school, family,

---

[42] Driscoll, 'Thinking Like a Fish', 129.

work, and community? John Goodlad labelled this interdependence 'the new ecology of schooling'.[43] From our vantage point, this new interdependence is well established and firmly rooted in a recognition that the integration of work life and family life is a cultural priority in an era of competitive labour markets, dual-career families, and the social pressure to succeed materially in both work and family (including schooling) endeavours. In the twenty-first century, the family has been made visible in the social milieu of work life and school life. Thus, what 'sense of place' defines Jewish day school communities? Where are Jewish day school communities situated along the continuum of social integration? Management? Engagement? Coalition? What school culture and organizational priorities coalesce to produce this particular model of school community? Who decides?

[43] Goodlad, *The Ecology of School Renewal*, 39.

Bibliography

Bronfenbrenner, U., P. Moen, and J. Garbarino, 'Child, Family, and Community', in R. Parke (ed.), *Review of Child Development Research: The Family* (Chicago, 1984), 283–328.

Bryk, A., and M. Driscoll, *The High School as Community: Contextual Influences and Consequences for Students and Teachers* (Madison, Wisc., 1988).

—— V. Lee, and P. Holland, *Catholic Schools and the Common Good* (Cambridge, Mass., 1993).

Burch, P., 'Circles of Change: Action Research on Family–School–Community Partnerships', *Equity and Choice*, 10/1 (1993), 11–16.

Chrispeels, J., 'Effective Schools and Home–School–Community Partnership Roles: A Framework for Parent Involvement', *School Effectiveness and School Improvement*, 7/3 (1996), 7–33.

Coleman, J. S., and T. Hoffer, *Public and Private High Schools: The Impact of Communities* (New York, 1987).

Comer, J., *School Power* (New York, 1980).

Cookson, P., and C. Persell, *Preparing for Power: America's Elite Boarding Schools* (New York, 1985).

Davies, D., 'Schools Reaching Out: Family, School and Community Partnerships for Student Success', *Phi Delta Kappan*, 72/5 (1993), 376–82.

Delgado-Gaitan, C., 'School Matters in the Mexican-American Home: Socializing Children to Education', *American Educational Research Journal*, 29/3 (1992), 495–513.

Driscoll, M., 'The Sense of Place and the Neighborhood School: Implications for Building Social Capital and for Community Development', in R. Crowson (ed.), *Advances in Research and Theories in School Management and Educational Policy* (Greenwich, Conn., 2001), 19–42.

—— 'Thinking Like a Fish: The Implications of the Image of School Community for Connections between Parents and Schools', in P. Cookson and Barbara Schneider (eds.), *Transforming Schools* (New York, 1995), 209–36.

Epstein, J., *School, Family, and Community Partnerships: Your Handbook for Action* (Thousand Oaks, Calif., 2002).

Epstein, J., 'School and Family Partnerships', in Marvin Alkin (ed.), *Encyclopedia of Educational Research*, 6th edn. (New York, 1992), 1139–51.

Galinsky, E., J. Bond, and D. Friedman, *The Changing Workforce: Highlights of the National Study* (New York, 1993).

Goldenberg, C., 'Accommodating Cultural Differences and Commonalities in Educational Practice', *Multicultural Education*, 4/1 (1996), 16–19.

Goodlad, J., *The Ecology of School Renewal: Eighty-Ninth Yearbook of the National Society for the Study of Education* (Chicago, 1987).

Harry, B., 'An Ethnographic Study of Cross-Cultural Communication with Puerto Rican-American Families in the Special Education System', *American Educational Research Journal*, 29/3 (1992), 66–85.

Henry, M. E., *Parent–School Collaboration: Feminist Organizational Structures and School Leadership* (Albany, NY, 1996).

Hochschild, A. R., *The Time Bind* (New York, 1997).

Lightfoot, S. L., *Worlds Apart* (New York, 1978).

Mapp, K., 'Having their Say: Parents Describe Why and How They Are Engaged in their Children's Learning', *School Community Journal*, 13/1 (2003), 35–64.

Meyer, J., and B. Rowan, 'Institutionalized Organizations: Formal Structure as Myth and Ceremony', *American Journal of Sociology*, 83 (1977), 340–68.

National Education Goals Panel, 'Executive Summary', *National Education Goals Report 1995* (Washington, DC, 1995).

Newmann, F., and D. Oliver, 'Education and Community', *Harvard Educational Review*, 37/1 (1968), 61–106.

Peshkin, A., *God's Choice: The Total World of a Fundamentalist Christian School* (Chicago, 1986).

Raywid, M. A., 'Community and Schools: A Prolegomenon', *Teachers College Record*, 90/2 (1988), 197–209.

Schemo, D., 'Report Cards are Due, only this Time for Parents', *New York Times*, 24 Nov. 2000, A23.

Schor, J., *The Overworked American: The Unexpected Decline of Leisure* (New York, 1992).

Shields, P., and M. McLaughlin, *Parent Involvement in Compensatory Education Programs* (Stanford, Calif., 1986).

Smrekar, C., *The Impact of School Choice and Community: In the Interest of Families and Schools* (Albany, NY, 1996).

—— 'Lessons (and Questions) from Workplace Schools on the Interdependence of Family, School and Work', in R. Crowson (ed.), *Advances in Research and Theories in School Management and Educational Policy* (Greenwich, Conn., 2001).

—— and L. Cohen-Vogel, 'The Voices of Parents: Rethinking the Intersection of Family and School', *Peabody Journal of Education*, 76/2 (2001), 75–101.

—— and E. Goldring, *School Choice in Urban America: Magnet Schools and the Pursuit of Equity* (New York, 1999).

—— J. Guthrie, D. Owens, and P. Sims, *The March toward Excellence* (Washington, DC, 2001).

Swap, S. M., *Developing Home–School Partnerships: From Concepts to Practice* (New York, 1993).

Tönnies, F., *Community and Society*, ed. and trans. C. Loomis (New York, 1963).

US Bureau of Labor Statistics, *Handbook on Labor Statistics* (Washington, DC, 2000).

US Department of Education, *Strong Families, Strong Schools* (Washington, DC, 1994).

Waller, W., *The Sociology of Teaching* (New York, 1932).

Compassionate Conservatism

On Schools, Community, and Democracy

DEBORAH MEIER

WHEN I WROTE my friend Miriam to say I was coming to Jerusalem to talk about Jewish education, she wrote back, and I quote, 'You? On Jewish education?'

I admit, I had virtually no formal Jewish education. As a student I went to independent private schools. The schools I have been involved in as a teacher and principal have all been public schools, in the US sense of that phrase, and it so happens they were all schools serving predominantly low-income African American and Latino students and families, located in largely ghetto communities of colour and poverty. In some of these there was a small white population, and probably half of those were Jews.

So much for my qualifications to address this topic.

On the other hand, I have a strong sense of my Jewish identity, which is connected to my absurd belief that in fact I had a deeply Jewish secular education at the hands of a family that was immersed in New York City's Jewish life as well as its intellectual life. Both of my parents were prominent leaders of Jewish organizations: my father was head of the UJA-Federation for his entire adult life, and my mother was president of both the International and National Councils of Jewish Women. Our dinner table was always the centre of my education, and their library a challenge: would I ever read it all?

So I had a rather romantic and egocentric notion of what lay at the heart of being a Jew, and it had to do with the habits of heart, mind, and work that epitomized my own experience as a Jew in New York City. I imagined Jewish education was built around the idea of the young being immersed in the culture, or, as I later would say, in the company of the adults they aspired to join and believed they were destined to become; that being 'educated' was a process that started with immersion, exposure, and acceptance.

I assumed Jewish education was also argumentative, questioning, doubting, and yet also loving and caring. It was, I took for granted, grounded in respectful uncertainties but not therefore one whit less passionately dedicated to the truth. And I assumed, because my family's life was also immersed in social and political struggles for defending and expanding democracy, that these were also the habits of mind suited to a democratic society. I imagined, in turn, that as Jews we had a special affinity with the idea of democracy.

*

The United States has had a long run at something like a democratic society; one that has steadily expanded the definition of who's 'in'. We've done this with wisdom and luck, and because of the unrelenting pressure of 'the people', organized in one way or another. That accounts in part for my long-term optimism. Still, looking at history's long haul, democracy seems a fragile and almost unnatural idea. And we can hardly argue that we've given a lot of time or attention to considering how it gets passed along from generation to generation. Mostly, we count on word of mouth and the happenstances of growing up. Now we are entering a century that will challenge the ideas underlying democracy as never before, and the odds on its survival seem about even, so long as we depend on word of mouth and happenstance.

But forty years of experience in schools reminds me of the amazing capacity for 'abstract' learning and empathy within every child. This, in turn, leads me to believe that while democracy is hardly the natural state of the species, it is not unnatural either.

These twin capacities—open-minded intelligence and empathy—make the idea of democracy fragile but not utopian; feasible for the long haul if we don't depend too much on luck but rely instead on nourishing both minds and emotions.

As long as education remains a topic rarely discussed jointly by practitioners and 'intellectuals', much less ordinary citizens, it seems unlikely that we will use schools to pass on the democratic idea. And we never have used them very well to pass on plain practical smarts. What an extraordinary waste of an extraordinary period in the life of a human being! It is a time when kids are bursting with energy, intelligence, and capacity for learning—and we spend it boring the majority of them to death, systematically disengaging them from their native intelligence and compassion.

Teaching democracy, if we took the job seriously, may be as hard as teaching modern science; at times it may be as counter-intuitive. Figuring out how to do the one is much like figuring out how to do the other; it might even make sense to think of them together. Study after study reports the same worrisome news: the average US citizen does not take the Constitution seriously and flatly disagrees with many of its key provisions, especially when it comes to the Bill of Rights. One recent study of high school students found that only 35 per cent of them agreed that people with profoundly disagreeable ideas had a right to publish their ideas. The good news is that this was up from 25 per cent before they took a course on the topic. It's worth noting that modern scientific ideas don't fare much better in public opinion polls.

The kind of scepticism and empathy needed to nourish science bears a similarity to the kind needed to foster democracy, and it comes only with a struggle. It does not come naturally to human communities. Such habits are not essentially alien to our humanness, but they are not naturally deeply rooted either. Our scepticism flourishes best in early childhood, when the world truly looks new and fresh, and scepticism is 'merely' a form of openness to the world's many possibilities. It tends to get narrowed into dogma as we grow older and as the need to conform to adult structures becomes more powerful. New ideas become threatening to the ongoing life of a community which rests on norms that are largely unquestioned, accepted, 'normal'. Similarly, while in childhood we might 'imagine ourselves' to be cats and dogs, cars and trains, and magical fairies, by the time we have reached pre-adolescence, maybe at age seven or eight, we have narrowed down such imaginings considerably, eventually mostly just to 'people like ourselves'.

It would take vigorous (I prefer this word to the current favourite in US circles, 'rigorous', with its connotation of inflexibility and harshness) and sustained training to create habits compatible with empathy and scepticism; habits that could withstand the pressures and stresses of real life. As I often point out, I know how to put away my keys so that I can always find them when needed. The problem is that, especially in times of stress, I forget to do so.

What a good education for democracy requires is the development of habits that are especially strong and hard to abandon in times of stress. When all is well, and life is going your way, it's easy to respect views one finds distasteful, or to allow a disagreeable neighbour to co-exist with you on the same block, or to put yourself in the shoes of the harmless beggar in the street. But when that beggar threatens your way of life, or the neighbour chooses a lifestyle that offends you deeply, it gets harder. And the same goes for nation-states as well.

People as individuals or collectives have a harder time respecting their neighbours when they feel threatened themselves. And we all have a harder time imagining ourselves the losers if most of our lives we've been winners. So, both those accustomed to dominate and those accustomed to being a minority have different reasons to struggle with scepticism and empathy. How do we hold on to a difficult, deviant stance if we admit to uncertainty? How do we imagine being losers if all of life has taught us that losers probably deserve their fate in some fashion?

Can schooling overcome such barriers to the qualities of heart and mind critical to the long-term nourishing of democracy? It's a tall order. And perhaps a utopian one.

Is democracy passé then? Possibly.

Is it because these ideas are too abstract and difficult? I don't think so.

I learned as a teacher of 5-year-olds many years ago about the amazing potential of young people for tackling difficult ideas. For example, I was teaching a simple prescribed lesson on living and non-living things. There I was, with a collection of items to be placed in one of two bins—living or non-living. It all seemed uncontroversial, except to Darrell, who interrupted as I was steamrolling a rock into the non-living box: he had a contrary opinion. After a half-hour discussion, Darrell's view was winning, so I set the rock aside; we would think more about it. In the ensuing weeks, I discovered how complex the neat division actually was. If rocks were hard to classify, how about a few leaves that were once on trees? Was non-living the same as dead? What had been a dry lesson turned into a fascinating month-long adventure—on a topic nearly as complex as democracy!

I shouldn't have been surprised, for childhood play is the essence of scepticism and empathy. Growing up has traditionally involved a trade-off between keeping that early inventiveness and 'fitting' better into the existing social order. Can 'schooling' do both?

We depended historically in the United States on face-to-face communication within local communities of peers to teach us about respect and power and compromise and, in some cases, democracy. Democracy rested on the previous existence of communities. But what happens to the idea in the absence of such communities? Can schools recreate the idea of community? Should they? And if not at school, where do we learn about the reciprocal nature of community and how democracy in general, and any particular form of it, works?

Sometimes I try to return to the vision I have of the family dinner table as a possible metaphor for what schools are about.

This style—the dinner-table conversation—of young people joining in company with adults, would of course not look the same in every family or community; but whatever the style, the assumption that you were learning to become an adult through keeping company with adults was pretty universal until a few centuries ago, and largely alive and well until perhaps half a century ago. But today not only the family farm, but also the family dinner table, may have disappeared. And even my vision of it—which included a good deal of the egalitarianism and contentiousness suitable to democracy—may have been far from universal.

Too easy agreement was, at my father's table, seen as something of which to be suspicious. One of his favourite stories involved his commitment to spend Friday nights at his parents' home even after he married my mother. The question was how to make the time pass more quickly. So he decided on a strategy. Whatever his father said, he'd agree with him, figuring that that would soon allow him to take his leave. After a few rounds of this, however, his father exploded: 'Such disrespect from my oldest son I didn't expect!' he thundered.

While not all families are like ours was, I have found enough similarities elsewhere to believe that tough conversation of the kind that my father and grandfather expected is universally possible. We are, I believe, naturally capable of arguing about, and learning about, hard questions, and of imagining ourselves in the shoes of others, even shoes we'd really rather not be in. It is possible—but not inevitable—that democracy can win.

So I try to imagine an educational system devoted to nurturing democracy. Yet such a system is hardly even a third-placed contestant in most reform packages. For example, not one of the six goals for twenty-first-century schooling listed in a front-page article in the prestigious journal *Education Week* of 7 May 2007 even mentioned democracy in passing! Nor did the US governors in their utopian goals under the first Bush administration, in the course of which they proclaimed that by 2000 the nation would score tops in mathematics!

Occasionally 'citizenship' makes it. But it's not only democracies that have citizens; and citizens everywhere have obligations—just different ones depending on the kind of political system in which they live.

In 1983 *A Nation at Risk*, the basic text of the current wave of US school reform, argued that if an enemy power had sought to overthrow our nation's way of life, it would have designed America's schools. But, in fact, despite the long Cold War on behalf of 'democracy', the word lost resonance, and became to the country's young citizens more and more an empty term.

Young people yawn about elections, as fewer and fewer vote in my beloved land. They may or may not know that cynical gerrymandering—redrawing district lines for electoral advantage—has made voting pointless in the vast majority of the districts that elect our Congress. Everyone complains, but the gerrymandering somehow slipped us by. We were busy looking elsewhere. Another example: while we worry about citizens who don't study calculus in high school, we are apathetic about citizens who are easily fooled by 'statistics'. We barely even teach the subject, so concerned are we about algebra. Meanwhile, decisions we might have a say in making if we understood statistics are made without our voice because we can't tell a rigged graph from a useful one. When I ask audiences how many of them know Robert's Rules of Order, few if any teachers or students raise their hands, and afterwards they ask me what in the world I was talking about—even though these are the rules governing virtually every powerful decision-making body in our land.

While the well-off can hire 'thinkers' and 'doers' (lobbyists) to tell their story and protect their interests, and be experts on Robert's Rules, the less well-off have to scramble to make sense of things. The collective bodies that once did some of this 'thinking' and 'acting' on behalf of the lower and working classes have been hard hit of late. Old standbys such as labour unions no longer play as central a role as they did in my youth in telling and then enacting a different story. Less than 10 per cent of the working people in the United States today belong to unions.

And the leisure that democracy requires of its citizens—the leisure to contemplate, reflect, and exchange ideas with one's fellows; leisure the Greeks once thought democracy required—hasn't been so scarce since the end of the nineteenth century, when the forty-hour week at last became 'secure'. Then the United States was ahead of the world's working-time norms. Today we are far behind. We barely have time to contemplate our own children, much less their schooling. Compassion for our fellow citizens is the first victim of such stress. The second is authentic learning. It takes too much time.

And in America this is a bipartisan act of long standing. For the first time in our history, we have more, not fewer, drop-outs from school—all in the name of 'rigour' and 'high standards'. The motives of the supporters of our latest fix-it legislation, introduced under the slogan 'No Child Left Behind', which writes into law our misplaced obsessions, vary considerably; still, together they have helped to remove even a hypocritical semblance of democracy from our schools.

People like us who advocate a childhood based on open-ended play and empathy—one that provides us with the chance to invent alternative worlds and imagine 'what if', pretend to be other species as well as other people, and not merely to imagine but to construct with our hands and hearts—are on occasion labelled elitist. We fail, it is said, to confront the gap between advantaged and disadvantaged children, which requires us to throw overboard the frills of childhood. Along with the frills of local democracy.

What the poor need, our critics argue, is something different, something more like a boot camp, with a boot-camp approach to intellectual skill and authority. And to this end, they say, we must give up our love affair with local democracy. We must, regrettably, take control away from the bleeding hearts—parents and teachers alike—and focus on what the higher authorities can measure.

Every parent, not just the authoritarian ones, knows that there are times when saying 'no' may seem mean and heartless but is, in fact, essential in the child's long-term interests. But this is not such a case. The poor need democracy as much as the rich (and surely as much as the Iraqis), and they need a real education—not test prepping—even more than the rich. And part of that 'real education' is witnessing at close hand how adults disagree and yet make decisions. No one should be for fluff, or softness, or too much focus on affect or mindless self-esteem. No one, right or left, would sacrifice our children's future for the sake of a frivolous present. But it's the current focus on narrowly defined 'academics' that is, I would argue, a frill. The current test-oriented approach to defining 'academic' deprives the least powerful of precisely what academia at its best offers: the ability to use one's mind freely, with agility, and with self-discipline.

That cannot happen in settings where everything that arouses young people's curiosity (and, incidentally, their teachers')—such as when a leaf ceases to be alive—and everything that appeals to their enthusiasm for challenge and risk-taking, is labelled a frill. It can't happen where we avoid uncertainty because it doesn't fit the multiple-choice format, or where children's thirst for independence or their hands-on delight with real craftsmanship is called fluff—too time-consuming, untestable. How exciting it was for me to see that the conservative American Enterprise Institute had issued a call to remember the 'value of play'! Play is not a partisan topic. And the hand, as an extension of the mind, designed to do more than turn the dial, is still critical for building the future.

The ending of recess, the ignoring of arts and crafts, of shop and music—these are signs of peril to human intellect, grandiose as this will sound. Democracy rests on both intellectual scepticism and empathy, which are the underpinnings of play. Yes, that's what play is all about!

Equally dangerous is our mindless acceptance of the idea that the real villains are the people who know the kids, their families, and their circumstances best—the local community, not to mention parents, above all mothers. If the polls show that parents trust their teachers (even as they'd like a second opinion from time to time), then it's due, so we're told, to their self-interested bias. Who's being elitist now? For the last fifty years, first in the name of civil rights, we have moved the big educational decisions from the school to the state and now the federal level. It was a modest and essential step when it came to civil rights. But in the process some of us grew over-fond of the idea that federal intervention is the answer to everything. Others saw a chance to dismantle public education 'as we know it' through federal mandates. A proudly conservative Republican administration has become, in New York Times columnist David Brooks's words, 'the accountability cop' over America's communities—because our government doesn't trust us. To those in power, the very *idea* of a local community is a source of anxiety and suspicion.

In most places in America neither parent, nor teacher, nor principal has the power to decide if it's in the child's best interest to be held back while the rest of the class goes up a level; or to decide what is the best way to teach Jack—not 'Jacks', but this Jack in particular—how to read; or whether science or history should be taught at all in the early grades, and if so, exactly how; or what punishment fits what crime. Our children are at risk in this vast shift of power away from the home, the school, and the local community. Even if tests were far better than they are—and in fact they are appallingly limited even at measuring important skills (and are likely to get worse in our rush to produce more and more of them)—the relentless focus on tests that carry high stakes betrays our mission as educators and the appropriate use of tests. If meeting deadlines, accepting responsibility, speaking clearly, weighing evidence, working with others, trying stuff out— if all this counts, as the people who know the kids know it does, then we need an alternative examination system, because none of the above counts a whit in the only tests our children now sit.

America's prominence in science and technology was built upon our respect for imagination and the practical arts. To preserve that respect we have to tamp down our enthusiasm for text-based learning as the sole source of achievement or competence. It doesn't work. No wonder my contractor in upstate New York complains that he hires graduates who passed the maths test but don't know how to use a ruler.

Children need to see that adults care about getting things right for reasons beyond scores; and they need to live in settings where they witness grown-ups with real standards, in societies with greater purposes than being economically and militarily competitive.

*

At a recent gathering at Amherst College, one of America's elite schools, the president described how the school was expanding its diversity—more scholarships and more affirmative action—without, in his words, 'lowering our standards', by which he meant SAT scores, rank-in-class.[1]

What is worth arguing about is his definition of 'standards'. He's assuming that standards and test scores are equivalent. But as Lani Ginier, a noted legal scholar, once pointed out, there is a direct link between LSAT scores and pro bono work—in reverse order. While high LSAT scores might correlate with higher income after law school, we might get a quite opposite result if we asked ourselves how LSATs correlated with the public, common good.

[1] The SAT (Scholastic Achievement Test) and LSAT (pre-law school test) are standard US college admissions tests. In high schools, children are ranked first, second and third in each class on the basis of the grades they achieve, which are increasingly based on standardized tests, and these rankings weigh heavily in college admission procedures.

What kind of intellectual habits serve the common good? What habits help sustain a democratic society? What measures might we invent to help us see whether our schools are serving such public purposes?

The kind of schools as communities, or communities as schools, that young people need to be part of seem to me consistent with both a democratic and a Jewish education; they unite us across generations, drawing together people and diverse interests in a shared sense of purpose and humanity.

Young people, first of all, need to belong to communities that have standards. Second, the young must also witness adults taking responsibility for their decisions and standing by them, exercising that fundamental capacity of citizenship: human judgement. Third, they need schools that provide safe opportunities to explore their own life-sustaining and joyous powers under the guidance of adults the world respects. Fourth, they need schools that belong to their communities and families, and know them well. They must, in short, be surrounded by grown-ups they can imagine becoming and would like to become.

Is any of this possible in schools? Yes. Not easily, but it *is* all do-able. In fact, for a decade or longer before the test craze hit us, hundreds and hundreds of such schools were founded that demonstrated that this kind of schooling needn't be the exception, that it isn't a frill, and that parents of all persuasions, incomes, and colours can embrace such schooling. Schools that aim at authentic work, attested to by independent experts, are able to produce productive members of their communities. This old-fashioned idea was reinvented in modern guise.

It's not a 'right' or 'left' idea. We still all agree, for example, that only a small part of the task of becoming a driver involves reading the driver's manual and learning to pass the written portion of the driver's test, no matter how arduous we might make the test. There's always that other part, the road test. Woe unto us if we decide that rigour requires us to dispense with the road test altogether, which is effectively what we are doing in our schools. It might save us money; it won't save lives.

Schools that base their practice on road tests are not easy to replicate. They are built around real people in real communities, and as such are not intended to be replicable to order. But they are destroyable to order, and many have been destroyed in the recent decades of federally backed high-stakes testing. Like Starbucks, the best schools share many characteristics;

but unlike Starbucks, each rests on the authority of those who know the kids best. And this is a form of adult authority too sadly lacking.

Tolstoy notwithstanding, all happy families are not alike, although, like all happy schools, they do have some things in common. One of the things that happy schools have in common is that their students and teachers think they are special, not standardized, not mass-produced, not shaped to someone else's prescription. The proof of their success lies in the longitudinal stories of their graduates, all of them. The best schools keep their eye on the prize—the kids—and not just on the anonymous higher authorities. They see the job of adults as one of nurturing intelligence and empathy and openness to the world, while cherishing their children's uniqueness. Schools for democracy are always quintessentially an act of collaboration with families and communities—they are expressions of grass-roots vitality and ingenuity. They will often be traditional to the core, and many will not live up to the potential I see in them. But that's a matter for argument and persuasion; and the alternative to persuasion in this case is a cure worse than the disease.

*

I went to visit a new school that was in its first year of trying to become such a place as I have just described. It was a small high school in San Francisco, named June Jordan. My friend and I spent a day visiting, and were much impressed. They invited us to stay for their after-school meetings. We did. They began with some kvetching. One teacher said, in an irritable voice, 'The kids act at times as if they owned the place.' Another noted that they ought to close off one of the two doors into their large shared staff room because the kids kept coming in one door and going out the other, just taking a look-see on their way from class to class.

They finally turned to us. I told them that Mark and I had spent a wonderful day, punctuated in early afternoon by Mark's turning to me and saying, 'You know, they act as if they owned the place.' It was a comment made in response to the ways in which the students accepted responsibility for getting to places on time, taking pride in the work on the walls, greeting each other, holding doors open for us, and so on. And then we noted how rare it is that young adolescents are interested in what the faculty is doing when not in class, and what a remarkable tribute it was to the culture of the place that the kids were dropping by to see what their teachers were doing when not with them!

We all had a good laugh. But behind that laugh is a reminder of how high and solid are the walls we have built between ourselves and our young, and how damaging that is to their becoming citizens of a shared culture, not just a 'me first' one.

Steven Mintz, in the closing chapter of his astute history of childhood, *Huck's Raft*, reminds us that Huck and Tom, for all their sorrows, had 'many ties to a host of adults, some of whom were family members, but many of whom were not. Today, connections that link the young to the world of adults have grown attenuated.' Study after study tells us that our children's futures depend on reconnecting. And the adults on the television and computer screens are not a substitute.

We have created this untenable fact of life, this divide between the real world of adults and the real world of schools. It wasn't written in the stars. We did not intend to let our young drift, subject to the relentless pressures of a consumer-driven, media-driven society, but we did it, in our own life-times. When I was born there were 200,000 school boards in the United States; today, with a population many times as large, there are fewer than 15,000 boards, mostly powerless except for borrowing from the banks in order to raise school funds. Our challenge is to reverse the process.

It will, however, take more than schools to close the real achievement gaps—not just the tested kind. That gap closely mirrors the ever-growing economic and social inequalities in our society. But schools are also the essential vehicle for tackling the citizenship gap, the hopefulness gap, the kid/adult gap. And in the process they'll probably do a damn sight better at narrowing the testing gap, though test scores alone cannot be the measure of their success. More importantly, they will provide the groundwork for tackling the awesome divide between the haves and have-nots.

Huck was in many ways an abused child, but he enjoyed something, notes Mintz, that 'too many children today are denied and which adults can provide'—the opportunity to use childhood in ways that sustain dreams, not just worries and fears. We can start by renouncing the mania that's driving our kids into ever narrower grooves, starting at an ever earlier age. Current policy leads to more and more centralized power over children and family life, as well as to intellectual rigidity and narrowness. We should choose another direction, reclaiming the intellectual openness and ingenuity on which democracy relies.

Whenever we're about to say, 'but the people are not ready . . .', we need to remember that old Conservative British prime minister's warning: 'Democracy is a thoroughly flawed and ridiculous idea, until one considers the alternative.'

FOUR

A Response to Deborah Meier

JOSHUA ELKIN

IN THIS BRIEF CHAPTER I want to respond to and elaborate on a few key points made by Deborah Meier, both in the preceding chapter and in her other writings. It is an honour to do so, for Deborah has been a great inspiration both as a teacher and as a role model to very many educators, including myself.

The first point takes me back to the first time I heard Deborah speak. It was on National Public Radio, where she was being interviewed by Christopher Lydon. I ordered a copy of the tape, summarized the interview, and gave it out to my staff, because it was so profound. I recall being deeply moved, particularly by her firm belief that our children need to have much more contact with many more adults than most of them do today. As she has said in her chapter in this volume, keeping the company of adults must be built into schooling.

What makes Deborah such a credible advocate for this belief is that, both at the Central Park East School in Harlem and at the Mission Hill School in Boston, she actually built such schools. So she herself is proof that these kinds of school *are* possible, that such beliefs are not pie in the sky. Her work, then, serves as a challenge to *all* of us. Why more adults? Because young people need to watch adults do what they do in the real world. Young people need to have things to which they can aspire, based on the adult models they see.

Increasing adult contact for our children represents to me a vitally important principle for Jewish day schools—in general education, in the Judaic part of the programme, and in those parts of the curriculum that are integrated, that is, where general and Judaic education are blended. This contact is vitally important to the theme of this volume, for adults can and do serve as bridges connecting the school and the broader community.

Let me offer a few brief examples. In the area of the general academic disciplines, we should be bringing in scientists, mathematicians, artists, and retired people who have had distinguished careers in various fields. Today, an increasing number of Jewish day schools in North America are locating their permanent campuses right next to assisted living or senior citizens' facilities. They do so largely for reasons having to do with the availability of land. Maybe they have some sense that day school students will have an opportunity to learn what it is to take care of the elderly. But let us turn the idea around: what about bringing the senior citizens into the school, not because they're old and not because they're challenged, but because they have wisdom, knowledge, and craft to share with the young? We have much to do in this area. It's a real challenge to build these connections.

We face a similar challenge within the Judaic component of schooling. We have leaders of Jewish organizations; we have synagogue leaders; we have rabbis; we have federation leaders; we have writers; we have commentators; we have scholars—all of whom remain outside the walls of our schools. I know how hard it is to arrange interactions between figures such as these and school students; I know there are so many more immediately pressing things to do; but in the schools that are doing this (and there *are* Jewish day schools that are doing this), the impact can be profoundly important.

In terms of integrated learning, we have people whose lives embody work of both general and Judaic significance. We have politicians such as Joseph Lieberman; we have Hollywood personalities; we have *shomer shabat* journalists; we have *tsedakah* and *tikun olam* heroes. There are many people who are doing important work and who have a place inside our schools, but we have to invite them in.

As Deborah has written, people learn in two ways. They learn by observing others and they learn by trying things out for themselves. I think both of those types of learning happen when you increase dramatically the number of adults in the school.

Increasing the number of adults within our schools also connects to Deborah's comments about education for democracy. If we care about democracy, our students need to see adults *doing* democracy. Deborah emphasized two qualities, or habits of mind, essential to education for democracy. It is interesting that she chose to capture one of these with the term 'scepticism'. In an earlier draft of her chapter she used the term 'open-minded intelligence', that is, wrestling or fighting with ideas that are the very opposite of fundamentalism. This is one of the qualities that we need to develop. The second one is the quality of empathy.

We need to expose our students to adults who have personally cultivated and developed these two habits—open-minded intelligence and empathy. One hopes that teachers and school administrators have done so; but there are also many other adults whom we can bring into our schools from the communities around them who have demonstrable experience in exercising these qualities. These habits of mind cut across all the disciplines; they cut across the general domains of learning, the Judaic domain, and all the integrated sections of the curriculum.

It is noteworthy that the habits of mind that Deborah has commended are actually quite compatible with Jewish teaching and values. In the area of open-minded intelligence, for example, I couldn't help but think about the first *berakhah*, the first petition in the daily Amidah where we praise God as being *ḥonen hada'at*, a bestower of knowledge. This is something we say three times a day. We have a tradition of *maḥaloket*, of disagreement. Going even further, there's such a thing as a *maḥaloket leshem shamayim*, disagreement for the sake of heaven: it's lofty to disagree. The whole Gemara would probably be one-third of its size if we took out all the second opinions and the third and fourth. We have a culture that has nurtured this quality, and so we have a running head start in our schools in the attempt to make this habit come alive.

On the empathy front, we have texts in our Torah like *ve'ahavta lere'akha kamokha*, 'love your neighbour as yourself' (Lev. 19: 18), and in rabbinic literature like *al tadin et ḥaverakh ad shetagia limekomo*, 'don't judge your fellow until you stand in his/her place' (Mishnah *Avot* 2: 4). We possess material within our own heritage that dovetails very nicely with the qualities that Deborah has thrown out to us as essential to the cultivation of democracy and to the building of a certain kind of community within our schools and within our Jewish community as a whole. Bringing in more adults of different ages from within the academic domains, as well as adults who exhibit these essential habits of mind, can, I believe, create over time a two-way relationship between school and community. You can bring people into the school from the outside, and you can also take the young people and their teachers from the school out into the community.

By developing this two-way relationship we can build a school setting where children and adults of various ages spend much more time together. We can break down the barriers between the school and the outside world. We can allow children of different ages to mingle more, and thereby make the school much more like the community outside it.

Parenthetically, I would like to mention one other angle on this multi-generational perspective. A wonderful volunteer leader in the New York area, Matthew Maryles, threw out a challenge to us all in arguing that financing Jewish day school education has to be seen as a multi-generational phenomenon. It's not about one generation carrying the load. It's about parents; it's about grandparents; and it's about senior citizens in the community all coming forward to share responsibility.

I would like to touch very briefly on four additional points arising from Deborah's remarks and the process of thinking through my response.

1. John Dewey's famous work *The School and Society* raises some questions about the relationships between schools and the communities beyond their walls. Does school prepare for the existing society or does school challenge the existing society? Let's look at this issue through the lens of the Judaic mission of our day schools, and in particular of community, non-denominational schools. Let's get a sense of exactly how tough answering Dewey's question is for these schools.

Some of those involved in community day schools—teachers, administrators, parents— believe that these schools are the revolutionary force, the wedge that will grow into into Jewish renewal, Jewish renaissance, and Jewish values for the future. Others see the Jewish day school as merely a gateway into the workforce, into an elite university—environments where the Jewish stuff will be at best tolerated. These two perspectives are on a collision course; any day school that has adherents of both within its four walls faces a serious challenge in accommodating such different conceptions of the relationship between what is going on in the school and the society outside it.

Yossi Prager of the AVI CHAI Foundation has written eloquently on the dangers of the Judaic mission of these schools being reduced to some lowest common denominator. We really must be concerned about this. There exists tremendous tension that pulls at the fabric of the relationships between these schools and the wider community.

2. There is a perspective very different from Dewey's that skirts the whole 'school and society' question. Walter Ackerman, another wonderful teacher, who taught at the Melton Centre in Jerusalem, at Ben-Gurion University in Beersheva, and at the Mandel Institute, issued a challenge to the world of Jewish schools—not just Jewish day schools but any Jewish school. In an excellent book edited by David Sidorsky, entitled *The Future of the Jewish Community in America*, Ackerman asked: Where in our schools is the supreme value of *torah lishemah* (learning for its own sake)? Deborah addressed this question in her chapter by talking about fostering scholarship and lifelong learning. Forget about whether schools are supposed to overturn the society and create a Jewish renaissance, whether they are gateways into higher education, or whether they are just a bunch of fancy Jewish prep schools. Ackerman asks different questions. What about the joy of learning? What about the idea of *havruta*, people studying in peer-mediated instruction? What about the here and now? What about the value of lifelong learning? What about cultivating this kind of learning, not only for our students but for their teachers, for their parents, for the grandparents, for the entire community?

3. Those of you who follow the publications of the AVI CHAI Foundation will probably know Jack Wertheimer's *Linking the Silos*. I think this work makes a very important contribution to Jewish education in North America, but I think it also applies to Jewish day schools anywhere around the world. The key question Wertheimer poses is: How broadly does the Jewish day school see its role and its reach? Is it operating in silo-like fashion and minding its own business, or is it genuinely connected to the rest of the Jewish community? I would assert that day schools cannot and should not be isolated islands. They must build bridges to synagogues, to JCCs, to federations, and to early childhood centres. Day schools need to be rooted in the broader community and need to be seen as a valuable and integral communal asset, not only for their current users but for the community as a whole. There are even day schools that reach out beyond the Jewish community because they believe that, as institutions of learning, they are a resource from which the entire general community can benefit.

4. My final comment is inspired by Deborah's book *The Power of their Ideas*, in which she writes about education as a shared responsibility. She describes teachers talking together and taking responsibility together for what's happening with the young in their school. This concept applies equally to Jewish day schools. Jewish day schools are a shared responsibility, not just the responsibility of the users. They should be valued as an essential Jewish communal asset. We have to make day schools more integral to the fabric of Jewish community.

We need school leaders who say that the Jewish community needs these schools; that they are not just about who is inside the four walls right now, but are organic institutions of the community and an integral part of the landscape of a literate, vibrant Jewish future.

Finally, I want to conclude with some words from Deborah herself. In her book *The Power of their Ideas* she writes: 'What makes me hopeful, no matter what bad news tomorrow brings, is our infinite capacity for inventing the future, imagining things otherwise.'[1] I find this to be an inspiring idea; it's the essence of vision. And this is Deborah's challenge to each of us—to envision and to dream the rich possibilities of interplay between day schools and the communities that surround them. Her wisdom calls out to each of us. Let us seize the moment!

[1] Meier, *The Power of their Ideas*, 184.

Bibliography

Ackerman, W., 'The Jewish School System in the United States', in D. Sidorsky (ed.), *The Future of the Jewish Community in America* (New York, 1973), 176–210.
Dewey, J. *The School and Society* (Chicago, 1991; first published 1889).
Meier, D., *The Power of their Ideas: Lessons to America from a Small School in Harlem* (Boston, 1995; 2002).
Prager, Y., 'All Things to All People', *Sh'ma*, 31 (Oct. 2000), 6–7.
Wertheimer, J., *Linking the Silos: How to Accelerate the Momentum in Jewish Education Today* (New York, 2005).

FIVE

Community as a Means and an End in Jewish Education

JON A. LEVISOHN

I N A D E L I G H T F U L but underappreciated book entitled *Back to Basics*, Fran Schrag opens by posing a question about the purposes of education in general. What, he asks, are our most fundamental aspirations for any particular educational endeavour? The question may seem intractable, but Schrag offers a helpful method for thinking about it. Adapting a thought experiment from the political philosopher John Rawls—the thought experiment that generated Rawls's *Theory of Justice* and launched a revitalization of liberal political theory—Schrag suggests that we try to imagine what aspirations might hold true not just for contemporary education but for the education of our great-grandchildren.[1]

The virtues of the thought experiment are, first, that we cannot claim to know what society will be like for our great-grandchildren, what their status will be within that society, what the culture will value, or what will be necessary for the common good; but second, that we may be presumed to *care* about our great-grandchildren. In other words, the thought experiment allows us to abstract our enquiry from accidents of history on both the societal and individual level, while also maintaining a personal connection with it sufficient to motivate a deep commitment to the welfare of the students. For Schrag, the thought experiment generates what he calls 'three key aspirations'. First, *students will care about arguments and evidence*. Second, *stu-*

The author acknowledges contributions by Aaron Bayer, Steven Cohen, Adam Mayer-Deutsch, Shuli Passow, Dan Pekarsky, Alex Pomson, Israel Scheffler, Chaim Strauchler, David Wolkenfeld, and the anonymous reviewers of the manuscript.

[1] In Rawls's thought experiment, citizens are (hypothetically) placed in an 'original position', behind a 'veil of ignorance' that prevents their knowing any of their own characteristics that are deemed morally irrelevant—socio-economic status, race, gender, religion, innate abilities, etc. From that original position, they must determine the organizing principles of the society. Thus, the thought experiment is intended to generate principles that are just, i.e. fair for all, regardless of social (or other) location.

dents will be disposed to continue learning. And third, *students will acquire the capacity to continue learning.* These aspirations, he believes, can withstand the test of time, and can apply to students in widely varying situations.

Now, for those who have attended to recent discussions of 'vision' in Jewish education,[2] many of which have focused on defining and articulating visions of the 'educated Jew' as the ideal outcome of Jewish education, Schrag's arguments may be intriguing. After all, he is presenting a vision of an educated person; he is taking a stand on what such a person will consider most important, and what education can aspire to provide or promote. Schrag is not concerned here with Jews in particular, of course, and some readers may wonder whether his arguments stand in tension with the goals of Jewish education, as they understand them. But the basic approach— developing an image of what the ideal product of an educational system ought to know or be able to do, or, more fundamentally, who she ought to *be*—may be applied to Jewish and general education alike.[3]

Note, however, that in this model educational purposes are considered only in terms of the individual student as the paradigm product of an educational institution. Schrag is certainly not alone in adopting this approach. For one thing, he is following the tradition of philosophical enquiry into the 'educated person'.[4] More generally, educational theorists commonly develop their ideas around what individual students ought to do or encounter in an educational setting. To take just one example, consider Philip Jackson's classic essay on 'The Mimetic and the Transformative'. Jackson describes what he calls two 'traditions', two fundamental orientations towards the task of teaching and the purpose of education, each with its own intellectual justification and each with its own history, one aiming at the transmission of accumulated knowledge and the second aiming at growth and development through the educational experience. Both of these, however, are focused on the individual student.

---

[2] These discussions have been stimulated by the publication of Fox et al. (eds.), *Visions of Jewish Education*, and the Mandel Foundation's Visions of Jewish Education Project, of which that volume is a part. See esp. the work of Daniel Pekarsky: his study of a vision-guided school, *Vision at Work*; his earlier essays, 'The Place of Vision in Jewish Educational Reform', and 'Vision and Education'; and his more recent 'Vision and Education: Arguments, Counterarguments, and Rejoinders'.

[3] I choose to interpret Schrag's aspirations in characterological (i.e. virtue) terms—rather than in terms of knowledge and skills—following his own embrace of a virtue model in his earlier work on thinking. See Schrag, 'What is Thinking?'

[4] For the classic source, see Peters, *Ethics and Education*.

But what if this way of considering the purposes of education is too narrow? What if the focus on the educated person, or the educated Jew, overlooks a function of education that is more communal? I do not mean only that individuals are or ought to be members of communities, that they have certain responsibilities to others, and that they derive certain benefits from being in association with others. In education, building school communities is *instrumentally* valuable for any number of reasons: because it facilitates engagement (both emotional and financial), because it lowers barriers of resistance to institutional goals, because it creates loci of meaning that contribute to individual human flourishing. Kaplowitz, for example, citing Merz and Furman, argues that 'when a sense of community exists in a school, formal school relationships can become less dependent on contractual agreements and more focused around mutual commitments'.[5] All these benefits are generated by having good and healthy communities in the schools, or created by the school, or with which the school interacts.[6]

However, my aim in this chapter is to consider the possibility that communities are not only instrumentally but also intrinsically valuable; that they are ends rather than or as well as means.[7] What are the educational implications of thinking about communities as ends in themselves, rather than as means to individual fulfilment and flourishing? What happens if, in our construction of visions of Jewish education, we seek to establish not only what is an educated Jew but also what is an ideal Jewish community? Is it even possible to sustain an enquiry into this question, or does any discussion of educational aims inevitably collapse into individualistic terms?

*

Schrag's thought experiment, like that of Rawls upon which it is based, draws its power from a picture of the individual as free agent, a picture in

---

[5] Kaplowitz, 'Community Building', 37. Kaplowitz's article includes an extensive discussion about the use of community rhetoric in Jewish day school contexts, articulating multiple levels of 'benefits'—that is, ways that community is instrumental to some other ends.

[6] Communities can also be *dangerous*, of course. See e.g. Noddings, 'On Community', 258: 'Is there a way to avoid the dark side of community—its tendencies towards parochialism, conformity, exclusion, assimilation, distrust (or hatred) of outsiders, and coercion?' These pathologies are real, but their reality does not undermine the value and necessity of strong and healthy communities.

[7] The chapter thus proceeds from an idea that I broached in an earlier essay, 'Ideas and Ideals in Jewish Education'. See, too, Pekarsky's response to that essay, 'Some Moral and Social Dimensions'.

which everything in our lives is up for grabs, apparently forcing us to reconsider the behaviours and associations that we take for granted. It is a picture of the individual as a radically autonomous *chooser*. One reason why this picture is so powerful is that it calls upon a moral intuition about fairness, an intuition that rules apply equally to everyone—because underneath our differences, in our essential humanity, we are all alike.

But it is precisely this picture that is challenged by Rawls's critics.[8] Michael Sandel, for example, calls this a 'picture of the unencumbered self': '[In this picture,] there is always a distinction between the values I *have* and the person I *am* . . . No role or commitment could define me so completely that I could not understand myself without it. No project could be so essential that turning away from it would call into question the person I am.'[9] There are values, roles, commitments, and what philosophers ever since existentialism have called 'projects' that I may choose to adopt, but these do not define me, they are not essential to me, they do not constitute my identity. In other words, the picture of the unencumbered self 'rules out the possibility of what we might call *constitutive* ends'.[10]

The problem with the picture is that some roles or commitments *do* define me; some projects *are* essential to my identity; some ends do *constitute* who I am rather than just being ends that I have chosen to pursue. Living out certain commitments, Sandel writes, 'is inseparable from understanding ourselves as the particular persons we are—as members of this family or community or nation or people, as bearers of that history, as citizens of this republic. Allegiances such as these are more than values I happen to have.'[11] I am not merely a chooser of projects. Rather, I come to my choices constituted by certain commitments, and by my history, and by the historical situation in which I find myself. When I think of who I am, these roles—parent, spouse, Jew, American, teacher—constitute my identity as deeply as anything I can imagine about myself.

Nor is this merely a matter of certain people whose identities happen to be bound up in deep commitments to family or country. Human nature, Sandel argues, is fundamentally 'encumbered'. This is the way things ought to be, and indeed the absence of these encumbrances would be

---

[8] My purpose here is limited: I merely want to introduce a way of thinking about community that is associated with the set of theorists known as 'communitarians'. I do not intend to take a stand on Rawls's actual views, or to jump into complicated debates in contemporary political theory.   [9] Sandel, 'The Procedural Republic', 86.   [10] Ibid.   [11] Ibid. 90.

nothing less than pathological: 'To imagine a person incapable of constitutive attachments . . . is not to conceive an ideally free and rational agent, but to imagine a person wholly without character, without moral depth.'[12] Far from Rawls's (and Schrag's) picture of an agent making pristine moral choices in the 'original position', protected from corruption by the 'veil of ignorance', Sandel imagines a moral monster, devoid of values, committed to nothing.

All this is too quick. Followers of Rawls, naturally, will reject this caricature of his position; and moreover, the discussion of encumbrances lacks a careful argument about the nature of our obligations towards the roles or projects or communities that constitute those encumbrances. And so, to examine the issues more carefully, I will turn (in a moment) to another theorist often associated with the communitarians, Charles Taylor. But Sandel's language of the 'unencumbered self' is helpfully evocative, because it draws a stark contrast between the liberal conception of the self as, essentially, a chooser among projects, and the communitarian critique of that conception.[13]

According to that critique, we are not essentially unencumbered; we come to our choices with encumbrances—as we might say in colloquial terms, with 'baggage'. We are still autonomous, free to move from traditionalist religion to liberalism (or vice versa), free to leave law school and become artists (or vice versa). We do make choices; but we do so against the background of the situation—personal, familial, cultural, historical—into which we are, as Heidegger said, 'thrown'. A person might divorce her spouse, but then she becomes not just a single woman but an 'ex-wife'. A person can choose to pursue a new career, but then he becomes not just a teacher, say, but a 'career-switcher'. All modern Jews may be, as we now say, 'Jews by choice'—but that slogan obscures the way in which those choices are all encumbered by prior commitments.

What do these encumbrances have to do with communities? At one level, community affiliations are one kind of encumbrance that we carry with us. I am a free agent, but I am also at the same time a member of a community (or several communities). More fundamentally, however, a community is composed of people who share a particular project or set of

[12] Sandel, 'The Procedural Republic', 90.
[13] The term 'liberal' is used here, of course, in its political-theoretical sense, not in its ideological sense.

commitments. For the unencumbered self, communities are like email listservs, joined on a whim and unsubscribed from at no cost. But in Sandel's picture a community is composed of 'fellow participants in a way of life with which my identity is bound'. The paradigm is a 'constitutive community' with a set of shared purposes, rather than merely a 'concatenated collectivity'.[14] Again, while I can certainly choose to leave a community, that choice is deeper and more complicated than merely ceasing to pay my dues to the club, because the community constitutes—or perhaps, more modestly, contributes to constituting—my own sense of who I am.

Communities, then, are central to identity in a way that liberal theorists, with their attention to individual choosers, do not fully appreciate. What is not yet clear is how this idea of a 'constitutive community' should affect our thinking about education; and for that connection we can turn to the work of Charles Taylor. Like Sandel, Taylor is also often associated with the communitarian camp, because of his critique of some fundamental assumptions of contemporary liberal political theory.[15] For example, in a classic essay from 1979, Taylor targets a set of doctrines in political theory 'which try to defend . . . the priority of the individual and his rights over society', which he labels 'primacy-of-rights' views.[16]

According to primacy-of-rights views, one's rights are fundamental and unconditional; obligations, on the other hand, are secondary or derivative. A person has rights because of who she is as a human being; a person has obligations only when she consents to them, or because of choices that she makes, or when they are to her long-term benefit. These views present 'a vision of society as . . . constituted by individuals for the fulfilment of ends which [are] primarily individual'; in other words, they 'present a purely instrumental view of society'.[17] In arguing against these views, then, Taylor will advance a view of society as not merely instrumental but rather, in a sense which will require careful articulation, as possessing inherent value.

Taylor's own label for the set of doctrines he contests is 'atomism', a term he uses as the title of his essay. According to this view, human individuals are or can be self-sufficient, independent of society or community. The bulk of his argument, then, is devoted to working out the relationship between primacy-of-rights theories, embraced by many political theorists, and the

[14] Sandel, 'The Procedural Republic', 90.
[15] Taylor himself does not accept the label. See e.g. his essay 'Cross Purposes'.
[16] Taylor, 'Atomism', 187.   [17] Ibid.

rather more controversial theory of atomism. Primacy-of-rights theorists typically argue that their view rests on no particular theory of human nature—that it is *neutral* with respect to competing ideas of human flourishing—so Taylor's linkage to atomism is designed to be provocative, and requires some clarification.

His argument begins with the claim that we ascribe rights to an individual on the basis of a belief that an individual deserves *respect* in some specific area. But that belief is, in turn, based on some belief about that individual's capacities. This defines not only who the bearers of rights *are* but what they have rights *to*. '[An individual] has a natural right to [do some activity] . . . if doing or enjoying that [activity] is essentially part of manifesting [the individual's essentially human capacities].'[18] What does this mean? It may be helpful here to consider a specific example.

Taylor refers to 'the right to one's convictions': not the *legal* right enshrined (for example) in the 'free exercise' clause in the First Amendment to the Constitution of the United States but a shared intuition about a *moral* right on which the authority of that law depends. We believe (do we not?) that we ought to respect the fact that other people have convictions of their own. To be sure, from time to time we might want to persuade them of the error of their ways. And in cases where we believe that those erroneous ways cause harm to others or to themselves, we may want to interfere. But in general, our efforts of persuasion are limited by our own sense that, ultimately, it is more important that individuals hold convictions in a genuine way than that they might be coerced or manipulated into 'correct' convictions by others (that is, by us).

At first glance, this right seems to represent the paradigm of liberal neutrality: we do not impose any particular view about human nature or human flourishing on others, but merely restrict people from imposing their views on others. Live and let live! But now, consider the fact that we do not imagine we ought to extend the right to one's convictions to non-human animals. We do not believe that Fido's convictions are worthy of our respect and non-interference. Indeed, it sounds ridiculous even to suggest such a thing; what would it mean? What this demonstrates is that the right to one's convictions makes sense only because of some underlying judgement about human nature, namely, that making decisions in accord with deeply

---

[18] Taylor, 'Atomism', 195.

held beliefs is fundamental to our sense of what it means to be human. It is not fundamental, on the other hand, to our sense of what it means to be a non-human animal.

If this is so, then the right to one's convictions is not so neutral after all: 'to affirm the worth of the human capacity to form moral and religious convictions goes far beyond the assertion of the right to one's convictions'.[19] Specifically, it entails a far greater and deeper set of obligations than mere non-interference with others' choices.

It also says that I ought to become the kind of agent who is capable of authentic conviction, that I ought to be true to my own convictions and not live a lie or a self-delusion out of fear or for favour, that I ought in certain circumstances to help foster this capacity in others, that I ought to bring up my own children to have it, that I ought not to inhibit it in others by influencing them towards a facile and shallow complaisance, and so on.[20]

This is a rather robust list of oughts! Consider the stark contrast between this list and the cool detachment of Schrag's three key aspirations. Nor is the list even complete: the obligation 'to help foster this capacity in others' might easily be expanded to include all kinds of educational institutions and interventions. Of course, there is significant potential here for abuse; Taylor's caveat 'in certain circumstances' signals the deep concern for individual rights that got the argument going in the first place. In other words, we always worry about justifying, say, censorship on behalf of the public good. Nevertheless, Taylor's argument helps us see that even a purportedly neutral ascription of rights—purportedly neutral with respect to competing visions of the good life—depends on our convictions about the human capacities that we value, and that those convictions carry with them not just respect for rights but indeed obligations to foster those capacities in others.[21]

But this is only half the argument, because Taylor also wants to extend the point to a consideration of communities and societies, by linking primacy-of-rights political theories to atomist theories of human development. Atomism, here, is concerned not with physical survival, but rather with the development of whatever capacities are distinctively human: the

---

[19] Ibid. 194.   [20] Ibid.
[21] For those familiar with Isaiah Berlin's famous essay 'Two Concepts of Liberty', Taylor—while sympathetic to many of Berlin's concerns—may be understood to be undermining the dichotomy between negative and positive liberty that Berlin advanced in that essay.

atomist denies that humans require communities or societies to develop their essentially human characteristics. In other words, it denies what Taylor, following Aristotle's conception of the human as, fundamentally, 'political', calls the 'social nature of man'. Instead, atomism affirms the developmental self-sufficiency of the individual.

But why would the primacy-of-rights theorists embrace such a questionable view? Taylor's strategy is to show that they are driven to this position (even if unknowingly) because of a desire to protect freedoms from restrictions imposed by society. Obligations imply restrictions: if I am obliged to do something, I am (morally) restricted from not doing it, and hence less free. So, to protect freedoms to the greatest degree, primacy-of-rights theorists have to avoid obligations at all costs. If humans are fundamentally self-sufficient, then we can safely and coherently avoid any obligation to belong to and support society. That's why primacy-of-rights theorists are driven, implicitly, to endorse atomism. But if humans are *not* fundamentally self-sufficient, if they *require* communities or societies of particular kinds to develop certain capacities, if atomism is a mistaken view of human nature, then those societies may rightly claim certain things from individuals. In other words, *obligations*, rather than rights, are primary.

Taylor makes the abstract point more concrete by focusing on 'freedom of choice', the fundamental right to choose a life path, which is central to liberal political theory.

The view that makes freedom of choice [an] absolute is one that exalts choice as a human capacity. It carries with it the demand that we become beings *capable* of choice, that we rise to the level of self-consciousness and autonomy where we can exercise choice, that we not remain enmired through fear, sloth, ignorance, or superstition in some code imposed by tradition, society, or fate.[22]

Taylor, the anti-atomist, asks us to acknowledge that this kind of development is impossible to imagine in the absence of a society that strives to overcome superstition, that rejects blind obedience, that celebrates independence, that values the very capacities that we are trying to nourish.

The free individual or autonomous moral agent can only achieve and maintain his identity in a certain type of culture . . . [with the support of] institutions and associations which require stability and continuity and frequently also support

---

[22] Taylor, 'Atomism', 197, emphasis added.

from society as a whole—almost always the moral support of being commonly recognized as important, but frequently also considerable material support.[23]

It is even of importance to him what the moral tone of the whole society is—shocking as it may be to libertarians to raise this issue—because freedom and individual diversity can only flourish in a society where there is a general recognition of their worth.[24]

The atomist, on the other hand, will have to argue that we can do all this on our own.

What are the implications of this argument for education, and specifically, for the role of community in education? Above, Sandel helped us to see that we are not unencumbered selves; instead, we are connected to communities characterized by shared projects, 'constitutive communities' rather than 'concatenated collectivities'. Taylor takes us one step further: we are not merely connected to communities but are in fact shaped by them in fundamental ways. We are not self-sufficient individuals, who develop our characteristically human capacities on our own; on the contrary, we develop those capacities—the capacities that we most value—only within communities or societies of certain kinds. Our obligation, therefore, is not merely to respect the rights of others, but to belong to communities that represent the values that we affirm, and furthermore to support those communities' or societies' continuation and flourishing—not only for the sake of others but for our own sakes as well.

The obligation is quite straightforwardly an educational one, because education—along with politics—is a primary mechanism for the development of both individual capacities and the supporting structures in society. Above, I cited without explanation Taylor's characterization of atomism as presenting a 'purely instrumental view of society'. We are now in a position to understand this better. The individual can choose to join a group, for some particular purpose, or choose not to, and hence sees that group as nothing other than a means to his own end, a means to the satisfaction of some desire (and a non-fundamental one at that, because it is one that he can choose to go without). And thus, even when the individual does choose a certain commitment, and accepts the obligations that flow from that choice, those obligations are derivative, conditional, always subservient to the free agent who chose to take them on.

---

[23] Ibid. 205.   [24] Ibid. 207.

But Taylor has argued that this view is incoherent. Rather, society has formed the individual; society has nurtured the capacities that the individual now claims to value and the rights that the individual now wants to protect. And thus the individual is obliged to support the society. 'The free individual, the bearer of rights, can only assume this identity thanks to his relationship to a developed liberal civilization . . . The free individual who affirms himself as such *already* has an obligation to complete, restore, or sustain the society within which this identity is possible.'[25] Rather than being derivative and secondary, obligation is primary. Society or community is now seen to have a kind of *inherent* value rather than a merely instrumental value; it is not simply a means to my own end, but rather has value or status independent of me.

Now, if we are convinced by Taylor's argument, we ought to wonder about its implications for education in general and for Jewish education in particular. What kind of educational institutions, general or Jewish, contribute to a 'developed liberal civilization' of the sort that Taylor is talking about? How should educational institutions, general or Jewish, fulfil our obligation to 'complete, restore, or sustain' society? How can educational institutions, general or Jewish, foster the capacity to form moral and religious convictions—not just in their direct educational impact on individuals (and perhaps not through didactic measures at all) but through their creation of communities in which such convictions are nurtured? How do Taylor's arguments shape our educational visions, general or Jewish?

These are vitally important questions, questions that (one hopes) might generate serious reflection alongside—and perhaps in constructive tension with—the question of 'Who is an educated Jew?' I want to commend these questions to thoughtful practitioners and theorists alike. But immediately, our application of Taylor's perspective to Jewish education must be qualified by two important considerations. First, the careful reader will have noticed that I have conflated Taylor's term 'society' with 'community' throughout the discussion. This conflation, however, should not go unexamined. Can a *community*, as opposed to a *society*, support the kinds of capacities that Taylor is describing? There is a reasonable case to be made that it cannot, at least not if we have in mind a modern community situated within a larger society. After all, it is not merely the community that supports freedom of choice, according to this argument, but the larger society.

[25] Taylor, 'Atomism', 209.

In fact, Taylor goes even further. 'The kind of freedom valued by [many of us]', he writes, allying himself with liberal political theory in this regard,

is a freedom by which men are capable of conceiving alternatives and arriving at a definition of what they really want . . . This kind of freedom is unavailable to one whose sympathies and horizons are so narrow that he can conceive only one way of life . . . Surely this is something which only develops within an entire civilization.[26]

So it turns out that Taylor, rather than celebrating community, wants us to embrace a *civilization* that makes multiple forms of life available in a meaningful way—by which he means Western liberal democratic civilization. Any defence of community as an end in Jewish education, therefore, will have to offer an argument for how a Jewish community can accommodate this kind of autonomy. That is, any defence of community as an end in Jewish education will have to acknowledge and confront the reality that strong communities tend not to provide conceptual alternatives to the 'one way of life' that they embody.

Perhaps, one might say, the Jewish education system can avoid the demand to provide conceptual alternatives because such alternatives are so readily available from the larger culture that surrounds it. That may well be true. But even if it is, that response only absolves Jewish education from having to provide conceptual alternatives. It does not deal with the fact that Taylor's arguments, as outlined here, support a commitment to that larger society in a way that they do not support a commitment to the sub-communities of which it is built. I do not mean to suggest that Taylor is opposed to religious or ethnic communities. It seems more accurate to say that Taylor *supports* sub-communities to the extent that their existence does not threaten the existence of the larger society composed of multiple sub-communities, the presence and visibility of which provide the developing individual with the opportunities to 'conceive alternatives'.[27] But I do mean to offer a caution about the ease or haste with which we might borrow his arguments for other purposes.

Beyond this cautionary point, however, is it correct to say that Taylor would defend community as an educational end in itself? It is certainly true, as argued above, that community has a *kind* of inherent value in Taylor's theory, in contrast to the instrumental value that it has in primacy-of-rights theories. It is true that our obligations to community are primary, in

---

[26] Ibid. 204.   [27] My gratitude to Dan Pekarsky for helping me to see this point.

Taylor's view, rather than secondary to our rights as individuals or merely derivative of the free choices that we make to associate. Communities are not merely there for our use, as it were; as Sandel claimed, they are constitutive of who we are. And so it is true, too, that Sandel and Taylor open the door to the argument that our educational aspirations ought not merely to include the inculcation of the liberal virtues of autonomy and rational decision-making, as in Schrag's three key aspirations, but to extend deeper and further—that we may coherently argue for the development of certain kinds of communities and for the immersion of individuals within them. This perspective can provide a helpful corrective to educational ideologies that, implicitly or explicitly, adopt a kind of atomist individualism.

And yet we must not overlook the fact that Taylor's argument relies upon the role of the community in the development of the fundamental human capacities of . . . the *individual*. This is the whole point of his anti-atomism: that individuals require societies to develop. The community may have a kind of non-instrumental value. It may be worthy of respect and generative of obligations. We may well want to consider how our actions and policies serve the promotion of strong and healthy communities, rather than merely focusing narrowly on promoting strong and healthy individuals. But this is still not yet a claim about community as an educational end in itself. 'In general', write Avineri and de-Shalit in an overview of communitarianism, 'communitarians regard the community as a need';[28] but a *need*, while possibly important or even essential, is still in the service of the thing that needs it. Taylor and Sandel may help us articulate a vision of human flourishing in which the good life is a life led by the individual embedded in healthy and vibrant communities. But the idea of the community itself, as an end, seems to slip through our fingers.

*

Where are we left, then, with the question of community as an end in Jewish education? The communitarians have helped us to see some of the weaknesses of a liberal individualistic model for educational theory (even when that model is pursued within a Jewish educational context). Schrag has served as a foil here. His three key aspirations may serve a noble purpose in reorienting educators away from factual knowledge and technical

---

[28] Avineri and de-Shalit, *Communitarianism and Individualism*, 7.

abilities and towards the intellectual and moral virtues, away from transient goals and towards enduring ones. But once one encounters Sandel's conception of the encumbered self and of constitutive communities, once one follows Taylor's arguments about our obligations to develop and support societies that can sustain the individual capacities that we cherish as essential to human flourishing, Schrag's list of three key aspirations begins to look rather anaemic.

Instead of, or in addition to, pursuing an educational vision as the answer to the question 'What is an educated person?' we might ask, as I wrote above, what kind of educational institutions, general or Jewish, would contribute to the development of a liberal civilization. We might ask how educational institutions, general or Jewish, ought to fulfil our obligation to sustain a society. We might ask how educational institutions, general or Jewish, can and should foster the capacity to form moral and religious convictions. These fundamental philosophical questions, occluded both by Schrag's explicit liberal individualism and the implicit liberal individualism of 'What is an educated Jew?', emerge from the encounter with the communitarians.

This chapter, though, has sought not merely a richer set of questions but, more specifically, a conception of community as an end in itself—and this, I have claimed, has slipped through our fingers. I asked in my introduction whether it is possible to sustain an enquiry into this question, or whether any discussion of educational aims collapses inevitably into individualistic terms. The argument to this point has suggested that the latter might be the case. However, in my final sentences I would like at least to raise the possibility of an alternative way of thinking about this issue.

If contemporary political theory cannot provide an articulation of community as an end in itself, perhaps such an articulation must be found elsewhere. Perhaps, that is, one must look *within a particular tradition* to discern, or develop, a conception of community that can stand on its own, that can serve as its own end.[29] Perhaps we might develop, out of the sources of a particular tradition, a conception that, while rooted in the tradition and hence particular, is nevertheless intelligible and defensible in universal terms.

[29] I am proposing, in other words, the approach of Michael Walzer's *Jewish Political Tradition* project. See Walzer et al. (eds.), *The Jewish Political Tradition*, i: *Authority* and ii: *Membership*. Subsequent forthcoming volumes will focus on 'community' and 'political vision'.

What would this look like? In the Jewish case, a conception of community might be developed by asking about those *mitsvot*, commandments or obligations, that apply to the community. These *mitsvot* are the exceptions, because most *mitsvot* apply to individuals. But some do not: establishing a judicial system, for example, or carrying out certain rituals, or educating children when parents are unable to do so. An analysis of these communal obligations, and others, suggests a three-part taxonomy. Some communal obligations derive from or suggest a conception of community as acting *in loco parentis* (as in the case of educating children). Others derive from or suggest a conception of community as a corporate agent, acting not merely as a collection of individuals but as a corporate entity (as in the case of certain communal rituals). And others derive from or suggest the communal expression of certain deeply held values (as in the case of the establishment of a judicial system, embodying the values of justice and order).

If we then ask our educational question, about the pursuit of community as an educational end in itself, this taxonomy may provide some guidance. Community is certainly a means towards individual human flourishing. But it is also valuable in itself in its capacity to step in where individuals fail; it may also be considered a corporate agent for certain purposes; finally, and most interestingly, it may also embody or express certain deeply held values. Thus, for example, Yitz Greenberg has recently written (about Jewish day schools in particular) that 'the day school gives educators the opportunity to create a world which can embody the holistic holy community which is our dream for the world'.[30] There is nothing in this vision about the *benefit* of holism for individuals, or the *purpose* of holy communities. Instead, a 'holistic holy community' is an end in itself, as an expression of our deeply held ideals on the community-wide or indeed global scale. Perhaps, then, these conceptions of community, derived from traditional Jewish sources, might enable us to develop Jewish existential visions at the communal level— visions not merely of the ideal individual but of the ideal Jewish community.[31]

---

[30] Greenberg, 'Judaism and Modernity', 3–4.
[31] I have been able only to gesture towards these ideas here, but I plan to develop them in a forthcoming paper.

Bibliography

Avineri, S., and A. de-Shalit, *Communitarianism and Individualism* (Oxford, 1992).

Berlin, I., 'Two Concepts of Liberty' (1958), in id., *Liberty* (Oxford, 2002).

Fox, S., I. Scheffler, and D. Marom (eds.), *Visions of Jewish Education* (Cambridge, Mass., 2004).

Greenberg, Y., 'Judaism and Modernity: Realigning the Two Worlds. An Edited Transcript of an Address by Yitzchak Greenberg', *Perspectives on Jewish Education*, iv (Ramat Gan, 2006), 33–4.

Jackson, P., 'The Mimetic and the Transformative: Alternative Outlooks on Teaching', in id. (ed.), *The Practice of Teaching* (New York, 1986).

Kaplowitz, T., 'Community Building: A New Role for the Jewish Day School', *Journal of Jewish Education*, 68/3 (2002), 29–48.

Levisohn, J., 'Ideas and Ideals in Jewish Education: Initiating a Conversation on *Visions of Jewish Education*', *Journal of Jewish Education*, 71/1 (2005), 53–66.

Merz, C., and G. Furman, *Community and Schools* (New York, 1997).

Noddings, N., 'On Community', *Educational Theory*, 46/3 (1996).

Pekarsky, D., 'The Place of Vision in Jewish Educational Reform', *Journal of Jewish Education*, 63/1–2 (1997), 31–40.

—— 'Some Moral and Social Dimensions of Vision-driven Practice', *Journal of Jewish Education*, 71/2 (2005), 243–4.

—— 'Vision and Education', in H. Marantz (ed.), *Judaism and Education: Essays in Honor of Walter I. Ackerman* (Beersheba, 1998).

—— 'Vision and Education: Arguments, Counterarguments, and Rejoinders', *American Journal of Education*, 113/3 (2007), 423–50.

—— *Vision at Work: The Theory and Practice of Beit Rabban* (New York, 2006).

Peters, R. S., *Ethics and Education* (London, 1966).

Rawls, J., *A Theory of Justice* (Cambridge, Mass., 1971).

Sandel, M., 'The Procedural Republic and the Unencumbered Self', *Political Theory*, 12/1 (1984), 81–96.

Schrag, F., *Back to Basics: Fundamental Educational Questions Re-examined* (San Francisco, 1995).

—— 'What is Thinking?', in id. (ed.), *Thinking in School and Society* (New York, 1988).

Taylor, C., 'Atomism' (1979), in id., *Philosophical Papers*, ii: *Philosophy and the Human Sciences* (Cambridge, Mass., 1985).

—— 'Cross Purposes: The Liberal-Communitarian Debate', in id., *Philosophical Arguments* (Cambridge, Mass., 1995), 181–203.

Walzer, M., M. Lorberbaum, N. J. Zohar, and Y. Lorberbaum (eds.), *The Jewish Political Tradition*, i: *Authority* (New Haven, Conn., 2000).

Walzer, M., M. Lorberbaum, N. J. Zohar, and A. Ackerman (eds.), *The Jewish Political Tradition*, ii: *Membership* (New Haven, Conn., 2003).

PART II

Cross-Cultural Insights

Do Jewish Schools Make a Difference in the Former Soviet Union?

ZVI GITELMAN

INTENSIVE JEWISH EDUCATION is seen in many countries, including Israel, as the most promising antidote to the assimilation of Jews—meaning the loss of Jewish identity and commitment. Full-day schools especially have been seized upon by Jews in the former Soviet Union (FSU) and their foreign supporters as the optimal solution to the lack of Jewish education, institutions, public life, and private religious practice among the 400,000 or so Jews left in the FSU.[1] This conclusion is based on extrapolation from Western Jewry's experiences. Common sense would also lead one to believe that viable Jewish life—that which engages people in private and public Jewish behaviours and transmits commitment across generations—depends on education, and not of children alone.

One crucial difference between the West and the FSU is that in the West Jewish education is conveyed in a wider context of Jewish commitment and activity: the family, organized peer and interest groups, a communal structure, religious and cultural institutions, and family and group traditions. In the FSU Jewish schools exist in a partial void. Jewish public institutions

---

[1] The number of 'Jews' in the FSU depends on how one defines a 'Jew', and on political and institutional agendas. There are at least four conceptions of Jews in the FSU. The first encompasses Jews according to halakhah: those born of a Jewish mother who had a Jewish mother. This category is assumed to be quite congruent with those who identify themselves as Jewish on post-Soviet censuses. The most recent censuses cite, in Russia, 259,000 Jews; in Ukraine, 103,700; and in Belarus about 27,800. In addition to these 390,500, there are perhaps 5,000 Jews in the Baltic states, and several thousand in the central Asian republics and in Moldova. The second includes *Khok-hashvutnye evreii*, or Jews according to the Israeli Law of Return, who need have only one Jewish grandparent to qualify for Jewish status for the purpose of immigration to Israel (though not for marriage or burial there). The third includes all those who describe themselves as Jews, and the fourth includes those who qualify as Jews under the first and second conceptions but do not choose to identify themselves as Jews. Note that in Russia and Ukraine people no longer have to identify themselves by nationality (ethnicity) on their internal 'passports', as they did in the Soviet era.

were abolished by the Soviet authorities after 1948 when the wartime Jewish Anti-Fascist Committee was dissolved and many of its leaders were arrested. In 1930 the Jewish Sections of the Communist Party were dissolved, and earlier still Jewish religious, Zionist, and/or Hebrew schools had been closed.[2] Although the USSR was the only state in the world to provide full funding for a network of Jewish schools, these were all run in Yiddish. No Hebrew was taught, Judaism was referred to only to criticize it, and Jewish history was limited to the modern era in the Russian empire and the USSR.[3] There were about 1,100 Soviet Yiddish schools in 1931, in which 130,000 students were enrolled. Of all the Jewish children who attended school at all in Belorussia and Ukraine, in the former Pale of Settlement, nearly half were enrolled in Yiddish schools. But urbanization, industrialization, and the attractiveness of Russian culture as the key to social, economic, and political mobility led most Jewish parents to choose Russian (sometimes Ukrainian, rarely Belorussian) schools for their children.[4] Most of the Yiddish schools were elementary, and if one wanted to go on to secondary and higher education, Yiddish schooling was a disadvantage. Thus Soviet Jews sent their children to state public schools to gain the tools for moving up the social and economic ladders, just as American or British Jewish parents did. After the Second World War, when Soviet policy towards Jews changed radically, no Jewish schools were reopened, with the possible and very brief exception of a single school in Vilnius.[5]

There had been no Jewish school of any kind for the 2.5 million Jews of the USSR for at least half a century when Mikhail Gorbachev's policy of perestroika, launched in the late 1980s, opened up opportunities for private cultural, political, and economic initiatives. By 1989 Jewish Sunday schools—many of which served both parents and children—some day schools offering both Judaic and general education, and supplementary schools were beginning to appear in all parts of the USSR. What effect have the day schools had on their students and their families, and on the Jewish population at large? The short answer seems to be that we don't know.

---

[2] For details, see Gitelman, *A Century of Ambivalence.*
[3] On Jewish education in the Russian empire and the Soviet Union, see Halevy, *Jewish Schools under Czarism and Communism.*   [4] Gitelman, *Jewish Nationality and Soviet Politics,* 337.
[5] On Soviet Jewish schools, see Weiner, 'The Politics of Education'; Schulman, *A History of Jewish Education in the Soviet Union*; Siilin-Vinograd, 'The Jewish Schools in the Soviet Union' (Heb.); Mark, 'Evreiskaya shkola v Sovetskom Soyuze'.

Shifting Jewish Agendas, West and East

As differences between 'Eastern' and 'Western' countries diminish, their Jewish agendas begin to converge. Struggles for legal equality and social acceptance have been won by Jews in the West and also, eventually, by those in the Soviet Union. After the revolutions of 1917 Soviet Jews enjoyed full legal equality with other Soviet citizens, and the government promoted social equality for the nearly 200 'nationalities' of the USSR, including Jews. However, from the 1940s until nearly the end of the Soviet period these policies were reversed. During these years Jews became second-class citizens. Acculturation, generally to Russian culture, was vigorously promoted, but assimilation—the ability to change one's identity from Jewish to Russian—was denied by the obligatory registration of nationality on one's internal 'passport'. Nationality or ethnicity was important in determining educational, vocational, and political opportunities. Whereas Jews had been prominent in Soviet government, the Communist Party, the military, and culture and science in the 1920s and up to about 1937, by the 1950s they had nearly disappeared from these elite groups.[6] Under the post-Soviet regimes of Presidents Boris Yeltsin in Russia and Leonid Kravchuk and Leonid Kuchma in Ukraine, Jews rose to high positions in government and business. In Russia, Jews served as finance, foreign, and prime ministers; Ukraine had a Jewish prime minister and two Jewish mayors of large cities. An extraordinarily high proportion of the economic 'oligarchs', later repressed by Vladimir Putin, were Jews.[7]

In West and East alike, Jewish public agendas have shifted from struggles for acceptance and acculturation to struggles to preserve Jewish identity and, maximally, to imbue Jewish people with Jewish culture, Judaism, and commitment to Jewish causes. In the United States, United Kingdom, and France, Jewish culture is conceived largely in terms of Judaism, since secular Jewish cultures based on Yiddish, Hebrew, or socialism have lost out to the dominant languages of those societies and to capitalism.[8]

[6] Gitelman, 'Ethnicity and Terror'. Details on the numbers of Jews in high and mid-level positions can be found in Pinkus, *The Jews of the Soviet Union*, 235–41.

[7] See Goldman, 'Russian Jews in Business'.

[8] Jitlovsky, 'What Is Jewish Secular Culture?', 92, 93, 95. Some believe that the new Jewish literature produced by the generation after Roth, Malamud, and Bellow, and suffused with more explicitly Jewish content, is a new basis for non-religious identity and constitutes a form of cultural Judaism; but no matter how large the Jewish reading public, this seems hardly likely to sustain Jewish commitment or activity, though it probably buttresses Jewish sentiments.

From the 1950s to the 1980s Jewish 'ethnic entrepreneurs', those concerned with the preservation and promotion of Jewish identity and commitment, identified the State of Israel and the Holocaust as pillars of contemporary Jewishness. However, in the 1980s, if not earlier, Israel began to lose its lustre in the light of Palestinian intifadas, the embourgeoisement of Israeli society, and constant bickering between nominally religious and nominally secular Israelis. More recently still, Israel has been 'repackaged' for younger generations as a place of 'sun 'n' fun'. Its place as a historic homeland, a haven for oppressed Jews, and a cultural and spiritual centre—once the most salient features of the 'miraculous' Jewish state—is emphasized less.

At the same time, the introduction of 'Holocaust education' into Jewish and general school curricula, the outpouring of literature on the Shoah, and the proliferation of Shoah museums, monuments, and commemorations have routinized what was once an unimaginable horror. In some sectors of Western populations, not excluding Jews, 'Holocaust fatigue' seems to have set in. Among some young people, constantly exposed to violence in the media, the Holocaust no longer shocks.

Education as 'the Answer'

The organized American Jewish community was forced to reconsider its priorities when it discovered that about half of all American Jews marrying in the 1980s and thereafter were marrying non-Jews, and that rates of Jewish affiliation and giving to Jewish causes were slowing. Federations, led largely by non-Orthodox Jews who did not send their own children to Jewish day schools, began to shift allocations from Sunday and supplementary congregational schools to day schools, especially as the latter became more popular among Conservative Jews. A consensus emerged, sometimes reluctantly, that day school education, once suspect as an instrument of 'segregation', 'ghettoization', and inferior general education, was the most effective single instrument for the maintenance of Jewish identity and the acquisition of Jewish culture and religion.

Fragmentary research on Jewish schools in the United States suggests—and no more than suggests—that a student with seven or more years of supplementary Jewish education, and even fewer years of day school education, is more likely to marry another Jew, and that this education is likely to have a 'positive impact upon Jewish identity'. Using the 2000–1 National Jewish Population Survey, Steven M. Cohen and Laurence Kotler-Berkowitz conclude: 'In general, attendance at a day school seven years or more exerts the most positive impact upon Jewish identity . . . Former day school students surpass the other schooling categories, controlling for the Jewish background and demographic factors, on almost all measures of Jewish identity.'[9] This is one of the very few studies that attempts to disaggregate the effects of schooling on Jewish identity from related and possibly causal items such as Jewish denomination, parental observance and education, location of respondents, and so on. Though other studies reach similar conclusions, they do not separate out the influence of Jewish education from other relevant considerations such as religiosity, parental background, synagogue affiliation, and peer group composition.[10] This allows no assessment of the *independent* effects of Jewish schooling. In the West it is hard to assess the likely impact of Jewish schooling where it occurs *without* parental knowledge, religious commitment, communal affiliation, and peer support to buttress it. Yet just such a situation is offered by the FSU, where Jewish schools are not complemented by the extensive cultural, familial, and institutional Jewish support that exists in Western countries.

The Lonely Jewish School in the FSU

After the Soviet Union collapsed, foreign Jews rushed in to help graft the Soviet branch back on to the trunk of world Jewry. Local Jews interested in developing free, meaningful public Jewish life lacked funds, experience, and, in most cases, knowledge of Judaism, Jewish history, and Jewish culture. Schools were among the first institutions to be constructed, largely by local initiative and with local educators, but soon forging partnerships with foreign professionals and activists.

The potential for Jewish schools in the FSU was considerable. First, Soviet Jews had the highest levels of general education among the Soviet

[9]　Cohen and Kotler-Berkowitz, 'The Impact of Childhood Jewish Education', 14, 15.

[10]　See e.g. Schiff and Schneider, 'The Jewishness Quotient'; Kosmin and Keysar, 'Four Up'; Rimor and Katz, 'Jewish Involvement of the Baby Boom Generation'; Fishman and Goldstein, 'When They Grow Up'; Himmelfarb, 'The Impact of Religious Schooling'. A bibliography of earlier studies of American Jewish education may be found in Brickman, *The Jewish Community in America*, 147–65. I wish to thank Dina Pittel, formerly a student at the University of Michigan, and the Partnership for Excellence in Jewish Education, for identifying some of these works.

nationalities. The 1959 census showed that on average five times as many Jews as members of the rest of the population had received a higher education. By 1970 the proportion of Jews who had completed higher education was about four times as high as that among urban Russians and Ukrainians.[11] Second, the Soviet system had provided for education in the languages, and to some extent the cultures, of territorial nationalities, as long as that schooling took place within the titular republics. The geographically dispersed Jews did not benefit from that provision, except in Birobidzhan, but it was easy for a Soviet person to conceive of a Jewish school system, especially since there had been one prior to the Second World War. Third, some Soviet Jews were eager to learn about Judaism and Jewish culture. Finally, external assistance with finance, curricula, and in some cases personnel was available for the establishment of Jewish schools.

Yet the prospects for such schools were dimmed by the fact that none had existed for several generations. The last religious schools had been shut down almost seventy years earlier. There were no teachers, books, curricula, alumni, administrators, buildings, or funds. A Jewish school had to start from nothing. Moreover, whereas the majority of Jewish schools in the West had a religious coloration, Soviet Jewry is an overwhelmingly secular one, and even religious believers do not necessarily link their belief in God to Judaism.[12] Most important, there was only a nascent organized community within which the school could function. Therefore, the role of external agencies was magnified.

Among the first to assist in the construction of educational institutions were the Memorial Foundation for Jewish Culture, the Chabad Lubavitch and Karlin-Stolin hasidic movements, the Israeli rabbi Adin Steinsaltz, and Bnei Akiva, a religious Zionist youth movement. They were soon joined by the American Jewish Joint Distribution Committee, the major provider of welfare services in the FSU, and by Agudat Yisra'el, ORT (Organization for Rehabilitation and Training), and the Conservative movement. Then, having decided that Jewish education in the FSU was not antithetical to immigration to Israel, the Jewish Agency, Lishkat Hakesher (the liaison bureau of the Israeli prime minister's office), and the Israeli ministry of education joined in. The Reform and Modern Orthodox movements have made only modest efforts at Jewish schooling, with the notable exception of Kharkov,

---

[11] Altshuler, *Soviet Jewry since the Second World War*, 108, 111.
[12] Gitelman et al., 'Religion and Ethnicity'.

Ukraine, where the Union of Orthodox Jewish Congregations of America co-sponsors a highly successful school.

The Structure of Jewish Education in the Former Soviet Union

The Baltic states have distanced themselves from the rest of the FSU,[13] but their Jewish educational profiles are similar. In Riga, Latvia, there is a Simon Dubnov secular Jewish comprehensive school and a Chabad school. The Dubnov school had 229 students in 2005–6 and the Chabad school 89. In Lithuania there is a secular Sholem Aleichem school in Vilnius, with about 200 students, but attempts to found a Chabad school seem to have failed.[14] Estonia has a secular Jewish school in Tallinn.

In Russia and Ukraine there seem to be four types of day school with Jewish components. There are public schools 'with a national component' (for example, Ukrainian, Jewish, or Armenian) which, it is said, receive 15–20 per cent of their budgets from the state, allocated to general studies teachers' salaries and maintenance; semi-private schools sponsored by the state but where Jewish organizations take responsibility for renovated premises in which Jewish instruction is given; 'schools within schools', wherein a part of the premises is set aside for Jewish instruction; and entirely private Jewish schools, almost all religious. In state schools the number of hours assigned to each subject is strictly regulated. Jewish subjects are usually allotted no more than four to eight hours a week, though sometimes other subjects—for example, art and music—are infused with Jewish content. An example of a 'school within a school' is the Bialik School in Minsk, Belarus, which operates within State School no. 132. Here, it is said, 275 students 'with Jewish backgrounds' receive seven hours a week of instruction in Hebrew and in Jewish history, literature, and geography. This is the only government-supported Jewish school in Belarus.[15] Note that there is no instruction in the Bible or Judaism, nor are there any religious activities. This is true of similar schools in Russia and Ukraine, because the

[13] Estonia, Latvia, and Lithuania are members of the European Union and are involved with NATO, unlike other former Soviet republics.
[14] Chabad and the officially recognized Lithuanian Jewish community clashed to such an extent that neither group would allow the other to control the only synagogue in the capital; as a result the synagogue was closed for several months.
[15] Naiman and Meisel, 'Fulfilling our Promise'. I thank Mr Naiman for providing the report.

three Slavic states have hitherto maintained a strict separation between religion and the schools, though the Orthodox Church is constantly pressing to insert prayers and religious instruction in Russian Federation schools. 'Russian nationalism and Russian Orthodoxy have emerged as the major theoretical foundations for moral education in state schools.'[16]

Private religious schools provide lunches and transport, major attractions for the poorer segments of Jewish society. Some, such as Or Sameach in Odessa, or the schools in Kiev under the aegis of Rabbi Yaacov Bleich, have dormitories which house students from outside the respective cities and those who come from broken or troubled homes. Many schools encourage students and their parents to emigrate to Israel. Some parents, though far fewer now than in the early 1990s, see any form of Jewish schooling as a preparation for life in Israel, offering students a facility in Hebrew and a familiarity with Jewish history and culture which should help them to integrate socially in Israel.

In 1997–8 the Institute for Jewish Education of Petersburg Jewish University surveyed Jewish education in the FSU. It found fifty-one Jewish day schools—nineteen in Russia and sixteen in Ukraine—with 10,700 students and nearly 1,600 teachers (including teachers of general studies). This was a substantial increase from 1992–3, when there had been only twenty-eight such schools. The institute also found 213 Sunday schools with 10,000 students and 1,000 teachers. Together, there were 296 schools, nearly 22,000 students, and over 2,800 teachers. Despite the fact that 77 per cent of the schools were supplementary, rather than comprehensive, nearly half the students were in day schools. But the institute noted that the numbers of schools and students were levelling off, probably as a result of continuing emigration and perhaps also because of low Jewish birth rates.[17]

Since then, the numbers of schools and students seem to have declined significantly, though an AVI CHAI Foundation report from 2002 says, 'As far as we can ascertain, there are about seventy day schools in the FSU, with a combined enrollment of nearly 12,000 students, grades one through eleven.' The authors note that there are about 2,000–3,000 students in Jewish-sponsored nursery, kindergarten, and pre-school programmes, but they acknowledge that on all forms of Jewish schooling 'precise statistics are difficult to come by, if only because certain institutions that are for broad

---

[16] Glanzer, 'Postsoviet Moral Education in Russia's State Schools', 1.
[17] Gitelman, 'Former Soviet Union'.

purposes identified as Jewish day schools may in fact not merit that identification. There is also apt to be a measure of exaggeration in enrollment claims.'[18] In 24 full-time Jewish schools in Russia and Ukraine studied in the 2004–5 school year there were about 6,300 students, including at least two high schools (*litsei*), with enrolments in individual schools ranging from 57 (New Jewish School in St Petersburg) to 483 (Or Sameach, Odessa).[19] The following year, in the same schools, total enrolments had dropped by nearly a hundred.[20] If one adds the students from the Baltic states, Belarus, and other former Soviet republics, perhaps about 7,000–10,000 students are studying in such schools at present, a drop from the previous 'nearly 12,000'.

Jewish emigration from the FSU has declined precipitously, and there may be more Jews returning there, at least temporarily, than leaving their countries. But the demographics of post-Soviet Jewry explain at least part of the decline in enrolments in Jewish schools. As early as 1994 only 6 per cent of the 'core' Jewish population (those who, when asked, identified themselves as Jews in the census, or children who were identified as such by their parents) were 14 years old or younger, and only 13 per cent of the 'enlarged' Jewish population (core Jews and non-Jewish household members) were in that cohort.[21] Significantly, 21 per cent of FSU immigrants to Israel were in this youngest age category, as the young are almost always overrepresented in migrations. Rising intermarriage rates—more than 80 per cent of Jews in the FSU who marry now marry non-Jews—and a drastic decline in the number of births to endogamous Jewish couples in Russia and Ukraine mean that there are fewer and fewer Jewish children in the FSU. According to Mark Tolts, in 1988–9 the total birth rate of Russia's Jewish population was 1.5, and was estimated to have fallen to 0.8 by 1993–4.[22] Thus, Russian Jews are having less than one child per family, on average. It is generally assumed that 2.2 children per marriage are needed to maintain a group's population.

[18] Rozenson et al., 'Avi Chai and Jewish Life in the Former Soviet Union'. The report was kindly made available to me by David Rozenson.
[19] The schools in the Russian Federation are located in Moscow, St Petersburg, Kazan, and Novosibirsk. The schools in Ukraine are in Kiev, Kharkov, Dnepropetrovsk, and Odessa. The Dubnov and Chabad schools of Riga are included, but the Vilnius and Tallinn schools are not.
[20] The data were kindly supplied to me by David Rozenson of the AVI CHAI Foundation in Moscow, 7 Dec. 2005. I am grateful to Mr Rozenson for his willingness to share not only the data but his analysis of them. Of course, he is not responsible for my interpretations.
[21] Tolts, 'Demography of the Jews in the Former Soviet Union', 173, 180.   [22] Ibid. 190–1.

Other constraints on the numbers of students in Jewish schools include the inability of these institutions to compete with the best schools. Many of the ablest Jewish children go to non-Jewish schools. One observer of Moscow Jewish schools argues that they have become dumping grounds for less able students, migrants from other republics, and returnees or sojourners from Israel. The presence of problematic children discourages parents of other children from sending them to these schools. Another problem is that families often see Judaic studies as the least important component of the curriculum. Most are unfamiliar with the material and unable to help their children with it.

On the other hand, some of the schools are regarded as academically superior to the neighbourhood schools children would otherwise attend. Classes are smaller, and drug abuse and sexual experimentation less prevalent than in the state schools. Because of the poor academic reputation of Jewish schools in Moscow, an attempt is being made to offer elective studies in Judaica in elite schools that have significant enrolments of Jewish children (for example, State Schools nos. 2, 56, and 57). Graduates of those schools are being trained to teach the Jewish subjects. The relatively large numbers of Jewish teachers in such schools constitute another potential resource for teaching Judaica. Some administrators are cool towards the idea of classes in Jewish subjects but will allow extracurricular 'clubs of Jewish interest'.

Finally, some of the religious schools will accept only children who are Jewish according to halakhah, meaning those who have a Jewish mother whose own mother is Jewish. The high intermarriage rates make this a limited category.

The Heftzibah programme (*ḥinukh formali tsioni yehudi biverit hamo'-atsot leshe'avar*—Formal Jewish Zionist Education in the FSU), formerly sponsored by the Lishkat Hakesher and now supported by the Jewish Agency, oversees the Jewish component in forty-four schools in the FSU. This component is heavily oriented towards Israeli history, geography, and culture, though sometimes the Bible is included as part of the literary heritage of Israelis. Many of the students do not meet halakhic criteria for Jewishness but are eligible for *aliyah* (emigration to Israel), the major motivation of those who established and maintain the programme. Some make no claim to any form of Jewishness. The ninety or so Judaica (more properly 'Israelica') teachers in these programmes are often unable to communicate in Russian, let alone Ukrainian, and are not necessarily trained as language teachers or as teachers of any other subjects. They usually serve for a year or two and then return to Israel. Since the sponsors aim to encourage *aliyah*, the curriculum is not structured for building Jewish communities in the FSU.

Ironically, these schools have found a new constituency among returnees from Israel. It is very difficult to estimate the numbers of these— some put them as high as 50,000 or even 90,000—since some shuttle back and forth between countries. Children from Israel excel in Hebrew and Judaica, but generally lag behind in mathematics, science, and Russian.

Religious schools are funded and staffed largely by the hasidic groups Chabad and Karlin-Stolin, the latter active in Belarus and Ukraine. In Moscow, St Petersburg, and Kiev, the three largest cities of the FSU, most Orthodox schools are not Chabad-affiliated, though Chabad regards the FSU as its 'home territory' since the movement originated in Belarus and spread thence to Ukraine. Chabad maintained an 'underground' presence in the European and Central Asian USSR throughout the Soviet period, so it was only natural, especially given the movement's commitment to 'outreach', that it rushed into the FSU when the Soviet regime collapsed. The movement claims to have permanent rabbis in 105 cities, all of whom seem to designate themselves 'chief rabbi', and others who serve 321 towns where there is no permanent rabbi.[23] Chabad has effectively displaced Adolf Shayevich and Pinchas Goldschmidt from their roles as chief rabbis in Russia and transplanted the Italian-born, American-trained Berl Lazar as 'chief rabbi of the Russian Federation'. A marriage of convenience has been consummated between President Putin, who conducted a widely publicized campaign against several well-known Jewish 'oligarchs', and Rabbi Lazar. Putin regularly appears at Chabad-sponsored events and Rabbi Lazar praises the president for his friendliness to the Jewish population.

In Ukraine, Chabad's attempt to upstage the American-born chief rabbi Yaacov Dov Bleich seems to have been largely unsuccessful, certainly while President Kuchma was in office. The charismatic Rabbi Bleich, fluent in both Russian and Ukrainian, presides over a dormitory school in Kiev with about 400 students, though it too has seen a decline in numbers.

[23] Mark, 'Habad's Global Warming'.

The main funder of Chabad activities in the FSU is Lev Levaiev, a native of Uzbekistan and a diamond entrepreneur who has built up a multifaceted and multinational economic empire. He is said to provide 60 per cent of the budget of the Or Avner school network, estimated by some at over $10 million a year. The American businessman George Rohr is another major contributor to Chabad institutions, especially in Russia. The central Or Avner office in Moscow reported to the AVI CHAI Foundation in 2002 that its network encompasses 42 schools and 5,178 students.[24]

The Conservative movement has a small presence in Chernivtsi, Ukraine. The Reform or Progressive movement has no visible educational presence in the FSU, though a few rabbis have been trained at the Leo Baeck Seminary in London.

Looking at twenty-four schools in Russia, Ukraine, and Latvia for which information was available for 2005/6, it appears that of 6,131 students enrolled at the beginning of the year,[25] roughly a third (1,993) were enrolled in schools affiliated with Chabad; 27 per cent (1,646) were in other Orthodox schools; and 40 per cent (3,639) were in secular schools, some affiliated with Israel, or ORT.[26]

Data are available for the major Russian cities of Moscow and St Petersburg (where over half of Russian Jews now live), and Kiev and Dnieprope trovsk in Ukraine. Enrolment figures for 2002 show a total of 4,680 students (see appendix).

The distribution of the types of school varies by city. Chabad schools encompassed about 21 per cent of the students in Moscow, 28 per cent in Riga, 30 per cent in St Petersburg, 40 per cent in Kiev, and 100 per cent in Dniepropetrovsk. In the last city there are three day schools; in Riga, two; in Moscow, nine; and in St Petersburg, six.[27]

Not surprisingly, almost all these schools suffer from a lack of qualified teachers—a shortage that stems from the absence of any Jewish teacher training programmes since the 1930s. Jewish schools generally pay better than others and are sometimes able to attract well-trained and experienced

---

[24] Rozenson et al., 'Avi Chai and Jewish Life in the Former Soviet Union', 13.

[25] I am told that enrolments often rise slightly because of late arrivals.

[26] This breakdown is misleading because some schools—e.g. those in Minsk, Vilnius, and Tallinn—are not included in this list. Moreover, many schools have several sponsors. For example, the 'Lipman School' in Moscow (School no. 1131) is supported by the city government, private donors, the Jewish Agency or Lishkat Hakesher, and Or Avner (Chabad).

[27] For more details, see the appendix to this chapter.

teachers for general subjects, but there is as yet no cadre of specialists in Jewish subjects.

For similar reasons, there is a lack of age-appropriate texts in Jewish subjects and in Hebrew instruction, though great efforts have been made in Israel and elsewhere to develop and distribute such texts and other educational materials.

Irrespective of sponsorship, schools are said by Russian Jewish education analysts to lack 'clear and well formulated common goals', the absence of which 'reflects a more general problem: the crisis of goals and national ideas of the Jewish diaspora as a whole'.[28] Rotman and Rokhlin point out that there is no comprehensive eleven-grade curriculum for a single Judaica subject. Curricula are frequently designed without pedagogical competence; there is no consensus on the body of knowledge to be acquired by students; nor are teaching methods co-ordinated.[29]

However, the AVI CHAI survey of teachers showed that half the Jewish history teachers had more than eight years' teaching experience. It is likely that general or Russian history teachers have switched to teaching Jewish history. Even a third of the Hebrew teachers claimed at least eight years' teaching experience, some of them having started out in *ulpanim* (intensive Hebrew language courses) or, even earlier, in semi-legal Hebrew circles in Soviet times. But only nine of twenty-four teachers of 'tradition', instructors in religion or customs, had more than eight years' experience, as might be expected in countries where religion was not taught at all until recently.[30]

Efforts have been made to provide 'on-the-job training' for Judaica teachers, through weekend seminars, educational trips to Israel, and various forms of tutorials. A training institute is said to have opened in St Petersburg.

Probably typical of some educators in the FSU is a Chabad principal (head teacher) whom we can call 'B.'. University-trained as a chemist, she says she grew up with a strong Jewish identity because of antisemitism. One grandmother was a Communist, the other a committed Jew. B. has been to seminars in Budapest and at Bar-Ilan University. She says she

[28] Rozenson et al., 'Avi Chai and Jewish Life in the Former Soviet Union', 9.
[29] Ibid. 12–13. For detailed, specific evaluations by teachers of the materials available to them when teaching Hebrew and Jewish history and tradition, see Rotman and Rokhlin, *Sostoyanie uchebno-metodicheskogo kompleksa*, ch. 4.
[30] Rozenson et al., 'Avi Chai and Jewish Life in the Former Soviet Union', 20.

knows all about rituals, laws, and customs, but observes few of them herself. She does not keep kosher but has proudly worn a family heirloom *magen david* since she was 12. B. is acutely aware of the complexities of Jewish identity and schooling in the post-Soviet space, and of the need to be sensitive to parental backgrounds, affiliations, and concerns. For example, the one non-Jewish student in her school was taken in as an orphan, but does not participate in daily prayers. The students in B.'s school get along very well with those in a secular Jewish school and they participate together in camps and other activities. But her school teaches nothing about modern Israel and emphasizes ancient history. The secular school does the opposite.[31]

What's Jewish about the 'Jewish Schools'?

In light of the demographic situation described earlier, it is not surprising that some students in Jewish schools are not Jewish by anyone's definition, including their own. This holds in Hungary, Poland, and other post-Communist countries, as well as in some schools in the United Kingdom and United States. Some argue that the non-Jewish students absorb some Jewish culture and gain respect for Jews and their culture or religion. Is this a persuasive justification for Jewish organizations appealing for funds to provide Jewish education to Jewish children? Perhaps, but no one seems willing to raise the question publicly. Moreover, might there not be a two-way traffic in influence? Might not non-Jewish students impart their cultures to the Jewish students in the same measure as they imbibe Jewish culture? I have not heard these questions addressed openly, perhaps because many fear that funders would shy away from schools that have substantial numbers of non-Jewish students. However, a reasonable argument could be made that in order to provide Jewish students with Jewish education, given the small number of those students it is economically and pedagogically necessary to include non-Jewish students in these schools. Moreover, the Jewish students are already thoroughly imbued with the non-Jewish culture.

In six schools studied in Moscow in the late 1990s, of the 540 students responding to a survey 17 per cent said they did not consider themselves Jewish and another 12 per cent said they did not attribute any nationality to

[31] Information obtained by Dina Pittel.

themselves; 64 per cent saw themselves as Jews (as did 74 per cent of the parents).[32] Almost a quarter of the students said their mothers were not Jewish and 36 per cent said their fathers were not. Only 11 per cent expressed a 'definite desire' to study at a Jewish college or university after finishing school.

Few students or parents claimed to observe the sabbath or *kashrut*, even irregularly. Two-thirds of the students and over 80 per cent of the parents had attended synagogue services no more than two or three times in the previous year. Only a quarter of the students and their parents said they had fasted on Yom Kippur. Though over 70 per cent of both students and parents said they believed in God or were inclined to such belief, only 47 per cent said that Judaism was the religion most attractive to them (15 per cent of students and 11 per cent of parents identified Christianity as most attractive; 13 per cent of students and 17 per cent of parents said no religion was attractive). Nearly half the students thought it 'makes no sense' that Jews should choose a Jewish spouse.[33] However, only 30 per cent of parents agreed, while 55 per cent said Jews should marry other Jews (74 per cent of the parents identify themselves as Jews, but only 45 per cent have a spouse who is fully Jewish).

As Table 6.1 clearly shows, students and their parents (mostly mothers) regard Jewish subjects as far less important and useful than others. Undoubtedly, this is not unique to Russian Jewish parents—or their children. But it is striking that both parents and children rank the importance of subjects in precisely the same order (with the exception of physics). No Jewish subject is considered by a majority of students to be 'of major importance'. Hebrew comes closest, but it is likely to be valued more for its practical utility than for its cultural significance and the access it gives to primary Jewish sources. Religious subjects ranked lowest of all, though if one were to analyse the findings by type of school, it may be that they rank more highly among those in religious schools (half the schools surveyed were Orthodox). Parents also do not feel religious subjects are important and see all Jewish subjects as less important than all general ones (again, with the exception of physics).

These findings would be shocking and disappointing to American Jews

---

[32] It is worth noting that four of every five parents responding were mothers.
[33] Shapiro and Chervyakov, 'The Jewish School in Russia Today and Tomorrow'. I thank Professor Shapiro for making the report available to me.

Table 6.1

Students' and parents' assessment of importance of subjects taught in six Moscow schools, 1990s

Subject	Respondents regarding subject as of 'major importance' (%)	
	Students	Parents
Foreign languages	95	97
Mathematics	80	85
Russian	73	82
Literature	50	75
Physics	50	54
Hebrew	48	67
Jewish history	36	60
Jewish traditions	33	48
Torah	30	39
Basic Judaism	24	30

who see Jewish education as the best instrument for achieving Jewish commitment and continuity. But the data must be seen against the backgrounds of the students and in the context of developing Jewish infrastructures. Moreover, a strikingly large majority of the Moscow students say they like their Jewish schools better than the schools they attended previously. Almost four out of five say that 'it is interesting/somewhat interesting for me to study in this school'. Nearly half say the school 'fully satisfies' them, and another 38 per cent say it does so 'somewhat'. Just over half say they would continue studying at their school even if all Jewish studies were dropped. Thus, students are strongly attached to at least these six Moscow schools, though they regard Jewish subjects as of little importance.

Might it be that the attraction of Jewish schools lies more in their ethnic character than in their academic offerings? Just over half the student respondents say that, being in a Jewish school, they do not miss contact with Russian peers, though only 20 per cent say that outside school their friends are mostly Jews (35 per cent say they are mostly Russian and 26 per cent say they are both Russians and Jews). When asked to identify the nationality of their three closest friends, respondents divide their answers evenly on average between Jews and non-Jews, and strongly reject the notion that people should choose friends on the basis of ethnicity.

Shapiro and Chervyakov interviewed 289 parents of children in the Jewish schools (80 per cent of these parents were mothers; about 15 per cent of the children report that they live with their mothers and not fathers). Parents are at least as positive about the Jewish schools as their children: over 90 per cent say they made the right decision to send them there. However, 42 per cent say their main motivation in sending the children to a Jewish school was that they would mix with other Jews and be in a Jewish milieu. The only reason they would change schools—and a third say they would never do so—would be to improve their children's learning of general subjects.

Some believe not only that Jewish schools will produce future generations of committed, knowledgeable Jews, but that as a result of the students' influence their parents will become more involved in Jewish affairs and practices. Indeed, it was common in the early 1990s for parents to learn along with their children in Sunday schools, though the number of such schools has declined. When asked how their children's attendance at a Jewish school had influenced them, 45 per cent of the Moscow parents surveyed by Shapiro and Chervyakov said that they had gained knowledge of Jewish subjects, but 24 per cent denied any influence at all. A quarter of the parents chose the answer 'I began to feel Jewish to a greater degree'. Only 3 per cent maintained that Jewish schooling had provoked conflict between them and their children. Over a third of the parents hoped that their children would emigrate from Russia; a majority of these saw the Jewish schools as facilitating that end. Both students and parents favoured secular Jewish schools and higher educational institutions. Only 6 per cent of the parents wished to see a religious institution of higher learning, where only Jews are accepted and 'strict observance of Jewish traditions is required'.

In 2004 Shapiro surveyed 1,050 Jewish residents of St Petersburg, using a 'snowball' technique to construct the sample.[34] His findings do not differ much from the earlier ones in Moscow. Parents feel good about the local Jewish schools, though they would like less religious instruction and prac-

[34] In the 'snowball' technique, researchers assemble a diverse panel of potential respondents and then ask each to identify further potential respondents, sometimes specifying particular characteristics that are being sought (e.g. age, gender, educational level, residence).

tice and, like their Moscow counterparts and their children, more sports and physical education. Between a third and a half of those whose children do *not* now attend Jewish schools would like them to do so, primarily in order to gain a better knowledge of their people's history and culture. Very few parents hope their children grow up as *religious* Jews.[35]

Judaic curricula vary, of course, with the sponsorship of the school, even within one network, such as Or Avner. In the religious schools in Kiev (Orach Chaim) the boys are taught by a Judaica staff of eight. They are supposed to study Torah, Mishnah, and Talmud for nine hours a week each, *mitsvot* for five hours, Hebrew language for four, and history for one. This amounts to thirty-seven hours a week devoted to Jewish subjects.[36] If this is accurate, it leaves little time for anything else. By contrast, the Chabad school in the same city, staffed by thirteen teachers, teaches no written or oral Torah, and divides the eleven and a half hours a week of Judaica among prayers, Hebrew, history (one hour), and 'tradition'. A third curriculum in Kiev, that of the ORT school, offers eight hours a week of Hebrew, history, and 'tradition' (one hour). The Dubnov school in Riga devotes only four hours a week to a combination of Hebrew, history, and 'tradition', though it claims a Judaica staff of five. The Jerusalem school in St Petersburg teaches Israeli music, Hebrew, history, and tradition, all in six hours a week.[37]

The Impact of Jewish Schools in the FSU

What has been the impact of Jewish schools on their students', and their students' parents', Jewish identification, knowledge, commitment, and activity? There are no systematic, comprehensive studies that would tell us. We have no idea how the schools have influenced the larger Jewish population, if at all. We cannot even extrapolate from what we think we know from Jewish schools in Western countries, from which the FSU is very different in several respects. Aside from the doubtless larger proportion of non-Jews among the students, the distinctive characteristics of Jewish schools in the FSU that set them apart from their Western counterparts include the following:

[35] Shapiro, 'Jews of St Petersburg Today and Tomorrow'. Unfortunately, I had access only to the report and not to the data or the more than 120 tables provided in an index.
[36] In the parallel girls school, there is a total of only 19.5 hours of Jewish studies, and, if the AVI CHAI report is accurate, no written or oral Torah is studied.
[37] Information supplied by the AVI CHAI Foundation, to whom I again express my gratitude.

1. Very few hours are devoted to Jewish studies in many Jewish day schools.

2. There are generally no supportive parents or grandparents to supplement and reinforce what the children acquire in school.

3. In most places, there are no strong communal structures to support the schools. Very few young people attend synagogues regularly. Many synagogues are primarily venues for the provision of meals and welfare services, especially to the elderly. There are few youth organizations, other than Hillel, which attract young people who have left high school. For some students there are trips to Israel and visits by their peers from foreign countries. The array of Jewish summer and winter camps reinforce what is acquired and learned in the schools.

4. The numbers enrolled in Jewish schools remain small, so students do not have the psychological support that large 'communities' of students afford (basketball or soccer leagues, for example).

5. Finally, in the FSU and Poland, though perhaps less so in Hungary, Jewish schools exist in something of a void. As in the West, schools are expected to do far more than transmit knowledge. They are charged with addressing social problems, feeding and sometimes housing and clothing children, acting *in loco parentis*, and almost single-handedly doing Jewishly what synagogues, secular organizations, families, libraries, camps, Jewish community centres, and youth groups do elsewhere. The burden they are being asked to carry is perhaps heavier than anywhere else.

I was able to gain a picture of one school, which may or may not be typical, and its impact on students and others, from Iryna Gubenko, a student who had attended the eleven-year Sha'alvim school in Kharkov, Ukraine, albeit only for the last two years of high school.[38] Founded in 1993, Sha'alvim has about 300 students, with boys' and girls' dormitories in different parts of the city (about a third of the students come from outside Kharkov). It is funded by the Orthodox Union (USA), the JDC ('Joint'), and 'Israeli friends'. Though it is an Orthodox religious school, in Iryna's

[38] Interview with Iryna Gubenko, Budapest, 22 Feb. 2006. I thank Ms Gubenko for the interview.

estimation 'only one or two' families who send their children there are religiously observant, though all the Judaica teachers are. The principal is not religious but, in deference to the character of the school, 'he wears a *kipah* [skullcap] all the time'.[39]

It is important to note that the school is located on a community 'campus'. A synagogue, dining hall, communal offices, computer room, housing for boys and for Jewish studies instructors and their families, and club rooms are all located there. This exposes students to communal institutions and activities, and facilitates serving meals to the students.

According to Iryna Gubenko, birth certificates are examined and only halakhically Jewish students are accepted into the school, while other students with Jewish identification go to School no. 170, another Jewish state school which is linked to Israel and emphasizes Hebrew. She thinks the issue of Jewish status is handled with sensitivity and understanding. The majority of general studies teachers are Jewish. Some teach not only for the relatively good pay but out of Jewish commitment. She rates the faculty high, pointing out that the head of the school has professorial status at the university (as a biologist) and that English and mathematics are strong suits of the curriculum, which appeals to parents. Teachers from America and Israel make the school 'more interesting'. Israeli teachers—only two of whom were born in the USSR—generally know no Russian but pick up some at the summer camps they attend before starting to teach. After some time they are able to teach the lower grades in Russian, but they cannot do so with 'really serious material' like Jewish studies. Therefore, each class has a translator.

Jewish studies are taught in the first half of the day. There is a religiously determined dress code, mostly for girls. Iryna comments that these stipulations are initially accepted as school rules, then resented and violated, but finally students appreciate that at least in school they should be observed. Kharkovites are encouraged to stay in the dormitories over sabbath. Students participate in services and a sabbath meal, 'but after sabbath activities were over we would go out and eat non-kosher food'.

Some children from less well-off families get free meals, dormitory accommodation, and camp tuition. No tuition fees are charged to anyone in

---

[39] It is obviously problematic to rely on a single informant, but I came to trust her judgement during an intensive course I taught at Central European University. Nevertheless, the reader should remember the limitations of this information.

the school, but students who wish to enter higher grades must pass an examination and an interview. There is some rivalry with School no. 170, but Iryna claims that their common Jewishness, shared camp experiences, and growing social networks bind all the young Jews together.

Iryna's impression is that about half of the school's graduates used to emigrate from Ukraine, and some, especially girls, became religious. She is the only one of eight girls in her class who remained in Ukraine. Now emigration is rare and some of the students are returnees from Israel who regret their parents' return migration but whose readjustment is eased by attending Sha'alvim.

How did her two years at the school influence Iryna Gubenko's life? Coming from a completely Jewish, completely non-religious family, she now recites the Shema twice a day and occasionally attends religious services, speaks fluent Hebrew and English, and has served as a point of liaison between foreign and local Jewish students. She has been to Israel, and completed an MA in Jewish Studies at Central European University (Budapest). She is delighted that she chose Sha'alvim. Though she says she never experienced antisemitism, she 'felt better in this environment'. Tellingly, she remarks: 'This was not just a school, but a community, a place we could hang out. They have sports, we loved communicating with Israelis and Americans . . . In no other school in Ukraine could you go to the principal with a problem.' As every educator knows, it is not only what is taught in the classroom that makes a school an educational institution. Sha'alvim organizes communal holiday celebrations that bring in alumni and parents. On Rosh Hashanah and Pesach the dining room is packed and another facility has to be rented for religious services.

In Iryna's estimation very few parents, if any, have become more religious as a result of their children's education, though some students have. Attempts by these students to influence their parents are usually unsuccessful. Although many families now participate in the holiday celebrations, it is not out of religious motives but out of solidarity with their children and with Jews generally, and because these are enjoyable activities.

Thus we have a portrait of an institution which is more than just a school, but less than what its sponsors probably desire. It creates multigenerational commitments to and knowledge of Jewishness, but not Judaism.

Dare We Know More?

When people make an investment, especially one amounting to millions of dollars, they are normally curious about how the investment is paying off. Apparently this is not the case with FSU Jewish schools; were it so, there would be systematic and comprehensive, perhaps periodic, assessments of their educational and social performance. Why is the most questioning people on earth so shy about making such enquiries? Perhaps donors and sponsors assume Jewish schools have to be a good thing so they don't need to see empirical tests of outcomes. Or maybe they are afraid to know the outcomes. Or perhaps it is too early—first we build, and only later do we evaluate. As Vladimir Lenin said, supposedly quoting Napoleon, 'On s'engage, et puis on voit.'

But it may be time we did evaluate outcomes, for students, parents, and communities, whether defined by *aliyah* numbers, observance, knowledge, or commitment and activity. Are imported models appropriate or should there be an entirely different type of school for environments so different from those of the United Kingdom, United States, France, Canada, and other Western countries? Is a Chabad school the most appropriate for a largely non-religious, scientifically oriented, culturally sophisticated population which prides itself on secular educational achievement? If not, what models should or could be developed for the very different circumstances of the FSU? Might non-religious Jewish schools in Latin America or Europe be more relevant than the English, French, or North American religious day school? To be sure, secular Jewish schools based on Yiddish or Hebrew have largely disappeared in North America, and secular non-ideological schools do not exercise the suasion enjoyed by religions or ideologies. Would the FSU, with its traditions of ethnic schools, be a place where such schools could succeed? All sponsors have their own agendas, so this question should be addressed much more to Jews who live in the FSU. If they are to mould schools to the form that is most appropriate for them, they must either develop their own resources or find external backers who share their outlooks.

In assessing the influence of the schools, one should make comparisons across time and space. A comparison with the United States may be instructive. For several decades American Jewish education was nurtured by European- or Israeli-born educators. It seems that, though unfettered by government policy, before the Second World War most Jewish schools failed to produce knowledgeable, committed Jews, for reasons possibly including their formats, the strivings of immigrants for acculturation, the excellence of public schools, and the unsuitability of teachers and administrators. After the war, American Jewry became financially and educationally capable of supporting serious Jewish schooling, though it has failed to produce enough qualified teachers and to make such education financially accessible to all. Can one reasonably expect those who started little over a decade ago, with no financial or educational resources of their own, to develop schools the likes of which had never been seen in that part of the world, except for the most traditional yeshivas? They enjoy Thorstein Veblen's 'advantage of the latecomer', but are also handicapped by it.

Striving

Jewish interconnectedness remains even when shared thick culture has eroded or disappeared. In some places, interconnectedness has grown and Jewish networks have expanded and become denser. In Hungary, Poland, Russia, and Ukraine, Jewish schools, camps, social and cultural organizations, and religious institutions attract people who share experiences and discover that they share values. In Budapest, graduates of the Jewish schools gather regularly at certain cafés. There connections made earlier are reinforced and new connections are made. In Warsaw, where there are far fewer Jews, connections are made through cultural and religious events. But where there are very few Jews this cannot happen, because networks will be too small and uninteresting.

Thus, a prerequisite for the development of this kind of 'social Jewishness' is a critical mass of people. Where there is such a mass, network development is facilitated (indeed, perhaps made almost inevitable) by the sharing of values, which some claim are secularized versions of traditional Jewish values, and demographic characteristics. In Europe and in the Americas, Jews are highly urbanized and highly educated. They cluster in certain professions—law, medicine, and academia—and in commerce, once in retail and small-scale business, increasingly in finance and real estate. They associate because of their common professions and vocations. In most countries their politics fall clearly on the liberal end of the spectrum, and in many countries this is a 'Jewish issue'.

In discussion with a young Jewish couple in Budapest in February 2006, when I probed what made a highly educated, thoroughly Magyarized professional couple Jewish, the answer was shared political and social values which led them to associate largely with Jews, almost unconsciously. Surely, I argued, there are Hungarians who share these values, so why are these uniquely 'Jewish'? The answer given was that those values had been imported into Hungarian society by Jews. To the extent they had been accepted by ethnic Magyars—and, in their view, that was not all that great—Jews had simply succeeded in persuading others to share their outlooks. Whatever the accuracy of this analysis, it is important that it is believed by young post-Communist people and that its consequences are the formation and sustaining of Jewish social networks. Jewish schools in the FSU may have already achieved that. There are other important goals to pursue as well.

APPENDIX: Enrolments in Jewish Day Schools in the Former Soviet Union

Table 6. A1

Moscow

School	Number of pupils											Girls	Boys	Total 2002	Total 2001	Maximum capacity of school
	Grade															
	1st	2nd	3rd	4th	5th	6th	7th	8th	9th	10th	11th					
Lipman	43	30	29	26	25	25	39	25	26	27	17	172	140	312	280	400
Achei Tmimim (Or Avner)	14	17	28	26	25	18	22	26	32	20	25	109	144	253	260	At capacity
Eitz Haim (Goldshmidt)	17	18	41	—	32	32	32	36	34	41	20	154	149	303	315	340
Beit Yehudit	6	10	9	—	8	15	8	—	13	8	15	73	19	92	120	150
ORT School	—	—	—	—	30	45	59	77	62	58	44	166	209	375	375	450
Migdal Or (Boys)	—	—	—	—	—	8	10	14	15	17	18	—	82	82	95	120
Migdal Or (Girls)	—	—	—	—	—	8	7	13	14	12	15	69	—	69	77	90
Mesifta (Boys)	—	—	—	—	3	7	8	17	22	14	9	—	80	80	46	At capacity
Gan Chama	12	16	—	11	8	—	—	—	—	—	—	26	21	47	50	At capacity
Machon High School	—	—	—	—	—	—	—	—	—	9	7	16	—	16	14	30
Total	92	91	107	63	131	158	185	208	218	206	170	785	844	1,629	1,632	—

Source: AVI CHAI Foundation

Table 6. A2

St Petersburg

School	Number of pupils											Girls	Boys	Total 2002	Total 2001	Maximum capacity of school
	Grade															
	1st	2nd	3rd	4th	5th	6th	7th	8th	9th	10th	11th					
Migdal Or (Boys)	9	7	9	–	–	12	10	12	7	16	9	–	91	91	90	110
Migdal Or (Girls)	2	7	1	–	–	–	6	–	10	8	10	44	–	44	70	80
Beit Sefer Menahem	19	9	18	–	10	11	30	23	18	13	16	76	91	167	150	At capacity
Beit Sefer Yehudi	8	12	14	–	10	10	16	16	9	19	15	62	67	129	150	170
Shorashim	26	26	26	26	26	26	26	26	26	26	26	160	126	286	286	At capacity
Beit Sefer Yerushalayim	22	28	25	21	29	49	44	41	28	27	25	161	178	339	356	435
Total	86	89	93	47	75	108	132	118	98	109	101	503	553	1,056	1,102	–

Source: AVI CHAI Foundation

Table 6. A3

Kiev

School	Number of pupils											Girls	Boys	Total 2002	Total 2001	Maximum capacity of school
	Grade															
	1st	2nd	3rd	4th	5th	6th	7th	8th	9th	10th	11th					
Simha (Chabad)	41	56	55	56	36	62	53	56	33	26	23	264	233	497	505	730
Bleich (Boys)	10	21	14	–	16	17	25	17	27	12	12	–	171	171	200	300
Bleich (Girls)	5	19	16	–	21	20	24	15	18	25	19	182	–	182	200	300
Or Avner	23	24	–	–	–	–	–	–	–	–	–	23	24	47	23	At capacity[a]
School No. 128 (school within school)	22	27	28	–	26	32	19	22	19	19	–	100	114	214	220	220
ORT/Israeli School	–	–	–	–	–	–	21	48	56	77	56	121	137	258	225	360
Total	101	147	113	56	99	131	142	158	153	159	110	690	679	1,369	1,373	–

[a] Owing to a large kindergarten, the space for grades 1 and 2 is limited.
Source: AVI CHAI Foundation.

Table 6. A4

Dniepropetrovsk

School	Number of pupils											Girls	Boys	Total 2002	Total 2001	Maximum capacity of school
	Grade															
	1st	2nd	3rd	4th	5th	6th	7th	8th	9th	10th	11th					
Jewish day school	59	64	63	—	51	55	62	55	63	52	54	264	237	501a	n/a	At capacity
Machon (Girls)	2	9	7	—	6	6	2	4	6	2	4	48	—	48	n/a	At capacity
Yeshiva (Boys)	6	7	9	—	6	10	8	13	6	5	7	—	77	77	n/a	At capacity
Total	67	80	79	—	63	71	72	72	75	59	65	312	314	626[a]	526	

[a] Discrepancies in total figures in source data.

Source: AVI CHAI Foundation.

Bibliography

Altshuler, M., *Soviet Jewry since the Second World War* (New York, 1987).

Brickman, W., *The Jewish Community in America* (New York, 1977).

Cohen, S. M., and L. Kotler-Berkowitz, 'The Impact of Childhood Jewish Education on Adults' Jewish Identity: Schooling, Israel Travel, Camping and Youth Groups', Report 3 to the United Jewish Communities, July 2004.

Fishman, S. B., and A. Goldstein, 'When They Grow Up They Will Not Depart: Jewish Education and the Jewish Behavior of American Adults', Cohen Center for Modern Jewish Studies (Brandeis University) and Jewish Educational Services of North America, 1993.

Gitelman, Z., *A Century of Ambivalence: The Jews of Russia and the Soviet Union, 1881 to the Present*, 2nd edn. (Bloomington, Ind., 2001).

—— 'Ethnicity and Terror: The Rise and Fall of Jews in the NKVD', paper presented at meeting of the Association for the Study of Nationalities, Columbia University, New York, April 2005.

—— 'Former Soviet Union', in *American Jewish Yearbook 2000* (New York, 2001), 396–404.

—— *Jewish Nationality and Soviet Politics* (Princeton, NJ, 1972).

—— V. Shapiro, and V. Chervyakov, 'Religion and Ethnicity: Judaism in the Ethnic Consciousness of Contemporary Russian Jews', *Ethnic and Racial Studies*, 20/2 (1997), 280–305.

Glanzer, P., 'Postsoviet Moral Education in Russia's State Schools: God, Country and Controversy', *Religion, State and Society*, 33/3 (2005), 207–21.

Goldman, M., 'Russian Jews in Business', in Z. Gitelman (ed.), *Jewish Life after the USSR* (Bloomington, Ind., 2003), 76–98.

Halevy, Z. [Harry Lipset], *Jewish Schools under Czarism and Communism: A Struggle for Cultural Identity* (New York, 1976).

Himmelfarb, H., 'The Impact of Religious Schooling: The Effects of Jewish Education upon Adult Religious Involvement', Ph.D. diss., University of Chicago, 1974.

Jitlovsky, C., 'What Is Jewish Secular Culture?', in J. Leftwich (ed.), *The Way We Think*, 2 vols. (South Brunswick, NJ, 1969), i. 91–8.

Kosmin, B., and A. Keysar, 'Four Up: The High School Years, 1995–1999', unpublished paper, Ratner Center for the Study of Conservative Judaism, New York (2000).

Mark, J., 'Habad's Global Warming', *Jewish Week*, 2 Dec. 2005.

Mark, Yu., 'Evreiskaya shkola v Sovetskom Soyuze', in Ya. G. Frumkin, G. Ya. Aronson, and A. A. Gol´denveizer (eds.), *Kniga o Russkom Evreistve 1917–1967* (New York, 1960), 244–50.

Naiman, A., and L. B. Meisel, 'Fulfilling our Promise, Fulfilling their Promise: Helping the Jews of the FSU', report to United Jewish Communities, National Young Leadership Cabinet, New York, 2006.

Pinkus, B., *The Jews of the Soviet Union* (New York, 1988).

Rimor, M., and E. Katz, 'Jewish Involvement of the Baby Boom Generation', unpublished paper, Israel Institute for Applied Social Research, Jerusalem, Nov. 1993.

Rotman, K., and Z. Rokhlin, *Sostoyanie uchebno-metodicheskogo kompleksa predmetov evreiskogo tsikla v obshcheobrazovatel´nykh shkolakh s etnokul´turnym evreiskim komponentom* (St Petersburg, 2002).

Rozenson, D., M. Warshaviak, and M. Schick, 'Avi Chai and Jewish Life in the Former Soviet Union', report submitted to AVI CHAI Foundation, 9 May 2002.

Schiff, A., and M. Schneider, 'The Jewishness Quotient of Jewish Day School Graduates: Studying the Effect of Jewish Education on Adult Jewish Behavior', unpublished paper, David Azrieli

Graduate Institute of Jewish Education and Administration, Yeshiva University, Apr. 1994.

Schulman, E., *A History of Jewish Education in the Soviet Union* (New York, 1971).

Shapiro, V., 'Jews of St Petersburg Today and Tomorrow', final report submitted to the American Jewish Joint Distribution Committee, Jewish Community Federation of Cleveland, and Jewish Federation of Palm Beach County, Moscow and St Petersburg, 2004.

—— and V. Chervyakov, 'The Jewish School in Russia Today and Tomorrow, Part One', report submitted to the Memorial Foundation for Jewish Culture (New York, 1999).

Siilin-Vinograd, D., 'The Jewish Schools in the Soviet Union and their Decline' (Heb.), *Behinot*, 5 (1974), 97–109.

Tolts, M., 'Demography of the Jews in the Former Soviet Union', in Z. Gitelman (ed.), *Jewish Life after the USSR* (Bloomington, Ind., 2003), 173–208.

Weiner, L., 'The Politics of Education: Jewish Education in the Soviet Union from 1917 to 1939', Ph.D. diss., Hebrew University of Jerusalem, 1980.

SEVEN

Jewish Pupils' Perspectives on Religious Education and the Expectations of a Religious Community

The Jewish High School in Berlin

CHRISTINE MÜLLER

IN THIS CHAPTER I present a case study of the Jewish High School in Berlin— the only Jewish secondary school in contemporary Germany. My focus is on the re-establishment of this school in 1993 and the associated hopes of the religious community, on the one hand, and the religious self-understanding and expectations of the pupils regarding religious education, on the other.[1]

I begin by setting out current developments in the Jewish educational system in Germany and the hopes that Jewish parents and religious communities have of it. I then give an account of the re-establishment of the Berlin Jewish High School and its Jewish profile. This makes it possible to understand the unique composition of the student body in its religious, cultural, and social heterogeneity. I then present quantitative data that provide an insight into the religious self-understanding of the young Jews in the school: how they think of themselves as Jews in Germany, what is associated with this self-understanding, and what religious behaviour arises from it. The analysis focuses on the similarities and differences between young Jewish people from German and Soviet backgrounds.[2] This focus is chosen because of the mix of expectations and anxieties within the Jewish community associated with immigration from the former Soviet Union (FSU). I then move on to a qualitative analysis of the expectations and desires of the pupils in relation to their religious education.

This study was funded by a Minerva Short Term Research Grant.

[1] A conception of Jewish identity can be influenced by other factors (e.g. the relationship to the State of Israel, the Holocaust, history, and the Jewish people). This article is limited to religion.

[2] The allocation to different groups of origin is based on the socialization of the pupils, not on the origin of the parents. The parents of the children with 'German backgrounds' also originated from many different countries. Other criteria (e.g. sex, religious affiliation of both parents) might also be relevant, but remain unaccounted for because of the specific subject matter of this paper.

In the final section I discuss what, realistically, might be the outcomes of an approach to Jewish religious education that embraces a student community so diverse in religious, cultural, and social terms.

Developments in the German Jewish Community's Educational System

Since the beginning of the early 1990s Jewish life in Germany has been revitalized. As a result of immigration of Jews from the states of the FSU, the Jewish community in Germany has quadrupled from 30,000 to 120,000 individuals and the age structure has become younger.[3] This revival has been most apparent in the establishment of Jewish educational institutions, both new foundations and re-establishments, since the mid-1990s.[4] In 1993 the first Jewish high school to operate since the Second World War began to offer classes.[5] The first Jewish primary school in North Rhine–Westphalia was also opened in 1993, in Düsseldorf.[6] In 2002 the Jewish primary school in Hamburg opened its doors again, sixty years after being closed by the Nazis.[7] The composition of the student body at this school reflects the changes that have occurred within the Jewish commu-

[3] The Jewish community in Berlin, with 12,000 members, is the largest Jewish community in Germany today. To understand this community it is important to know that the religious situation within the Jewish communities in Germany is unique because of historical circumstances. After the Second World War only a small number of Jewish survivors found themselves in Germany. There were not enough Jews to found separate communities for different religious groups and denominations, and consequently so-called *Einheitsgemeinden* (unity congregrations) were established that all Jews—regardless of their religious preferences—could join. The first communities tried to enable every Jew to take part in the religious services, and therefore used only Orthodox services, because Liberal or Conservative Jews can take part in Orthodox services, but Orthodox Jews cannot join liberal services.

There is still only one Jewish community in Berlin, but the religious situation has become more diverse within the last few years. Today there are six synagogues, and six Orthodox, Liberal, and Conservative rabbis serve the community. Although the religious situation is beginning to diversify, it remains difficult to live up to the expectations of all these religious interests under one roof.

[4] The big Jewish communities in Germany maintain Jewish kindergartens and primary schools. At the moment, there are primary schools in Munich (since 1967), Frankfurt (since 1966), Berlin (since 1986), Düsseldorf (since 1993), Cologne (since 2002), and Hamburg (since 2002). Another secondary school is planned in Frankfurt.

[5] Herz, 'Jüdisches Gymnasium in Berlin eröffnet'.

[6] Freund, 'Zur Arbeit in den Jüdischen Gemeinden', 256.

[7] For the history and the re-establishment of the Jewish school in Hamburg, see Czudnochowski-Pelz (ed.), *Talmud Tora-Schule*; Dohnke, 'Pausenklingeln und Kinderlachen'; Hartung, 'Integration hinter Stacheldraht.'

nity: five of the eleven pupils in the first class originated from countries of the FSU.[8]

The (re-)establishment of these schools became possible as a result of immigration by Jews from the FSU. Yet their creation cannot be explained by the mere fact of immigration alone. Ginzel, for example, has argued that the generation of Holocaust survivors who remained in Germany after the war rejected Jewish schools because they were afraid of a new isolation. Today, this fear has been displaced by another one: the present generation of Jewish parents want a Jewish education for their children because they are concerned that a non-Jewish environment might alienate their children from their religion.[9]

Jewish parents, then, have invested high hopes in the educational work of these schools. But it is difficult to develop appropriate concepts for these schools as long as nothing is known about the religiousness of their pupils, and the extent of their interest in religious education. The empirical study on which this chapter is based attempts a preliminary investigation of the desires and expectations of the pupils.

Before turning to the study itself, it is necessary to provide an overview of the history of the Jewish High School in Berlin, its re-establishment in 1993, the pupils, and the special profile of the school.

The Jewish High School in Berlin

History and Re-establishment

The history and tradition of the Jewish High School in Berlin—the first Jewish school in Germany in which Jewish and Christian children had the opportunity to study religious and secular subjects together in one classroom—may be traced back to the eighteenth century. Modern Jewish education began with Moses Mendelssohn (1729–86). Up until the eighteenth century, Jewish children were only taught a small amount of writing and arithmetic; the Bible and Talmud were at the centre of their education.[10] State schools were based on Christian principles and excluded Jewish pupils. This situation changed as the Enlightenment progressed. Mendelssohn imagined an ideal of a modern Jewish citizen who intermixes faith

8   Hartung, 'Integration hinter Stacheldraht', 62.
9   Ginzel, 'Ein Leben zwischen Extremen?', 22.
10   Hehlke, 'Die Geschichte der Jüdischen Freischule', 26.

and knowledge without contradiction, combining his religious life with his work in society.[11] In 1778 David Friedländer, Isaak Daniel Itzig, and Moses Mendelssohn founded the Jüdische Freischule in Berlin in the service of the new ideals, to meet the need for a modern Jewish education.[12]

The National Socialists ended this tradition. On 15 April 1942 the school was shut down, and for the next three years it was used as a camp for Jews awaiting their deportation to concentration camps.

In 1986, even before the first substantial waves of immigration from the FSU reached Germany, a Jewish primary school in Berlin was re-established. Later, at the beginning of the 1990s, questions about the further school career of these primary pupils arose.[13] After the peaceful revolution in the former East Germany it became possible to use the building of the Jüdische Freischule—the original Jewish high school— in the eastern part of Berlin as a Jewish school. In 1993 this building, at Großen Hamburger Straße 27, was restored to its original use and opened its doors as a comprehensive secondary school with eighteen pupils and a junior high school with nine pupils.

The former chairman of the Jewish community in Berlin, Alexander Brenner, articulated three fundamental concerns that led to the re-establishment of the school in 1993:

1. The desire to continue the tradition of the Jewish Free School.

2. The desire to improve knowledge about Jewish history, religion, and Hebrew; to strengthen the connection of young people with Judaism; and to sensitize the pupils to antisemitism and to the conflicts in the Middle East.

3. The desire to educate Jews alongside non-Jews, in the hope of improving tolerance and mutual understanding and eradicating prejudice.[14]

The Jewish High School's mission statement reveals that the school sees itself as an example of 'living Judaism in Germany'.[15] It makes the point that teachers are trying to strengthen the Jewish identities of the pupils, and

---

[11]   Stein, 'Traditionelle und moderne Erziehung', 18.
[12]   Eliav, *Jüdische Erziehung in Deutschland*; Behm, (ed.), *Jüdische Erziehung und aufklärerische Schul-reform*.   [13]   Mull, 'Über die Anfänge der Schule'.
[14]   Brenner, 'Grußwort (Vorsitzender der Jüdischen Gemeinde zu Berlin)', 7.
[15]   The mission statement is accessible to the public at <http://www.josberlin.de>.

that with this end in view it is necessary for pupils to learn the Hebrew language and to take part in Jewish religious education.

Composition of the Student Body

From the time it re-opened in 1993 the school has accepted pupils from several countries and a wide variety of cultural, religious, and social backgrounds. These included many non-Jewish boys and girls. In fact, at the time of its re-opening only one-third of the pupils were Jewish. The school has always included a high proportion of Jewish immigrants. Even in 1993 40 per cent of the pupils originated from the states of the FSU, and the proportion has increased since then. During the 2003/4 school year, about 300 students from 14 different countries of origin with many different religious backgrounds attended the school.[16] It is not clear what proportion of the students in the school today are Jewish, as the school makes available only aggregate numbers of pupils, wishing to emphasize the unity of Jewish and non-Jewish pupils. At the beginning of the 2006/7 school year, 380 pupils attended the school. The school plans to increase this number to 480 pupils in the 2010/11 school year.

Jewish Profile and Religious Education

Jewish schools in Germany are awarded state recognition and are grant-aided; 90 per cent of their expenditures are financed by the state. In addition to the national curriculum, these schools offer special in Hebrew, Jewish religious education, and German language classes for immigrants.

The special Jewish profile of the Jewish High School in Berlin is reflected in its daily practice, its general organization, and its curriculum. The school kitchen is kosher, grace after meals is recited, and male pupils wear the *kipah* (skullcap). The school calendar and timetable are configured around the Jewish holiday calendar, and the national school curriculum is augmented by study of the Bible, religion (mainly Jewish, though with some comparative content), Jewish philosophy, and Hebrew.

Participation in Jewish religious education is compulsory for both Jewish and non-Jewish pupils. All students have to attend two classes of Bible studies and one class in religion each week from seventh grade to tenth grade. In tenth grade there is an additional class comprising an introduction to Jewish philosophy. In addition to this, tenth-grade pupils have the

---

[16] Witting, 'Vorwort', 15.

opportunity to learn Jewish prayers.[17] From eleventh grade up to thirteenth grade (the highest), the pupils can choose from a range of different streams and classes that take place over four or five hours a week. At this level, all students also learn the history of the Jewish people up to the present.

Religiousness of Jewish Pupils

The empirical material presented below was obtained in November 2003.[18] A questionnaire was given to fifty-eight Jewish pupils in grades ten to thirteen during their religious education classes.[19] The questionnaire was divided into two different parts: the first consisted of multiple-choice questions that dealt with students' religious self-understanding and practice; the second of two questions requiring written answers about the role of religion in everyday life and about students' experiences concerning their religious education.[20] In this article I concentrate on just a few of the topics covered in the questionnaire.

The pupils were divided into two groups on the basis of whether they originated from Germany, Israel, and Iran, or from the states of the FSU.[21] I judged this to be a meaningful distinction because of the socialist-inclined, mostly non-religious education provided in the states of the FSU. In the analysis that follows, the similarities in pupils' answers will be presented first; thereafter the focus will be directed towards the differences between the two groups. This empirical approach provides the basis for a sub-

[17] Ehrlich, 'Bibel/Religion/Philosophie'. 80.

[18] These empirical data are part of the research for my Ph.D. dissertation (University of Hamburg, Faculty of Education), dealing with the meaning of religion for young Jews in contemporary Germany. For my research, I conducted twelve 'expert' interviews (i.e. with rabbis and teachers) as well as nine biographical interviews with young Jews, and carried out both a quantitative and a qualitative case-study at the Jewish High School in Berlin. The dissertation was published in February 2007: C. Müller, *Zur Bedeutung von Religion für jüdische Jugendliche in Deutschland* (Münster).

[19] There are 174 Jewish and non-Jewish pupils in these grades. The questionnaire was given to 58 Jewish and 24 non-Jewish pupils. They could choose between two versions of the questionnaire: one contained questions for Christian and/or non-religious pupils, the other contained questions for Jewish pupils. These self-definitions were accepted for the purposes of the analysis. The contribution here is restricted to the Jewish pupils.

[20] The multiple-choice part included questions about religious self-understanding; involvement in community action; attitude towards religious reforms, towards the Torah, and towards some aspects of religious practice and basic tenets of faith.

[21] Half of the Jewish respondents were born in states of the FSU, and half were born in Germany, Israel, or Iran.

sequent discussion of the pupils' desires and expectations concerning their religious education.

Before turning to the specific results of the questionnaire, a note of caution is in order. Although these answers provide us with an impression of the religious self-understanding of these pupils, they should be considered carefully, bearing in mind the difficulties inherent in applying a quantitative approach to this subject. For example, strongly religious people may well assess themselves as 'not very religious' because they take religious leaders as their measure, while less religious people with a less exacting standard might assess themselves as 'very religious' even if they have only comparatively little affiliation to their religion. These difficulties show the limitations of a quantitative approach and the necessity of employing an additional, qualitative, approach in analysing religiosity.

Religious Self-Understanding

The pupils were asked about their religious self-understanding in the form of the following question: 'How would you define yourself—Orthodox, Liberal, Conservative, or other? Please choose the category that fits your personal religious preferences best. If you like you can explain your position below.'

Most respondents, in both groups of origin, tended to identify themselves as Conservative or Orthodox (see Table 7.1).

Table 7.1

How would you define yourself as a Jew? (%, rounded to nearest integer)

Pupils	Orthodox	Conservative[a]	Liberal	Other
All Jewish	36	40	18	6
With German, Israeli, or Iranian background	30	41	26	4
With FSU background	43	39	11	7

[a] I am using Conservative not as a synonym for Orthodox, but as a specific denominational alternative. The term is quite problematic because the term 'conservative' has a meaning in the German language as being 'old-fashioned'. I explained my use of the word to the pupils during the survey.

Table 7.2

Do you believe in God? (%, rounded to nearest integer)

Pupils	Definitely not	Probably not	To a large extent	Yes, definitely
All Jewish	7	16	26	51
With German, Israeli, or Iranian background	4	18	28	50
With FSU background	11	15	22	52

Belief in God

The pupils were first asked about their belief in God and then answered a series of follow-up questions. As noted above, a quantitative approach to this question contains some difficulties. People might indicate that they do not believe in God, but they might believe in something that they just do not call 'God'. This shows again the need for an additional, qualitative, line of analysis. In order to gain deeper insight into basic tenets of faith through the quantitative approach, additional questions were put about faith in a 'higher power', in the strength of prayer, and in the appearance of a messiah or the coming of a messianic age.

As can be seen from Table 7.2, faith in God is of high importance for these young people, irrespective of their national origins. The answers to the questions about a higher power and the strength of prayer showed similar tendencies. Faith in the appearance of a messiah, however, the central element of an Orthodox self-understanding, does not loom large for either group.

Religious Practice

Frequency of synagogue attendance The young people taking part in the questionnaire were asked about the frequency of their attendance at synagogue (Table 7.3).[22] This time, the answers given by the two groups were markedly different. While 46 per cent of the young people from an FSU background attended synagogue only on High Holy Days, 71 per cent of the

[22] It should be noted that affiliation with a religious community can also have social or economic imperatives. The frequency of synagogue attendance provides us with information about behaviour but not about the motives behind this behaviour.

Table 7.3

How frequently do you attend synagogue? (%, rounded to nearest integer)

Pupils	Never	On High Holy Days	Once a month	At least once a week
All Jewish	11	36	34	19
With German, Israeli, or Iranian background	4	25	50	21
With FSU background	18	46	18	18

young people from a German, Israeli, or Iranian background attended synagogue at least once a month. A discrepancy between an Orthodox self-understanding and personal religious practice is noticeable within both groups of origin. As Table 7.1 shows, both groups of origin tend towards a Conservative or Orthodox self-understanding, and yet at the same time a comparatively small percentage of both groups attend synagogue regularly, that is, at least once a week.

Sabbath Since perceptions of the sabbath day vary so much among Jews, respondents were asked whether they make a principled difference between the sabbath and other days (Table 7.4). As in responses to the question about synagogue attendance, differences appeared between the groups. Seventy per cent of the young people from the FSU never or seldom make such a distinction; for young people from a German, Israeli, or Iranian background the proportion is lower, though it still amounts to half the group.

Preliminary Conclusions

The findings presented above allow a few preliminary conclusions to be drawn about the beliefs and practices of those who participated in the survey.

It is apparent from the responses to these questions that the presumption that young Jews from the FSU are less religious than others is unfounded. Moreover, for these young immigrants at the school, migration to Germany seems to have brought about neither a religious revival nor a complete turning away from religion. More broadly, it is not appropriate to

Table 7.4

Do you observe a principled difference between the sabbath and other days? (%, rounded to nearest integer)

Pupils	Never	Seldom	Sporadic	Always
All Jewish	27	33	24	16
With German, Israeli, or Iranian background	18	32	32	18
With FSU background	37	33	15	15

speak of a general secularization or indifference towards religion. Claims of this sort need to be differentiated according to religious practice and faith.

The two groups hold similar attitudes towards religion in general, their location within Judaism, and the basic tenets of faith, while differing in their approach to religious practices such as sabbath observance and synagogue attendance. In a majority within both groups, liberal everyday practice is combined with a Conservative or Orthodox self-understanding.

It is not clear what kind of meaning those respondents who do observe the sabbath and attend synagogue associate with these practices—for example, whether these express affiliation to the religion or to their family traditions. Also, it may be that young immigrants identify themselves as 'religious Jews' simply because they wish to identify with a group, not because of religious affiliation. If so, they may abandon this self-identification once they feel settled in Germany.

Jewish Pupils' Attitudes towards Religious Education

The second part of the study examined respondents' perceptions of their religious education. Although participants were ready to comment on many different aspects of their religious education, I shall concentrate here on just a few of the issues that surfaced.

The pupils overall were very willing to engage with religion as a subject, having received up to five hours of religious education per week since the seventh grade. Given the special significance ascribed to religious education in the formal school curriculum, it seems appropriate first to analyse the attitude of the pupils towards its place in their school life. Thereafter I shall turn to the expectations, criticisms, and suggestions of the pupils. This opens the way for a concluding comparison between the perspectives of the pupils and those of the religious community.

Significance of Religious Education within the School Curriculum

The pupils do not agree upon a preferred role for religious education within the school curriculum. On the one hand, there is a demand that it be kept out of the marking system:

In my opinion religious education should not be evaluated.

(17, f., Potsdam, Germany)[23]

On the other hand, there is a desire to strengthen the position of religious education:

I would double the number of hours, since I think that religious instruction is very important.

(19, f., Halle, Germany)

The Bible/religious education should become a main subject.

(16, f., Berlin, Germany)

Some of the respondents see religious education as an opportunity to recuperate from the rest of the school day because they feel less pressure in these hours. Others appreciate the opportunity to ask critical questions:

In general I really like religious education. First of all because it differs from all other subjects, e.g. during holidays and when we get the opportunity to influence the lesson through critical questions.

(17, m., Berlin, Germany)

I see Bible instruction as a very good and informative chill-out hour!

(17, f., Poltava, Ukraine)

Desires and Expectations

All respondents agree in their rejection of any kind of proselytism. They emphasize that a teacher must not try to convince pupils of certain beliefs or to urge them to make certain statements:

---

[23] In setting out the pupils' comments, I have identified each respondent by age, sex, and place of origin.

I would not only teach about a certain religion, but about the largest religions of the world in religious instruction, without conclusions reached by the teacher concerning which religion is the correct religion. The pupil must decide whether to follow a religion or not and what religion to choose.

(21, m., Odessa, Ukraine)

Some pupils hope to get from religious instruction a deeper understanding both of their own traditions and customs and of their personal relationship to God:

Religious education gives me the possibility of understanding Judaism better. I did not have the possibility in the Ukraine to take part in such instruction and so I hardly knew anything when I came here. The lessons helped me to understand and determine my relationship to God.

(21, f., Ukraine)

For these young people, religious instruction can be of practical assistance in their lives:

The topics are very interesting and could make life easier for humans.

(16, f., Berlin)

For other pupils, religious education does not have an impact on their own religiousness. They nevertheless appreciate the lessons for the opportunity they provide to improve their knowledge about different religions:

I like religious education, but I do not learn to believe or anything like that.

(16, m., Berlin)

One has to know a little bit about all religions, but one does not have to believe in them.

(17, f., Riga, Latvia)

I like religious education. It is simply good for general education.

(17, f., Riga, Latvia)

Religious education in the upper grades of the school is philosophically orientated. The pupils react to this in different ways, corresponding with their expectations concerning religious education in general. Some of the pupils hope for instruction on religious practice during their religious education classes:

More religious education in the form of everyday life (morning prayers). More learning of the Talmud etc. Less philosophy.

(18, m., Ramat Gan, Israel)

Other pupils value the philosophical approach to religious education:

I like religious instruction a lot, because there is a high philosophical level, which I have not experienced in a school institution before.

(18, m., St Petersburg, Russia)

Critique and Suggestions for Improvement

Some pupils criticized specific aspects of the lessons:

He [the teacher] cannot answer our questions. He thanks God that He has brought the Nazi period to an end. If he is asked why God has allowed it in the first place, he cannot find an answer. I only participate in religious education because I have to.

(17, m., Berlin, Germany)

There is a widespread view that a broader variety of subjects and methods should be taught. The pupils criticize the fact that 'Judaism' recurs as a theme in every grade of the school and feel that the lessons are constantly being repeated over the years:

One should not always repeat the same topics in class 1–9. They should try to teach as many different topics as possible.

(16, f., Ukraine)

Instruction is interesting, but I would like to learn different topics such as fascism

(18, m., Afghanistan)

The pupils hope to acquire basic knowledge about other religions in their lessons. This knowledge is seen as part of a good general education that should be offered in religious education but is too often neglected:

Some things you have to know, for example who were Jesus and Moses and why did God give the Torah to the people.

(17, f., Riga, Latvia)

I think it is a pity that we hardly learn anything about other religions because I would like to find out more about how others think and their life.

(16, f., Greifswald, Germany)

Religious education would be interesting if there were something about other religions in the curriculum but, unfortunately, many teachers do not consider that.
(16, f., Germany)

Final Considerations

It is difficult to identify with confidence the possibilities for and constraints on religious education in the Jewish High School in Berlin, in particular given the heterogeneity of its pupils, in cultural, religious, and social terms. Nevertheless, the very fact that the composition of the student body is so different from that found in Jewish secondary schools in other countries makes it especially interesting to attempt to understand how religious education works in this school. In other countries, such as Britain and France, there are different schools for the various Jewish denominations; in Germany there is only this one secondary school for all denominations. The school is seen as a 'flagship' for the whole religious community. These expectations pose great challenges for religious education in the school, because it has to deal with many kinds of different Jewish religious affiliations within one classroom, in addition to many non-Jewish faiths.

All in all, there is a willingness among the pupils to participate actively in religious education. Teachers would be well advised to respond to this willingness and consider the needs of the pupils during the course of the lessons. First of all, it is important to note that all the pupils reject any form of proselytism. Most of the respondents to the study do not regard the school as a place to 'learn religion'; this, they suggest, must remain the responsibility of the religious communities. The respondents show a strong interest in different religions. This is remarkable, because many are in a 'double minority situation' with regard to both their religion and their country of origin. Rather than leading to a separatist impulse, this leads to openness towards other religions. Some individuals see religious education as an opportunity to learn about their own religion; others wish to improve their level of general knowledge. The preferred designs of lessons set out by respondents reflect these expectations. Some would like to see philosophical debate about religion and religions; others wish to practise religion.

In addition to these huge differences in expectations and the common rejection of proselytism, there is a discrepancy between the hopes of the community for a religious revival through religious education, and the needs of the pupils. As noted above, the school was opened with the specific intention of strengthening students' connection with Judaism. But it is not evident that religious education can contribute to this outcome, at least not in this complicated context.

Perhaps the task of interdenominational religious education in this environment can only be to emphasize the different kinds and levels of knowledge and different forms of religious self-understanding that are available. The strong interest in other religions could be used to direct attention to differences between strands of Judaism and to contribute in that way towards the integration of old-established and new community members.

Bibliography

Behm, B. L. (ed.), *Jüdische Erziehung und aufklärerische Schulreform. Analysen zum späten 18. und frühen 19. Jahrhundert*, Jüdische Bildungsgeschichte in Deutschland 5 (Münster, 2002).

Breidenbach, B., *Lernen jüdischer Identität. Eine schulbezogene Fallstudie* (Weinheim, 1999).

Brenner, A., 'Grußwort (Vorsitzender der Jüdischen Gemeinde zu Berlin)', in Jüdische Oberschule zu Berlin (ed.), *Festschrift. 10 Jahre Jüdische Oberschule. 225 Jahre Jüdische Schule in Berlin* (Berlin, 2003), 7.

Czudnochowski-Pelz, I. (ed.), *Talmud Tora-Schule. Mehr als ein Gebäude . . .* (Hamburg, 1993).

Dohnke, K., 'Pausenklingeln und Kinderlachen. Hamburg: Jüdische Schule kehrt an den traditionsreichen Standort im Grindelhof zurück', *Jüdische Allgemeine. Wochenzeitung für Politik, Kultur, Religion und jüdisches Leben*, 13 Mar. 2002, 13.

Ehrlich, A., 'Bibel/Religion/Philosophie', in Jüdische Oberschule zu Berlin (ed.), *Festschrift. 10 Jahre Jüdische Oberschule. 225 Jahre Jüdische Schule in Berlin* (Berlin, 2003), 80–1.

Eliav, M., *Jüdische Erziehung in Deutschland im Zeitalter der Aufklärung und der Emanzipation* (Münster, 2001).

Freund, M., 'Zur Arbeit in den Jüdischen Gemeinden', in G. B. Ginzel (ed.), *Der Anfang nach dem Ende. Jüdisches Leben in Deutschland 1945 bis heute* (Düsseldorf, 1996), 252–9.

Ginzel, G. B., 'Ein Leben zwischen Extremen?', in G. B. Ginzel (ed.), *Der Anfang nach dem Ende. Jüdisches Leben in Deutschland 1945 bis heute* (Düsseldorf, 1996), 15–36.

Hartung, M. J., 'Integration hinter Stacheldraht. Die neue jüdische Schule in Hamburg wirbt auf Russisch um Nachwuchs', *Die Zeit*, 29 July 2003, 62.

Hehlke, R., 'Die Geschichte der Jüdischen Freischule und der Mittelschule der Jüdischen Gemeinde zu Berlin', in Jüdische Oberschule zu Berlin (ed.), *Festschrift. 10 Jahre Jüdische Oberschule. 225 Jahre Jüdische Schule in Berlin* (Berlin, 2003), 26–34.

Herz, C., 'Jüdisches Gymnasium in Berlin eröffnet', in U. Kaufmann (ed.), *Jüdisches Leben heute in Deutschland* (Bonn, 1993), 103–5.

Mull, U., 'Über die Anfänge der Schule', in Jüdische Oberschule zu Berlin (ed.), *Festschrift. 10 Jahre Jüdische Oberschule. 225 Jahre Jüdische Schule in Berlin* (Berlin, 2003), 56–8.

Müller, C., 'The Case of the Jewish High School in Berlin: A Denominational School Dealing with Diversity' *British Journal of Religious Education*, 27/3 (2005), 239–51.

Stein, D., 'Traditionelle und moderne Erziehung. Jüdische Erziehungskonzepte von Moses Mendelssohn, Samson Raphael Hirsch und Franz Rosenzweig', in Jüdische Oberschule zu Berlin (ed.), *Festschrift. 10 Jahre Jüdische Oberschule. 225 Jahre Jüdische Schule in Berlin* (Berlin, 2003), 18–25.

Witting, B., 'Vorwort', in Jüdische Oberschule zu Berlin (ed.), *Festschrift. 10 Jahre Jüdische Oberschule. 225 Jahre Jüdische Schule in Berlin* (Berlin, 2003), 14–15.

Mutual Relations between *Sheliḥim* and Local Teachers at Jewish Schools in the Former Soviet Union

IRA DASHEVSKY AND URIEL TA'IR

THE SYSTEM of formal Jewish education in the former Soviet Union (FSU) began to develop during the final years of the Communist regime in major cities such as Riga, Vilna, Moscow, St Petersburg, and Kiev. Since the establishment of the Dubnow Jewish school in Riga in 1989, dozens more Jewish schools have opened throughout the FSU. The first day schools were established at the initiative of local activists, but the major surge came during the 1990s, in the wake of active intervention by Jews overseas. The parties to this endeavour included the Liaison Bureau in Israel ('Nativ'), the Chabad movement, Karlin hasidim, strictly Orthodox groups of Lithuanian origin, and the Conservative movement.

The Heftzibah Support Programme for Formal Jewish Zionist Education in the FSU was established within the Israeli ministry of education in the early 1990s, on the initiative of the late minister Zevulun Hammer, to support Jewish schools within the territory of the FSU. In fact, the FSU is the only region in the diaspora where the Israeli ministry of education is involved with Jewish education. The aim of those who founded this unique programme was to provide the Jews of the FSU with the Jewish education that had been forcibly denied them for about seventy years. The programme includes financial support for school infrastructure, informal activity related to celebration of Jewish festivals, support for Jewish studies teachers, and the provision of *sheliḥim* (emissary teachers) from Israel.

Few non-religious Jewish schools in the FSU received support from the programme during the 1990s. Today, however, about forty-three schools participate in the programme; most of their students, who in total number more than 9,000, are Jewish, at least in the sense of qualifying for entitlement to migrate to Israel under the Law of Return.[1] Some seventy

---

[1] Although to be halakhically Jewish one has to have a Jewish mother, to qualify for immigration to Israel it is sufficient to have one Jewish grandparent on either side.

sheliḥim, along with more than 200 local teachers, are currently teaching Jewish studies (Hebrew, history, tradition, etc.) at these institutions.

The Heftzibah programme brings together professional teachers (local as well as *sheliḥim*) of very different social, cultural, and personal backgrounds. Even among the *sheliḥim* themselves there is great diversity: some are just starting out on their path in education, while others are close to retirement; some are parents whose children will accompany them on their assignments, others are single or divorced; some are fluent in Russian while others, born in Israel, are taking their first steps in the new language; bearers of a secular world-view have colleagues who are strictly Orthodox or traditional; Ashkenazim work alongside Sephardim.

What is common to them all? First of all, a sense of mission: a will to pass Jewish and Zionist knowledge on to students in Jewish schools in the FSU. In addition, every *shaliaḥ* must be in possession of a teaching diploma recognized by the Israeli ministry of education, and at least five years' proven experience in educational work with children.

Interaction between Local Teachers and *Sheliḥim*

The Jewish school in the FSU brings together *sheliḥim* and local teachers. Members of the two groups meet daily at school, and both are involved in running any informal activity that is connected to Judaism or Israel. To this extent they are partners in the shared work of Jewish schooling. At the same time, the status and situation of the two groups in schools are fundamentally different. Local teachers are familiar with the local scene, while *sheliḥim* require a year or two to accustom themselves to the new environment and to understand what is going on around them. On the other hand, *sheliḥim* enjoy a more elevated status than that of local teachers. They are emissaries of the State of Israel, and their position is comparable to the extraterritorial status of, for example, an ambassador to a foreign country.

Pomson and Gillis researched the situation of *sheliḥim* at Jewish schools in Toronto.[2] They defined the situation of the Israeli teacher as that of a 'foreign worker'. The very fact that *sheliḥim* have come from a different environment, ostensibly for a limited period (according to their contract, *sheliḥim* are obliged to return to Israel after five years), emphasizes their alienation from their working environment, including the local teachers.

[2] Pomson and Gillis, 'The Teacher-as-Stranger'.

Sheliḥim and local teachers work side by side for long hours at school, day after day, sometimes for several years. During the course of their work they are in prolonged and intensive contact with one another. In an article summarizing the activity of *sheliḥim* at Jewish schools in the United States during the 1960s and 1970s, Kessler writes that most of the *sheliḥim* regarded themselves as agents of Zionism, carrying out a national mission 'to bring the light of Zionism to the Diaspora'.[3] This, unsurprisingly, caused friction and a lack of understanding between them and their local colleagues in schools. Likewise, Wolf and Kopelowitz found that in teams of counsellors at Jewish summer camps in the United States the Israeli counsellors maintained a certain distance from their local colleagues, believing that familiarity would have an adverse effect on their mission 'to bring the children closer to Israel'.[4]

The subject of the relations between the two groups of teachers has not previously been researched. Nor has any in-depth study yet examined the phenomenon of *sheliḥim* at Jewish schools in eastern Europe in general, or the relations between these teachers and the local personnel in particular. We hope that our pioneering study will contribute to a clearer understanding of how the two groups of teachers interact and prompt further discussion of these important questions, which penetrate to the heart of Jewish education in the FSU.

The Research

To gather data for our study we interviewed thirty teachers—twenty local teachers and ten *sheliḥim*. Each of the participants was interviewed for forty to sixty minutes by members of the research team. During the interviews we focused our questions on five main subjects:

1. What was the contribution of each *shaliaḥ* to the school during the period of his or her stay?

2. What sort of interpersonal relations prevailed between local teachers and *sheliḥim*?

3. How were working relations conducted, within the school framework, between local teachers and the *sheliḥim*?

[3] Kessler, 'Israeli Teachers in American Jewish Schools', 55–61.
[4] Wolf and Kopelowitz, 'Israeli Staff in American Jewish Teacher Camps'.

4. How did *shelihut* influence the *shaliah*, personally and professionally?

5. How did the students at the schools relate to the *shelihim*?

The interviews were recorded and translated (where interviewees were Russian-speakers), transcribed, and analysed. The findings will be presented below in relation to two broad topics: interpersonal relations; and differences of approach to education and the professional relationship.

Findings

Interpersonal Relations

Social interaction outside the study framework There appear to be few deep—or, for that matter, even superficial—ties of friendship between the two groups of teachers. In general, the joint involvement in teaching was all that connected them. Virtually the only possibility for meeting outside school was at the home of the *shaliah* on the sabbath or a festival. Local teachers, for their part, almost never invited *shelihim* to their homes or initiated any sort of meeting outside school. All the local teachers praised those *shelihim* who invited them to their homes to celebrate a Jewish festival or sabbath, or alternatively spoke disparagingly of those who did not. S., a local teacher at a school in Samara, said: 'Shaliah A., who taught here at the school a few years ago, invited me to his home and endeared Israel and Judaism to me. Those who came after him didn't do much inviting; the last *shaliah* didn't invite me at all.'

A similar picture arose from the responses of the *shelihim*. It seems that the *shelihim* themselves regard such hospitality as obligatory, or at least as an effective method of outreach and of amplifying their influence on the locals. (It is important to note that the briefing to *shelihim* includes no directive to invite people to their homes.) *Shaliah* S., from the Yerushalayim School in St Petersburg, explained: 'This is my fourth year. Throughout the years [here] I have invited locals to my home; that's how I learned about life here, and that's how I've been able to influence them, in an informal atmosphere.'

Home hospitality, then, is a one-way street; it is not customary for any of the local teachers to invite *shelihim* to their homes, even where there are no concerns about *kashrut* issues in the local teacher's kitchen (*shelihim* being, on the whole, more punctilious than the local teachers in their observance of *kashrut*).

***Sheliḥim* as authorities on Israel** All the local teachers noted that the *she-liḥim* represented, for them, a prime source of information about Israel. Local teacher A. from the ORT School in Moscow said: 'Today, most people have [access to the] internet, but there's still a need for authentic information and an "Israeli view" of what's going on in Israel. I speak and read Hebrew, but if something happens, I go to Sharon and ask for her opinion.'

Local teacher T., from the ORT School in Samara, formulates the idea as follows: 'Just as I, during my stay in Israel, am a representative of Russia in the eyes of Israelis, so he [the *shaliaḥ*] is a representative of the State of Israel for us. He has the power to make a positive impression, to draw people towards Israel, towards Hebrew and Judaism, and conversely to chase them away from anything Israeli or Jewish.'

***Sheliḥim* as authorities in matters of Judaism** Most of the *sheliḥim* teach Hebrew, not Jewish tradition. However, since they are graduates of the Israeli education system and have lived in Israel, in the eyes of the locals they possess religious authority and are perceived as a source of reliable information on Jewish matters. This phenomenon is clearly manifest at the ORT (non-religious) network of schools, especially in the more remote towns. *Shaliaḥ* A., from the ORT School in Kazan, said:

When I invited the teachers to our home on Hanukah, they showed interest in every detail: how to light the candles, what to eat, etc. Most had celebrated the festival in the past, but I felt that it was important for them to see how I, as an Israeli, went about it. One teacher was moved to tears. After this incident I became a sort of local rabbi.

Even *sheliḥim* who lack any connection to Jewish tradition are transformed into authorities in this realm, especially during the period of the festivals. *Shaliaḥ* A., at the school in Novosibirsk, noted in her interview: 'I studied a course on tradition at the Lewinsky College, but I'm a Jewess from Odessa: Jewish tradition and I don't get along. Here, at the school, I became a supreme authority, rendering halakhic decisions. Whatever I didn't know, I read in books; I didn't disappoint them.'

This attitude towards *sheliḥim* as the source of information and authority in the realm of tradition forces them to change their approach towards Jewish tradition. A *shaliaḥ* from Novosibirsk reports: 'Today I don't define myself as even traditional, but my attitude towards [Jewish] tradition has changed completely. It's not foreign to me, it's part of my identity; I also mark all the festivals now—as a secular person, obviously.'

Teacher S., from the ORT School in Moscow, a sabra spending her fifth year in the city, defines herself as traditional: 'I come from a secular family, I don't observe the commandments, but life here has done something to me. By virtue of my position as the Israeli second-in-command at the school, I work extensively with the local Jewish studies teachers. They ask me questions; I've started reading a lot on the subject of Judaism, it began to interest me a lot.'

The *shelihim* are aware that their knowledge of Jewish tradition is superior to that of the local teachers. *Shaliah* M., from the Tehiya School in Moscow, recalls:

We worked together on a Purim production. One teacher was certain that Haman's wife was called Vashti, [so] I corrected her. She said to me, 'We've also been working on these productions for fifteen years already.' I told her that I appreciated that, but that she was wrong. A vocal argument broke out, at the end of which she admitted her mistake. Since then I've become an authority at the school. No religious event takes place without them consulting me on matters of religion and tradition.

Familiarity vs foreignness Both *shelihim* and local teachers, for the most part, reported normal working relations, and mutual appreciation in both the professional and the personal realm. At the same time, the *shelihim* are conscious that they are at the 'giving' end of the relationship, and that it is only through giving that they can become familiar, or create good relations, with the local teachers.[5]

Sometimes a personal closeness develops between the *shaliah* and the local teacher against the background of a family problem, or even a personal tragedy. A history teacher from Nizhniy Novgorod recounted: 'We had good relations with the *shaliah*, Hani. My eldest daughter was about to finish her schooling. We didn't know what to do afterwards, because I'm a widow and

---

[5] At this point the question could be asked: were the interviewees sufficiently honest with us? We assume that, for the most part, they were. We made it clear to all participants, prior to the interviews, that their anonymity would be maintained and that our purpose was, first and foremost, research. The form and content of the interview were not threatening. Our impression was that the interviewees had nothing to gain from distorting their experiences. It is important to note that both members of the research team worked for years with a large number of the participants in the interview, and during that period relations of trust developed between us. Therefore the teachers had no fear that the information about specific individuals would be passed on to other bodies. They wanted to share with us the experiences and dilemmas that they face.

don't have the means to finance continued studies. Hani found a good study framework for her. I'm very grateful to her for that.' And the local deputy principal at the Ets Hayim School in Moscow told of the closeness between her and *shaliah* A., during the year when her father passed away:

He helped me with everything, even without my asking; he organized things at the time of the burial and the shiva. My mother remembers his assistance to this day. He helped me at school. None of the local teachers knew how to help, but he did. I appreciate that greatly, and since then we've been friends; he consults me and I consult him.

It seems that familiarity with the way local people think, and with the language, helps a great deal both in day-to-day work and in developing interpersonal relations. The local deputy principal at the Moscow Ets Hayim School reported that it took her a few months to understand *shaliah* A.'s speech (he is not a native Russian-speaker). In contrast, *shaliah* N., who teaches the lower grades at the same school, attributes some of her social success to the fact that she speaks Russian: 'I have not the slightest doubt that my popularity among the local teachers is connected to the fact that I am well acquainted with the language and the mentality.'

A note of frustration is discernible in the words of *shaliah* S. (who does not speak Russian), from the Yerushalayim School in St Petersburg: 'I've already been here for four years on *shelihut*. I've come to understand a lot, I've done a lot, they appreciate me, but I'll always be "someone who came and then left" at the end of his *shelihut*. I'm a foreigner here; they know that.'

A., a local Jewish studies teacher at the ORT School in Moscow, summarizes his relations with the *shelihim* who have taught there as follows: 'It's true that they're different and they aren't familiar with the mentality, but they learn to work and live with us. Without their presence the school would be different; we would be different. This encounter is important to me personally.'

Differences of Approach to Education and the Professional Relationship

There is a marked difference between the two groups of teachers in respect of their professional background and experience. Both Israeli-born *shelihim* and those who migrated to Israel from the FSU have undergone professional training in Israel and have worked for many years within the Israeli educational system. Their status is fundamentally different from that of the local teachers. The latter are employed by the Russian ministry of education or by the local rabbi. The *shaliah*, on the other hand, is employed by the Israeli ministry of education and also holds the status of an emissary of the Jewish Agency as part of the Heftzibah project. The average salary of a *shaliah* is ten times that of a local teacher (an issue to which we shall return below). In addition, there is the matter of tenure at the place of work: local teachers are an integral part of the school system; they have worked there prior to the arrival of the *shaliah*, and will continue to work there after the *shaliah* returns to Israel, although the erosion in salaries of the local teachers—and especially Jewish studies teachers—has led to a brisk turnover of personnel in the Jewish schools, especially in the major cities. At the same time, Chabad emissaries come not only to work in schools, but to remain in the places of their *shelihut* 'until the coming of our righteous Messiah, who will redeem the entire nation of Israel', as one interviewee put it to us.[6] Nevertheless, the general rule is that *shelihim* serve their *shelihut* officially for no more than five years; thereafter they cease to be emissaries of the State of Israel and of the Jewish Agency. In practice, most *shelihim* return home after an average of three to four years in the job.

In many respects these two groups of teachers can be said to come from two different worlds that intersect in the Jewish school. Within the framework of this limited study we were not able to explore in depth the professional dynamic between the two groups, but during the course of the study a number of interesting issues arose, and these we address below.

The differences between Israeli and local teachers stand out with particular prominence in certain educational issues relating to the nature of instruction, attitude towards the students, and sticking to the curriculum and the textbooks. These differences may be categorized under the following pairs of contrasts:

1. *Initiative vs passivity.* From our interviews with both groups of teachers it became apparent that two opposing modes of behaviour were in operation: the *shaliah* initiates, is active, and leads all the teachers at the school, while the local teacher by contrast remains passive.

The following are a few comments on the subject, quoted from inter-

---

[6] The Chabad emissaries are members of the Heftzibah programme. However, many of them are simultaneously emissaries of Chabad too, and may stay on in the latter capacity when they finish their terms of office with Heftzibah.

views with the Israeli teachers. S., from the ORT School in Moscow, said: 'The local teachers I work with are excellent. Two of them studied for a year in Israel . . . They initiate—but not enough, and they expect me to get things moving. This small-mindedness irritates me; I'm going to back to Israel while they remain behind; who will help them?' S., from the Shorashim School in St Petersburg, added: 'I've seen no local initiative—neither in Hebrew instruction nor in Jewish studies instruction. The teachers are capable of initiating, but they're used to the Israeli *shaliah* having to initiate and promote things.'

It seems that the local teachers agree with these assessments. L., from ORT Moscow, said: 'What can we do? We're just simple teachers; who cares that I studied in Israel?' B., from the Ets Hayim School in Moscow, reported: 'A. organized a Purim fair at our school. When he came to us with the idea, we literally attacked him: "You don't understand the reality here: Chabad, not Chabad; religious, not religious." He remained silent and started doing. In the end, we joined with him. We would never have initiated such an impressive event.' K., principal of the Ahei Temimim School in Moscow, expressed his opinion thus: 'Israeli teachers are idealistic (not all, but most). They have educational and Jewish objectives. There are very few local teachers like that in Moscow; most have already emigrated to Israel.'

2. *Experience vs knowledge.* Many local teachers expressed their appreciation of the *shelihim* for introducing new teaching methods which arouse the children's interest in informal ways in the classroom. Local teacher B., from the Ets Hayim School in Moscow, said: 'They always invent something new, popular and fresh . . . We're just heavy-footed Soviets.' N., from the same school, agreed: 'Anything that is innovative and interesting was brought here by the Israelis. I understand that one has to first of all be interesting to the child, and afterwards to give him knowledge.'

As for the *shelihim*'s comments on the educational approach of the local teachers, N., from the Ets Hayim School in Moscow, reported:

All that's important to the local teachers is knowledge. Every child has to be an Einstein. Even a psychologist who was brought to our school asserted that many children are traumatized by their parents' and teachers' demands for achievement. Some of the young [teachers] have begun changing their teaching methods, but the 'knowledge above all' model is still very strong here.

S., from the Shorashim School in St Petersburg, made a similar point:

Knowledge and more knowledge. The teacher is evaluated according to his knowledge of the discipline, and the student is likewise evaluated on the basis of knowledge. It's difficult for me to come to terms with this; what is going on in his head? What is he feeling? Does it satisfy him? I'm always fighting with this 'local' approach, without much success.

Some of the local teachers did not agree with the Israelis' assertion that they had superior experience in teaching. For instance, G., from the Ets Hayim School in Moscow, argued:

They know the language [Hebrew], but we teach it better. We have experience in teaching a foreign language, while they do not. It's not enough to be a speaker of the language and to give the students experiences. In the case of our *shaliaḥ*, not all [his students] know how to read [Hebrew]. In my class, everyone knows how to read, and they understand what they're reading!

Sheliḥim and local teachers also have very different perceptions of the ideal graduate. Local teachers would like to see their students graduate as good people, with extensive knowledge—including, obviously, in Jewish matters. In contrast, the *sheliḥim* emphasize the emotional, experiential aspect: 'I want Judaism to be part of the identity and day-to-day experience of the student; if in the future he wants to know more, he can sit and study', said M., a *shaliaḥ* from the Tehiyah School in Moscow.

3. *Seriousness vs 'playing around'*. The local teachers note, sometimes deprecatingly, the lack of seriousness of the Israelis, and relate this to the visitors' 'experiential' inclination. Our impression is that some of the *sheliḥim* internalize this message. A., from the ORT School in Kazan, told us:

Over here, everyone is so serious; it's work–home–work–home. If someone wants to speak with me, I know it's about work. There's no atmosphere here like there is in Israel: teachers sitting in the teachers' room, joking about the students, or about themselves, just chatting. And something else: here at the school everyone is dressed in suits and ties. I also adopted the practice pretty quickly when I understood its importance and its contribution to the school atmosphere. When the inspector from Israel visited me a few months ago, I was dressed like one of the locals. She asked me, 'What festival is it today?' I told her, I dress like this every day. If I respect myself, then everyone respects me.

A.'s practice was adopted by *sheliḥim* at other schools. The *sheliḥim* relinquished their typical Israeli characteristics—such as sitting on the floor or on a table, or forgetting to greet a colleague in the teachers' room. Many adopted local manners and dress.

4. *Strictness vs flexibility.* If it was easy for the Israelis to get the hang of local manners, it was more difficult for them to come to terms with certain characteristics of the local teachers, such as their lukewarm attitude towards the Jewish studies curriculum. Many also viewed askance the way local teachers behaved towards the students, noting in the interviews their concerns about strictness as reflected, for example, in punishments handed out to anyone who had not prepared homework or completed some other task, examination evaluations, and the exaggerated importance attached by local teachers to grades.

On the other hand, local teachers accused the Israelis of destroying norms of behaviour at the school, making such comments as: 'They don't give the students homework'; 'A teacher cannot let the class go before the bell rings'; 'A teacher has to follow the curriculum, otherwise what's the point of its existence?'; 'The lesson has to look like a lesson, and not like a game.'

Some of the *sheliḥim* were aware of these criticisms, and reported that the local teachers did not accept their 'softness and consideration' towards undisciplined students. One insisted: 'I don't accept the local norms towards students who have failed; I always give a chance to a student who has failed.'

Of all the Israeli teachers, only one expressed a willingness to combine the Israeli approach and the local approach towards the students. S., from the Shorashim School in St Petersburg, explained:

I attach value to the contact with the student in the lesson. The study curriculum isn't holy, but it's important. Here I haven't changed my opinion: the student must be at the centre of the learning, and the bond between him and the teacher is important. Perhaps the local teachers are correct in that the breaking of the distance between teacher and student is perceived, by the student, as weakness. We should give more homework, we should maintain distance, and we must not break the local modes of teacher–student relations.

Tensions and their Resolution

It is clear from comments made in the interviews that there were some tensions between the two groups of teachers. Although the interviewees did not address this subject at length, we were able to glean some important information from the little we heard.

The local teachers are clearly scornful of inexperienced *shelihim* who regard themselves as missionaries dispatched to attend to 'savage children'. 'The main thing for the *shaliah* to understand is that he has to integrate into the teaching staff of the school, and not to be above it', wrote a local teacher from the ORT School in Kazan. A., from the Tehiyah School, described the phenomenon explicitly:

There were *shelihim* at our school who treated us like Indians with feathers on their heads, as though everything came from Israel: education, knowledge, manners. I told them: You think we came down from the trees? Professor Vygotsky was born and studied here, and many others. We're familiar with Piaget and Chomsky, we read English, German, and French. Even knowledge of Judaism isn't entirely absent here. In Moscow, Hebrew was always studied; our Hebrew teacher studied with local experts. They want to educate us? Let them go home and educate their own children. They want to share their experience with us? By all means.

Sometimes tension arises from divergent expectations of how teachers work. Israeli teachers are more accustomed to teamwork, with everyone tackling a common mission together in a collective and often voluntary effort. Local teacher A., from the ORT School in Moscow, said: 'With all due appreciation to *shaliah* S., the other teachers and I had to get used to her expectation that we would all work together, and voluntarily, in preparation for the Jewish festivals. Apparently, she wanted us to feel as though we were working together. We didn't like her "kibbutz habits".'

This unwillingness to take part in joint efforts was particularly evident among the non-Jewish local teachers who taught Hebrew. *Shaliah* S., who at the time of the research was working at the ORT School in Moscow, told us about her work at her previous place of employment, the Tehiyah School in the same city.

The school employed three non-Jewish girls who taught Hebrew. They came to this Jewish school with crosses around their necks, they weren't interested in anything: not the ceremonies, not the festivals. Nothing! Only Hebrew instruction. My argument was that if you're part of the staff at a Jewish school, you have to participate in everything educational that takes place at the school. My position received no backing from the local Jewish teachers, who accepted this absurd situation as self-evident. I was left to battle it alone; it broke me, and I left that school for ORT Moscow.

As noted above, there are significant differences in salary between the two groups of teachers. We asked the Israelis whether they sensed any jealousy on the part of local teachers on this account. In only two interviews with Israeli teachers did we receive any indication that such emotions might have been at work. It is possible that the local teachers hide their feelings when they come into contact with their Israeli colleagues. But when we addressed the same question to them, they expressed understanding for the discrepancy in salaries, and in the same breath expressed their hope for an improvement in their own remuneration.

It appears that the tensions that arose in the ordinary interplay between teachers working together were solved in most instances by virtue of the common desire of both sides to reach appropriate solutions for the benefit of the school and the students. As M., the local teacher from Kazan, put it: 'There are tensions, but there are also solutions. If the argument centres around the interests of the school and the students, and not the personal interests of some teacher, then the solution will be found.'

Summary: From Foreignness and Alienation to Active Partnership and Mutual Fertilization

In the previous section we addressed the divergence in educational approach between the two groups of teachers. We saw that they differ significantly in their perceptions with regard to central questions such as: What is the best way to educate young people? What is more important in instruction—the educational experience or the acquisition of skills and knowledge? What is the image of the ideal student?

Our findings should not be viewed as generalized characterizations. Local teachers do not categorically repudiate experiential elements in education, nor do *shelihim* disdain the inculcation of knowledge and skills at school. Not every Israeli teacher supports the lessening of the distance between teachers and students, and not every local teacher is opposed to more democratic teacher–student relations. Nevertheless, the findings do present discrepancies which indicate a difference in educational values, as reflected not only in the interviews, but also—and more importantly—in the actual educational endeavour.

It is easy to understand that these discrepancies arise from different cultural environments, different educational schools of thought, and different perceptions of the role of the teacher and the school in the life of the community. It is well known that Soviet society valued achievement and broad academic knowledge, placed great weight on authority, and did not encourage private initiative. Long years of absolute supervision by the governing regime over the workplace and any form of social organization gave rise to distrust of social organizations and scepticism towards the value of voluntarism.[7] Sheliḥim, in contrast, have grown up in a family-oriented society, based mainly upon informal relations as an accepted—and even desirable—norm. They have been educated through youth movements, where they have been taught to volunteer, to contribute to society, and to work together with friends.

It is worth noting that the local teachers belong to a society that has undergone ideological and social upheaval in the not-so-distant past. The former Soviet republics have yet to achieve economic and social stability, and a new system of social values has not yet been consolidated in place of the old one.[8] Israeli teachers, by contrast, come from a society with stable social foundations and moral values. For the most part, they identify with the social sector to which they belong, and therefore they usually have a solid Jewish identity. These and other factors influence the respective world-views and educational philosophies of the two groups of teachers.

Sheliḥim are perceived by the local teachers as being stationed in their schools by external forces interested in providing instruction in Hebrew and Jewish studies. On a personal level, local teachers are able to develop friendly relations with sheliḥim and to regard them as authorities in matters related to Judaism and Israel, but on a professional level sheliḥim will never be integrated as equals among the teaching staff. Their status remains somewhat elevated. Local teachers and sheliḥim alike are conscious of this imbalance, and there is conspicuous human and professional distance between them. This strengthens the sheliḥim's feeling of foreignness.

Sheliḥim are constantly initiating and leading educational processes. The directorate of the Heftzibah project, the directorate of the school, and their teaching colleagues all expect this of them. Local teachers, in contrast, have no support—either within the school or outside it—comparable to the support of the State of Israel enjoyed by sheliḥim. The professional training of local teachers is perceived as inferior, not only by the sheliḥim but also in

[7] Fridgut, 'The Silent Majority' (Heb.), 96–111.
[8] Kontorer, 'The Crisis of Identity' (Heb.), 32–9.

the eyes of the school directorate. This perception that the local teachers are of secondary status goes a long way towards explaining their passivity and lack of initiative. The system does not expect them to initiate or lead any educational process, or to consolidate a new approach to Jewish education. They feel like workers hired to teach a certain discipline. We may assume that this causes local teachers to feel a certain degree of alienation from everything going on around them in schools.

In our estimation, the present situation does not allow for genuine dialogue between *sheliḥim* and local teachers. Local teachers need to understand that they have the power and responsibility to consolidate their school's educational approach, with all that this entails in terms of their relationships with students and parents, and their contribution to the shaping of both general subjects and Jewish studies. The *sheliḥim* also suffer from an unnatural situation in that they represent an external body that lacks sufficient familiarity with the educational context within which the schools exist and the local culture.

Conclusions and Recommendations

The study summarized in this chapter may be regarded as a snapshot of a complex and changing reality. The opinions and positions of the *sheliḥim* and their local counterparts may change over time, as may the quality of the relations between them. An in-depth study conducted over a longer period could track any such changes in the attitudes and identities of the teachers and compose a fuller and more complex picture.

We, as researchers, are not able to change the current reality. Change has to come about from within the system, not from outside. At the same time, we are able to offer a number of practical suggestions for improving the situation that could be implemented in the short term:

1. A course of special preparatory workshops for *sheliḥim* prior to their dispatch. These workshops would focus on familiarity with the local situation and dealing with existing problems at the schools where they are to work.

2. Preparatory workshops for the local teachers prior to the arrival of new *sheliḥim*. These workshops would focus on such issues as getting to

know the 'other', and the intercultural encounter as a source of growth for both parties and for the school.

3. Joint courses for *sheliḥim* and local teachers held throughout the school year, as well as workshops on group dynamics at the school.

4. Establishment of a 'learning community' within the school, for groups of *sheliḥim* and local teachers.

5. Encouragement and support of the local teaching staff with regard to creating curricula and special projects.

Implementation of these measures could help the local teachers to consolidate a Jewish educational approach of their own, and to become a complementary educational force working with the *sheliḥim*, thereby benefiting the entire system of Jewish education in the FSU.

Bibliography

Bruk, S., 'Formal Jewish Education in the Former Soviet Union: Survey Conclusions Draft', Jerusalem Fellows Programme (Jerusalem, 1995).

DellaPergola, S., 'A Census of Jewish Schools in the Former Soviet Union for the 1993/4 School Year', *Journal of Jewish Education*, 63 (Winter/Spring 1997), 20–31.

Fridgut, T., 'The Silent Majority' (Heb.), in D. Prital (ed.), *Jewish Intelligence in the Soviet Union* [Inteligentsiah yehudit bibrit hamo'atsot] (Jerusalem, 1982), 96–111.

Galperin, A., 'Motivation of Teachers in Jewish Schools of Belarus' (Rus.), *Yevreiskaya Shkola*, no. 4 (1994), 129–37.

Kessler, A., 'Israeli Teachers in American Jewish Schools', *Journal of Jewish Teaching*, 4 (1973), 55–61.

Kontorer, D., 'The Crisis of Identity: Israelis and Russian Emigrants' (Heb.), *Eretz Aḥeret*, 19/6 (Jerusalem, 2003), 32–9.

Pomson, A., and M. Gillis, 'The Teacher-as-Stranger as Model and Metaphor' (forthcoming).

Rochlin, Z., and H. Rotman, 'Jewish Day Schools and Jewish Supplementary Schools: What the Principals Won't Speak About' (Rus.), *Yevreiskaya Shkola*, no. 12 (2002), 180–90.

Shneider, Y., 'Classical Jewish Sources in the Eyes of Jewish Teachers in Jewish Schools of the FSU' (Heb.), *Mayim midalyo: Yearbook of Lifshitz Academic College* (Jerusalem, 1998), 175–86.

Sobkin, V. S., and A. M. Gracheva, 'On the Psychology of Jewish Identity' (Rus.), in V. S. Sobkin (ed.), *Etnos, identichnost', obrazovanie* (Moscow, 1998), 105–41.

—— P. S. Pisarsky, and Yu. O. Kolomiets, *Uchitel'stvo kak sotsial' no-professional'naya gruppa* (Moscow, 1996).

Ta'ir, U., 'Jewish Identity of Teachers in Jewish Schools in Russia in the 1990s' (Heb.), Ph.D. diss., Hebrew University of Jerusalem, 2000.

Vershlovsky, S. G., *Research of Attitudes towards Values of Teachers in Jewish Schools in St Petersburg and the Russian Provinces* [Issledovanie tsennostnykh predstavlenii u uchitelei evreiskikh shkol v S. Peterburge i rossiiskoi provintsii] (St Petersburg, 1998).

Wolf, M. F., and E. Kopelowitz, 'Israeli Staff in American Jewish Teacher Camps: The View of the Camp Director', report commissioned by the Development Unit, Department for Jewish Zionist Education of the Jewish Agency for Israel (Jerusalem, 2003).

Community School versus School as Community

The Case of Bet El Community in Buenos Aires

YOSSI J. GOLDSTEIN

IN THIS CHAPTER I present two different views of the relationship between the Jewish day school and the Jewish community. I focus on one case—that of the Bet El community in Buenos Aires, Argentina, founded in 1962 by Rabbi Marshall T. Meyer. A study of the Bet El Conservative School sheds light on the emergence of Jewish community schools that has become, since the 1970s, the leading trend in Jewish education in Argentina. Bet El, an institution regarded as the flagship school of the Conservative movement in Argentina, was founded as a kindergarten in 1967, some five years after Rabbi Meyer's establishment of the Bet El community as a nucleus for the development of the Conservative movement in Latin America. The elementary school began operating in 1974, at the same time as an application was made to establish a Conservative high school—an application that was approved by the public authorities but not taken further owing to the need to consolidate and strengthen the elementary school.

The figure of Rabbi Meyer loomed large over Argentinian Jewry from his arrival in Buenos Aires in 1959 until his return to the US in 1984. He came to Argentina as a young rabbi having just completed his studies at the Jewish Theological Seminary in New York, where he was one of the closest disciples of Rabbi Abraham Joshua Heschel. Meyer contributed significantly to the consolidation of a new type of Jewish community in Argentina, different from the accepted model built around central and centralized institutions, or around Zionist parties. Meyer's vision was of a synthesis between American and Argentinian modes of Jewish existence within a Western society undergoing extensive change. From the 1970s, however, he became a controversial figure, at once admired and vilified. He symbolized an innovative spirituality that attempted to combine traditional Judaism, Zionism, and human rights, integrating Jews into civic life and the struggle to attain a society that was democratic, pluralistic, and multicultural. Despite his seminal influence, there is almost no research that addresses his impact on Argentinian Jewry in particular and Argentinian society in general.[1]

In this chapter I discuss Meyer's moulding of the Bet El School as an institution embodying two fundamental views of the connection between the Jewish community and the Jewish school. I survey the main approaches to conceptualizing the relationship between schools and communities since the 1980s, within the context of fundamental changes that have occurred in the relationship between general society and organized Jewry, and the profound penetration of globalizing processes into Argentinian society. My main concern is with the measure of overlap between the community built around the Conservative synagogue and the community day school. I examine, on the one hand, parental involvement in the life of the community school and, on the other hand, the involvement of the Bet El community in communal education, in Jewish communal life in general, in the Conservative movement, in the environment close to the school, and in Argentinian society.

Theoretical Background and Research Questions

The theoretical starting point for this research is the growing literature on the connection between school and community. From Sergiovanni's conception of the school as not only an organization but also a community to Furman's exploration of the 'school as community', it is clear that in the postmodern era schools play a far-reaching role in nurturing communal belonging. They assert and maintain the connection among various social elements—from the family to society in general—as an objective in itself, beyond organizational, instrumental expediency.[2]

Most of the research literature dealing with these matters focuses on public (state) rather than private schools.[3] But in recent years research has been undertaken to examine the Jewish day school as the focus of

---

[1] During 2006 a doctoral thesis was completed by Daniel Fainstein at UNAM University in Mexico City, addressing the philosophies of Martin Buber, Abraham Joshua Heschel, and Marshall Meyer. See Fainstein, 'Secularización, Profecía y Liberación'.

[2] Sergiovanni, *Building Communities in Schools*; Furman, introduction to ead. (ed.), *School as Community*, 1–8.   [3] Furman, introduction to *School as Community*, 11.

communal Jewish life, for instance through adult education and work with parents.[4]

Furman places at the centre of her enquiry the question of how to build community *within* a school. She aspires to promote shared community values within public schools. From the perspective of Jewish education, even more challenging is the problem of how a community school can promote shared communal values while remaining grounded in a particular worldview or affiliated with a certain ideological stream. This chapter focuses accordingly on a case that reflects the development of a school in a community spirit, but within a given communal/ideological framework, in this case, the Conservative movement in Argentina. This is a case study of a Jewish community school that plays a significant role outwardly, both towards the institutions of the Jewish community and towards Argentinian society in general.

Furman draws a distinction between the 'school–community connection', on the one hand, and the 'school as community', on the other. In contrast to these two concepts, she proposes a new research direction, which she terms the 'ecological model', combining assumptions borrowed from both approaches.[5] I follow her example in assuming that school and community represent not two separate entities but rather an integrated and interdependent system, and I adopt her definition of community in postmodern terms. Schools, as she puts it, reflect the multilingual, multicultural diversity of the postmodern world. Throughout this chapter, then, I take 'community' to mean the experience of being *in community*—'the sense of belonging, trust of others, and safety'.[6]

These assumptions find expression in the case of the Bet El community from two different perspectives:

1. *The 'school as community' perspective.* According to this view, the school is at the centre of communal life and serves not only those closest to it—the students and their families—but also the neighbourhood or the Jewish community in its wider sense (that is, members of the community itself, members of sister communities belonging to the Conservative movement, and the broader public). In our context, the important question is whether

---

[4] Pomson, 'Day School Parents and their Children's Schools'; id., 'Schools for Parents'.
[5] Furman, introduction to *School as Community*, 8–10.
[6] Furman, 'Postmodernism and Community in Schools', 52.

the Bet El School is open to members of the community and to the non-Jewish environment. What is the significance of the concept of an 'educational community', and how does it find expression in school policy? Does the school also serve the community of parents and assign them a significant role, beyond the recruitment of additional students?

2. *The 'congregational day school' perspective.* According to this view, the community is grounded in an ideological–religious foundation, and a day school is one of a range of services offered to its members. This view, developed by Mordecai Kaplan in the United States, sees the community as a civilization, that is, an entire system with a synagogue at its centre, including a community of believers and a social framework. Originally, in the United States, this view of a community with a school was applied to supplementary education, to Sunday schools, and to educational frameworks offering preparation for bar/bat mitzvah. This view began to be challenged in the 1970s, and in the 1990s some talked of a 'paradigm shift' concerning the envisioning of the communal supplementary school.[7] In this view, the school served better as a supplementary vehicle for the socialization of values provided by the community, along with youth movements, camps, and adult education. In the Argentinian context of the early 1970s, an innovative view began to take shape of a day school belonging to the Conservative movement which placed the synagogue at the centre.

Below I analyse the tensions between these two perspectives, the first placing the community school at the centre, the other giving pre-eminence to the broader community. These tensions find expression at the structural–organizational level as well as at the ideological level. They rest upon differences of opinion on issues such as the place of the school within the community, and parental involvement in school life and in the life of the synagogue community. My discussion focuses on Furman's question: Is the view of community in general, and of a learning community in particular, based upon a modernist view of the nurturing of belonging and sameness, or is it grounded in a constructivist approach according to which 'belonging' also means a sense of responsibility towards and co-operation with the other, and where community is conceived as a 'network that is connected to a global communal network'?[8]

7 Aron, 'From the Congregational School to the Learning Congregation', 56–77.
8 Furman, 'Postmodernism and Community in Schools', 57.

Historical Background: The Jewish Day School in Argentina

Research literature on communal Jewish education has emphasized the connection between the school and some form of Jewish community, whether conceived as an institution, a stream, a social movement, or even a geographical region. In the context of Argentinian Jewry this connection had historically been between the Jewish school and a party or ideological movement. In Argentina during the first decades of the twentieth century Jewish schools became quite manifestly agents of socialization into a consolidated, historical Jewish world-view. In this sense, 'community' meant a party or movement, and in the context of the growing power of the Zionist parties leading up to the 1940s the community school was an instrument used by the Zionist movement for 'conquest' of the community.[9] The school was conceived as a bulwark against a majority society characterized by a strong Roman Catholic culture and antisemitic animosity towards Jewish organizations.[10]

By 1965 four Jewish day schools were operating in the greater Buenos Aires area. Five additional day schools were opened that year, and another six in 1966. The turning point in the institutionalization of day schools was General Onganía's military revolution in June 1966. With the revival of right-wing Catholic trends in government and society, and the establishment of a public school system grounded in deeply conservative Catholic values, the Jewish day school decisively triumphed over the supplementary school as the preferred model for Jewish education. In 1968 eleven new day schools were established, bringing the number operating in the Buenos Aires region to twenty-six. By 1970 all but two Jewish elementary schools in the area were day schools.[11] Members of the Jewish community discovered, in the new, 'integral' model of the day school, a second home that protected them from external threats.[12]

The Bet El elementary day school was founded in 1973, but actually began operating in 1974 on the foundations of a kindergarten that had been established in 1967 and that now numbered more than a hundred

---

[9] Schenkolewski-Kroll, *The Zionist Movement and the Zionist Parties* (Heb.), 231–95.
[10] Avni, *Emancipation and Jewish Education* (Heb.), 91–138.
[11] Rubel, *Las Escuelas Judías Argentinas*, 23–8.
[12] Avni, *Emancipation and Jewish Education* (Heb.), 139–62.

children.[13] In the community's view, the school reinforced the inculcation of traditional Judaism in a modern spirit, paying attention to every age group and aspect of community life.[14] In other words, the holistic or 'integral' view embodied by the school arose from a conception of communal life as consolidated in the Bet El community, and was not the result of external antisemitic pressure on the part of Argentinian society. In this sense, the development of the Bet El day school was unique and quite different from that of most day schools in Argentina. The first articles of constitution of the Bet El community set down its goal of creating, within the framework of education 'to disseminate knowledge of the Hebrew religion, tradition and language', an elementary and a high school (and even an institution of tertiary education) 'in an independent manner, or together with institutions close to us'.[15] In an initial agreement with industrialist Ezra Teubal, one of the founders of the community, who in 1962 contributed a plot of land and the community's first home, it was set down that within ten years an elementary community school would be established.[16] The Bet El community was exceptional at that time in placing the synagogue at its centre, as well as in its appeal to a broad public including both Ashkenazi and Sephardi Jews. Founded by middle-class Jews and located in the new middle-class neighbourhood of Belgrano, Bet El was far removed from existing centres of institutionalized Jewish life in Buenos Aires. Under the influence of its new American rabbi, the community aimed to encompass an entire collection of values embodied in the very term 'Jewish community'.

The Philosophy of Rabbi Marshall T. Meyer

Starting in the 1960s, against the backdrop of the growth of the Conservative movement in Argentina, a new vision of the character and essence of the community school began to crystallize. In the wake of Rabbi Meyer's arrival in the country in 1959, efforts began to build institutions that would embody an American vision of community. The Bet El community, and thereafter the Bet El School, were plainly products of this trend. The young American rabbi who landed in Buenos Aires at the end of the 1950s was not

[13] According to the testimony of Susana Shulansky in the 'Bar Mitzvá Book' of the Bet El community (1976), unpaginated.
[14] See also Fainstein, 'Secularización, Profecía y Liberación', 290–6.
[15] Estatutos de la Comunidad Bet El.
[16] Interview with Batia Nemirovsky, Dec. 2005.

at first the main player in the search for a new sort of community and community life, but he soon became a key figure in the consolidation of a process of communal renewal that sought an antidote to dwindling synagogue congregations and the relegation of religious life to the margins. At the time, the spiritual and cultural life of Argentinian Jewry developed around Zionist parties and parties of the non-Zionist left. Argentina was being swept up in a wave of antisemitism that began in 1959 as a worldwide phenomenon with local manifestations, and grew in the wake of the kidnapping of Adolf Eichmann by the Israeli Mossad in 1960. Hostility towards Jews was inflamed by the antisemitic populist rhetoric used by ultra-nationalist opponents of the democratic regime of President Frondizi, which was not stable and thus was unable to realize its promise of social progress.[17]

From a Jewish perspective, the early 1960s were a period of experiment and institution-building. In Buenos Aires the Tarbut Day School (consisting of a kindergarten, elementary school, and high school) was established as a synthesis of old communal norms and a search for new solutions.[18] Zionist youth movements flourished, and there were record levels of *aliyah* (migration to Israel), especially in 1962 and 1963 following the end of Eichmann's trial and his execution.[19] One of the leaders of Jewish communal renewal was Adolfo Weil, deputy president of the CIRA congregation (Congregación Israelita de la República Argentina, the country's oldest Jewish communal organization), whose city-centre synagogue on Libertad Street symbolized the essence of institutionalized religious Jewry. Weil's memoirs depict a situation in which, at a certain stage, it was not possible to innovate from within the existing framework, and it became necessary instead to forge a revolutionary new path.

At the outset, the main innovations proposed by Rabbi Meyer concerned work with young people: special prayer services and, most importantly, the establishment of Camp Ramah, a summer camp for children that offered an informal environment imbued with Jewish values. A second step was to initiate the establishment of a rabbinical seminary open to the entire South American continent, with a view to training a new generation of rabbis in

---

[17] Rein, *Argentina, Israel and the Jews* (Heb.), 133–60.

[18] Avni, *Emancipation and Jewish Education* (Heb.), 188–90.

[19] Rein, *Argentina, Israel and the Jews* (Heb.), 212–14. See also Bar-Gil, *In the Beginning There Was a Dream* (Heb.), 45–58.

the liberal Conservative spirit. The first group at the rabbinical seminary—Seminario Rabínico Latinoamericano—numbered four students, and their studies commenced at the CIRA centre on Purim 1962. By the end of that year the chasm between reformers and conservatives within CIRA had deepened, and conflict became unavoidable. A contingent led by Adolfo Weil (one of Rabbi Meyer's most enthusiastic supporters) broke away to form a new community, with a different, innovative spirit—the Bet El community.[20] Rabbi Meyer had planned to return to the United States at the beginning of 1963, following the launch of Camp Ramah, having intended to serve for only two years in Argentina. Efforts were made to persuade him to remain in Argentina, including correspondence with L. Finkelstein (president of the Jewish Theological Seminary of America), Martin Buber, and Abraham Joshua Heschel. Eventually it was agreed that Rabbi Meyer would stay for an additional two years to contribute to the establishment and consolidation of the Bet El community. This commitment was extended over and over again, so that eventually Rabbi Meyer was to spend twenty-five years in Argentina.[21]

Meyer's innovative approach was based on his perception of a need for a new type of spirituality, pluralism, and sense of belonging. He launched this approach from the Bet El community and from the rabbinical seminary, from where he aimed to export young rabbis to small communities within Argentina and other Latin American countries.[22]

The Bet El community came into being at the end of 1962 with twenty families. Towards the end of Rabbi Meyer's tenure, in 1984, it numbered close to a thousand families, with two rabbis who had graduated from the rabbinical seminary at its head. Rabbi Meyer's philosophy included a strong connection with the State of Israel, and the encouragement of *aliyah*. During his 25-year tenure, more than 1,800 Jews moved to Israel from his community, from the rabbinical seminary, and from Camp Ramah. He was committed to involvement in the processes of democratization and the advancement of individual rights in Argentinian society.[23]

The Bet El community introduced several significant innovations into Jewish communal life in Latin America. The most important of these was the transformation of the synagogue into a space where contemporary

---

[20] Weil, *Orígenes del Judaísmo Conservador*, 85–90.
[21] Fainstein, 'Secularización, Profecía y Liberación', 262–90.
[22] Ibid. 91–5.   [23] Freund, 'Somos Testigos', 28–32.

issues were addressed. Another concerned the realm of worship, into which Meyer introduced a 'neo-hasidic' approach which he claimed to have inherited from Heschel.[24] This was in addition to highlighting the family dimension of prayer (with a removal of the separation between the sexes). Ultimately, Meyer established an 'Argentinian synagogue', which brought together Ashkenazi and Sephardi components and reflected the particular conditions of social and cultural integration and upward social mobility under which the Jews of Argentina lived.[25] Meyer had been one of the founders of the Jewish Movement for Civil Rights in Argentina, and was active on behalf of Jewish prisoners during the years of dictatorship. It was for this reason that his opponents called him the 'red rabbi' or the 'communist rabbi'.[26] In his view, the military dictatorship which ruled Argentina between 1976 and 1983, and was responsible for the disappearance and murder of tens of thousands of citizens (including a large number of Jews), was a fascist regime that perpetuated the Nazi model.[27] He termed the period of that final military dictatorship a 'minor holocaust' in which much innocent blood had been spilt. As he saw it, until those who had been responsible for the atrocities that had taken place were appropriately punished, it would not be possible to create a true democracy.[28]

Meyer believed that the future of Jewish existence in Latin America depended on establishing a true democracy, social justice, and civil rights. He upheld a philosophy of 'multiple loyalty'—to Argentina, to the State of Israel, to Jewish tradition suited to the spirit of the times, and to a just society in the universalist, humanist sense of the term. Despite his American origins he adopted Argentina as his homeland and spoke extensively of a 'better, democratic and pluralistic' society there.[29]

From the start of his work in Argentina, Meyer promoted a new vision of the relationship between school and community. His veteran students assumed that his educational view did not, at first, include the day school model, but was centred rather on an attempt to duplicate the American communal model which concentrated on informal education and supplementary study.[30] On the contrary, however, Meyer regarded the day school

[24] Fainstein, 'Secularización, Profecía y Liberación', 292   [25] Ibid.

[26] Meyer, 'Consideraciones sobre América Latina', 5, 7–9.

[27] Meyer, 'El Judaísmo y el Cristianismo', 358, 364; Isay (ed.), You Are My Witness, 149 ff.

[28] Meyer, 'Escoged, pues, la vida', 38; Fainstein, 'Secularización, Profecía y Liberación', 328–41.

[29] Meyer, 'Educación Judía Hoy', 22.

[30] Interviews with Batia Nemirovsky, Jerusalem, 28 Dec. 2005, Buenos Aires, 2 Aug. 2006; Graciela Jinich, Buenos Aires, 31 July 2006; Daniel Fainstein, Jerusalem, 3 July 2006.

as the pinnacle of his educational vision. He believed that it was necessary to nurture the community in a new sense, on the basis of emotional connection and a sense of belonging. The three foundations of the rejuvenated community were:

1. The synagogue-as-congregation, maintaining a strong connection with Torah and with the State of Israel, serving as a warm home for Jews of different strata, and presenting itself to Argentine society as a whole as a model of solidarity and social justice.

2. An open house of prayer, exuding family spirit and equality, which did not discriminate against women, did away with the specially designated women's section, and was characterized by enthusiasm and emotional identification.

3. A *beit midrash* (study centre) that encouraged all forms and methods of study, including a *talmud torah*, Camp Ramah, a kindergarten, and an elementary school.

In Meyer's view, all of life is a school, and a Jew's mission is to 'celebrate life', to sanctify it, and to exalt it as a Godly creation. On the inauguration of the new building for the day school in 1983, Meyer described the school as 'the most important building for our nation, for Argentina today'.[31]

Meyer's educational vision included grappling with the crisis of faith in the postmodern world. His search for spirituality in an alienated, information-based environment served as the foundation for his educational–communal vision. The ultimate aim, for him, was to create 'significant spiritual communities capable of providing comfort, consolation and a challenge'.[32] However, he viewed this as an almost impossible task that few had managed to fulfil; and so, as a minimum, he sought 'to create a living, dynamic synagogue with open doors, open arms, and open hearts'.[33] This openness was directed not only towards Jews but also towards the non-Jewish environment, including the society within which the Jews lived.

According to research by Babis-Cohen, from 1970 onwards twenty-five Orthodox synagogues in Buenos Aires were transformed into lively Conservative community centres on this model. However, few included their own day schools, and so the Bet El community maintained its uniqueness as a

---

[31] Meyer, 'Educación Judía Hoy', 24–5.   [32] Meyer, *Antología*, 5–6.   [33] Ibid. 10.

'mother community' strongly connected to the Latin American Rabbinical Seminary of Buenos Aires. According to various estimates, by the end of the twentieth century close to 50 per cent of Argentina's Jews identified themselves as Conservative or expressed a connection with one of the synagogues and communities affiliated with the movement.[34]

Bet El Community vs Bet El Day School

Although the Bet El day school was originally intended to serve as a contributory element in the community's system of communal services, in practice the relationship between the school and community was not always harmonious. In this respect the school's situation and development reflected social processes and forces that shaped all of Argentinian Jewry. I shall briefly present here some of the stages in that development and some of the dilemmas characterizing its unique situation, with a focus on the period following the terrorist attack on the central community institutions in Buenos Aires on 18 July 1994.

Views of the School during the Years 1982–1993

During Bet El's first twenty years Rabbi Meyer had at his side another rabbi who contributed greatly to the consolidation of the community: Rabbi Mordechai Edery, who also served as deputy director of the rabbinical seminary up to the beginning of the 1980s. Rabbi Edery, who had been born in Tangier, was known as an educator with an excellent command of the Hebrew language, and as a teacher of Talmud and Bible. During the 1970s he was considered the spiritual leader of the Bet El day school. In 1982, however, there was a split between him and Rabbi Meyer—for personal and unclear reasons—following which Edery left the school and the rabbinical seminary. This crisis threatened the delicate balance which had hitherto prevailed between the school and the community. During the period prior to his departure, two *minyanim* were held at the Bet El synagogue; Rabbi Edery's was conducted exclusively in Hebrew. The figure who served as a bridge between the school and the community during the years after 1982 was the school principal, Batia Nemirovsky. In her view, the departure of Rabbi Edery sharpened the differences in outlook between those who

---

[34] Babis-Cohen, 'From Orthodox Synagogue to Conservative Community Center' (Heb.), 19.

viewed the day school as a central element in the life of the community, and those—the majority within the community—who took the view that the core educational work with the community's young people took place on *shabatot* and at Camp Ramah. The head of general studies at the school during the years 1984–90, Graciela Jinich, also emphasizes the tensions and differences in approach within the community's executive committee. In her view, this inner tension resulted in the deterioration of the school during those years. Jinich attributes this tension to the ambiguity of Meyer's legacy concerning the relationship between school and community and the crisis that occurred in the wake of his departure. Ultimately, the more traditional model, viewing the school as only one factor in the inculcation of a Conservative religious world-view, prevailed.[35]

The appointment of Rabbi Baruch Plavnick to replace Rabbi Edery as deputy rabbi facilitated a division of labour whereby Rabbi Plavnick became a prominent spiritual figure among the teachers of the school, where his presence was strongly felt. A rabbinical student was appointed to liaise between the community and the school. The division of labour also facilitated a smoother transition to the post-Meyer era, in so far as it prepared the community for his departure in 1984. After Rabbi Meyer's departure from Argentina Rabbi Plavnick was appointed as presiding rabbi of the community.

Following Rabbi Meyer's departure, Rabbi Darío Feiguin was made responsible for youth activity and for informal education. Rabbi Feiguin remained active in Bet El until the end of 1988, when he moved to the Tarbut School, which briefly (and ultimately unsuccessfully) attempted to convert the day school into the centre of a new Conservative community.

Batia Nemirovsky moved over to serve as principal of the Tarbut School at the beginning of 1990, but continued to attend the Bet El synagogue. Her departure reflected the escalation of tensions between the school and the community. In 1992, however, she was appointed general director of the Bet El community, and in 1993 she returned to the position of principal of the community's day school. Throughout these years the kindergarten numbered some 80 children, and approximately 220 were registered in the elementary school.[36]

[35] Interview with Graciela Jinich, Buenos Aires, 31 July 2006.
[36] Interview with Batia Nemirovsky, Jerusalem, 28 Dec. 2005.

The Crisis of 1994–1995

Rabbi Meyer visited Buenos Aires for the last time in August 1993, and during his visit to the Bet El community he expressed his concern that the 'ardour had subsided'.[37] His words suggest that even prior to the terrible terrorist attack on the community's institutions there were indications of a communal crisis. The year 1994 was especially difficult, witnessing threats by the president of the Bet El community to close down the day school and lay off approximately thirty teachers in the middle of the year, without consulting the directorate of the school or the parents' committee. This crisis led to a schism and the departure of the principal of the kindergarten, a senior educational figure at the institution.[38]

In 1995 a large number of students left the school. Some moved to the new Arlene Fern School, recently established by the charismatic Rabbi Sergio Bergman. Setting out to generate a turnaround in the educational perceptions of the Jews of Argentina and to correct the deficiencies of the average Jewish school, Bergman established this new, private institution with none of the traditional links to Zionist parties or to the view that upheld the dominance of Hebrew (as a national and cultural language) in Jewish day schools. Established within the framework of the Emmanuel Reform community, the Arlene Fern School promised an innovative educational approach, giving preference to study in English, along with Spanish. Hebrew was optional after the early years and Jewish studies were integrated with English. Leah Weiner, a former principal of the kindergarten at Bet El and a central figure in the life of that community until her departure in the wake of the crisis in 1994, was appointed principal of the new institution.

Under these circumstances, efforts were made to rehabilitate the Bet El School, but it was a slow process. In addition to the internal crisis, there was also the security threat that needed to be addressed, in view of the possibility of a third attack on a Jewish institution, following those on the Israeli embassy in March 1992 and on AMIA—Asociación Mutual Israelita Argentina, the central organization of communal life—in July 1994. Security concerns greatly occupied community leaders, and gave rise to a community-wide decision to place concrete barriers on the streets facing all

---

[37] Based on the testimony of the school's principal from 1993 to 2000, Batia Nemirovsky.
[38] Interview with Batia Nemirovsky, Buenos Aires, 2 Aug. 2006.

Jewish communal institutions. This situation left no room for any discussion of a community school that was open to the street and to the neighbourhood. The Bet El School, through its staff and directors, projected a sense of acute distress, and it is doubtful whether the school at this time could have been accurately described as an educational community. During this challenging period the school was subjugated to the needs and priorities of the parent community, which supported the decision on the security measures.

However, the Bet El community could not ignore its educational *raison d'être* as envisioned by Rabbi Meyer, who had passed away in the United States in December 1993. The turning point came between the terrorist attack of July 1994 and the first *yahrzeit* of Rabbi Meyer. Seeking to commemorate the memory of Rabbi Meyer, a community journal, *Kol Bet El*, was launched to promote a communal educational vision that would involve in its implementation both the parents of the students at the school and community members in general. The editorial board of the new journal was aware of the importance of nurturing a connection between members of the community and the parents of the day school students. Their declared objective was to nurture the traditional Conservative Jewish worldview and 'to revive our unity with the State of Israel', while also pursuing integration with the surrounding culture. According to Rabbi Mario Roisman, the presiding rabbi in that year, writing in the first issue of the journal, the challenge was to 'Judaize' to a greater degree the homes of the members of the community and the approximately one thousand Jews who prayed every Friday evening at the Bet El synagogue.

The following issues of the journal addressed with a light-handed educational approach not only Jewish matters, but also the kinds of universal subjects discussed by Rabbi Meyer, such as human rights and the urgent need to solve the mystery of those who had 'disappeared' during the period of dictatorship. Rabbi Daniel Goldman, the deputy rabbi of the community, who was also responsible for youth activities, regarded it as an obligation to continue this work, highlighting the danger posed by the phenomenon of genocide at the end of the twentieth century.

The final print issue of the journal was published in August 1995, soon after the memorial ceremonies commemorating the victims of the terrorist attack on the AMIA building a year earlier. It was devoted mainly to the theme of the sabbath and its place in the life of a Conservative Jew, and included an article on *havdalah* by Naomi Meyer, widow of Rabbi Marshall Meyer. *Kol Bet El* also published in Spanish a special booklet—'Guide to Family Celebration of the Sabbath'—accompanied by a special cassette with recordings of sabbath *zemirot*, and explanations by the rabbis of the community. The introduction to this booklet emphasized its educational value; the aim of 'Judaizing' the members of the community is plainly manifest. The booklet includes explanations in Spanish along with the words of several prayers in Hebrew.

The failure to continue publication of this journal, owing to a severe shortage of funds, reflects the Bet El community's inability to institutionalize changes and to deepen its spiritual vision; but this was at a time when all communal bodies in Argentina were focused on security needs and financial difficulties.

The Information Revolution, 2002–2005

The economic and political crisis that befell Argentina in December 2001 brought about a turning point in the approach of the Bet El community, leading to a drive for efficiency that found expression, *inter alia*, in the creation of an electronic edition of *Kol Bet El*. The community gathered a database of addresses and began sending the newsletter to thousands of people in Buenos Aries and throughout the world. A systematic analysis of this electronic newsletter over a period of three years (mid-2002 until mid-2005) uncovered a number of points of importance to our discussion.

1. *Structure of* Kol Bet El *Online.* The newsletter's main heading clearly conveys the community's self-image: 'The Community of Jewish Renewal'. Every edition in the sequence studied included the following elements, always in the same order: a quotation from a prominent thinker associated with the Conservative movement; weekly news (events, conferences, Camp Ramah, etc.); 'Hineni' (donations of food and medicines to the needy); rabbinic activity (contact with the two rabbis of the community and prominent activity on their part); youth news and activities; the school; courses and activities for adults; notices; committees; and community life (including the weekly Torah reading).

2. *The place of the school in the community.* Despite the fact that school notices appear some way down the running order, the school occupies an important position in every issue, highlighting the image of an educational community that maintains its ideological link with the community and with the Conservative movement. This link finds expression through joint activities between the school and Rabbi Daniel Goldman, and through the school's promotion of the value of honouring the Torah and observing the commandments, as well as of the values of justice and democracy. It is notable, however, that the role of parents is relegated to the margins, for example as organizers of end-of-year parties, or within the framework of *kabalat shabat* with first-grade students. From time to time the directorate of the school also published messages, highlighting, for example, the joint responsibility of the community and the school together, and of parents in particular, for educating young people in Jewish and universal values.

3. *The rabbi's place in the community.* Over the years, Rabbi Daniel Goldman increasingly came to be perceived as a spiritual leader who was continuing on the path forged by Rabbi Meyer. The rabbi became a central bridge between the school and all parts of the community. He confirmed the image of the Bet El community as an open community involved in Argentinian social life in general, both through his articles in the general press and by virtue of his position as deputy president of an important human rights organization.[39] Rabbi Goldman also received several prizes and honours which contributed to the positive image of the community in Argentinian public opinion. His speeches and articles on the subject of the 'disappeared' were renowned during those years, and were cited at length in the electronic edition of *Kol Bet El*.

School and Community Today

Today, the Bet El School presents itself as a trilingual community school (teaching Spanish, Hebrew, and English) with approximately 500 students ranging in age from kindergarten to seventh grade,[40] in whom it seeks to inculcate the values of tolerance and diversity, with the aim of nurturing personal abilities as well as a 'true culture of solidarity'. The school prides itself on being an 'educational community situated in the present and obligated to the present', for the sake of 'building a more just society'. On the

[39] Asamblea Permanente por los Derechos Humanos (APDH).
[40] Data supplied by the school principal from 2003 to 2007, Aliza Minowitz, and the parents' committee. This figure signifies considerable growth of the school during the past two years.

Jewish level, the school aims 'to strengthen positive Jewish identity' through recognition of the values of the Torah, the cultural tradition, and Jewish sources.[41] However, the official website of the school makes no mention of the synagogue or of the significance of the concept of an 'educational community'. The parents are markedly absent as an important link in the educational process; they are depicted as unwilling consumers who must be persuaded to send their children to the school. In the school news section of *Kol Bet El Online*, the parents are mentioned from time to time, but not as an active factor.[42] Courses are sometimes offered for the voluntary leadership, but the parents' council seems only a shadowy body with no clear status. The role of the mothers on the parents' council is principally to raise funds for the school, for example to expand the library, or to prepare an annual reception for new families. It is interesting that when 'Bet El news' appeared on the school website for the first time in May 2004, the website was presented as a 'meeting point for families and the school'. In other words, the encounter is virtual, distanced, and does not exist as part of a perception of an educational community or as part of an intention to open the school to real activity for parents that would contribute towards their Jewish identity and their connection to the community.

There is no organic relationship between membership of the congregation and belonging to the school community. Members of the Bet El congregation who send their children to the school enjoy a discount on tuition fees, but there is no real attempt to draw new families at the school towards the community itself. According to the school director, only about 10 per cent of the parents at the school are members of the congregation.[43] The distinct impression arising from various interviews that I conducted is that the school and synagogue are two separate entities which exist under the same umbrella, with a bridge between them in the form of the rabbi, who nurtures the school's commitment to the fundamental values of the community. The school is completely reliant on the community for its funding (a fact which led to tensions in the past), but its annual budget is managed independently. All of the personalities active today in leadership of the community and of the school emphasize the harmony that prevails between the council of the community and the directorate of the school, and their shared

---

[41] <http://www.betel.edu.ar>.
[42] <http://www.betel.edu.ar/newsletter/news/htm>.
[43] Interview with Aliza Minowitz, Buenos Aires, 1 Aug. 2006.

identification with the community's system of values. The school, according to its lay leadership, respects the legacy of Rabbi Meyer and is open to the wider community on the basis of a philosophy of tolerance and acceptance of the other.[44]

It should be emphasized that in Rabbi Meyer's vision there was no justification for a separation between the two entities; on the contrary, the school was intended to be just one link in the realization of a liberal Jewish world-view. At the same time, the acute crises that the community encountered in 1994 and in the early 2000s led to a degree of separation between itself and the school, with a view to ensuring better functioning and a certain independence for the school. The rabbi of the community defines Bet El as a 'religious community that believes in the Torah, worship, and acts of loving-kindness', on the basis of social solidarity and a bridging between Jewish and Argentinian identity, and as a democracy that respects human rights. From this perspective the school is well integrated into the community's self-perception, and 'it would be impossible to imagine the community without the school'.[45] For this reason, there is no significance to the question of which is at the centre—the school or the synagogue—since in the postmodern world the meaning of centrality changes depending on needs and circumstances. This perception conforms to Furman's call for a new definition of community in general and of school community in particular.[46]

According to Rabbi Goldman, it is possible today to join Bet El day school and to subscribe to its philosophy without being a dues-paying member of the community; therefore there is no justification for requiring the parents of pupils at the school to join the community as members. The most important point is that most of the parents were married within the community, and also send their children to informal activities on the sabbath and to Camp Ramah.

According to Edgardo Band, president of the community in 2006–7, the Bet El community has changed from a 'rabbinocracy' into a model of joint management, whereby the senior rabbi serves as the deputy president of

[44] Interviews with Aliza Minowitz, Buenos Aires, 1 Aug. 2006; with the president of the community, Edgardo Band, Buenos Aires, 2 Aug. 2006; and with the rabbi of the community, Daniel Goldman, Buenos Aires, 9 Aug. 2006.

[45] Interview with Rabbi Daniel Goldman, Buenos Aires, 9 Aug. 2006.

[46] Furman, 'Postmodernism and Community in Schools', 54 ff., 60–3.

the community and is a partner in the entire process of decision-making, while the principal of the school is a member of the community executive council. The aim of this model is to maintain harmony while separating professional from voluntary leadership.[47] This harmony is evident in the unanimous belief among all the senior personnel I interviewed that Bet El has become a distinct and well-known 'brand name', and that the school is perceived as a community institution that highlights its family orientation, Jewish values, and a strong connection with Tanakh (Bible) and the Hebrew language.

Conclusions

The tension between the two models of day schools in Argentina reflects the uniqueness of Argentinian Jewry and its process of transition from a situation of insecurity (existential and economic distress, instability, and uncertainty regarding the future of its existence), to a postmodern diaspora existence (freedom of association, multiple identities in dynamic consolidation, and social mobility). The Jewish day school went through a crisis during the 1990s as processes of globalization penetrated on all levels—the economic, the ideological, and the sociological. This meant a transition from a Zionist ethos directed towards the Jewish nation and the State of Israel to a postmodern ethos highlighting personal careers, personal needs, competitiveness, and utilitarianism. From this perspective, the Bet El community represented a model of a community school based on education oriented towards values (Jewish and universal), in contrast to other more technocratic and materialistic models.

We may say that the Bet El community has created a model that integrates community and school, in a postmodern spirit, nurturing a sense of belonging on the basis of respect for the other, social solidarity, and the construction of a global communal network.[48] From this perspective there can be no doubt that both the adaptation of the American Jewish model to communal life in Argentina, and the need of Argentinian Jewry to grapple with the crisis of globalization and the instability characterizing the country during the past decades, contribute important elements to an understanding of the uniqueness of the Bet El community.

[47] Interview with Edgardo Band, Buenos Aires, 2 Aug. 2006.
[48] Furman, 'Postmodernism and Community in Schools', 56–7.

Bibliography

Aron, I., 'From the Congregational School to the Learning Congregation: Are We Ready for a Paradigm Shift?', in I. Aron, S. Lee, and S. Rossel (eds.), *A Congregation of Learners: Transforming the Synagogue into a Learning Community* (New York, 1995), 56–77.

Avni, H., *Argentina y las migraciones judías: de la inquisición al Holocausto y después* (Buenos Aires, 2005).

—— *Emancipation and Jewish Education: A Hundred Years' Experience of Argentine Jewry 1884–1994* [Ha'emantsipatsiyah veḥinukh yehudi: me'ah shenot nisyoneiha shel yahadut argentina 1884–1994] (Jerusalem, 1985).

Babis-Cohen, D., 'From Orthodox Synagogue to Conservative Community Centre: Changes in the Communal Organization of the Jews of Buenos Aires' (Heb.), MA thesis, Hebrew University of Jerusalem, 2001.

Bar-Gil, S., *In the Beginning There Was a Dream: Graduates of the Pioneer Youth Movements from Latin America in the Kibbutz Movement, 1946–1967* [Bereshit hayah ḥalom: bogrei tenu'ot hano'ar haḥalutsiyot me'amerika halatinit beitenuah hakibutsit] (Jerusalem, 2005).

Coleman, J. S., 'Schools and the Communities They Serve', *Phi Delta Kappan*, 66/8 (Apr. 1985), 527–32.

Estatutos de la Comunidad Bet El, fundada 11 de Diciembre 1962, con personería jurídica del 27 de Diciembre de 1963 [Regulations of the Bet El Community, founded on 11 December 1962, with juridical recognition on 27 December 1963].

Fainstein, D., 'Secularización, Profecía y Liberación: La desprivatización de la religión en el pensamiento judío contemporáneo. Un estudio comparativo de sociología histórica e historia intelectual', Ph.D. diss., Universidad nacional autónoma de México, 2006.

Feierstein, R., *Historia de los Judíos Argentinos* (Buenos Aires, 1993).

Freund, R., 'Somos Testigos—We Are Witness: The Jewish Theology of Liberation of Rabbi M. T. Meyer', *Conservative Judaism*, 47/1 (Fall 1994), 27–38.

Furman, G. C. (ed.), *School as Community: From Promise to Practice* (Albany, NY, 2002), 1–19.

—— 'Postmodernism and Community in Schools: Unraveling the Paradox', in ead. (ed.), *School as Community: From Promise to Practice* (Albany, NY, 2002), 51–75.

Isay, J. (ed.), *You Are My Witness: The Living Words of Rabbi Marshall T. Meyer* (New York, 2004).

Meyer, M. T., *Antología: seleccionada por B. Plavnick* (Buenos Aires, 1989).

—— 'Consideraciones sobre América Latina', *Majshavot*, 26/2 (Apr.–June 1987), 5–13.

—— 'Educación Judía Hoy', *Majshavot*, 22/4 (Oct.–Dec. 1983), 22–6.

—— 'El Judaísmo y el Cristianismo frente a la Violencia Estatal: El Caso de la Argentina, 1976–1983', in L. Senkman and M. Sznajder (eds.), *El Legado del Autoritarismo: Derechos humanos y antisemitismo en la Argentina contemporánea* (Buenos Aires, 1995), 355–64.

—— 'El Judaísmo en el Mundo Post-moderno', in *Masortí: Entre Ideología y Comunidad* (Buenos Aires, 1994), 5–10.

—— 'Escoged, pues, la vida', *Majshavot*, 23/2 (Apr.–June 1984), repr. in *Nuestra Memoria*, 27 (June 2006), 35–9.

Pomson, A., 'Day School Parents and their Children's Schools', *Contemporary Jewry*, 24 (2003/4), 104–23.

—— 'Schools for Parents: What Parents Want and What They Get from their Children's Jewish Day Schools', in J. Wertheimer (ed.), *Family Matters: Jewish Education in an Age of Choice* (Hanover, NH, 2007) 101–42.

Rein, R., *Argentina, Israel and the Jews: From the Division of the Land of Israel to the Eichmann Episode*

[Argentina, yisra'el vehayehudim: lemin halukat erets yisra'el ve'ad parashat eikhman] (Tel Aviv, 2002).

Rubel, I., *Las Escuelas Judías Argentinas (1985–1995): Procesos de evolución y de involución* (Buenos Aires, 1998)

Schenkolewski-Kroll, S., *The Zionist Movement and the Zionist Parties in Argentina, 1935–1948* [Hatenuah hatsionit vehamiflagot hatsioniyot be'argentina, 1935–1948] (Jerusalem, 1996).

Sergiovanni, T. J., *Building Communities in Schools* (San Francisco, 1994).

Weil, A., *Orígenes del Judaísmo Conservador en la Argentina: Testimonio* (Buenos Aires, 1988).

Beyond the Community

Jewish Day School Education in Britain

HELENA MILLER

A HISTORY TEACHER sits with an adviser from the local education authority to discuss implications for her school of changes to the national curriculum history syllabus. A school principal meets with a government official from the Department for Education and a senior educator in the community to discuss arrangements for the forthcoming inspection of the school.

These meetings could be taking place on a typical school day in any state school in Britain. What makes the situation unusual, possibly unique, is that they are taking place in a Jewish state school in Britain. The British context, which has allowed the growth and development of Jewish day school education through legislation providing for denominational schools, has considerably shaped Jewish schools in Britain: their structure, their curriculum, and their accountability. This chapter identifies and discusses the impact of the relationship with the state on Jewish schooling in Britain, in terms of both the opportunities this relationship presents and the challenges it poses.

While some Jewish schools in Britain are private institutions, funded by trusts and individuals within the Jewish community, most Jewish primary and secondary schools are located within the state sector. The rights of religious groups to establish their own schools have been enshrined in law in Britain since the mid-nineteenth century.[1] The case for denominational schooling in Britain was accepted as early as 1839, more than thirty years before the 1870 Education Act that paved the way for compulsory education for all.[2] At that time, the government's Committee for Education stated that if promoters of schools could prove that their intention was to combine secular and religious studies, and that the curriculum would include the read-

---

[1] Wolffe (ed.), *The Growth of Religious Diversity*.   [2] Miller, 'Meeting the Challenge'.

ing of the Authorized Version of the Bible, then their schools would be eligible for government grant funding. The government took the view, at that time, that the religious requirements in Jewish schools did not match their own statement closely enough and state funding was withheld, just as it was also withheld from Catholic schools. After several attempts to redress the situation, a pressure group headed by the philanthropist Sir Moses Montefiore finally prevailed in 1851, when the government agreed that Jewish schools would be permitted to receive grants in the same way that other denominational schools were, provided they agreed to read the scriptures of the Old Testament every day and provided they were also prepared to submit to government inspection. In 1853 the Manchester Jews' School received state funding, for the first time putting a Jewish school on equal terms with other denominational schools. The proportion of state funding remained minimal, however, until the end of the nineteenth century, by which time it had increased to cover all the running costs of the school apart from the Jewish education and the maintenance of the building.

By 1880 nearly 60 per cent of Jewish school-age children attended Jewish schools, with the remaining children attending Church schools or no school at all.[3] Between 1880 and 1914, despite an influx of 100,000 Jews from eastern Europe into Britain during these years, Jewish schools declined in popularity: the immigrants thought that if their children attended non-Jewish schools they would become accepted as English men and women, and integration into the host community was encouraged. The Education Act of 1944 held out the prospect of substantial state aid for denominational schools, but British Jewry, with less than 20 per cent of its children in Jewish schools at that time, did not take advantage of the offer.[4]

By the late 1960s Jewish education in Britain had reached a watershed. Then, in 1971, the chief rabbi of the United Synagogue, Lord Jakobovits, launched the Jewish Education Development Trust,[5] which significantly raised the profile of Jewish education within the Jewish community. Communal efforts at raising funds, of which less than 10 per cent a year had hitherto been earmarked for education, began to place more emphasis on projects within Jewish education. By the 1970s the focus of fundraising initiatives reflected sociological and historical needs, of which education was paramount.[6] Today, more than 60 per cent of Jewish children in Britain are

---

[3] Black, *JFS: The History of the Jews' Free School*.   [4] Cesarani, *The Making of Anglo-Jewry*.
[5] Sacks, *Will We Have Jewish Grandchildren?*   [6] Miller, 'Meeting the Challenge'.

educated in Jewish schools,[7] the majority of them within the state system. These schools thus take advantage of the public funding that supports this system, and are at the same time fully accountable to the government in all aspects of the secular education that must be provided in state-aided schools.

These two issues, of funding and accountability to the government, are the keys to understanding Jewish day school education in Britain today. They will be examined in the next few pages, as will the matter of curriculum, which has also been shaped by the relationship between Jewish schools and the government. Clearly, these are not completely separate fields of concern, and throughout the chapter links and connections between them will be made as appropriate.

Funding

The British government began subsidizing education to a limited degree, in the form of treasury grants, as early as 1833, but it did not assume the role of instigator for educational provision until the following century.[8] Instead, different faith groups were instrumental in promoting education with a strong inculcation of religious values,[9] and this began a tradition of denominational schooling in Britain that has continued until today. After the Education Act of 1870, which legislated for compulsory schooling for all children in Britain, religious groups could not afford to meet the needs of schooling for all. From that time to the present, and through successive Education Acts, these religious schools have been supported financially by the state.

The implications of state aid to Jewish day schools are significant. The state provides funds to cover all expenditure, apart from that related to Jewish education. Thus all secular teaching costs (salaries, resources, school maintenance) are taken care of through the budget provided by the government and the local education authority. Of course, this budget is not open-ended or unlimited. The budget for British state schools is calculated on a per-pupil basis and careful management is required by the principal and governors of the school. State funding of Jewish schools does not cover the

---

[7] Unpublished data provided by Board of Deputies of British Jews, 2007.

[8] Armitage, *Four Hundred Years of English Education*.

[9] Wolffe (ed.), *The Growth of Religious Diversity*.

Jewish religious education provided. It does cover general religious education, which all state schools are expected to teach, and for which up to one
hour or so each week may be allotted. Jewish schools, however, expect to
spend far longer each week teaching Jewish studies than the amount of
time allotted to religious education, in order to provide a full and meaningful Jewish education for their pupils. To pay for the human and material
resources needed to ensure a Jewish, as well as a secular, education of high
quality, each school asks for a voluntary annual financial contribution from
each family whose child is a pupil. Compared to paying private school fees,
which in England range from about £6,000 to over £10,000 a year, this
figure is minimal—between about £250 and £750 a year for each pupil. No
state school, however, is permitted to make any compulsory charge towards
the education provided, a prohibition which includes contributions towards
religious studies. As a result, in most Jewish schools only around 70 per
cent of parents do pay the voluntary levy. In one elementary school in London, as few as one-third of parents pay the levy.[10] Some of those who do not
pay cannot afford to, a situation accepted unreservedly by all schools, but
others choose not to pay, a situation accepted with frustration by all schools.
A shortfall in parental contributions is sometimes compensated for in part
by fundraising, but the outcome often seen in schools is poor resourcing
of Jewish studies departments. In an extreme case reported in the British
Jewish press in 2006, a Jewish primary school in the north of England was
threatened with closure because the proportion of those parents paying the
voluntary contribution was so low that the school could apparently not
afford to remain open.[11]

Funding arrangements for Jewish education have implications for
teachers as well as for resources in Jewish studies departments. In some
schools funding is used to offer salaries above the UK national teaching
scales, to attract Jewish studies teachers. More often, however, the opposite
happens: insufficient funding means that Jewish teachers are paid below
the UK national teaching salary scales. Good, experienced teachers are not
attracted into Jewish studies posts and morale remains low, as these teachers compare their lot with teachers of secular subjects in the same school.
Even where a full complement of capable teachers is in place, there has frequently been insufficient funding to run rich programmes of professional

[10] Personal correspondence with head teacher.
[11] 'Faith Schools'.

development or to support classroom programmes. Currently, this problem is being addressed by initiatives taken by central Jewish agencies in Britain, and an increasing range of initial and in-service training opportunities are now available for Jewish studies teachers.

More positively, the financial relationship between the state and faith-school systems in Britain does allow access to Jewish schooling for all Jewish students, regardless of family income. This situation, which is almost unique in the Jewish diaspora, guarantees schools a stable level of funding that relieves them of the need to engage in burdensome fund-raising programmes. At the same time, by accepting state funding, schools face a perennial problem of working within a budget that is never gener-ous enough and of having to attempt to raise sufficient additional funds through the voluntary parental levy.

In a recent survey of Jewish schools in the UK it was found that two-thirds of the twenty-seven schools inspected in a three-year period between 2000 and 2003 were inadequately resourced.[12] The growth of information and communications technology in the wider world has not been matched by progress in this area in Jewish studies departments, in terms of either hardware or software, and most schools require substantial additional resources to support all aspects of the Jewish education being provided. Although this situation has arisen in part because there has not been a suf-ficient range of good-quality educational resources available for purchase by schools, in the last few years an increasing number of publishers and authors have produced high-quality materials; a greater problem is that schools have insufficient funds available to resource their Jewish studies classrooms to the standards now common in secular studies. Should schools increase the voluntary levy to a level that would generate a realistic and sufficient budget for all aspects of Jewish education? Would such a move be self-defeating and prevent a larger proportion of parents from pay-ing at all? Should schools increase their efforts at substantial fundraising within the community? Although education is high on the communal agenda, it has to compete, in fundraising terms, with many other charitable causes, both local and overseas. In addition, the very fact that Jewish school-ing is 'free' in Britain means that there is a perception in the community that Jewish schools do not need substantial additional funds.

---

[12] Miller, *Inspecting Jewish Schools.*

Curriculum

All state schools in Britain are subject to legislation in respect of curriculum. Interestingly, until the Education Reform Act of 1988 the only compulsory subject in the British state curriculum was religious education. In 1988 the first version of a national curriculum for the entire age range from 4 to 18 was introduced into state schools, identifying core and foundation subjects that should form part of a balanced curriculum. Core subjects for pupils from 5 to 16 years old are English, mathematics, and science. Foundation subjects that provide a broadening of the curriculum are information and communication technology, geography, history, art, design and technology, music, physical education, languages, and citizenship; the last of these has been compulsory for pupils at secondary level since 2002.

Alongside these subjects is religious education, which must be taught in every state school, and 'daily collective acts of worship', which have been compulsory since the 1944 Education Act. In non-denominational schools, these 'daily collective acts of worship' are usually morning assembly times for year groups or for the whole school. Content varies and may include some or all of the following: prayers, hymns or songs, a story from scripture or of moral value, performance or contributions from pupils, general reports of school life, and announcements. In Jewish schools 'daily collective acts of worship' will usually include *shaḥarit* (morning prayers) or *minḥah* (afternoon prayers) as well as the non-religious items listed above.

The national curriculum gave structure to a curriculum which, particularly in primary schools, had from the 1960s to 1980s been seen by some as non-conformist, individualistic, and eccentric, and by others as creative and inspiring. For Jewish state schools, although it provides pupils with the framework for a well-balanced secular education, the national curriculum poses various challenges. First, the number of hours required to teach the national curriculum takes up the whole school day. Even using the allotted time for collective worship and religious education, no more than three hours each week are available for Jewish education. While the government stipulates that there must be 190 days of schooling per year, the number of hours of schooling each day is set by individual schools. So Jewish state schools make the time for Jewish education by extending the school day by one hour or more. The school day in most non-denominational schools lasts approximately seven hours. It is not unusual for an eleven-year-old pupil in a Jewish state school to be in school for eight hours or more. In addition, the pupil is expected to complete up to two hours of homework each day for national curriculum subjects. Add to this a homework requirement for Jewish studies and you have a very long working day, five days a week. Some Jewish schools have addressed this issue by extending the number of days in the school week from five to six, making schooling compulsory on Sundays. The majority of mainstream Jewish state schools, however, try to keep the teaching week to five days. The result is that often relatively little time is devoted to Jewish studies and Hebrew in these schools.

In jurisdictions where Jewish schools do not have to take account of state legislation, Jewish studies can take up half the school day; this is the case, for example, in many Jewish schools in North America. In state-aided Jewish schools in Britain, Jewish studies is more likely to occupy something between forty-five minutes and two hours each day. The implications of this situation are clear: the greater the number of hours devoted to Jewish studies, the more knowledgeable and confident students are about their Jewish education.

In some Jewish elementary schools in Britain, to compensate for the relatively few hours available for Jewish studies, the Jewish and general studies curricula are integrated. Zeldin and others have put forward powerful arguments for a single unified curriculum in which deliberate efforts are made to bring Judaism and the culture of modernity in contact with one another.[13] Zeldin charts a variety of structural ways in which this can happen in a school context, referring to them as co-ordination, integration, and interaction. The constraints of the national curriculum mean that, at best, interaction is what usually takes place in British day schools. Interaction is where, according to Zeldin, there are separate opportunities for Jewish and general learning, and times when deliberate efforts can be made to bring the two together.

The content of the national curriculum poses potential challenges to some Jewish state schools. In science and literature, for example, some of the more Orthodox Jewish state schools look for opportunities to select options within the national curriculum which enable them to avoid teaching what they regard as unacceptable material. For example, they try not to

---

[13] Zeldin, 'Integration and Interaction', 579–90.

use a recommended novel if it includes content of a sexual nature. On a positive note, there are also opportunities for Jewish schools to use the curriculum to select material that can integrate Jewish education with national curriculum topics. For example, they may be able to study the land and geology of Israel within a geography topic, or focus on the paintings of Chagall during an art topic on twentieth-century European artists. This approach to subject matter enables more time in the school day to be devoted to Jewish studies than in a timetable where there are rigid divisions between Jewish and non-Jewish content.

Where integration or interaction is possible, the onus is on the teacher to ensure that he or she has the ability and experience to teach the material. The traditional staffing structure in state primary and secondary schools in Britain does not lend itself to integration in this manner. Separate staff teams are employed to teach either secular or Jewish studies. In order for subject matter to be integrated, teachers must begin to integrate as staff teams in the first place. But these staff teams often have little professional contact in school; sometimes they even use separate staff rooms. In some British Jewish primary schools integration and interaction do take place because all teachers in those schools are employed to teach both Jewish and secular studies. This places a great deal of responsibility on the teacher and the school to ensure that both secular and Jewish studies are taught to a high standard. It has not yet proved possible to achieve this level of integration in a state Jewish secondary school because of the constraints of curricular and examination requirements; nevertheless, in some Jewish secondary schools a degree of integration and interaction has been possible within non-public examination syllabuses, and with younger pupils (11 to 14 years old).

As mentioned above, citizenship education is now a compulsory element in the UK national curriculum.[14] All students from 4 to 18 years old in all state schools must be taught aspects of its three interrelated components: social and moral responsibility; community involvement; and political literacy. Citizenship education aims to provide students with the knowledge, skills, and understanding to become informed citizens, aware of their rights, responsibilities, and duties, and capable of playing an effective role in their local, national, and international communities.[15] Making

[14] Department for Education and Skills, *Raising Standards*.
[15] Department for Education and Skills, *Making Sense of Citizenship*.

citizenship education an entitlement for all students is both right for them as individuals and to the benefit of democratic society as a whole. But it is a challenging task. The Jewish community has always taken its citizenship in Britain very seriously. In every mainstream synagogue in Britain, on every sabbath, a prayer for the royal family of Britain is read, usually in English, even where no other English would be used during the *tefilah* (prayer). Jewish schools give their students opportunities to play effective roles within the local Jewish and wider non-Jewish community, both through religious and community initiatives and through social and political initiatives.

In addition, some Jewish schools encourage the study of world faiths as part of the general curriculum. They promote links with local schools in other faith communities, particularly through the arts and sports, emphasizing what different communities have in common as well as what distinguishes them from one another. One Jewish primary school in London each year pairs a group of pupils with the equivalent age group at their neighbouring Catholic school. The children have visited each other's festival preparations and celebratory concerts; they have interviewed each other about religious practice; and their teachers have met to exchange lesson ideas on Christianity and Judaism. They have also played each other at football and other sports, and undertaken art projects together.

While these activities are certainly part of citizenship education, they also address the mandate that requires religious education to be taught in all state schools in Britain. Up to now, Jewish schools have been able to use the time allotted for religious education for Jewish studies. Soon this situation will change in state-funded faith schools of all denominations in the UK. In accordance with British government regulations, the Board of Deputies of British Jews has called for all Jewish schools to teach about world faiths as well as about Judaism.[16]

Many Jewish schools are resistant to this idea. The origins of their resistance can be traced back to the Torah. In Deuteronomy 12: 30, the Israelites are told not to enquire about pagan religions and ask, 'How did these nations worship their gods?' It was feared that such curiosity might lead to imitative idolatrous practices. If Israel was to be cleansed from paganism, it was best to prohibit the very knowledge of these dangerous ways. Gunther Plaut observes that the purpose of this view was quite clear: in order to

[16] 'Faith Schools'.

establish God as the supreme ruler of all Israel, all other religious practices and ideologies were ruled out of bounds and the very knowledge of them considered inadmissible.[17] While Jewish practice has rarely been determined by direct reference to biblical verses, these concerns have resonated down the years, especially during periods when looking outwards at other faiths has left the Jewish people vulnerable, insecure, and persecuted.

In the light of these concerns, how might mainstream Jewish schools in Britain be convinced that teaching about other faiths is not something to be feared? Integration into the host community has certainly been encouraged throughout the centuries. In 1911, some thirty years after the beginning of the mass immigration of Jews from eastern Europe to Britain, the Reverend S. Levy told the Conference of Anglo-Jewish Ministers that the national system of compulsory and free education was enabling Jews 'to acquire English habits of thought and character'.[18] This integration into English life was seen as the only way for Jews to move beyond the poverty in which they were living. The children of immigrants wanted desperately to be accepted as Englishmen and women. Adapting to English culture and principles as well as learning to speak English was therefore considered vital. However, while integration to the fullest extent was encouraged, assimilation was not, and adherence to Jewish practice and custom was emphasized. We now know, nearly a century later, that there is a fine line between integration and assimilation.

The challenge for Jewish schools today is, on the one hand, to respond to the call from the government to teach about other faiths and, on the other hand, to remain true to their own religion. In the three progressive/pluralist Jewish primary schools in the UK a response to this dilemma has been grounded in an expectation that if pupils are clear about their Jewish identity and knowledgeable in their Judaism, they are able to look outwards at the wider community, appreciating it without wishing or needing to embrace it as their own. All three schools teach world faiths as part of a religious education syllabus, and all three make good links with other faith communities, visiting each other's places of worship and faith events, as well as getting to know each other in social and educational contexts. The schools expect that if they have educated their students to have a love for Judaism, those young people will be able to learn about the world and all its variations of human existence secure in a well-developed Jewish identity.

[17] Plaut (ed.), *The Torah*.   [18] Lipman, *Social History of the Jews in England*.

Accountability

The Office for Standards in Education (OFSTED) provides a national schools inspection service for all state schools in Britain. While OFSTED inspects all secular provision for education, there is a statutory requirement in Britain that schools also have their denominational religious education assessed. In response to this requirement, a body named Pikuach, meaning 'supervision', was set up in 1996 by the Jewish community to provide Jewish schools with a framework and structure for evaluating Jewish education provision in schools. This framework parallels that of OFSTED in an attempt to ensure that the status of Pikuach inspections, and therefore the status of Jewish education in schools, is comparable to that of OFSTED. To date, Pikuach has carried out more than sixty inspections, evaluating schools according to their own aims and goals. This individualized approach has been necessary because there is no shared aim or set of standards for Jewish education across the Jewish community. A report on the first years of Pikuach inspections shows that accountability through inspection has benefited the schools.[19] On the whole, schools were found to perform well against the standards they set themselves. Areas highlighted for development, in particular teacher training and curriculum development, were also beginning to be addressed. Schools are inspected every three to five years and, virtually without exception, those schools that underwent a second Pikuach inspection between 2000 and 2003 showed improvement in the areas identified during their first inspection.

There are challenges for Pikuach. For example, as OFSTED evolves, so Pikuach must develop too. In 2006 OFSTED radically revised its method of inspection to focus on a self-evaluation process for schools, supported by external inspection to interrogate the judgements of the school themselves, in place of a sole reliance on externally evaluated inspection. Consequently, Pikuach had to reorganize its framework and inspection process to parallel OFSTED's requirements.

National initiatives related to faith schools and religious education also have an impact on the Pikuach process. The British government is moving towards a situation where all faith schools will have to demonstrate that they are teaching major world religions and not just their own, ensuring that they take full account of the multicultural character of British society.

[19] Miller, *Inspecting Jewish Schools*.

While Pikuach was developed to inspect the Jewish educational aspects of schools, it may well be that in the future its inspectors will also have to look at the wider teaching about religion, as part of the broader 'Jewish life' education taking place.

Unusually within British Jewry, Pikuach was established as, and has remained, a cross-communal initiative. The practical issues of training Jewish educators to become Pikuach inspectors and the sensitivities needed for one agency to deal with a very wide range of Jewish schools across a diverse Jewish community are significant. Pikuach has shown that it is possible for Jewish education to transcend denominational differences within Judaism. Schools are able to choose inspectors who are religiously acceptable to their own populations, but all inspector training and discussion is conducted cross-communally, under the auspices of the Board of Deputies of British Jews, itself a non-denominational body.

Just as OFSTED inspections require schools to look at themselves critically and identify areas for development, Pikuach does the same. Key issues are targeted for improvement and form the basis of the school's action plan. Since 1999, as a direct result of the first Pikuach inspections, the Jewish community has put into place several new teacher-training and development initiatives to address the need for a workforce that is more professional and better prepared for its task. Areas for action identified through Pikuach inspections between 2000 and 2003 included the following:

1. implementation of strong and efficient management structures in schools;

2. provision of fully developed programmes for the systematic and relevant in-service training of teachers;

3. raising of standards in biblical Hebrew skills by re-evaluating curricula, providing continuity and progression;

4. development of the provision for special educational needs;

5. improvement in the resources available to support Jewish studies teaching.

Efforts are being made by the central Jewish education agencies to address these issues, and some of them have already made a qualitative difference in certain sectors of the community. For example, one group of elementary schools has instituted a year-long programme focusing on teacher and curriculum development. A nine-day seminar in Israel for twenty teachers supported by a programme of in-service training sessions in London has led to definite progress in curriculum development, staff development in relation to Jewish identity, and professional expertise. This same group of schools had previously invested considerable time and energy in developing a shared vision of what it means to be a pluralist/progressive Jewish elementary school. But these efforts are not national or cross-communal, so although development can be seen, the end results are pockets of excellence rather than any sense of national improvement in quality and standards. Again, the lack of financial resources to improve the quality of Jewish education across UK state schools is one, albeit not the only, factor contributing to lack of progress in this area.

*

Jewish education has been a communal obligation for over 2,000 years, and the establishment of schools has remained a priority for all Jewish communities. The Jewish community in Britain has undergone its own educational journey, aided and significantly scaffolded by the relationship its schools have with the state, and by having to look outwards as well as inwards. While the relationship with the state poses challenges, it also presents opportunities that have enabled Jewish education to flourish and develop in Britain through the state school system.

As I write this, however, it is clear that we, in Britain, are about to face new and complicated challenges precisely because of the relationship our Jewish schools have with the state, and because of the religious, political, and social situation in Britain today. In October 2006 the government backed a proposed amendment to the Education and Inspections Bill which would have forced faith schools to give 25 per cent of their places to pupils from other faiths. This measure was intended to promote social cohesion.[20] While it would initially have affected only new schools, there was justifiable anxiety among all faith schools that it would then be applied to already existing schools. The Board of Deputies of British Jews co-ordinated a united Jewish community voice, in conjunction with other faith groups, to oppose this sudden call for quotas. On 26 October the proposal was

---

[20] Department for Education and Skills, Education and Inspections Act.

withdrawn. The 2006 Education and Inspections Act, within whose pages the new code of admissions will be enacted in 2008, will continue to allow faith schools to give priority to applications from pupils within their own faith. Although the faith schools won this particular battle, the likelihood is that the relationship between faith schooling and the state will continue to be a prominent political issue in the coming years. How this will play itself out, only time will tell.

Bibliography

Armitage, W., *Four Hundred Years of English Education* (London, 1964).

Black, G., *JFS: The History of the Jews' Free School, London, since 1732* (London, 1998).

Cesarani, D., *The Making of Anglo-Jewry* (Oxford, 1992).

Department for Education and Employment, Education Reform Act (London, 1988).

Department for Education and Skills, Education and Inspections Act (London, 2006).

—— *Making Sense of Citizenship* (London, 2005).

—— *Raising Standards* (London, 2002)

'Faith Schools: Multi Faith Aim', *Jewish Chronicle*, 3 Mar. 2006.

Lipman, V., *Social History of the Jews in England, 1850–1950* (London, 1950).

Miller, H., *Inspecting Jewish Schools 1999–2003* (London, 2003).

—— 'Meeting the Challenge: The Jewish Schooling Phenomenon in the UK', *Oxford Review of Education*, 27/4 (2001), 501–13.

Office for Standards in Education (OFSTED), *Every Child Matters: Framework for the Inspection of Schools in England from September 2005* (London, 2005).

Plaut, G. (ed.) *The Torah, a Modern Commentary* (New York, 1981).

Sacks, J., *Will We Have Jewish Grandchildren?* (London, 1994).

Wolffe, J. (ed.), *The Growth of Religious Diversity: Britain from 1945* (Newcastle, 1994).

Zeldin, M., 'Integration and Interaction in the Jewish Day School', in R. Tornberg (ed.), *The Jewish Educational Leader's Handbook* (Los Angeles, 1998), 579–90.

ELEVEN

Attitudes, Behaviours, Values, and School Choice

A Comparison of French Jewish Families

ERIK H. COHEN

THIS CHAPTER compares the background, attitudes, values, and practices of French Jewish families who send their children to Jewish day schools with those of other such families who send their children to public (state) schools or non-Jewish private schools. Choice of school plays a pivotal role in the formation and expression of French Jewish identity.

The issue of school choice and the struggle of French Jews to preserve their identity must be understood in the context of the long and rich history of the Jews in France. Throughout their many centuries in the country, the Jewish community waxed and waned as its members were subjected to periodic legal restrictions, punitive taxation, violent attacks, attempts at forced conversion, 'blood libel' trials, and expulsion orders. Despite all this, the Jewish communities in the region persevered; indeed, some of the most famous Torah scholars of all time came from France. The Enlightenment and the French Revolution brought political emancipation to the Jews. However, the equality extended to all French citizens under the republic was granted with the expectation that allegiance would be exclusively to the state, and that all affiliation with ethnic or religious communities would be strictly private and subordinate to citizenship. This philosophy, which discourages affiliation with ethnic or religious sub-groups, still guides the political culture of France.

Today, the Jewish community of France is the second largest diaspora community in the world,[1] and one of the most vibrant. The French Jewish community has experienced major demographic and cultural upheavals

Thanks to Allison Ofanansky for her editorial contribution in the preparation of this chapter.

[1] According to DellaPergola et al., *Between Thriving and Decline*, France is home to just under half a million Jews, while Russia has just under a quarter of a million. Other sources estimate the Jewish population of Russia as significantly higher, possibly making it the second largest diaspora population. On the basis of my familiarity with DellaPergola's work and methods, I accept his

since the Second World War. Under Nazi occupation during the Vichy regime a quarter of the Jews of France were killed or deported, and the institutional and educational structure of the community was almost completely destroyed. The psychological impact was equally traumatic. In the decades following the war, Jewish refugees from other European countries as well as half a million Jews from France's newly independent colonies in north Africa migrated to France. French Jews today, while patriotic and largely integrated into French culture, are attempting to navigate a path between expression of Jewish identity and respect for the republican ideals of universalism and *laïcité* (secularism).

Since the late 1990s, and especially since the first years of the current century, this struggle, which is simultaneously taking place on a larger scale throughout French society, has been described as a debate between 'republicans' and 'communitarians'. The term 'communitarian', which sometimes takes on accusatory or derogatory connotations, refers to those who are affiliated with a particular ethnic or religious community, while 'republicans' insist on loyalty only to the French nation.

This issue as it relates to schooling in France is complex. The public school system plays an important role in reinforcing French ideals of citizenship, with an emphasis on universalism and secularism. Sending one's children to a private, parochial school is viewed by some as bordering on unpatriotic.[2] However, the enforced secularism of the public schools may pose problems for traditional Jewish families. For example, neither students nor faculty members are allowed to display outward signs of religious affiliation such as *tsitsit* or a *kipah*, and classes are held on Saturdays.[3]

While the latent direction of French policy is to build a general French identity and not to foster sub-cultures, for many decades the French government has accepted the development of private schools (primarily Catholic and Jewish), providing finances and professional support for such schools under contract with the state. Recent improvements in the academic standards of Jewish day schools and the partial subsidizing of parochial schools, combined with an increase in drug use, violence, and antisemitic incidents in public schools, have contributed to the rise in enrolments at Jewish day

figure as the most accurate, but recognize the inherent difficulty in assessing the number of Jews remaining in Russia following the collapse of the Soviet Union.

[2] Shurkin, 'Decolonization'; Laborde, 'The Culture(s) of the Republic'.
[3] Wasserstein, *Vanishing Diasporas*; Shurkin, 'Decolonization'.

schools in recent decades, including pupils from non-religious families.[4] There has also been an increase in the number of Jewish students enrolled in non-Jewish private schools.[5] Families who take the latter course are withdrawing their children from the public school system but, for a variety of ideological and logistical reasons, choosing not to send their children to Jewish day schools.

Methodology

The data used in this article are drawn from a representative survey of the heads of French Jewish households conducted in January 2002. Since French census records do not include religion, a list of Jewish family names was compiled and a sample of heads of household with these last names was contacted by telephone. A total of 1,132 questionnaires were completed by household heads who defined themselves as Jewish or Israelite. In this comparison, only respondents with school-age children are included. Of the 817 school-age children in the families surveyed, 26 per cent were enrolled in Jewish day schools. The data presented in this article relate to the parents surveyed, comparing those with children enrolled in Jewish day schools with those whose children are not enrolled in Jewish day schools (no differentiation is made here between those in public schools and those in non-Jewish private schools).[6]

The results were first analysed using cross-tabulations. While there is much to learn from these tables, they do not make it easy to see the relationships among the various aspects of the data. In order to portray the 'structure' of the data graphically, a multidimensional scaling technique known as Smallest Space Analysis (SSA) was used.[7] In the SSA procedure, the correlations between the selected variables are plotted as points in a

---

[4]   Cohen, *Les Juifs de France*; id., 'Are There Potential Clients?'

[5]   Lefkovits, 'Third of French Jews Send Children to Catholic Schools'. My research on French Jewry conducted in 2007 is cited in this article.

[6]   It is likely that some families have chosen, for various personal reasons, to send some of their children to Jewish day schools and others to public or other private schools. However, the survey asked only if the family's children attend Jewish day schools or not, so such details are not included. Nevertheless, the numbers of families who use more than one school system are small and would not affect the overall results of this analysis.

[7]   For detailed information on the Smallest Space Analysis procedure see Guttman, 'A General Nonmetric Technique'; id., 'Facet Theory'; Levy (ed.), *Louis Guttman on Theory and Methodology*; Canter, *Facet Theory*; Borg and Lingoes, *Multidimensional Similarity Structure Analysis*.

Euclidean space called 'smallest space'.[8] The points are plotted according to an intuitively understood principle: the greater the correlation between two variables, the closer they will be located on the map; the weaker the correlation between two variables, the further apart they will be.[9] This procedure enables us to consider the correlations among all variables simultaneously. In the resulting map, contiguous regions of related variables may be recognized and interpreted in relation to the theoretical basis of the study.

Once the map of the original variables has been created, external variables such as sub-populations may be added to the map. This feature distinguishes the SSA from other, similar, multidimensional data analysis techniques. A correlation matrix is calculated between each of the external variables (in this case, French Jewish families with and without children enrolled in Jewish day schools) and the original variables. The external variables are then placed one by one into a 'fixed' map in such a way that the original structure is not altered. In other words, the placement of the external variables is determined by the original variables, but the placement of the original variables is not affected by the external variables.[10]

Results

General Background

As the French Jewish population is approximately 70 per cent Sephardi, the overwhelming majority of Jewish families with children in either Jewish day schools or in public and other private schools is Sephardi. However, Ashkenazi families are proportionately less likely to enrol their children in Jewish day schools. Families with children in Jewish day schools are somewhat more right-leaning politically, though not dramatically so. Respondents with children in Jewish day schools are 10 per cent more likely than those whose children attend other schools to have reported being victims of

[8] This is done using the Hebrew University Data Analysis Package. See Amar and Toledano, *HUDAP Manual with Mathematics*; id., *HUDAP: Hebrew University Data Analysis Package*. In this case the monotonicity correlation, a non-linear coefficient of correlation, was used. The non-linear MONCO correlations are always higher than the more traditional, linear, Pearson correlations because MONCO measures whether or not two items increase or decrease in the same direction. It is more sensitive (though less useful as a predictor), and recognizes a wider variety of correlations as 'perfect'.

[9] Guttman, 'A General Nonmetric Technique'; Levy (ed.), *Louis Guttman on Theory and Methodology*.　　　[10] Cohen and Amar, 'External Variables'.

antisemitism within the past five years, although it is not clear which is the cause and which is the effect. While the rise of antisemitism has contributed to the rise in day school enrolment,[11] attacks on Jews may be more common around synagogues and Jewish schools.[12] 'The majority of antisemitic acts, particularly verbal attacks on Jewish students, take place in schools.'[13]

Attitudes towards Israel

Overall, the Jews of France feel connected to Israel, as Table 11.1 indicates. The level of connection is stronger among those with children in Jewish day schools, who are somewhat more likely to describe their connection to Israel as 'very close'. The families with children in Jewish day schools are somewhat more likely to have close relatives in Israel (68 per cent, compared to 53 per cent of the other families), but the vast majority of French Jews have family and friends in Israel. The families whose children attend Jewish day schools are somewhat more likely to have made multiple trips to Israel, although the frequency of visits among families with children in other types of school is also high. Almost a fifth of the families who do not send their children to Jewish schools have never visited Israel, compared to only 7 per cent of those with children in private Jewish schools. The Jewish day school families are significantly more likely to be considering making *aliyah* 'very soon' and are more enthusiastic about supporting their children making such a move. A hypothetical question asking respondents to choose a religion and nationality if they could be 'born again' enabled them to express feelings about living in Israel without considering practical obstacles. Far more of the parents with children in Jewish day schools said they would prefer to have been born Jewish in Israel. While no one said they would prefer to be non-Jewish, almost a fifth of the parents whose children are not in Jewish day schools said religion and nationality would not be important to them, compared with only 5 per cent of those with children in Jewish day schools. This indicates the more widespread acceptance of universal values among families who chose non-Jewish schools, an issue which will be revisited below.

[11] Cohen, *L'Étude et l'éducation juive*; Trigano, 'French Anti-Semitism'.
[12] Cohen and Ifergan, *La Jeunesse juive*.
[13] Suzan and Dreyfus, *Muslims and Jews in France*, 6.

Table 11.1

Attitudes towards Israel

Question and response	Parents selecting each response (%)		
	Parents of children not in Jewish day school	Parents of children in Jewish day school (kindergarten, elementary, or secondary)	Total
How close is your feeling of connection to Israel?			
Very close	43	66	48
Close	37	30	37
Distant	17	2	13
Very distant	3	2	2
What, if any, personal connections do you have in Israel?			
Children	4	4	4
Other close relatives	49	64	52
Distant relatives	24	22	23
Friends but not relatives	9	8	8
No one	15	3	12
How many times have you visited Israel?			
None	19	7	16
One or two	15	9	13
Three or four	16	18	17
Five or more	50	66	54

Community Life

Parents with children in Jewish day schools are much more active in the local Jewish community, as seen in Table 11.2. They participate more often and are more likely to volunteer to give their time. They are more than twice as likely to listen to Jewish radio programmes and read the Jewish press: 43 per cent of those with children in Jewish day schools listen daily to Jewish radio programmes and 48 per cent read the Jewish press often, compared to 21 per cent and 22 per cent, respectively, of the families with children in other school systems.[14] This indicates not only greater interest in news rele-

[14] For reasons of space, not all the data are included in the tables. The full data set is available upon request from the author.

Table 11.1 *(continued)*

Question and response	Parents selecting each response (%)		
	Parents of children not in Jewish day school	Parents of children in Jewish day school (kindergarten, elementary, or secondary)	Total
Are you considering making aliyah?			
Yes, very soon	5	30	11
Yes, later	18	34	21
I considered it but changed my mind	7	3	6
Eventually	18	14	17
No	52	19	45
If your children wanted to make aliyah, would you:			
Encourage them	44	60	48
Be pleased	41	32	39
Not oppose	10	6	9
Be disturbed	4	2	3
Oppose	1	0	1
If you could be born again, would you choose to be:			
Jewish in France	30	20	28
Non-Jewish in France	0	0	0
Jewish in another diaspora country	6	3	6
Jewish in Israel	45	72	50
Religion and nationality not important	19	5	16

vant to the Jewish community, but likely greater participation in community events, which are often announced through the Jewish media. Interestingly, the families with children in Jewish day schools are also slightly more likely to volunteer in general (not specifically Jewish) community projects, though the difference is less pronounced.

Religious Practice

The most dramatic difference between the two groups is in terms of religious practice, as seen in Table 11.3. Those with children in Jewish day schools are more likely to describe themselves as Orthodox or traditional, though it is worth noting that almost half of those with children in other

Table 11.2

Community life

Question and response	Parents selecting each response (%)		
	Parents of children not in Jewish day school	Parents of children in Jewish day school (kindergarten, elementary, or secondary)	Total
How often have you participated in the local Jewish community in the past two years?			
Never	17	0	13
Rarely	14	8	13
Occasionally	15	6	14
Often	20	14	18
Very often	34	72	42
Do you volunteer in the Jewish community?			
Yes	25	48	30
Do you volunteer in the general community?			
Yes	11	16	12

school systems also describe themselves as traditional. The parents of children in Jewish day schools are far more likely to observe religious commandments; but again, it is worth noting that over half the families with children in non-Jewish schools regularly practise traditions such as having a family sabbath meal, lighting candles, and making kiddush. Almost none (1 per cent) of the parents of Jewish day school students are married to non-Jews, whereas a third of the respondents in the other group of parents have non-Jewish spouses. As one would logically expect, the Jewish day school parents are also much more strongly opposed to their children marrying outside the faith.

Almost half the parents with children in Jewish day schools described themselves as more religious than their parents and also as having become more religious than they used to be. This increase in religiosity may be a cause or a consequence of the enrolment of children in Jewish day schools, or a combination of both.[15] Among the families with children in other

[15] Formal and informal Jewish educational settings have been found to have an impact on ritual observance in the participants' families. See Cohen, 'Executive Summary'.

Table 11.3

Religious practice

Question and response	Parents selecting each response (%)		
	Parents of children not in Jewish day school	Parents of children in Jewish day school (kindergarten, elementary, or secondary)	Total
How would you define your level of religious practice?			
Non-practising	30	1	24
Liberal	14	1	11
Traditional	47	69	52
Orthodox	9	29	13
Is your spouse:			
Jewish?	66	99	74
Non-Jewish?	33	1	26
A convert to Judaism?	1	0	<1
Do you eat kosher at home?			
Always	48	95	59
Do you eat kosher outside the home?			
Always	33	79	44
Does your family light candles on Friday night?			
Regularly	55	95	64
Does your family make kiddush on sabbath evening?			
Regularly	60	98	69
Do you refrain from working on the sabbath?			
Regularly	49	87	58
Do you have a family meal on the sabbath?			
Regularly	75	96	80
Do you go to synagogue on the sabbath?			
Regularly	28	65	37

schools, over a third of respondents said they were less religious than their parents, just under a third said they were more religious than their parents, and over a third said they were more religious than they used to be. Taken together, these results indicate a revival of Jewish practice among French Jews.

Attitudes about Education

Just under half of the parents with children in Jewish day schools thought the schools should strictly observe religious commandments and traditions. The rest, along with the majority of those who do not send their children to Jewish schools, thought the schools should observe the tradition to varying degrees, reflecting the traditional but not Orthodox character of the French Jewish population. Interestingly, there is little difference in the rating of the quality of French Jewish day schools between those who send their children to them and those who don't, indicating that other reasons (predominantly religious and ideological, although also possibly logistical and practical) motivate the choice of school system. At the same time, only 10 per cent of the parents who sent their children to non-Jewish schools said that giving their children a Jewish education was not important, and almost 60 per cent said it was very important. Some may send their children to formal or informal Jewish educational programmes outside normal school hours.

Structure of Values

The heads of household were given a list of values and asked to rate the importance of each. On the basis of these results, four profiles of French

Table 11.4

Profiles of French Jewish families

Question and response	Parents selecting each response (%)		
	Parents of children not in Jewish day school	Parents of children in Jewish day school (kindergarten, elementary, or secondary)	Total
Individualists	20	8	16
Universalists	23	6	20
Traditionalists	34	52	38
Revivalists	23	34	26

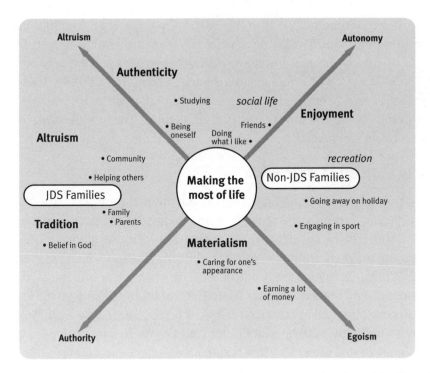

FIGURE 11.1. Cognitive map of values of French Jews showing location of families with children enrolled and not enrolled in Jewish day schools (JDS)

Jews were identified: individualists, universalists, traditionalists, and revivalists. Revivalists place emphasis on both traditional and individualist values. Table 11.4 shows the percentages of those with children in Jewish day schools and those with children in other schools who fit each of these profiles. The former group are more likely to be traditionalists. Although the traditionalists are also the most common profile among the families with children in other schools, this group also has significant percentages who fit the individualist and universalist profiles, which are rare among the Jewish day school families.

Figure 11.1 shows a graphic portrayal of the structure of values held by heads of French Jewish households. The two sub-groups of families with and without children enrolled in Jewish day schools are shown in relationship to this structure. The value 'making the most of life is at the centre of the typology, surrounded by regions of values which relate to enjoyment (social life and recreation), materialism, tradition, altruism, and authenticity. Additionally, within this map we see two axes: a political axis from autonomy to authority and a social axis from altruism to egoism. The families with children in Jewish day schools are between the regions of traditional values, which include items such as founding a family, honouring parents, and believing in God, and the region of altruism, which contains items such as community and helping others. Those with children in other schools are close to the centre of the map, in the enjoyment region.

Discussion and Conclusion

The issue of school choice provides insight into the difficult questions about identity faced by the Jews of France today. The French nation as a whole is undergoing an 'identity crisis' related to the integration of minority groups and the predominance of the republican values on which the state is based. While it is beyond the scope of this chapter to delve into the myriad, deep-rooted, and serious conflicts related to immigration and national identity that have emerged in France (and indeed across Europe) in recent years, it may be noted that the Jews of France find themselves in a delicate position. They are well integrated into the general population; they are strongly patriotic, and embrace the political emancipation granted to them by the secular state. Nevertheless, many in the relatively traditional French Jewish population do not wish to relegate their religious practice and culture entirely to the 'private' domain. A more public type of Judaism has emerged, including an expression of national identity through connection with the State of Israel. At the same time, the French Jewish population has been put on the defensive by anti-Israeli rhetoric and a resurgence of violent antisemitic acts, perpetrated primarily by young members of the growing French Muslim population. In response to this difficult situation, some Jews have questioned their future in France. A third of the heads of French Jewish households surveyed said they did not see themselves living in France within the next several years,[16] and the rate of *aliyah* from France rose by 27 per cent between 2004 and 2005.[17] Nevertheless, most French Jews are not leaving France, and are therefore in the process of negotiating the nature of their French Jewish identity. Various responses are possible, as seen in the profiles identified, ranging from stronger affiliation with the Jewish community to accelerated assimilation into the general population.

[16] Cohen, *Touristes juifs*; id., *Les Juifs de France*.   [17] Reuters, 'Suspect in Murder of French Jew'.

School choice is a critical piece in this puzzle. The results of this analysis show that the situation should not be oversimplified. Traditional, religious families may choose to send their children to public schools and secular families may choose to send their children to Jewish day schools. However, overall we can see that the families who send their children to private Jewish schools are more likely to observe religious traditions and practices, and are more strongly connected to Israel, than those with children in other school systems. The multidimensional analysis of values shows that the families with children in Jewish day schools place more emphasis on family, community, and religious belief, while those with children in non-Jewish schools emphasize the universal values of autonomy and personal enjoyment.

The impact and influence of the Jewish day school extends beyond the classroom. For example, students meet on Sundays and holidays for informal, social activities, and therefore their families meet, creating a community with the school at its centre. In addition, many families who do not live close to a Jewish day school are faced with the choice of either sending their children long distances by public, private, or school-organized transport or relocating to a neighbourhood near a Jewish school. As a result, apartments in neighbourhoods near Jewish day schools have become expensive and hard to find (as seen in the case of the school in Pavillons-sous-Bois).[18] As families with children in Jewish day schools concentrate in certain neighbourhoods, these schools take on the role of synagogue (on sabbath and holidays) and community centre.

Coda

Interestingly, the distinctive environment of a French Jewish day school may soon be carried into Israel. Surveys of French Jews have found that a very high percentage of both tourists and immigrants to Israel have children in Jewish day schools. Some community leaders and educators are advocating founding schools in Israel specifically for *olim* (new Israeli citizens) from France. This suggests that the French Jewish day school has a particular style and environment found neither in French public schools nor in any of the educational streams already present in Israel. The particular style of French Jewish day schools and of schools for French

[18] Rachel Cohen, principal of the school, pers. comm., 2005.

immigrants in Israel has not yet been analysed in the social scientific literature.

From my own familiarity with the field of Jewish education in France and Israel, I can offer a few observations. French Jewish parents are most likely to be looking for a school in which discipline is clear, in contrast to the *laissez-faire* approach more common in Israeli schools; they want a school with a fairly high level of religious practice and learning but one that is not ultra-Orthodox; they expect to be able to maintain their own level of religious practice in the home without the requirements and restrictions sometimes imposed by Israeli religious schools. Additionally, French *olim* may wish their children to continue to be familiar with French language, culture, and values, even while living in Israel.

In sum, in order to understand the roles Jewish day schools and public schools play in French Jewish society, the whole informal environment surrounding the school must be considered. Far from being an enclave for the most Orthodox families, the private Jewish day school has become a site for expressing Jewish identity and creating Jewish community among a population facing rapid social change. In the coming years, as social researchers observe and analyse the French Jewish community, it will be crucial to pay close attention to the role of the Jewish day school.

Bibliography

Amar, R., and S. Toledano, *HUDAP: Hebrew University Data Analysis Package* (Jerusalem, 2002).
—— ——*HUDAP Manual with Mathematics* (Jerusalem, 1997).
Borg, I., and J. Lingoes, *Multidimensional Similarity Structure Analysis* (New York, 1987).
Canter, D. (ed.), *Facet Theory: Approaches to Social Research* (New York, 1985).
Cohen, E. H., 'Are There Potential Clients for the Jewish Day Schools in France? An *a posteriori* Analysis of a Prognosis', in S. DellaPergola (ed.), forthcoming.
—— *L'Étude et l'éducation juive en France* (Paris, 1991).
—— 'Executive Summary', in id., *One Movement, Many Faces: Survey of Members of Bnei Akiva in the World* (Jerusalem, 2004).
—— *Les Juifs de France: Valeurs et identité* (Paris, 2002).
—— *Touristes juifs de France en 2004* (Paris and Jerusalem, 2005).
—— and R. Amar, 'External Variables as Points in Smallest Space Analysis: A Theoretical, Mathematical and Computer-based Contribution', *Bulletin de Méthodologie Sociologique*, 75 (2002), 40–56.
—— and M. Ifergan, *La Jeunesse juive: Entre France et Israël* (Paris, 2005).
DellaPergola, S., et al., *Between Thriving and Decline: The Jewish People 2004* (New York and Jerusalem, 2004).
Guttman, L., 'Facet Theory, Smallest Space Analysis, and Factor Analysis', *Perceptual and Motor Skills*, 54/2 (1982), 491–3.

—— 'A General Nonmetric Technique for Finding the Smallest Co-ordinate Space for a Configuration of Points', *Psychometrika*, 33/4 (1968), 469–506.

Laborde, C., 'The Culture(s) of the Republic: Nationalism and Multiculturalism in French Republican Thought', *Political Theory*, 29/5 (2001), 716–35.

Lefkovits, E., 'Third of French Jews Send Children to Catholic Schools', *Jerusalem Post*, 4 Apr. 2007.

Levy, S. (ed.), *Louis Guttman on Theory and Methodology: Selected Writings* (Dartmouth, UK, 1994).

Reuters, 'Suspect in Murder of French Jew Held in Ivory Coast', 23 Feb. 2006.

Shurkin, M. R., 'Decolonization and the Renewal of French Judaism: Reflections on the Contemporary French Jewish Scene', *Jewish Social Studies*, 6/2 (2000), 156–71.

Suzan, B., and J. M. Dreyfus, *Muslims and Jews in France: Communal Conflict in a Secular State* (Washington, DC, 2004).

Trigano, S., 'French Anti-Semitism: A Barometer for Gauging Society's Perverseness. An Interview with Shmuel Trigano by Manfred Gerstenfeld' (Jerusalem, 2004), <http://www.isranet.org/DataBank/FRANCE_ANTISEMITISM.htm>.

Wasserstein, B., *Vanishing Diasporas: The Jews in Europe since 1945* (Cambridge, Mass., 1996).

TWELVE

The School Ghetto in France

AMI BOUGANIM

THE JEWISH SCHOOL in France was never conceived or planned; it just created itself behind the backs of community institutions. The first modern Jewish institution in the country with a pedagogical vocation, the Alliance Israélite Universelle, was founded in 1860 and decided against opening schools in France. The Alliance did not see the need or demand for special Jewish schools; its pioneers could not conceive of a school for Jews that would not be a school of the republic. Its leaders, rabbis and the members of its central committee (which always included the most prestigious members of the community), gently shied away from such a proposition.

Nevertheless, over the course of the following century the Alliance was not reticent about opening schools elsewhere in Mediterranean communities. In Egypt, Morocco, Turkey, Iran, Iraq, Syria, Lebanon, Malta, Greece, and of course in Palestine, it created a number of establishments. Among those in Palestine was the famous agricultural school Mikveh Yisra'el, founded in 1870 and built on land leased by the sultan to Baron Rothschild, sponsor of the institution.

In France itself the Alliance was satisfied with directing the famous École Normale Israélite Orientale (ENIO), which was charged with training teachers for the Mediterranean schools. In order to further its interest in developing the moral and intellectual level of oriental Jews, weakened by the neglect that prevailed in their countries of residence, the Alliance willingly relocated its principals and teachers with little concern for their personal preferences. In 1914 the Alliance ran 188 schools with 48,000 students from Tangier to Tehran.

In 1960, a century after its creation and having survived the Dreyfus affair and the First and Second World Wars, this venerable institution was still not ready to recognize the Jewish school at Pavillons-sous-Bois, in

Seine-Saint-Denis, 10 kilometres north-east of Paris. The history of this school provides a good illustration of the way Jewish schooling expanded in France. It was founded at the beginning of the 1960s by a former principal of the Alliance in Morocco, without the support of the headquarters in Paris. It opened a first classroom and then a second one in a suburban house. Considering himself the holder of the pedagogical patrimony of the prestigious educational network, the principal dared to challenge the authority of its supervising organization and described his school as part of the Alliance.

When he retired, the headquarters in Paris named as his successor a former principal of the Alliance in Tunis. Nevertheless, the institution made no effort to renovate the derelict premises. Even when it decided, under the impetus of a new president, to collect funds for the restoration of the offices and library, it continued to show no interest in the school, believing in neither its necessity nor its viability. Until the middle of the 1990s the ever-growing student body shared unstable benches in prefab classrooms where they froze in the winter and roasted in the summer. Without a donation from the chief rabbi of Paris and pressure from the principal, the Alliance would not have invested a centime in this establishment, even though it possessed considerable financial and material resources. The school offended the 'Israélite' sensibility, according to which Jewishness was exclusively a religious identity, and violated the historical decision, taken at the very beginning of the Alliance's existence, not to open schools in France.

The Alliance was not politically ready to review its pedagogical vocation and had no institutional disposition to do so. For a century it did not cease speaking in France's name, promulgating the country's republican principles and cultural patrimony. The colonial vocation was so entrenched in its institutional fabric that it could not renounce its oriental impetus. When the ENIO reopened in 1946 with Emmanuel Lévinas as its new principal, he declared that this new beginning meant nothing less than 'creating . . . a centre of Jewish western spirituality that will know again how to contribute something new to Oriental Judaism'.[1] But the creation of the State of Israel and the 'ingathering of the exiles' reshuffled the cards, limiting the Alliance's function to supervising the dismantling of its educational net-

---

[1] See Lévinas, 'La Réouverture de l'E.N.I.O'.

work. The Alliance's representative in Israel was even decent enough to cede the lease on Mikveh Yisra'el's lands to the Israeli government.

Elsewhere, the Alliance renounced its prerogative to be the political representative of the French Jewish community in favour of the Conseil Representatif des Juifs de France (CRIF). Motivated by the award of the Nobel Peace Prize to its president, René Cassin (1943–68), father of the Universal Declaration of Human Rights, it reinvented itself as the promoter of human rights. It has never had anything to say about Jewish education in France, but repeats the formula about the creation of 'school environments where children and youngsters from different socio-economic, religious and intellectual horizons meet' and about 'the promotion of a community consensus' with the potential to become 'the embryo for a new Jewish *pharhesia*'. Two initiatives to open schools, one in Nice at the beginning of the 1980s and the other in Montrouge in the suburbs of Paris at the beginning of the 1990s, did not succeed. The Alliance fell into such disgrace that it left its own ENIO to deteriorate, to the point where it had become one of the worst schools in France prior to its closure in 1998.

In the middle of the 1990s it was finally decided to create a new school in France. The donor was Gustave Leven, grandson of Narcisse Leven—the long-standing president of the Alliance in its early years. Land was found in the twelfth arrondissement in Paris and an architectural competition was launched. The process took years to complete. When the new institution, the Établissement Georges Leven, finally opened its doors in 1997, it had neither a strategic plan nor a pedagogical vision. Its founders had not imagined that parents would not want to send their children to an elementary school that had no secondary school. Nor had they budgeted for the cost of the five probationary years the state required private institutions to operate before it would fund the salaries of teachers of general subjects—the heaviest expense in the budget of any school. The Alliance had to improvise. It relocated the ENIO to the new building to guarantee state funding, and to offer parents the prospect of a secondary school. During this period, the students in Pavillons-sous-Bois continued to attend classes in unhealthy conditions, unable to improve matters until the death of a neighbour whose property crossed the middle of the schoolyard offered an opportunity to expand. Despite the mayor's intervention, this brave and stubborn Gaul, in a stance heavy with symbolism, refused to cede his property to 'strangers'.

The history of Jewish schools in France is a reflection of what happened with the Pavillons-sous-Bois school. First, expansion was advanced by old Alliance school principals from North Africa, rather than by representative community institutions, such as the Fonds Social Juif Unifié (a secular institution) or the Consistoire (a religious institution). Second, this expansion responded to the needs of the Jewish immigrants from the Maghreb, rather than the wishes of the veteran Jews or of descendants of east European immigrants, who continued to prefer the secular republican schools. The first schools of the 1960s were the products of strange conglomerates like Le Refuge, an association entitled to collect employers' training taxes which, according to French law, go to philanthropic institutions and to training agencies. In practice, and somewhat dubiously, Le Refuge left its schools to the directors who were, by law, the only legitimate interlocutors of the government and its agencies.

A second group of schools was established under the sponsorship of Otzar Hatorah, an Orthodox network created in Morocco to compete with the Alliance and to reduce its influence, since the rabbis considered it overly assimilationist. Its devoted director in France was supported by a strange American character who played on his connections with the American Senate and Israeli leaders to pave himself a route to the corridors of power in France. A third network, even more Orthodox, was created by the followers of the renowned Lubavitcher Rebbe, based in Brooklyn. ORT, solidly supported by the Joint Distribution Committee, opened a series of professional schools; these, lacking enough pupils, accepted both Jewish and non-Jewish students.

In other words, the expansion of Jewish schools was not a result of the development of the old 'Israélite' community, anxious to renew itself after the Holocaust, but was actually the fruit of initiatives taken by Maghreb immigrants who could not find places in the few Jewish schools that existed before the war, such as Lucien de Hirsch (primary), Yavneh (secondary), and Maimonide (primary and secondary). This expansion was neither planned nor co-ordinated. Schools opened in areas with a high concentration of Jews, in the suburbs of Paris or in the provinces. Everywhere the process occurred with the same goodwill, the same dedication, and the same problems. The community representatives were usually absent, and even when they were present their support was usually symbolic. This expansion was big business: it involved large sums of money and, more importantly, contracts in the government sector for thousands of people.

The expansion of the Jewish school system in France cannot be understood independently of the debate about schools that divides France. The public (state) school system is the product of a series of disputes, breaks, and reconciliations between the Church and the Republic. Each side has been and continues to be entrenched in its positions. The public school sees its mission as integrating, at any cost, the children from all the provinces, from all social classes, and from all religions around a secularity that does not differentiate between one and another and that aims to 'convert' one and all into followers with an unconditional allegiance to republican principles. This did not stop French legislators from finally recognizing the legitimacy of private schools, and agreeing to a co-operation contract with each of these institutions by which the state commits to fund teachers of general subjects and also to supply a range of subsidies. For its part, the private school is contractually obliged to respect the curriculum as proposed by the supervising ministry and to avoid discrimination between pupils. In a Jewish school under contract, the teachers of general subjects, including Hebrew since it was declared a live language, are state employees. Nowadays, most Jewish schools are under contract. They benefit from large-scale state support and are required to uphold the various clauses of the contract.

From the beginning, the Jewish schools were built around small communities comprising members of one or several families who shared the same religious convictions. Their most pressing need was not to clarify their pedagogical vision so much as to conform to the instructions of the ministry, to perpetuate the traditions and pedagogical methods imported from the Maghreb or from the east, and to integrate the other teachers of Jewish subjects into the small founding community. The schools perpetuated what came to be known as voluntary segregation, reinforcing that which separates Jews from non-Jews rather than that which brings them together. In Morocco and in eastern Europe, this essential Jewishness was in the air and in the customs, accepted by Jews and non-Jews alike; in France, the situation was more delicate. Assimilation was threatening; the schools needed to protect themselves.

In the long run, the Jewish school revealed itself to be a blend of communal and faith school, forming a definition of Jewish citizenship that was peppered with commandments, prayers, and rituals, and leaving it to the street, the television, and the environment to provide instruction in French citizenship. The question of French citizenship is never raised in the Jewish school, and never has been. Therefore, the question of how a child born of immigrant parents understands his or her Jewish condition in France has not been raised either. These children are indoctrinated to know that they are Jewish, that the Torah contains all the wisdom in the world, that the commandments will protect them from any harm, that Israel is the country of the Jews, and that Hebrew is their language. Their parents were comfortable with this view while they saw themselves as part of a group that had immigrated from the Maghreb for whom France was not a final destination but a stop on the way to Israel. This position was so rooted in their being that their only concern was how to succeed in their professional careers while resisting the temptation of assimilation hidden under the republican duty of melting into the nation, speaking its language, wearing its colours, and celebrating the virtues and greatness of—according to the cliché that attracted so many would-be immigrants—'the most just, the most free, the most human of homelands'.

The Jewish school in France, therefore, took upon itself the preparation of neither Jewish citizens of French nationality nor French citizens of the Jewish faith. Instead, it concentrated on preserving 'the Jewish sparkle' in young souls exposed to assimilation, perpetuating threatened customs and creating protected spaces where young Jews could be among themselves. So completely unconcerned were they with devising a new Jewish–French citizenship, with integrating into the universal republic while preserving Jewish particularism, or with reconciling a double and even triple loyalty to France, Israel, and their various countries of origin, that forty or fifty years later, there are very few pedagogues of a high level in this community (which is not short of high-level intellectuals) who can—or would dare to—propose a citizenship credo at the Jewish school.

The Jewish school in France today maintains this same pedagogic approach. Every time its main actors and partners are invited to an educational discussion, the debate revolves round the same questions of teaching the Bible, the commentaries, or the Mishnah, or how to give model lessons on Jewish celebrations and commemorations. At best the participants are exposed to rabbinical sermons trying to reconcile Maimonides' or Shimshon Raphael Hirsch's view on *midrashim* dealing with teaching in the Talmud with brief snatches of the pedagogical theses that feed the current public debate. The rabbis show themselves even more relaxed than their

'Israélite' predecessors. Some say that they have abused their role as interpreters of the divine word in order to say nothing at all:

The sermon . . . has degenerated into either idle paraphrases, subtle and wasting breath on the simplest verses of the Scriptures (*drosh*), or into light jokes (*halatsa*), peppered by jovial anecdotes, not worthy of the subject or the place, or into controversies too elevated for the audience, that transformed the temple into a scholastic arena (*hloq*); on other occasions, into condemning and heated eloquence (*tokhaha*) that enjoyed terrifying the souls with dark descriptions, instead of lifting them by jovial perspectives.[2]

If there is a Jewish pedagogy in France, it is hopelessly apologetic; if there is a pedagogy of Jewish–French citizenship, it is not mentioned in reviews or colloquiums. The French Jewish school is, with a few exceptions, a 'ghetto-like' school. This means that it is concerned with protecting its pupils, their parents, and their teachers from the external influences that carry the threat of assimilation inherent in the republican integration project. This type of school would have faced no problem if it had wished to remain unchanged; if it had chosen, philosophically and politically, to retreat in order better to cultivate the intimacy and community of its partners; and, particularly, if it had not shown signs of communal dissidence, in which the threat of spiritual sclerosis and atrophy can be detected.

The absence of a reasoned Jewish pedagogy was not the result of a lack of intellectuals able to deal with such questions. First and foremost, it was the result of the absence of any genuine pedagogical reflection in France as a whole. For a century, up until the crisis resulting from the suburban violence of 2006, the republican school had not been troubled by pedagogical considerations. The responsible ministries dictated the curriculum. The teachers were trained within the same mould, and their privileges were protected by powerful teachers' unions. They were not particularly troubled by civil integration or by discipline problems (they eagerly used an 'orientation or exclusion' policy). The republican discourse was ingrained everywhere, and they deferred to the dominant French culture not only in letters but also in manners or tastes, so as to imprint it on the body, to transfer it to the senses, and to infuse it into the spirit. Nor were teachers much exercised about pedagogical methods—they privileged content, and expected their pupils to grind away and assimilate it. Looking ahead, the republican school

---

[2]   Wogue, *La Prédication israélite en France*, 9.

prepared its pupils for the best secondary schools, and these in turn prepared them for the best qualifications that offered them access to the best
colleges—the famous *grandes écoles* such as the Polytechnique and the École
Normale Supérieure, competing with the best universities. The children of
immigrants, still a minority in French classrooms, were expected only to
succeed in their studies in order to walk the golden path that leads from
success at school to the insertion and integration into the social structure
that are secured by a good career. Even though education was promoted to
the level of 'science', Jewish educators felt no need to invest in serious pedagogical reflection, allowing any intellectual to pronounce on questions that
required research and, moreover, classroom experience in problematic
schools.[3] The pressure to assimilate exerted in the public schools during
the first half of the twentieth century was such that the children of Jewish
immigrants from eastern Europe were among their best pupils and ex-
tracted themselves from the socio-economic condition of their parents,
becoming doctors, engineers, or researchers. Immigration was then a mar-
ginal phenomenon and the assimilation of immigrants was still possible.

The later influx, in the 1980s and 1990s, of millions of immigrant workers of a variety of colours, religions, and cultures different from those that
dominated the country provoked questions of integration and assimilation
that France was not ready to tackle. The country lacked the expertise and
experience to address the issue on such a large scale—despite its tendency
to rejoice in the success of past integration policies, referring to the Jews as
'a model of successful integration' or 'the historical example of the successful Judeo-republican synthesis'.[4] On the other hand, there was little willingness to challenge the model of national cohesion and republican principles
in order to articulate a better integration policy in the schools for the millions of children and grandchildren of immigrants. This policy of integration and assimilation inevitably led to clashes with the large concentrations

---

[3] Plato prescribed the death penalty for any 'busybody in the fields of education and law'. See
Laws XII, 952d.
[4] This second sentence belongs to Pierre-André Taguieff. See 'Communauté, communautaire, "communautarisme"', 98. These sentences, repeated ad nauseam, did not convince either
Jews or non-Jews—not at the time of the Dreyfus affair, not during Vichy, not today; nor will they
tomorrow. Only the lip service of the Jews of the Republic, detectable among the leaders of the
Alliance, before and after Vichy, stops the best analysts from seeing that the only integration tolerated by the republican universal is still assimilation and that the behaviour of the Jews from the
Maghreb, in terms of civil integration, is closer to that of their former Maghrebian compatriots
than to that of their 'Israélite' co-religionists.

of minorities and religious extremists in the poor suburbs. Today, France is still recruiting philosophers as education ministers and then seeing them fail; it is still willing to argue about multiculturalism, multinationalism, and multiloyalism, and to corner itself over multicolourism. It is still willing to send in the army to ensure civil co-operation in the most problematic cases, and to babble about positive discrimination when it does not know where to begin. France is willing to engage in a pedagogical debate that is prisoner to outdated political clichés charged with sociological distinctions so subtle that they mislead decision-makers more than they assist them.

In this context, Jewish education has once again latched on to the idea of establishing the ghetto in and around the school. This vision, unfortunate as it seems, makes its own contribution to the socio-political tension around the traditional concept of nation, shaken by the establishment of the European Union, by globalization, and by the general perception that life is about 'getting what you want'. This concept of the nation is also overwhelmed by the general use of English as a universal language and by the extension of communication channels. The French authorities seek to integrate and assimilate millions of foreigners, among them more than 6 million Muslims and several million Africans, without reviewing the republican model and its sacred principle of secularity. The Jewish school, however, decided to mobilize its rich historical experience and retreat into its own ghetto, admitting only children with Jewish mothers, paying symbolic tribute to civil instruction and republican principles (through visits to museums, and by participating in national rather than regional competitions), but showing no interest—with a diaspora defiance and a declared love for Israel—in the communal debate that shakes France.

The French model, deliberately Jacobin and centralized, ensconces itself behind the one and indivisible Republic. It leaves minorities no choice but to hide behind ghetto-like protections. France has not relinquished, even if some political scientists claim it has, its desire to reduce the number of immigrants. In the aftermath of the revolution, when, according to the formula of Clermont-Tonnerre, 'everything was accorded to the Jews as individuals and nothing as a nation', the vision was clearly one of assimilation. In spite of the progressive consolidation of Europe, the European notion of 'nation' remains essential. It does not tolerate cultural or linguistic erosion, even less being chipped away at by the particularistic claims of immigrant minorities that threaten national cohesion. The United States of America was constituted by national communities that experienced their crowning achievement in a political model that ought to be characterized as transnational, its constituent entities having come to terms with the communal phenomenon, multiculturalism, and multi-ethnicity (or, as Erik Erikson has said with reference to Jews, pseudo-ethnicity). By contrast, Europe is built as a puzzle of nation-states; the communal phenomenon that transcends borders presents a real menace to its delicate construction. While European national aspirations, be they in Brittany or Corsica, remain localized, Muslim 'national' aspirations risk taking on European proportions.

In a Europe that does not know what to do with its immigrants, the communal phenomenon is barely tolerated and is quickly reframed as communitarianism, menacing the national status quo and compromising the achieved respect for human rights. In this debate the Jews continue to enjoy the status of 'protected minority' that grants a variety of privileges, including visible and public communal expression of compensation for the political crimes committed against them in the past. Worthy of mention are the impressive demonstrations by French Jews in support of the Jews of Syria and the USSR, their mobilization in support of Israel, the public campaigns of the chief rabbinate of France calling its followers to participate in the gatherings known as the Torah Journeys, and the erection of a huge *menorah* in Trocadero Square for Hanukah. On the other hand, the European Jewish community, if there is one from Paris to Budapest, does not represent a dominant factor in the demographic map of Europe. Its spokesmen, from Shmuel Trigano to Alain Finkelkraut, are neither convincing nor interesting. An article in *Le Monde* should not conclude with a sentence as morally empty and politically hallucinatory as this: 'The debate about communitarianism would be clearer if, taking the Jewish experience as an example, we could wager that each group does not exist only for itself but as a participant in an exchange that sees humanity as its horizon.'[5]

The problem is that the ghetto, in spite of the positive connotations that it may have for those aware of the fragility of the modern Jewish condition and of the deceptive seductiveness of non-committal modernity, might save the Jews from assimilation but risks exposing them to a religious anaemia that could be fatal. Most pupils in France's Jewish schools exhibit what could be called a ghetto-like personality. They willingly display a French

[5] Bernhein et al., 'Les Juifs de France'.

spirit, but inside they are focused on Israel. They eagerly adhere to the regime of liberties; they engage with the republican lexicon; they display generous tolerance in public; in private, at home or at school, they are frankly intolerant, even racist. They engage willingly with contemporary cultural and social phenomena; however, they do not disengage from rabbinical, dogmatic, and anachronistic positions that challenge the most elemental sense of criticism. It is a fact that nowadays the French Jewish school produces Marranos, some more neurotic than others: Jewish in their hearts, French in their appearance; inside, citizens of nowhere, outside, citizens of France. Maybe it is the vocation of all Jewish education to educate towards dissidence in this world the better to prepare for the world to come. We risk, even with the general loss of religious faith that accompanies our growing understanding of other worlds, cultures and peoples, paving the way to the exaltation of one world over the other, choosing religious foolishness rather than Jewish understanding.

A second reason for the pedagogical carelessness of French Jewish schools lies in their association with strict Orthodoxy, to which most are bound by tradition. Most of the principals present themselves as Orthodox even if they allow themselves a more liberal way of life during school holidays. Most of the parents enjoy seeing themselves as Orthodox even if they drive their car after sabbath services. Most teachers of Jewish subjects declare themselves Orthodox—and in fact they are the only ones who really are Orthodox, sometimes for the worse rather than for the better. The Orthodox public persona is never challenged. It is assumed as protection rather than from conviction. People are afraid to criticize it for fear of alienating the rabbis, many of whom themselves represent no more than a caricature of Orthodoxy. The assumption of this religious mantle does not allow space for any pedagogical reflection. The complex and passionate questions that need to be asked about Jewish education cannot be posed without exposing religious convictions as well as political and civil positions. The kind of civic instruction that has to be dispensed in a Jewish school in France, or elsewhere in Europe, cannot be understood without identifying the seams between education for Judaism and education for citizenship.

Having said this, maybe it is time to reflect on the Jewish school in France. Within the main Jewish institutions, both elected lay leaders and professional staff are calling for such a process; so are the foundations and parents. Dominique Schnapper, heir to a long republican tradition, member of the Alliance's central committee, a revered partisan of administrative Jacobinism, and an advocate of the universal republic, recalls: 'For years I have tried to convince the Jews that for moral and political reasons they had to stop justifying any form of political "community" and adopt the republican affirmation, [leaving] individual citizenship and the transmission of Judaism's spiritual and historical tradition to the individual.'[6] She deplores the Jews' defiance of republican integration and their adhesion to multiculturalism in order to secure a better public expression of their particularism. In other words, Jewish public opinion has begun to ask itself discreetly about the best way of 'nationalizing' the Jewish school without compromising its achievements. Stakeholders wonder how to prepare new principals who have not known Morocco or Tunis, and how to prepare teachers of Jewish subjects who would be able, competently and critically, to argue with their general subject colleagues and infuse a real Jewish–French civility. Such a civility would neither return to an 'Israelitism' weakened by the draining of their passion for Judaism nor lean towards the exaltation of a real or imaginary Jewish genius, divine or human.[7]

But France's Jewish community, while losing impetus and prestige, is also confronted by the problems and dilemmas presented to French civil society by the partial Islamization of its demography, if not of its customs. The Jews have lost their status as a privileged minority in France. The Jewish minority is no longer alone on the public scene; there are Muslims, Buddhists, and animists as well. They are no longer, as a commentator at the beginning of the twentieth century called them, 'the cause for liberty of conscience, that the Jews had the honour and the misfortune of incarnating'.[8]

*

The complex of the Alliance in Pavillons-sous-Bois represents, in principle, what in the United States would be all that one could expect from a so-called community school. It has a synagogue open to teachers, parents, and all other local Jews. It offers a wide range of extracurricular activities engaging both parents and pupils. It has even succeeded in attracting a number of young couples who have relocated close to the school to secure places for

---

[6] Schnapper, 'L'Universel républicain revisité'.
[7] The 'Israélite' circles themselves call for some reinforcement of the 'love for the Republic' by the Jews of France as a reaction to the new varieties of antisemitism. See Wieviorka, 'Naissance, vie et déclin', 177.   [8] Levaillant, La Genèse de l'antisémitisme, 27.

their children. However, the disputes among parents, children, and teachers have not disappeared, be they about practical matters or about the conceptualization of Jewish subjects. Moreover, in spite of significant progress, the Jewish school has not become a school of excellence capable of competing with the best public schools that continue to attract the best pupils.[9] It does not stand out as an exceptional school or a school to be imitated. Muslims, who are searching for their own way of preserving their religion and cultural inheritance, are interested in the role that can be played by the school. They do not realize that the Jews, with long experience in challenging civil society, have now transplanted their ghetto into their schools.

[9] Only Yavneh school in Paris was on the list of the best 100 secondary schools in France in 2007.

Bibliography

Bernhein, G., et al., 'Les Juifs de France et la France, une confiance à rétablir', *Le Monde*, 30 Dec. 2003, 11.

Levaillant, I., *La Genèse de l'antisémitisme* (Paris, 1907).

Lévinas, E., 'La Réouverture de l'E.N.I.O', *Les Cahiers de l'Alliance*, 11 (1946–7).

Schnapper, D., 'L'Universel républicain revisité', in Y. Arfi (ed.), *Les Enfants de la République* (Paris, 2004), 131–55.

Taguieff, P. A., 'Communauté, communautaire, "communautarisme": Perspectives républicaines', in Y. Arfi (ed.), *Les Enfants de la République* (Paris, 2004), 55–108.

Wieviorka, M., 'Naissance, vie et déclin du "modèle français d'intégration républicaine"', in Y. Arfi (ed.), *Les Enfants de la République* (Paris, 2004), 157–84.

Wogue, L., *La Prédication israélite en France*, ed. A. Durlacher (Paris, 1890)

PART III

Insights through the Prism of Community

Relationships between Schools and Parents in Haredi Popular Literature in the United States

YOEL FINKELMAN

A S EMANCIPATION and increasing religious freedom gradually pushed the majority of modern Jews away from strict observance of Jewish law, a small group of Jews, referred to as Haredim or ultra-Orthodox, worked to shore up religious commitment by creating an insular community and protecting it from the perceived threats of contemporary culture. Grounded in the ultra-conservative ideology of the circle of the Hatam Sofer,[1] a leading nineteenth-century Hungarian rabbi, Haredi Judaism has spread from central Europe to eastern Europe, the United States, Israel, and other countries across the world. The various groups and sub-groups of Haredi Jews maintain slightly different practices and levels of acculturation, but all are characterized by a fear of outside culture and a desire to maintain strict observance of halakhah, Jewish law. As a protective strategy, Haredim adopt a deep religious conservatism, preserve distinctive dress and social norms, and work to isolate group members from outsiders.[2] Haredim try to construct an enclave culture in which a Jew can be socialized into the practices and values of the community. Two of the most important institutions involved in this socialization are the family and the school. Hence Haredi Jewry has put great emphasis on the religious significance of the family and on the network of Haredi schools, which have been created in every Haredi community. The religious atmosphere in these institutions, and the relationship between them and families, are matters of great concern for Haredi Jews.

This research was partially funded by a grant from the Memorial Foundation for Jewish Culture and by the Moshe Davis Memorial Fellowship from the Institute of Contemporary Jewry at the Hebrew University.

[1] Silber, 'The Emergence of Ultra-Orthodoxy'.
[2] For a good introduction to Haredim, see Friedman and Heilman, 'Religious Fundamentalism and Religious Jews'.

For many years there was significant tension between Haredi educational institutions and families. The years following the Holocaust were a time of deep crisis for the Jewish people, and in particular for that segment of devout east European Orthodoxy that had centred on the yeshivas, the advanced talmudic academies.[3] The survivors desperately sought to reconstruct what had been lost. Leading rabbis and their followers wanted to establish Haredi yeshivas where young men would be involved singlemindedly in full-time Torah study well into adulthood. However, many parents, even Orthodox ones, did not view this as an ideal for their own children. They had provided their sons with an Orthodox education, but hoped and expected them to move into socially and economically advantageous professions. A future studying in a yeshiva seemed a dead end.

Further, the yeshivas and the Haredi community they represented made exclusivist claims on students' time and values. There were no concerns outside the yeshiva, including those that parents and families might value, considered worthy of serious investment. Thus students who were attracted to yeshivas often found themselves at odds with their families. In order to compete more effectively for the students' allegiances, yeshivas sought to replace the family for students, and to this end worked to provide a warm and loving atmosphere in which students who were alienated from their parents and homes—or who the yeshivas hoped might become distanced from their parents—could find a replacement for what those homes had once supplied. In what Friedman calls a 'family–community model', yeshivas worked to provide a complete and totalizing environment for their students. At the time, the growth of yeshivas depended on their emerging victorious from their battles with families.

Today, the Haredi community has developed a very different 'family–community' model. Many contemporary Haredi parents are themselves second- and third-generation recipients of intensive Haredi and yeshiva education, or are *ba'alei teshuvah*, people who voluntarily adopt Orthodox observance after being raised in its absence. These parents generally identify with Haredi educational and religious values. Instead of being in conflict, parents and schools share an interest in co-operation. The goal

---

[3] Friedman, 'The "Family–Community" Model'. Friedman focuses particularly on the situation in Israel, but a parallel phenomenon existed in the United States as well. See Finkelman, 'Haredi Isolation in Changing Environments'. On yeshivas, see Stampfer, *The Development of the Lithuanian Yeshiva*.

remains the same: to surround youth in the warm and encompassing embrace of a totalizing Haredi environment. Yet, rather than doing so by separating children from their non-Haredi homes, both schools and homes aim to make themselves into bastions of Haredi Orthodoxy.

In this chapter I examine how this new family–community model is reflected in popular Haredi educational discourse in the United States. In recent decades, an extensive English-language Haredi popular literature has developed. Publishers such as Artscroll-Mesorah, Feldheim, and Targum Press have produced thousands of volumes of accessible and popular English-language Judaica. Spanning numerous genres—translations of and commentaries on classic Jewish texts, halakhic codes, self-help, inspirational stories, fiction, and history—this literature provides Haredi Jews, and other interested readers, with comfortable and user-friendly access to writing that reflects Haredi values and ideals.[4] These publishers are broadly associated with the more acculturated and less isolationist wing of the Haredim that is particularly prominent in North America. It is a community referred to by William Helmreich as 'strictly Orthodox'—fully observant of Jewish law—but with a wider general education, higher levels of professional training, and greater acculturation than the more isolationist hasidic groups.[5] It is a community in the sphere of influence of Agudat Yisra'el, a worldwide Haredi political and social movement.[6] This literature has been bitterly attacked by several modern Orthodox intellectuals,[7] but it has not been adequately mined as a resource for understanding the ways in which Haredi Jewry negotiates its complex relationship with general culture and tries to mould the character, values, and social alliances of its members.[8] This chapter examines this literature's portrayal of the relationships between schools and families, arguing that it presents conformity between schools and homes as an ideal, and that it calls upon parents to heed the

[4] The easiest way to get a sense of the nature and scope of this literature is to visit the websites of the various publishers, including <http://www.artscroll.com>, <http://www.feldheim.com>, and <http://www.targum.com>.   [5] Helmreich, *The World of the Yeshiva*, 54.

[6] On Agudat Yisra'el, and its role in forming Haredi identity, see Stolow, 'Transnationalism and the New Religio-Politics'.

[7] See Levy, 'Judge Not a Book'; id., 'Artscroll: An Overview'; id. 'Our Torah, your Torah and their Torah'; Helfand, 'Striving for Truth'; Schachter, 'Facing the Truths of History'.

[8] But see Finkelman, 'Medium and Message in Contemporary Ḥaredi Adventure Fiction'; id., 'Tradition and Innovation in American Haredi Parenting Literature'. See also Stolow, 'Communicating Authority, Consuming Tradition', where he examines Artscroll as outreach literature, for consumption by a non-Orthodox audience. It is nevertheless important to examine the way this literature functions within the Haredi enclave as well as outside it.

rabbis and educators who can teach them how to build homes that live up to Haredi standards. Yet, in addition to describing this hegemonic ideal, the popular literature also reveals places where actual practice does not live up to that ideal, and raises resistant voices that question aspects of the ideal itself.

My approach to this popular literature is a hybrid one. At one level, these texts are artefacts of an existing culture. As such they can teach us something about the reality in that culture. Their descriptions of relations between community and school can reveal something about how those relations play out in practice. At another level, such an approach can be oversimplified and naïve. These texts are also ideological, working to alter reality by changing the attitudes and practices of readers. As such, what they depict may be quite different from reality. I will attempt to combine these two approaches, comparing depictions of families and schools in this literature to some of the more complex social dynamics within the Haredi community. Such a task is difficult given that Haredi families and schools, and the interactions between them, have been largely neglected by sociologists and anthropologists.[9] Further research—including surveys, interviews, and ethnographic studies—will provide the basis for a more subtle discussion of the relationship between the ideology and the reality.

Socialization into the Haredi Enclave

Haredi Judaism views itself as the representative of authentic Judaism in the face of a contemporary culture it perceives to be entirely at odds with its ideals. 'Torah values are diametrically opposed to those of modern secular culture', one popular author boldly proclaims, in a fairly typical fashion.[10] Similarly, 'At no time has the contrast between the values Judaism stresses and those of the society around it been more pronounced than today.'[11] At the same time, Haredi Jewry is also deeply acculturated, and shares many values and cultural patterns with the contemporary society that it claims to reject.[12] This is particularly pronounced in educational litera-

---

[9] But see Hakak, *Spirituality versus Materiality* (Heb.) for a study of such issues in the Israeli Haredi environment.   [10] Tatz, *Worldmask*, 84.

[11] Abramov, *The Secret of Jewish Femininity*, 29.

[12] This has been studied in great detail in the articles collected in Caplan and Sivan (eds.), *Israeli Ḥaredim* (Heb.). Levels of acculturation among American Haredim are even higher. See also the comments of Fishman, *Jewish Life and American Culture*, 26–8.

ture, where Haredi assumptions about the child-centred nuclear family are fully grounded in American suburbia and contemporary conservative sensibilities.[13]

As a minority that perceives itself to be threatened in an open society, the Haredi community requires a great deal of willingness from individuals to conform voluntarily to certain group norms that are decidedly counter-cultural, even if Haredi rhetoric tends to exaggerate the differences between its own values and those of contemporary America. It prepares its members for this challenging commitment, in large part, through intense socialization into an enclave community. The enclave creates (or tries to create) a total cultural envelope for the individual, in which as many as possible of his or her personal, social, financial, religious, and intellectual needs are fulfilled within the confines of the community, thereby minimizing contact with the dangerous outside.[14]

This enclave serves as a 'plausibility structure': a network of social institutions and interpersonal relations that make a particular belief system or behavioural pattern seem plausible, if not inevitable.[15] When one is surrounded by people who behave or think in a certain fashion, those habits and ideas can take on an air of reasonableness and normality. Haredi education and socialization work to make the community's social and religious norms seem natural, commonplace, and taken for granted.

Nothing is more destructive of a community's ability to make its values seem inevitable as conflict between the family's practices and norms and those of schools. In a situation of conflict, children and young adults pick up contradictory messages and are forced to negotiate their confusion. They may reach ideological and operative conclusions that are unsatisfactory to both parents and educators, if not the students themselves. Hence it is an educational necessity in an enclave community to bring the family's values and those of the educational institutions into line with one another.

The Ideal of Harmony between Families and Schools

Haredi popular literature describes an ideal in which families and schools share the same values, thereby reinforcing them. This can be seen, for example, in a compilation of articles on education entitled *Timeless*

---

[13] See Finkelman, 'Tradition and Innovation in American Haredi Parenting Literature'.
[14] Sivan, 'The Enclave Culture'.   [15] Berger, *The Sacred Canopy*, 45 ff.

Parenting.[16] These articles exemplify mainstream Haredi popular literature in America. Culled from the pages of the *Jewish Observer*, a widely distributed monthly which serves as the official mouthpiece of Agudat Yisra'el in America, these essays were republished by the influential Artscroll publishing house as part of its Judaiscope series. They emphasize the necessity of continuity and conformity between families and schools. In an introductory essay, Rabbi Nisson Wolpin, editor of the *Jewish Observer*, explains that parents are the best educators of children; true education happens at home. The development of universal schooling, as indicated in a passage in the Talmud (BT *BB* 21a), 'marked a deterioration of the standard Jewish households of the times . . . The introduction of universal schooling must be seen as the response to . . . parents . . . [who] need[ed] all the help they could get . . . As life becomes more complex, and parents more harried than ever, they are forced to delegate more of their instructional responsibilities to others [namely, schools].' Today, 'teachers, seminary deans, and *mashgiḥim* [spiritual advisers]' fill in to help parents who can no longer educate their children on their own. 'Teachers are increasingly doing the work of parents . . . In some cases, teachers are the most dedicated parents imaginable.'[17] In Wolpin's vision, families should educate, but schools take on a familial role when families cannot fulfil their obligations.

The next essay describes the opposite, but complementary, vision. For Rabbi Yitzchok Kerzner, families must fill in where schools cannot. The goal of the Jew is to become 'complete', and 'this remarkable achievement' can 'best be realized . . . in our study halls'. Unfortunately, the 'family as an institution is in trouble' in contemporary society, and as a result, life can be 'cut off from the purity and wisdom of the *beis hamidrash* [study hall]'. Hence, it is necessary for families to turn to 'leading *rashei yeshivah* [yeshiva deans], who offer their insights on how to raise a Torah family'.[18] If for Wolpin the school is an extension of the ideal home, then for Kerzner the ideal home is an extension of the ideal *beit midrash*.

Another essay in the book ties the two themes together with an ironic rhetorical twist. Rabbi Yisroel Miller writes of 'Mrs Rosenberg's Yeshiva'— by which he does not mean that Mrs Rosenberg might serve as a real *rosh yeshivah*, but rather that this housewife's family is a yeshiva writ small, modelling itself on the lessons and styles of three famous east European

---

[16] Wolpin, *Timeless Parenting*.   [17] Ibid., pp. xvii–xx   [18] Ibid. 27–8.

yeshivas. Her family is

a carefully controlled atmosphere combining the best elements of Kelm, Slobodka, and Novardok . . . The yeshiva is small—only four students—but [Mrs. Rosenberg is] more concerned about quality than quantity . . . There's Dovid, 5 years old; Esther, 2; Shaindy, 6 months, and of course the oldest, who also helps in running the place, Shlomo, who's 31.[19]

The essay seems unaware of the potentially subversive gender implications of this image, which masculinizes the mother, feminizes the figure of the *rosh yeshivah*, and infantalizes the father. More important for our present purposes, however, is the rhetorical equation of family and yeshiva.

Rabbi Shimon Schwab, one of late-twentieth-century America's leading Haredi rabbis, states this connection particularly clearly. He explains that 'parents and schools' should be 'mutually dependent, mutually enriching', reinforcing each other's values in their conformity.

The Torah entrusts the teaching of *Yiddishkeit* [Judaism] to father and mother, but even the best of parents cannot do a complete job and carry out their sacred mandate without a Torah school and capable Torah teachers. Parents who expect the best kind of education for their sons and daughters can do very little without the proper school. Yet even the best school will accomplish next to nothing without the cooperation of the parents.[20]

This Haredi literature describes an ideal of harmony and co-operation between families and schools, created by fundamental agreement about educational and religious values. Many authors claim that this co-operation is created when parents learn from rabbis, as representatives of the tradition, how to educate their children and manage their households. According to Haredi ideology, norms are defined by the ancient texts of tradition, as interpreted by contemporary rabbis and teachers. This approach is reflected in the 'ethic of submission' that permeates Haredi ideology and life, and in the doctrine of *da'at torah*, which grants Torah scholars extensive authority over nearly every aspect of Jewish life, endowing them with virtual infallibility.[21] Laypeople, therefore, should accept the authority of the leadership, particularly regarding such critical issues as education and bringing up children. Families, as we have seen, must turn to 'leading *roshei yeshiva*,

[19] Ibid. 71–5. [20] Ibid. 191.
[21] On the ethic of submission, see Kaplan, 'Ḥazon Ish'. On the doctrine of *da'at torah*, see Kaplan, 'Da'as Torah'; Katz, 'Da'at Torah'.

who offer their insights on how to raise a Torah family'. This reflects a top-down model, in which rabbinic and school leaders teach, and parents learn.

This top-down model is implicit also in Lawrence Kelemen's parenting guide, *To Kindle a Soul*. The book claims to contain 'ancient wisdom' that was 'directly revealed' to the Jewish people 'more than 3,300 years ago at the foot of a mountain in the Sinai desert'.[22] Parenting style, like the other commandments revealed at Sinai, is not dependent on the personal proclivities or autonomous choices of individuals. It is dictated by God. Schwab reinforces the top-down notion when he declares that 'our *chinuch* [education] system' must set up a 'Parents' Department' to institutionalize numerous programmes for '*Chinuch Hahorim*—parents' education'. If parents are already '*frum* [devoutly religious]', then fathers should be taught how to review their sons' Talmud homework, and both parents should attend a series of classes on 'the science of "parenting"', in addition to a weekly 'friendly, but soul-stirring *mussar schmuess* [inspirational speech]'. In contrast, 'Modern Orthodox' parents, because of their religious inadequacy, require the approach of a '*kiruv* [outreach] professional' who will provide instruction in 'basic *halochos* [religious laws]' as well as 'fundamentals of *hashkafos* [religious ideology].' Non-observant parents should be invited for '*Shabbos* meals' to the home of the 'Parent Outreach Coordinator', in order to help 'win the parents over to a commitment to Torah'.[23]

Ironies in the Political Economy of Haredi Family–School Relations

It is no accident that these examples of the top-down model have been authored by male rabbis who work as teachers, educators, and rabbinic leaders. They represent the hegemonic voice of the tradition and its authority. But this is not, nor could it be, a conspiracy on the part of the establishment to control parents against their will.[24] Laypeople, who generally identify strongly with the leadership, and whose identity is deeply tied up with Haredi Judaism, have a similar interest in facilitating co-operation. If

---

[22] Kelemen, *To Kindle a Soul*, 19. As I argue elsewhere, Kelemen's claims of ancientness notwithstanding, the book is thoroughly modern (see Finkelman, 'Tradition and Innovation in American Haredi Parenting Literature'). [23] Wolpin, *Timeless Parenting*, 192–5.

[24] Systematic anthropological, sociological, and economic studies of Haredi educational life and its book market could help flesh out the following comments, which, given the state of the research, I have kept at a level of abstract generalization.

the parent body, or a least a sizeable portion of it, was not prepared to hear the message of the establishment, then popular parenting and educational books would not sell and the message would fall on deaf ears. As normative Haredi Jews, mainstream Haredi families share with the leadership a desire to see families conform to the high standards of the educators and rabbis. Indeed, this kind of literature could never develop, either in the Haredi community or in the general population, without anxiety and feelings of inadequacy on the part of parents, and a consequent sense that they need help from experts, an anxiety that the publishers of these books are only too happy to magnify in order to expand their market.[25] Furthermore, since rabbis and religious leaders in the United States wield no legal power, and since religious association is voluntary, the rabbinic authorities are dependent on the laypeople for their authority. Parents choose schools for their children, often from a wide range of options. Hence, educational leadership in the Haredi community is, to a great degree, charismatic. Paradoxically, the followers choose the authorities.

That is to say, the open market of educational ideas and private schooling is structured in such a way that like-minded educators and parents find one another because they are dependent on one another. Parents need educators to operate Orthodox schools for their children and to write books to provide answers to their parenting questions. Educators need parents to pay their salaries and buy their books. Parents who want a particular kind of educational system or parenting advice work to find schools and books that provide what they are looking for. Authors who do not write what some consumers want to read, and educators who do not educate in ways that a significant number of parents find desirable, may find themselves without a readership or student body. The conformity between schools and families is not simply created by the literature, or by the ideas that the literature expresses. Rather, a great measure of agreement is a prerequisite for the production and consumption of this literature. Much of the work in bringing families close to educators was done before popular parenting and educational literature came into existence.

This is not to say that parents and schools see eye to eye about all educational issues, or that there is perfect co-ordination between homes and educational institutions. The model of complete co-operation between

[25] On these paradoxes in the American parenting literature market, see Stearns, *Anxious Parents*; Hulbert, *Raising America*.

schools and homes, and the top-down authority of rabbis, is a hegemonic ideal; but it is neither a complete picture of the reality, nor the only voice heard in the popular literature. Haredi parents in the United States pay a great deal of money for the privilege of sending their children to private religious schools, and they are demanding customers. Like well-educated American parents of privately schooled children, Haredim have a great deal to say about the quality of their children's education. When existing schools do not satisfy the demanding criteria of these parents, the parents are at the forefront of moves to found new ones that more closely reflect their desires.[26] Parents wield a great deal of economic and political power in the Haredi educational system, and they can and do often use that power when they feel that it will benefit themselves or their children. The top-down model of parenting education, the doctrine of *da'at torah*, and the notion of strong rabbinic authority are ideological stances that may mask the social dynamics that in fact grant laypeople significant power.

Questioning the Top-Down Model

I will now examine two examples that question aspects of the hegemonic model. In both instances the writers agree that parents and schools ought to reinforce one another, but they question the top-down model. They suggest that in at least some cases parents may know better than educators and schools. In the first example, the female author of a parenting guide tries to balance criticism of the flaws in the educational system with concern for maintaining an image of agreement and co-operation. Bowing to the fear of discord and to the authority of educators, she indicates that it may be the task of parents and students quietly to sublimate their concerns and criticisms so as not to create the kind of overt conflict that could damage the mutual reinforcement between schools and homes.

In her guide to *Effective Jewish Parenting*—a work popular enough to have been published by three different Haredi publishers (Feldheim, Kest-Lebovitz, and Artscroll-Mesorah)—Miriam Levi considers how parents ought to react to conflict between students and inferior teachers. She

[26] More than once, while eavesdropping on adult conversation in the playground in Haredi neighbourhoods, I heard parents express their own dissatisfaction with aspects of their children's education. As one set of Haredi parents explained to me, when the numerous available schools did not match the criteria they had set for educating their own children, they became involved with a group of local parents to found a new school.

acknowledges that 'Teachers, sadly, are not always the perfect examples we would like for our children. Often they are far from the prescribed ideal.' Going on to note that 'poor teaching skills or poor control of the class' can lead to serious educational problems, she suggests that 'some of these [problems] can be solved by some tactical intervention on our [the parents'] part'. Still, she is deeply concerned about the dangerous consequences of conflict and tension. If problems are openly acknowledged and if conflict ensues, children might lose respect for teachers and the Haredi Judaism they represent. 'However dissatisfied we [parents] may be, we must never talk about it in front of our children, as this is likely to foster disrespect for their schools and teachers . . . No matter what difficulties he is having, the child must know that he has to respect his teachers, especially his Torah teachers.' Similarly, in conflict with a teacher 'the child should never see himself in the right. Certainly . . . he must never hear us berate the school or belittle the teacher.' Furthermore, when a student complains about a teacher, the parents cannot listen to the child before determining if the complaint qualifies as *lashon hara*, forbidden speech about others. Parents must be prepared to say, 'I'm so sorry [that] you're having a hard time, but you're not allowed to tell me *lashon hara*' about the teacher.'[27]

Levi is distanced from the top-down authority of the rabbis by virtue of being both a layperson and a woman. Indeed, she uses the term 'we' in this passage to refer to parents, highlighting her identification with the parents over and against the potentially problematic teachers. The passage from which the quotations in the previous paragraph are taken points to the ways in which families and homes may not be prepared simply to accept the advice and practice of educators and rabbis. Still, as a parent who sees co-operation between homes and schools as vital for Haredi educational success, Levi has too much invested in co-operation to risk undermining it by open criticism of the educational system. Ironically, then, this passage recommends both highlighting and concealing the flaws in schools, depending on the intended audience. Levi commends a bottom-up critique of schools and teachers by parents, arguing that education will improve if these criticisms are addressed tactfully, even as she repudiates any discussion of such matters in the presence of students. Adults, who are presumed to be already socialized into and committed to Haredi Judaism, can acknowledge tensions between homes and schools. Students, who are in

[27] Levi, *Effective Jewish Parenting*, 203–6.

the process of socialization, must not perceive the tension, since that perception might undermine the socialization process.

Not all writers are as cautious as Levi. In some contexts, parents voice their criticism of the educational system more strongly, even harshly, giving expression to bitterness, anger, and subversiveness. At times of educational and social crisis, when the community and its educational system are involved in collective introspection and self-evaluation, the image of unity between schools and parents may be undermined more boldly. Without denying the ideal of school–home harmony, parents and students sometimes openly attack the schools, overtly identifying flaws and failures in educators, rabbis, and schools.

In November 1999 the *Jewish Observer* devoted an entire issue to what it called 'Children on the Fringe . . . and Beyond'. The magazine was concerned with a perceived increase in dropout teenagers who reject communal norms and abandon Orthodox practice, falling into delinquency and substance abuse. The publication struck a raw nerve, and the publishers quickly ordered a second print run, making this issue the most widely circulated in the magazine's thirty years of existence.[28] A few months later, in March 2000, the magazine dedicated another issue to follow-up comment and readers' responses on the same theme. These two issues of the *Jewish Observer* are extraordinarily rich sources for examining many aspects of contemporary Haredi social and educational discourse, as writers and editors wend their way between self-criticism and self-confidence, fear of and embeddedness in general culture, conformity and individuality, concern and pride. In what follows, I focus on only one matter: relationships between schools and families.

These articles include discussion of the need for parents and schools to work together. One article, on 'Teamwork', argues that 'parents, students, the *rebbe* [male Torah teacher], the teacher, and the yeshiva' should work as a team. 'A fundamental concern of *chinuch* is whether the values and concepts taught in yeshiva are reinforced at home.'[29] Although this article emphasizes teamwork that moves in both directions—from schools to parents and vice versa—the discussion more often focuses on the top-down model, in which teachers and leaders dictate to parents how best to raise their children. 'Our *Rebbeim* suffer from the fact that many children who go

---

[28] See *Jewish Observer* (Mar. 2000), 6.
[29] Ibid. 46–9; also *Jewish Observer* (Nov. 1999), 29–34.

to *yeshivos* are the victims of the wrong *chinuch* received from their parents. We need desperately a school for parents to guide and advise them on how to *mechanech* [educate] their children.'[30] One contributor suggests that schools might refuse to accept any child whose parents do not participate in a school-run parenting class.[31]

Yet the editors also include the voices of parents and young people who undermine aspects of the discourse of co-operation and conformity. Some attack schools, in places quite severely, and call into question aspects of the top-down model. According to these authors, schools often fail to provide the warmth and individual attention that students need, and that, it is claimed, they receive at home. Schools are too institutionalized and too concerned with organizational reputation. This blinds them to the need to provide the kind of tender and individualized care that parents can.[32] One mother directs an uncompromising blast at her children's schools: 'The conventional mainstream yeshiva system nearly made rejects of my sons.'[33] Another parent makes the distinction between family and school more explicit.

At home I use many of those same [gentle and caring approaches] . . . to coax my son into attending early morning *minyan* [prayer services] and *shtaiging* [growing] in general. But, oh, what he's up against once he's in school, dealing with his 'frum' English teachers and administration. I feel like he comes home battle-scarred each day and I have to bandage his wounds.[34]

For these writers, it is the schools that fail to live up to the personalized care and loving role models provided at home.

The harsh tone and critical attitude of these attacks on schools differ from the more calm and controlled approach of Levi's parenting guide. Levi writes abstract and generalized advice about hypothetical situations in order to guide parents of otherwise normative young people who may be struggling with particular problems with particular teachers. In contrast, the parents writing to the *Jewish Observer* are describing the very specific and painful conditions of their own individual children, who have already abandoned so much normative practice. For these parents and their children, there is no longer an image of unity to maintain, and no possibility of convincing students that they ought to be satisfied with what the schools

---

[30] *Jewish Observer* (Mar. 2000), 15.   [31] Ibid. 48.
[32] *Jewish Observer* (Nov. 1999), 31, 39, 48; (Mar. 2000), 22, 26, 31, 37, 54, but cf. 20–1.
[33] *Jewish Observer* (Mar. 2000), 27.   [34] Ibid. 26.

offer. The young people have already demonstrated, through their delinquent behaviour, that they reject what both their schools and their homes stand for. Furthermore, the parents' letters appear in the context of a magazine issue designed to impress readers with the gravity of the situation. The angry rhetoric fits neatly with the *Jewish Observer*'s special 'crisis' issue, in contrast to the calm and controlled tone projected in the expert's parenting guide.

Even in the context of these parents' letters, however, there are ways in which the rhetorical defence of the schools and rabbinic leadership persists. The second parent quoted above encodes the notion that he or she is not criticizing the theory of ideal Jewish education as articulated by great rabbis. The letter is responding to 'the beauty of Rabbi Shlomo Wolbe's words'— Wolbe being a leading Jerusalem rabbi—which had been published in the first issue of the *Jewish Observer* on at-risk youth. The problem is not with the great rabbi or his ideas, but with the execution at the level of the school. Furthermore, it is not the Torah teachers in the school who cause the harm, but the '"frum" English teachers'. In addition, these particularly harsh criticisms of the school system, at least one of them expressed by a woman, are printed anonymously, in letters to the editor; evidently there are limits to how much criticism of the school system parents can voice openly, claiming to know better than educators and rabbis how to educate children. Parents, as noted, have a great deal of power in determining how schools function, but rhetorically it is preferable not to announce this power since it could undermine the ideology of strong rabbinic authority.

These limits on parental criticism are reflected in the contrast between the presentation of anonymous letters from parents, published relatively unobtrusively in the middle of the second issue, and that of the voice of a rabbinic leader, featured prominently on the inside cover of the first issue. Seemingly anticipating the parents' letters, the rabbi claims that

There are those who claim inaccurately and unfairly that fault lies with our heroic *mechanchim* [educators]. We reject that claim. Most *rabbe'im* and *morahs* [female teachers] are overworked, underpaid, underappreciated—and, yet, notably effective. Are they perfect? No. But they are far more devoted and caring than most of their detractors. And if all the critics of 'the system' would focus their energies on ensuring the financial viability and societal prestige of the *chinuch* profession in America, the face of Orthodox Jewry across the country would be unrecognizable.[35]

35 *Jewish Observer* (Nov. 1999), inside cover.

This passage acknowledges that teachers are imperfect, but argues that discussion of such imperfections is unwise and ineffective. The good that these imperfect teachers do far outweighs the bad. More importantly, it will be more effective to provide support for teachers than to question their relatively minor failings. In their presentation of this essay and the parents' letters the editors of the *Jewish Observer* seem to be making a statement that criticism of teachers, when voiced, comes merely from weak and anonymous parents, and has been pre-empted by the rabbinic elite.

Despite the fear of criticism and the marginalized status of some of the critical voices, there are important positive and constructive aspects to the tensions and criticisms. The relatively open and heated debate regarding issues of teenage dropouts did create increased awareness of the problem, and led to significant changes and innovations in Haredi education during the decade following the *Jewish Observer*'s first special issue on the subject. Several initial attempts have now been made to survey the extent of the problem.[36] New organizations and programmes, such as MASK (Mothers and fathers Aligned Saving Kids), have been founded to provide resources to struggling parents. Nefesh, the organization of Orthodox mental health professionals, has placed the problem of at-risk youth at the top of its agenda.[37] Furthermore, the Haredi community has created numerous programmes, like Camp Extreme and Agudat Yisra'el's Project YES, in addition to new schools and other educational institutions, to help these struggling youngsters find a place for themselves. Social support and psychological services, as well as drug counselling, rehabilitation centres, and other resources have become increasingly available within the Haredi community. Perhaps most importantly—though this is difficult to measure—parents and educators have become progressively more sensitive to signs of behaviour suggesting that children may be at risk and more astute and sensitive in their responses. While some suggest that this topic 'needs to be addressed, but not in the public arena', others, including the editors of the *Jewish Observer*, believe that 'these problems can and will be addressed' only if there is public debate about them.[38] Some aspects of Haredi rhetoric indicate that conflict weakens communal solidarity; other aspects point to ways in which this tension can be creative and constructive.

[36] See Danziger, *The Incidence of At-Risk Youth*; Metropolitan Coordinating Council on Jewish Poverty, *Teenage Orthodox Jewish Girls At Risk*.
[37] See Blumenthal and Russell (eds.), *Children in Crisis*; also Pelcovitz, *The At-Risk Adolescent in the Orthodox Jewish Community*.   [38] *Jewish Observer* (Mar. 2000), 7.

Conclusions

In this chapter I have examined some aspects of the relationship between Haredi popular discourse and the complex social reality of this devoutly religious group. As an isolationist community that feels threatened by the outside, Haredim view in-group harmony as critical for the maintenance of boundaries and for the construction of communal identity. Few institutions are so important in the effort to create such harmony as schools and families. The discourse in popular Haredi educational literature seeks continuity and conformity between homes and schools, and to a large degree the social reality reflects that ideal. By shoring up similarities between group members in terms of dress and practice, and by contrasting these similarities with differences, real and perceived, from outsiders, Haredi Judaism has had a great deal of success in maintaining itself in the seemingly challenging environment of contemporary America.

However, I have also painted a more nuanced picture of the popular discourse, one that reflects a more complex reality. Within the Haredi community, different sub-groups vie for political, social, and religious power, and popular literature is one location in which this power is negotiated. Rabbis and educators, voicing a hegemonic ideal, often call for a top-down model, in which cultural uniformity is created by laypeople learning from the leadership how to run their homes and raise their children. In reality, however, social and economic forces are at work that allow other voices to call this hegemonic authority into question. In an atmosphere of voluntary religious commitments, parents and laypeople in fact wield a great deal of economic and political power. They are the ones who choose schools and leaders for themselves and their families. At times they voice criticism of the educational leadership and challenge the top-down model that this leadership often advocates. At the same time, devout lay members of Haredi society desire in-group conformity no less than the leadership does as a way of maintaining the separatist socio-religious group of which they are members. Lay criticism of the leadership is balanced by acknowledgement of the necessity of conformity to rabbinic norms and of the cultural power of the rabbinic leadership.

Bibliography

Abramov, T., *The Secret of Jewish Femininity: Insights into the Practice of Taharat Hamishpachah* (Southfield, Mich., 1988).

Berger, P., *The Sacred Canopy* (New York, 1969).

Blumenthal, N., and S. Russell (eds.), *Children in Crisis: Prevention, Detection and Intervention* (New York, 1999).

Caplan, K., and E. Sivan (eds.), *Israeli Ḥaredim: Involvement without Assimilation?* [Haredim yisra'elim: hishtalvut belo temi'ah?] (Tel Aviv, 2003).

Danziger, Y., *The Incidence of At-Risk Youth in the Orthodox Jewish Community of Brooklyn, New York* (New York, n.d.).

Finkelman, Y., 'Haredi Isolation in Changing Environments: A Case Study in Yeshiva Immigration', *Modern Judaism*, 22/1 (2002), 61–82.

—— 'Medium and Message in Contemporary Ḥaredi Adventure Fiction', *Torah u-Madda Journal*, 13 (2005), 50–87.

—— 'Tradition and Innovation in American Ḥaredi Parenting Literature', in David Zisenwine (ed.), *Innovation and Change in Jewish Education* (Tel Aviv, 2007), 37–61.

Fishman, S. B., *Jewish Life and American Culture* (Albany, NY, 2000).

Friedman, M., 'The "Family–Community" Model in Haredi Society', *Studies in Contemporary Jewry*, 18 (2002), 186–97.

—— and S. Heilman, 'Religious Fundamentalism and Religious Jews: The Case of the Haredim', in M. Marty and R. S. Appleby (eds.), *Fundamentalisms Observed* (Chicago, 1991), 197–264.

Hakak, Y., *Spirituality versus Materiality in Lithuanian Yeshivas* [Ruḥaniut mul gashmiut bayeshivot halitaiot] (Jerusalem, 2005).

Helfand, J., 'Striving for Truth: Struggling with the Historical Critical Method', *Edah Journal*, 2/1 (2002), n.p.

Helmreich, W., *The World of the Yeshiva: An Intimate Portrait of Orthodox Jewry* (New Haven, Conn., and London, 1982).

Hulbert, A., *Raising America: Experts, Parents, and a Century of Advice about Children* (New York, 2004).

Jewish Observer, 32/9 (Nov. 1999), 33/3 (Mar. 2000), 39/1 (Jan.–Feb. 2006).

Kaplan, L., 'Da'as Torah: A Modern Conception of Rabbinic Authority', in Moshe Sokol (ed.), *Rabbinic Authority and Personal Autonomy* (Northvale, NJ, 1989), 1–60.

—— 'Hazon Ish: Ḥaredi Critic of Traditional Orthodoxy', in J. Wertheimer (ed.), *The Uses of Tradition* (New York and Jerusalem, 1992), 145–73.

Katz, J., 'Da'at Torah: The Unqualified Authority Claimed for Halakhists', *Jewish History*, 11/1 (1997), 41–50.

Kelemen, L., *To Kindle a Soul: Ancient Wisdom for Modern Parents and Teachers* (Southfield, Mich., 2001).

Levi, M., *Effective Jewish Parenting* (New York and Jerusalem, 1986).

Levy, B. B., 'Artscroll: An Overview', in M. L. Raphael (ed.), *Approaches to Modern Judaism* (Chico, Calif., 1983), 111–40.

—— 'Judge Not a Book by its Cover', *Tradition*, 19/1 (1981), 89–95.

—— 'Our Torah, your Torah and their Torah: An Evaluation of the Artscroll Phenomenon', in M. L. Raphael (ed.), *Truth and Compassion: Essays on Religion in Judaism* (Waterloo, Ont., 1983), 137–89.

Metropolitan Coordinating Council on Jewish Poverty, *Teenage Orthodox Jewish Girls At Risk: Study and Recommendations* (New York, 2003).

Pelcovitz, D., *The At-Risk Adolescent in the Orthodox Jewish Community: Implications and Interventions for Educators* (New York, 2005).

Schachter, J. J., 'Facing the Truths of History', *Torah u-Madda Journal*, 8 (1998/9), 200–76.

Silber, M., 'The Emergence of Ultra-Orthodoxy: The Invention of a Tradition', in J. Wertheimer (ed.), *The Uses of Tradition* (New York and Jerusalem, 1992), 23–84.

Sivan, E., 'The Enclave Culture', in M. Marty and R. S. Appleby (eds.), *Fundamentalisms Comprehended* (Chicago and London, 1995), 11–68.

Stampfer, S., *The Development of the Lithuanian Yeshiva* [Hayeshivah halitait behithavutah] (Jerusalem, 2005).

Stearns, P. N., *Anxious Parents: A History of Modern Childrearing in America* (New York, 2002).

Stolow, J., 'Communicating Authority, Consuming Tradition: Jewish Orthodox Outreach Literature and its Reading Public', in B. Meyer and A. Moors (eds.), *Religion, Media and the Public Sphere* (Bloomington, Ind., 2006), 73–90.

—— 'Transnationalism and the New Religio-Politics: Reflections on a Jewish Orthodox Case', *Theory, Culture and Society*, 21/2 (2004), 109–37.

Tatz, A., *Worldmask* (Southfield, Mich., 1995).

Wolpin, N. (ed.), *Timeless Parenting: Raising Children in Troubled Times—Understanding, Coping, Success* (New York, 2000).

FOURTEEN

The Impact of Community on Curriculum Decision-Making in a North American Jewish Day School

ELI KOHN

T HIS CHAPTER presents the first tentative results of a qualitative study of a curriculum development process undertaken with the Herzliah High School in Montreal. This is the largest community Jewish day school in that city, with two campuses in different locations. The results are tentative because the project is continuing, allowing for further refinement and enhancement of the curriculum and materials produced. The research focuses on the 'partnership model' of curriculum development in which administrators, teachers, parents, students, and curriculum experts create curriculum in a collaborative forum. This chapter examines how decisions are reached in this process, focusing on the following two central questions:

1. Who ultimately makes the curriculum decisions among those involved in the kind of partnership model described here?

2. What is the impact of 'the community' in the curriculum decision-making process?

Defining who and what we mean by 'the community' in the context of a Jewish community day school lies at the centre of my purpose in this chapter. I will show that although the curriculum development process described here began with a narrow view of the term 'community' as applying to the particular school where the project was situated, the research reveals the impact of the wider Jewish community on the process of decision-making. By 'the wider Jewish community' I refer to the influence of interest groups in the Jewish community that do not at present have any official connection to the school but exert influence over its educational direction.

Background and Context: Herzliah School

In October 2002, together with a colleague from Bar-Ilan University's Lookstein Centre for Jewish Education in the Diaspora, I visited the Herzliah School for a period of four days. The main goal of the visit was to review the school's Judaic studies programme, with particular attention to the high school, for the purpose of identifying possible changes in the syllabus.

In advance of our visit we received written information about the structure of the school, the make-up of the student population in each campus, the content of the Judaic studies programme at each grade level, the number of hours devoted to Judaic studies for each grade group, and details of the training and experience of Judaic studies teachers. This information helped us to put together our own initial picture of the school before the visit. During the visit we met with members of the school's board, Judaic studies teachers, groups of students from different grade levels, parents of current pupils, and graduates of the school. In addition, we conducted detailed discussions with the director of Judaic studies about the structure and content of the Judaic studies programme, examined curriculum materials, and visited a wide selection of Judaic studies classes.

According to the group's mission statement, the United Talmud Torahs of Montreal (of which Herzliah High School is a part) are independent, co-educational, private Jewish day schools offering a programme from kindergarten to secondary V (grade 11) to students from a diverse Jewish community encompassing a variety of philosophies, beliefs, and practices. As part of their mission, the schools wish to prepare their students to be knowledgeable and committed Jews who have a rich understanding of their Jewish heritage, values, traditions, and practices. The study and mastery of the Hebrew language, and its use as the language of instruction in all Judaic studies (through *Ivrit b'Ivrit*—the method of teaching Hebrew language and Jewish studies in Hebrew only), is central to the Herzliah High School's mission. In addition, it is an important part of the school's philosophy to foster a love for and attachment to Israel. It is interesting to note that the school has chosen not to define itself in relation to terms commonly used in the Jewish community such as Orthodox, modern Orthodox, traditional, community, or centrist. This has implications for the content of the Judaic studies curriculum and for the ensuing discussions about the school's identity to which I shall refer at the end of the chapter.

The high school has two campuses, one in the Snowdon neighbourhood and the other in St Laurent. The Snowdon campus has two sectors—a smaller English sector of 138 students and a larger French one of 193 students, making a total of 331. Herzliah High in St Laurent has a single, English, sector of 264 students. While all students are Jewish, they come from a wide range of Jewish backgrounds with varying commitments to Jewish tradition and practice. This diversity of Jewish backgrounds is also reflected in cultural differences between the large Sephardi community from which most students on the Snowdon campus are drawn and the almost exclusively Ashkenazi population in St Laurent. These differences came to the fore in our curriculum deliberations, especially with students, as will become clear below.

A substantial number of students join Herzliah for the high school years from feeder schools; these include not only Jewish schools such as Solomon Shechter and Akiva, but also a number of non-Jewish schools. The resulting annual influx of students with little or no Hebrew language facility or Jewish knowledge creates a challenge as regards the Judaic studies curriculum. The school has developed its Judaica programme to enable these students quickly to master basic skills and knowledge in Hebrew and to facilitate their speedy integration into the regular Judaic programme. Another important factor that has an impact on the school's population is the competition for new students between the various Jewish and non-Jewish schools in the city. Montreal is blessed with a rich diversity of day schools that offer their students an excellent education. This competition is healthy on the one hand, in that it forces schools to raise standards in order to attract students from a limited pool. On the other hand, the competition can create conflict, with various schools vying for the same students. In addition, there is a danger that in their desire to attract students schools may 'sell' themselves as being all things to all people. Such an attitude can impede the progress of curriculum definition, particularly in a community school, and can lead, as we shall see, to a lack of clarity as to the school's identity.

Herzliah's Judaic studies teachers come from a wide variety of religious and cultural backgrounds. Many are Israelis who feel comfortable with the school's all-Hebrew language policy, while some are locals who have themselves studied in the Herzliah system in their youth.

Theoretical Framework for the Process of Curriculum Development

Following our preliminary study of the school, the Lookstein Center was contracted to guide and facilitate the process of writing a comprehensive Judaic studies curriculum. Given the lack of professionally written curricula in many areas of Judaic studies in Jewish day schools worldwide,[1] we decided to embark on a process of designing a curriculum specifically suited to the needs of the Herzliah School.

Various theoretical models for the process of curriculum development were examined before formulating our partnership model. A 'top-down model', which was popular in North America and the UK during the 1960s and early 1970s and led to the development of so-called 'teacher-proof' curriculum, was considered first. In this model, the educational purposes of the school and the teacher play a subsidiary role to those of educational administrators and their discipline-based curriculum writers. The model aims to achieve high levels of fidelity between the conception and practice of curriculum change. However, research has shown the weaknesses of this approach.[2] Curricular innovations are invariably transformed between conception and implementation, with local forces, including the teacher and the school environment, playing a key role in this apparent 'slippage'. Curricular innovations fail to account for the social, economic, and cultural factors that limit and steer the possibilities for change in special contexts. For these reasons, other models were also considered in the Herzliah project. Two of them were school-based curriculum development and action research, both of which locate schools and teachers at the centre of curriculum reform efforts.[3] However, research has identified deficiencies in these approaches, too, showing that the curricula they generate are often insufficiently demanding, poorly resourced, and loosely assessed. Studies of teacher-initiated innovation report that even in these contexts 'slippage' occurs between the formal plan of the innovation and its implementation.[4]

---

[1] Schremer and Bailey, *Curriculum*, 69–81.
[2] Kirk and Macdonald, 'Teacher Voice and Ownership of Curriculum Change', 551–67.
[3] Kemmis and McTaggart, *The Action Research Planner*, 44–60.
[4] Fullan develops this thesis in his *The Meaning of Educational Change*.

At Herzliah we adapted a partnership model which involves collaborative relationships between school stakeholders, on the one hand, and external curriculum developers, on the other. Such partnerships involve, in Fullan's terms, 'across boundary collaboration'. For Fullan, curriculum change is multidimensional and is therefore most effective when both top-down and bottom-up partnerships are employed.[5]

Central to my work at Herzliah was the question of who exactly are 'school stakeholders' within the context of a Jewish community day school. I felt that we needed to refine Fullan's model to define more accurately the 'partners' in this process. Recognizing the important work of Schwab and Fox on the curriculum development process, I decided to integrate their ideas into my own work. Schwab argued that instead of focusing on the substance of a discipline, its basic concepts and findings, the curriculum should also, if not primarily, teach the syntax of a discipline, its methods of discovery and justification. In this enquiry-based curriculum, students learn the tools of investigation and critical assessment used by scholars to discover new knowledge.[6] Schwab recognized that designing such a curriculum is a complex process involving scholarly discussion and debate. This process, which he called 'curriculum deliberation', engages representatives of the essential elements of curriculum in dynamic discussions about how best to translate theory into practice. He called these elements 'commonplaces' and identified them specifically as teachers, students, subject matter, and milieu. Since there is no one right way to teach a discipline, the creation of practical pedagogic wisdom requires the 'art of the eclectic', an integrated application of the most compelling and relevant theories from both the subject matter itself and the study of how best to teach it. Schwab's student Lee Shulman was later to call this sort of practical wisdom 'pedagogic-content knowledge', the unique understanding that is accumulated in the teaching of an academic discipline.[7]

The Curriculum Development Process Adopted

The curriculum development process we adopted, therefore, was based on a synthesis of the theoretical underpinnings of Fullan's partnership model

[5] Ibid.
[6] Schwab, *Science, Curriculum and Liberal Education*. See also Fox, 'A Practical Image of "The Practical"'.
[7] Shulman develops this concept in his article 'The Practical and the Eclectic', 183–200.

and Schwab's 'commonplaces' concept. Accordingly, we invited representatives of the four commonplaces to be actively involved in deliberations on the curriculum. These included Judaic studies teachers led by the director of Judaica (teachers); student body representatives (students); Lookstein Center subject and curriculum experts (subject matter); and representatives of the school board (milieu). Learning from the curriculum development experiences of Holtz, we made explicit the central role of the curriculum expert within these deliberations.[8] First, in the role of curriculum expert, I acted as facilitator. This involved not only ensuring that the curriculum development process kept to its staged timetable and came to fruition, but also meeting with representatives of the commonplaces separately, given the difficulties of convening them all together. Through this form of 'shuttle diplomacy' (a term used in this context by Holtz), I aimed to ensure that the views of all the commonplaces were aired and understood by all parties. Second, beyond the role of facilitation, I trained the Judaic studies faculty in methodologies of curriculum development to enable them effectively to critique and provide feedback on the material produced. This was achieved by a series of professional development seminars which took place at the school over a number of years.

At the beginning of the project I presented participants with a four-stage model of curriculum development.

1. Definition of the school's 'ideal graduate'. Judaic studies teachers, student representatives, and school board members were all asked to determine this using the school's particular mission and ethos statement as their guide. This was organized under five headings:

   (a) beliefs and philosophies;

   (b) behavioural characteristics;

   (c) Jewish knowledge;

   (d) skills in Jewish learning;

   (e) general knowledge.

2. Identification of subjects to be taught and determination of the time to be allotted to each.

---

[8] Holtz, 'Making the Practical Real', 196–7.

3. Articulation of the overall goals of each subject in terms of content, skills, and values.

4. Definition of annual and semester goals for each subject in every grade level.

Stages 1 and 2 were completed in 2003. Stage 1 was particularly time-consuming since it involved a process of 'shuttle diplomacy' between the various commonplaces following the Holtz model described above. Stages 3 and 4 were undertaken through a series of twice-yearly workshops at the school, beginning in 2003 and continuing up to the academic year 2006/7. As the process developed, I took on more of a writing role, providing teachers with source material and detailed teacher guidelines. Student worksheets and materials were developed by the teachers themselves.

The Study

During the four years of the curriculum development process, interviews were held with representatives of the commonplaces to discover to what extent each group ultimately made curriculum decisions. Semi-structured interviews focused on the following three questions, the first two of which were posed at the beginning of this chapter:

1. Who, in your opinion, ultimately makes the curriculum decisions among those involved in the kind of partnership model we have developed?

2. What is the impact of 'the community' in the curriculum decision-making process?

3. What differences, if any, can you observe in the decision-making progress between the various four stages in the curriculum development process?

The interviews were semi-structured in that while these questions formed the basis for all of them, we allowed interviewees some flexibility in developing their responses.[9] The study involved interviews with the school's executive director, the director of Judaica, ten Judaic studies teachers, five board members, and ten students and school graduates.

---

[9] For more detailed references regarding the methodology of semi-structured interviews, see Seidman, *Interviewing as Qualitative Research*, and Spradley, *The Ethnographic Interview*.

Our study initially focused on stage 1 of the process—the definition of the school's 'ideal graduate'. This was the most fundamental stage on which all the others stages were to be based. We recognized that the specific identity of the school's 'ideal graduate' in terms of knowledge, skills, and values acted as the catalyst and engine for the curriculum development process.

The director of Judaica at the school was in no doubt about how the decision-making process operated, remarking in an interview: 'Yes, we do involve teachers and students in the process of defining our ideal graduate, but ultimately the ideal graduate is the vision of the school board, and a number of key figures in it. It is they who almost exclusively decide on the content of the "ideal graduate" model.'

In interviews with teachers, there was general concurrence with this perception. For example, a grade 9 Hebrew language teacher commented: 'There is general agreement among teachers as to the relative importance of Hebrew language in the "ideal graduate" model but much less agreement as to the place of Jewish tradition and practice. However, we assumed that ultimately it was the school board's decision anyway and so we did not fight over it.'

This view of the key role played by the board was also our perception as curriculum experts. Among the representatives of all the commonplaces, it was the 'milieu' or community representatives who had the strongest overt influence in the 'ideal graduate' deliberations. This is perhaps not surprising as it is the school board that sets school policy decisions. However, we also noted the very strong influence of the director of Judaica in the 'ideal graduate' decisions. A forceful proponent of *Ivrit b'Ivrit* studies, she had a strong influence in ensuring that this component of the curriculum remained a highly visible presence in the final 'ideal graduate' profile.

What was the role of the students in the curriculum decision-making process? Our research shows that they exercised a substantial influence on deliberations about the ideal graduate and ultimately on the final profile. They reflected, in fact, with some precision, divisions in the larger Montreal Jewish community which were revealed later in the process. In interviews with eleventh-grade students, held both as part of the initial curriculum deliberations and as part of this research, we discovered three major camps. In one camp, students emphasized the importance of learning about Jewish traditions and practices, while another camp focused on the value of acquiring competence in the Hebrew language, also giving a minor role to

Jewish law. In a third camp the focus was on learning about relevant issues, like 'Israel today' or 'Jewish communities throughout the world'; this camp saw Jewish traditions and practices, and proficiency in Hebrew, as far less important. It seems that these variant student views on the attributes of the 'ideal graduate' were representative of different community perspectives on these same issues. Some represent a more traditional Sephardi sector of the community that champions more Jewish practice in the school, while others seem to mirror perspectives charactereristic of other sectors of the community that wish to focus more on Zionism, Israel, or sociological issues within the Jewish people.

Our interviews with students shed great light on the differing perspectives within the community that influenced both the final 'ideal graduate' profile and the process by which it was reached. For, in order to satisfy the divergent perspectives concerning the 'ideal graduate' which arose from the student commonplace discussions, the school board attached a proviso to the final draft of the 'ideal graduate' profile about the importance of providing choice and offering electives in the curriculum so as to accommodate diverse community perspectives. Therefore, although overtly the school board ultimately made the ideal graduate decision, the students' deliberations had a major impact on board decision-making. The students' divergent perceptions, expressed in their deliberations about the Jewish identity of the ideal graduate, led the board to understand that electives needed to be provided in the new Judaic studies curriculum in order to reflect the variety of interests and religious affiliations within the community.

The extent of the student body's impact on decision-making about the curriculum is one of the more surprising findings of our research. While Schwab highlighted the 'student' as one of his four 'commonplaces', not much emphasis is commonly given among curriculum developers to the role of students as either consumers of, or decision-makers on, curricula.

When considering stages 2, 3, and 4 of the curriculum development process, interviewees expressed general consensus that in these stages the focus of decision-making moves from the school board to the Judaic studies faculty and curriculum experts. The board, having set guiding principles through the definition of the school's ideal graduate, put its trust in the school's professionals to define the curriculum details. In the words of one board member: 'The ideal graduate profile helped us in setting our target. We leave the details of the journey to the professionals.'

This does not mean that the board wished to bow out of the process. They asked to receive periodic written reports on the process of curriculum development. As curriculum experts, we also made regular presentations to the board on all our visits to the school. However, the details of stages 2, 3, and 4 were left mostly to the deliberations of the teachers and the curriculum experts. It is important to emphasize that students were consulted throughout the four-stage process and their opinions on the design and content of the new curriculum were actively considered. This was done both through interviews before the curriculum was designed at each year level and in continuing written evaluations after the curriculum was delivered.

In summary, our study shows that in determining the question of who ultimately makes curriculum decisions in a partnership model of curriculum development, the following two points need to be considered:

1. Distinctions should be made between different stages of the curriculum development process. The determination of the 'ideal graduate' profile in stage 1 is clearly in the domain of the school board, while decisions on stages 2–4 are largely the result of partnerships between the commonplaces of teachers and curriculum experts.

2. In our study, although the school board ultimately determined the 'ideal graduate' profile, its decisions certainly reflected wider community or 'milieu' concerns. As we learned both from our curriculum development process and from subsequent research, this occurred through the influence of the student 'commonplace' perspective. Students' divergent perspectives were seen by the board as reflecting authentic differences between elements of the wider Jewish community of Montreal, and this in turn had a practical impact on the need for curricular choice in the new Judaic studies curriculum.

Does the School Board Reflect the Community 'Milieu'?

The research study so far has been grounded in an assumption that in a community Jewish day school the school board is representative of the 'milieu' commonplace. However, as our study progressed we began to question this premise. Was the board the authentic representative of the wider Jewish community to which the school belonged? What in fact did Schwab himself mean by the 'milieu' or community environment? Looking back at Schwab, we found that he did not clarify this term precisely in his work. He writes: 'Curriculum is what is successfully conveyed to differing degrees to different students by committed teachers using the appropriate materials and actions . . . which are chosen for instruction after serious reflection *and communal decision* by representatives of those involved in the teaching of a specified group of students known to the decision makers.'[10] This 'communal decision' made by 'representatives' could refer to the school board, as was our original premise, but it is possible that the address for the community decision-makers lies elsewhere. Shulman and Fox, Schwab's students who interpreted and expanded on his work, did not clarify this issue further.

As the curriculum experts in this project, we interpreted the term 'milieu' as referring to the representatives of the school community, its board. But do board members in fact represent the wider Jewish community? As we will show, it seems that we may have applied too narrow a definition of the term 'milieu' as regards a Jewish community day school, attributing too much weight to the particular school community in view, as distinct from the general Jewish community of the city or even the collective of Jewish communities throughout North America.

This process of self-questioning arose out of a series of meetings that took place in 2005–6 between the school board and a group consisting of influential members of the wider Jewish community in Montreal. This group, with the tacit support of the Board of Jewish Education in Montreal, had been calling for curricular changes in the Judaic programme of the Herzliah School to bring it more into line with what they believed to be the needs of the Jewish community as a whole. As part of the study, a review of the written positions of key members of this group was made. The data from this review give us, we believe, valuable insight into the impact of community on curriculum decision-making.

In a series of statements Gil Troy, one of the most influential members of this group, made a strong case for being more flexible on the issue of *Ivrit b'Ivrit* in a community day school:

---

[10] Schwab, 'The Practical 4', 240 (emphasis added).

Parents and students of this generation are saying it loud and clear: they want more options, more flexibility, within the curriculum, in the approach to Judaism, in their school up and down and sideways. This requires a paradigm shift . . . Let's take the Ivrit B'Ivrit question as a case study. There is an issue of 'positive–negative' messaging, which goes far beyond PR towards the heart of an educational philosophy and approach to students. A 'Mechina' [*mekhinah*: preparatory] programme for students who 'cannot handle' the Hebrew in the present curriculum not only makes parents and students fear that those who opt for this approach will be stigmatized, but 'Mechina' means that that the goal is to prepare the students—for what? For getting up to par? More neutral language such as Hebraica/Judaica track, invites students to go down different paths . . . The school has to be willing to support students who for non-handicapped reasons choose not to study Ivrit B'Ivrit but nevertheless will be blessed with a top-notch Herzliah education and will contribute to the community in many ways.[11]

The argument is both forceful and compelling. A community leader is calling for a more open approach to *Ivrit b'Ivrit*, one of the pillars of the Herzliah Judaic curriculum. He argues that, by adopting such an approach, the school will be more inclusive of Jewish students across the community.

As regards greater flexibility about *Ivrit b'Ivrit* within the school, Troy's comments, and those of the group he represents within the Montreal Jewish community, have had a noticeable influence on curriculum decision-making in the school. In the 2006/7 academic year, the school resolved to launch an 'English-speaking' track called *Da'at* for the 2007/8 academic year. The *Da'at* programme was to be based on the same content as the school's regular *Ivrit b'Ivrit* curriculum but the textual sources presented were to be in Hebrew *and* English and the language of instruction was to be English. Students were to be 'recommended' to the *Da'at* programme by the school on the basis of their Hebrew-language capabilities.

It remains to be seen how many students will participate in the '*Da'at* option', and what impact this will have on the mainstream *Ivrit b'Ivrit* programme of the school. This is certainly a controversial move within the Montreal Jewish community which, unlike most Jewish communities in North America today, has a long tradition of *Ivrit b'Ivrit* as a matter of policy in a number of its day schools. Proponents of the *Ivrit b'Ivrit* policy maintain that the opening of a *Da'at* track endangers the established *Ivrit b'Ivrit* programme of the school.

[11] Troy, unpublished email correspondence with head of Herzliah school, Jan.–May 2005; published here with the writer's permission.

In further comments in the statement quoted above, Troy calls for more pluralistic practices in this traditional community day school. He writes: 'To build a school of excellence, which is also imbued with Jewish content, Jewish values and Jewish excitement, we would like to see . . . room for different kinds of Jewish expression, both by taking a more pluralistic approach to Jewish ritual, by building up prayer and holiday observance, [and] by finding more diverse Jewish role models or mentors.' Again, Troy offers a salient argument in support of pluralism in a community day school. By summer 2007, however, Troy's arguments regarding pluralism had had less of an impact on curriculum decision-making than his views on *Ivrit b'Ivrit*.

For curriculum developers the question, of course, is not the rights or wrongs of the argument. It is, rather: Who ultimately should make the decisions about curriculum in any particular school? Does Troy indeed express the sentiments of the Montreal Jewish community more authentically than the school board of Herzliah? Perhaps Troy's views are representative of an elite minority of Jews in the community. It can be stated with some certainty that many Sephardi community members would disagree strongly with a number of Troy's points. Who, then, speaks for 'the community' in a Jewish community day school? And, a more basic question still: Can there be in this context any such thing as *a* or *the* community for which any single group or individual can speak?

Conclusions and Further Questions for Consideration

Discussions continue within the Montreal Jewish community on these fundamental questions about the identity of their community school. Nevertheless, we can draw from this study a number of conclusions about the process of decision-making in a curriculum development process.

1. A synthesis of Fullan's partnership model and Schwab's commonplace concept can yield an effective process of curriculum decision-making in a community day school. Teachers express their sense of ownership of the curriculum produced when they are full partners in the process of arriving at it. In addition, students and board members have much to contribute to curriculum deliberations, as Schwab envisaged in setting out his concept of the four commonplaces.

2. The four-stage curriculum process, as described above, serves as a useful framework for applying the Fullan–Schwab model. It offers opportunities for meaningful curriculum discussions and interplay between various sections of the school community, allowing a range of voices to be heard both as a prelude to curriculum design and in partnership during the process itself.

3. While the formulation of the 'ideal graduate' profile clearly involves the active involvement of all four commonplaces, stages 2, 3, and 4 of the process are, more realistically, confined in large part to the teacher and subject matter commonplaces (the second represented in our case by the curriculum expert), albeit with significant student input.

4. While the determination of the 'ideal graduate' ultimately rests with the 'milieu', represented in our model by the school board, students can offer critical insights into divergent thinking within the community. In this case, it was these very reflections that actually had the greatest impact on board decisions.

5. The question of whether the school board in a community day school authentically represents the views of the wider Jewish community in the city seems to be moot. In this instance, the school seems subject to influence by trends in Jewish community day school education even beyond the confines of its own (Canadian) multilingual culture. This is both a troubling and a promising conclusion, and ought to be examined further. It raises the fundamental question: Which community (or communities) do Jewish community day schools in fact represent?

Bibliography

Floden, R. E., 'Reforms that Call for Teaching More Than You Understand', in N. C. Burbules and D. T. Hansen (eds.), *Teaching and its Predicaments* (Denver, Colo., 1997), 11–28.

Fox, S., 'A Practical Image of "The Practical"', *Curriculum Theory Network*, 10/49 (1972), 45–57.

Fullan, M., *The Meaning of Educational Change* (New York, 1997).

Holtz, B., 'Making the Practical Real: The Experience of the Melton Research Center in Curriculum Design', *Studies in Jewish Education*, 6 (Jerusalem, 1992), 196–7.

Kemmis, S., and R. McTaggart, *The Action Research Planner* (Geelong, Victoria, 1988).

Kirk, D., and D. Macdonald, 'Teacher Voice and Ownership of Curriculum Change', *Journal of Curriculum Studies*, 33/5 (2001), 551–67.

Schremer, O., and S. Bailey, *Curriculum: Real Teachers in Focus. A Study in Jewish Education* (Ramat Gan, 2001).

Schwab, J., 'The Practical 4: Something for Curriculum Professors to Do', in *Curriculum Inquiry*, 13/2 (1983), 240–8.

—— *Science, Curriculum and Liberal Education* (Chicago, 1982).

Seidman, I., *Interviewing as Qualitative Research: A Guide for Researchers in Education and the Social Sciences* (New York, 1998).

Shulman, L. S., 'The Practical and the Eclectic: A Deliberation on Teaching and Educational Research', *Curriculum Inquiry*, 14/3 (1984), 183–200.

Spradley, J., *The Ethnographic Interview* (New York, 1979).

FIFTEEN

Ideological Commitment in the Supervision of Jewish Studies Teachers

Representing Community

MICHAL MUSZKAT-BARKAN AND ASHER SHKEDI

THE COMMUNITY is a fundamental element of any educational process. Educational processes are motivated by ideological views that relate to a certain community. In teacher supervision the ideologies of teachers and supervisors, and their respective communal loyalties, find expression. This chapter recounts a study that set out to define the communities represented by the partners in the supervisory process, to characterize the nature of individuals' commitments to these communities, and to identify the influence of those commitments on the supervision of Jewish studies teachers in Israel. The ensuing discussion of the ideological aspects of supervision conferences may enrich our understanding of the processes of professional development undergone by teachers, and also enhance in-service teacher supervision.

Why Examine Ideology in Teacher Supervision?

'Pupil', 'teacher', 'curriculum content', and 'community' are the fundamental elements underlying curriculum planning and teaching. Those involved in curriculum planning need to understand the content of the instruction, but—no less importantly—they also need to understand the environment in which the learning is taking place: in other words, they need to have an awareness of the socio-cultural world of the students and the community within which those students are growing up. At the same time, they also need to be conscious of the background of the teachers—and particularly the biases that they bring with them as part of their own education. However, even assuming that curriculum planners are aware of the communal affiliations of the students and the ideological biases of the teachers, it is not clear how this awareness is translated into curriculum planning and teacher training.

This research was partially funded by a grant from the Memorial Foundation for Jewish Culture.

The process of curriculum planning represents a meeting between teachers, student population, and specific teaching material, within the framework of a certain community or society. The educator's perception of each of these elements is, by definition, subjective, and represents his or her vision and analysis of reality, and the social context within which he or she understands the educational situation. Ideology is an important element in every individual's evaluation of reality and personal commitment, as well as expressing his or her social affiliation.[1]

Ideology provides the individual with a map of social reality, creating a collective consciousness among the members of cultural groups.[2] Thus, according to this approach, any cultural discourse expresses ideology, which represents reality for the members of that society.[3] We must therefore assume that the ideology of the collective influences the structuring of educational processes. In the process of supervision of Jewish studies teachers there is an encounter between teachers and teacher supervisors, each with his or her own ideology. Hence the encounter is, inevitably, also an encounter between the ideologies of its participants.

The purpose of the study described in this chapter was to examine the connection between the ideologies of teachers and supervisors, on the one hand, and the ideology of the communities to which they belong, on the other. The study was based on research into processes of teacher supervision in Jewish studies in Israeli schools.[4] One of the prominent findings in the research concerned the prominent place of the collective—'society' or 'community'—in the ideologies of the partners to the supervision process. However, we found that the collective that is represented in the processes of supervision is not identical across teachers and supervisors. This chapter presents and discusses these findings.

Ideology in Education

The influence of ideologies in education is sometimes treated with suspicion, based on the concern that ideology in education may serve interests that are foreign to the educational ideal of an autonomous graduate, represent a means of indoctrination, and prevent the development of

---

[1] Althusser, *On Ideology* (Heb.), 70; Lamm, *In the Turbulence of Ideologies* (Heb.), 59.
[2] Geertz, *The Interpretation of Cultures* (Heb.), 204.
[3] Schremer, *Education between Radicalism and Tolerance* (Heb.), 121–4.
[4] Muszkat-Barkan, 'Ideological Encounters' (Heb.)

independent, critical students. In the training of teachers, too, ideology is sometimes perceived as a threat to the acquisition of objective knowledge.[5]

However, along with consciousness of the dangers inherent in ideological indoctrination, there is also an awareness of the unavoidable influences of ideology on the educational endeavour, and its contribution towards the orientation of the goals of that process. Ideology is present, whether consciously or unconsciously, at the foundation of every curriculum.[6] At the basis of every curriculum lies some perceived need, either explicit or implicit, and curricula serve as a response to the problems and needs of the individual and the community as identified by those responsible for developing them.[7] The curriculum expresses the prevailing beliefs held by the community with respect to what is worthy of being studied, and for what purpose. Therefore, ideology influences the setting of goals, the content of instruction, and the approved methods of teaching.[8]

Ideology in education, then, influences the curriculum and its instruction, as well as any understanding of the nature of the graduate whom the educational system seeks to produce.[9] Ideology influences the 'what' that is being taught (the content) as well as the 'how' (the pedagogic aspects, including goals, methods of instruction, and methods of learning). The exposure of the ideological aspects of the curriculum facilitates conscious choice and an assessment of their suitability in relation to the goals of the school and the views of the community.

Education that is cut off from its environment and community creates learning that is lifeless and impersonal, in contrast with learning that is connected to the community and to life itself. It is therefore important to understand the use of the concept of 'community' in order to discern its influences on the perception of ideologies in education.

'Community' in the Context of School Values

The development and use of the concept of 'community' in education research is related to the development of how schools and their relationship with their environment are perceived. Sergiovanni and others use the con-

---

[5] Apple, *Ideology and Curriculum*, 58–9; Schremer, *Education between Radicalism and Tolerance* (Heb.), 144–5.　　　　　　　　　　　　　　[6] Jackson, 'Conceptions of Curriculum'.

[7] Cohen, 'Proposals for the Arrangement of Teaching Jewish Thought' (Heb.), 76–9.

[8] Alpert, 'Concepts and Ideas in the Study of Curricula' (Heb.), 15–19.

[9] Muszkat-Barkan, 'Standards for Evaluating' (Heb.), 151–5; Alpert, 'Concepts and Ideas in the Study of Curricula'.

cept of 'community' with a view to analysing the crisis in which schools find themselves and to propose directions for reforms aimed at rehabilitating them.[10] In so doing, Sergiovanni uses the distinctions drawn by Toennies (1877–1957) between *Gemeinschaft*—community, assembly—and *Gesellschaft*, which is a pragmatic association that may be characterized as an organization or business partnership.

Various proposals for school reform have as their objective the strengthening of the communal dimensions of the school, and a change of metaphor for the school from 'organization' to 'community'.[11] These proposals are based on the notion that the main problem facing schools is a weakening of such values as unity, co-operation, social equality, and goodwill, identified with *Gemeinschaft*, as opposed to the values associated with *Gesellschaft*, such as efficiency, achievement, and accountability. The proposed new direction is aimed at raising the level of co-operation between teachers, parents, and students at the school by creating a 'community of mind' that is committed to core values. Some regard community as a curricular resource and view the life of the community in which the school is situated as part of the proper core content for curricular development.[12]

There is a duality in the use of the term 'community'. It is used by some authors to describe the interaction and interdependence of the environment and the school,[13] and by others to analyse the reality within the school.[14] In fact, if the partners in the educational process are ranged in a number of social circles, the school community is only one of them. Others include the residential environment, the synagogue, family affiliations, etc. An examination of separate and overlapping loyalties to these communities in the encounter between teachers and other partners in the educational process (principals, supervisors, superintendents, parents, students) may contribute to an understanding of how ideology influences the educational endeavour.

Ideologies of Teachers and Supervisors in Jewish Education

Educators are on the 'front line' when it comes to practical educational decisions within the school. Thus, teachers and teacher supervisors in the field

[10] Sergiovanni, *Building Community*, 5–14; Merz and Furman, *Community and Schools*, 18–20.
[11] Sergiovanni, *Building Community*, 13–14.   [12] Townsend, *Effective Schooling*, 112–13.
[13] Schwab, 'Translating Scholarship', 3–4.   [14] Sergiovanni, *Building Community*, 4.

of Jewish studies are required to decide on the nature of the connection between Jewish sources and the modern world in which they themselves, and the school's students, live. Teachers need to adapt the content of instruction to their students within the framework of the school, the community, and the society in which the educational process is taking place. This task gives rise to a great number of practical dilemmas.[15]

Teachers' decisions are based on a priori views which influence the choice of materials for instruction and the ways in which these materials (often texts) should be analysed and their relevant elements addressed. In this way, Jewish studies teachers express, through their practical pedagogic choices, ideological views.[16]

Several commentators, including Cohen and Shkedi and the authors of the 'Am Olam' report, note the central role of the teacher's world-view in moulding the curriculum.[17] Teachers represent a vital link in the planning and implementation of learning materials. Some have therefore proposed that the experience and world-views of the teachers be placed at the centre of the process of curriculum development.

Supervision of teachers for the purpose of curriculum development focuses on planning or reorganizing the curriculum for use in the classroom. Overseeing the development and implementation of the curriculum is perceived as the main contribution of teacher supervision, and represents the principal yardstick for evaluating the professionalism of supervisors.[18]

We have described above how ideology influences the choice of instruction content and teaching methods. Teaching and teachers' supervision are no more devoid of ideology. Various scholars have called for an examination of the role of supervision in exposing and clarifying teachers' ideologies, in order to build up their pedagogic knowledge and to improve their professional abilities, but there is a dearth of information from the field as to how the ideologies of teachers and supervisors affect the actual supervision

[15] Shkedi, 'Scholars' Theories about Teaching' (Heb.), 269.
[16] Muszkat-Barkan, 'Standards for Evaluating ' (Heb.), 161–3; Cohen, 'Jewish Thought' (Heb.), 181–2.
[17] Cohen and Shkedi, The Intent to Kill, 16–17; Goren', 'People and the World' (Heb.), 24–7.
[18] Glickman, Supervision of Instruction, 356–8; Oliva and Pawlas, Supervision for Today's Schools, 284.

process.[19] Nevertheless, it is clear that teachers and supervisors act within a context that is embedded in ideologies.

Teachers and Teacher Supervisors

In Israel, the supervisors appointed by the ministry of education are meant to nurture teachers and help them grow professionally while, at the same time, helping them implement the curriculum.[20] The planning of study units on, for example, the Bible, Jewish philosophy, prayer, or festivals, is the heart of the joint activity of supervisors and Jewish studies teachers. These planning processes are embedded in ideological influence. Researchers point to the supervisor's responsibility to ensure that teachers discern the influence of cultural structures that are perceived as self-evident in the learning environment of the classroom, and to their role in helping teachers develop sensitivity to the influence on the students of that which teachers take for granted in the contexts of culture, gender, and values.[21]

Ideology in Jewish Education

Ideologies pertaining to the connection between Judaism and Zionism have influenced—and continue to influence—the moulding of Jewish education within the state education system in Israel at various levels.[22] The translation of Jewish sources into classroom instruction requires teachers to grapple with and take decisions on value-related, social, and normative questions.[23] The discussion about what it is proper to teach within the sphere of Judaism, and the ways of translating a classical, traditional world into modern, secular language, covers ideological shades that range between continuity and replacement, criticism and identification.

The 'communal' element, in the context of the school, may therefore refer to various 'collectives', such as 'secular Israeli society', or 'the school community', or the 'synagogue community'. The ideology of each of these

---

[19] Britzman, 'Cultural Myths', 442–3; Muszkat-Barkan, 'Ideological Encounters' (Heb.), 48; Gudmundsdottir, 'Values in Pedagogical Content Knowledge', 50–1.

[20] Ministry of Education, Regulations of the Director-General; Rubinstein, *The Supervisor as a Professional* (Heb.), 43–4.

[21] Bowers and Flinders, *Culturally Responsive Teaching and Supervision*, 5–7.

[22] See e.g. Lamm, 'The Ideological Bases of Jewish Studies' (Heb.), 323; Goren, 'People and the World' (Heb.), 9.

[23] Cohen, 'Jewish Thought' (Heb.), 164–5; Fox, 'The Art of Translation', 266–70.

collectives can serve as a guiding force in the structuring of educational processes. Thus these processes may be influenced by the heterogeneous ideological backgrounds of the partners to the educational process. In the absence of open discussion of these issues, the influence of the ideologies of supervisors and of teachers in their joint work is relegated to their implicit presence in the processes of teacher supervision.[24]

The goal of the study described here was to describe the ideologies of teachers and supervisors as reflected in the processes of supervision of Jewish studies teachers, and thereby to examine the influence of the communities represented by teachers and supervisors respectively in the processes of supervision of Jewish studies teachers.

How the Study Was Conducted

Research Methods

The research was carried out using a qualitative constructivist methodology, its objective being an in-depth description of the phenomenon under examination, leading to the construction of a 'grounded theory'.[25] The study sought to understand the subjects of the research, through their language, their views, and their interpretation of the unique reality within which they are active.[26] The research was based on observations and on the subjects' comments on incidents that took place over the entire course of the supervision process. Our assumption was that relying on the participants' own accounts of incidents that took place would elucidate educational dilemmas and considerations, and thus deepen our ability to research the professional knowledge of the teachers and supervisors. In a study of this type, the testimonies of the subjects are regarded as facts.[27] Accordingly we constructed our understanding of the reality in question on the basis of both dialogue with the participating teachers and supervisors and the interpretation of the researcher, who inevitably also approaches the research in a subjective way.[28] An in-depth understanding of the incidents in question will aid in attaining the ability to generalize.

---

[24] Cochran-Smith, 'Editorial', 3–5; Grundy and Hatton, 'Teacher Educators' Ideological Discourses', 7–10.   [25] Strauss and Corbin, 'Grounded Theory', 278–80.

[26] Tsabar ben-Yehoshua, *Qualitative Research* (Heb.), 87; Shkedi, *Words of Meaning* (Heb.), 65.

[27] Connelly, foreword to Ben-Peretz, *Learning from Experience*, p. xvii.

[28] Shkedi, *Words of Meaning* (Heb.), 56–8.

Research Population

The researcher accompanied four Jewish studies supervisors and ten teachers who work with them. Each supervisor works with two or three teachers. The research followed the supervisory meetings between supervisors and teachers over the course of about a year, with between two and four meetings being observed for each supervisor.

Of the supervisors participating in the study, two represented the ministry of education's department for the supervision of Bible instruction, one represented the department for the supervision of Jewish philosophy instruction, and one represented the Tali Foundation.[29] The ten teachers who participated in the study ranged in teaching experience from one year to twenty years.

Data Collection and Documentation

The data collection included an in-depth interview of between one and two hours with each of the participants, and observations of supervisory meetings (between two and four for each supervisor), each lasting approximately ninety minutes. Following the observation, a second interview of between one and three hours was held with each of the participants. In total, some eight hours of interview time were devoted to each supervisor, and between two and four hours of interview time to each teacher.

In order to track the ideologies of the interviewees it was necessary to become familiar with their lifestyles and the backgrounds in which they had grown up.[30] Therefore, each participant was asked in the first interview to describe his or her personal history and the family and educational background in which he or she had grown up, with special attention to the matter of Jewish lifestyle. Since the participants did not always express their world-view directly, we sought to trace their ideologies through their comments on the fundamental elements of education, and especially through their attitudes towards the content of their teaching.[31]

[29] The Tali Foundation is an educational body founded by the Schechter Institute for Jewish Studies. It provides pedagogic and educational guidance to Israeli public schools that choose to intensify Jewish studies. Today the programme is run jointly by the Ministry of Education and the Tali Foundation (see Ministry of Education, Director-General's Circular 9(A)).

[30] Elbaz Lubish, 'Narrative–Biographical Research' (Heb.), 145.

[31] Alpert, 'Concepts and Ideas in the Study of Curricula' (Heb.), 23–4; Hillocks, *Ways of Thinking*, 43.

All of the interviews and observations were recorded and transcribed word for word.

Analysis of the Data

The data were processed using an analytical method aimed at giving significance and interpretation to, as well as generalizing, the phenomenon under examination.[32] Following transcription of the recorded interviews, an analytical tool was created through a process of multi-stage encoding. The analysis was based, first and foremost, on the interviews, with the understanding that only the explanation of those who had experienced the phenomenon under examination—in this case, the teachers and supervisors—could help in interpreting it.[33] On the basis of existing research, coupled with our analysis of the interviews with the supervisors and teachers, we arrived at several 'keys' that helped us identify the educational and cultural ideologies of the teachers and supervisors:

1. Direct reference by the interviewees to their world-views and their educational vision. This was expressed in conversation about their goals, aspirations, beliefs, and perceptions of what is desirable.[34]

2. Indirect references to their world-views and visions by the participants, during the course of the supervisory meetings and in interviews, in descriptions of activities, and in interpretations of supervisory meetings. Embedded in these references were diagnoses of the reality that must be addressed,[35] hidden assumptions concerning that which is desirable, and perceptions of what is considered self-evident.[36]

3. Manifestations of enthusiasm and a sense of commitment towards certain content.[37]

4. Commitment to a certain collective,[38] whether personal or institutional, and the identification of points of inner tension between such commitment and the perception of instructional content, as well as tensions

---

[32] Gvaton, 'Field-Grounded Theory' (Heb.), 208–9.
[33] Geertz, *The Interpretation of Cultures* (Heb.), 17–18.
[34] Nisan, '*Educational Identity*', 12–16; Hansen, *The Call to Teach*, p. xi.
[35] Lamm, *In the Turbulence of Ideologies* (Heb.), 72.
[36] Grundy and Hatton, 'Teacher Educators' Ideological Discourses', 7–8.
[37] Nisan, '*Educational Identity*', 19–22.   [38] Lamm, *In the Turbulence of Ideologies* (Heb.), 77.

observed during the course of the supervisory conferences between teachers and supervisors surrounding their respective commitments to the collective(s). These tensions led, at times, to decisions of a consciously ideological nature.[39]

In a multi-stage process of encoding and analysis, the findings were examined and a grounded theory was constructed.[40]

Findings of the Study

From the various categories that were created during the process of analysing the interviews and observations it appears that the ideologies of the teachers and supervisors may be characterized as 'lived ideologies'.[41] This type of ideology is not necessarily coherent, and finds expression in a combination of perceptions, ideas, and beliefs, along with behaviours arising from the personal and collective experience. We found the ideologies of the teachers and supervisors to be characterized by a sense of profound commitment. This sense of commitment is reflected in a desire for action and in the yardsticks by which they assess their educational work.

Ideology serves as a prism through which the teachers and supervisors understand the Jewish content of the Jewish studies that are taught, and through which they define their educational objectives and the needs of the students in relation to the community.

What Is the Community to which the Teachers Are Committed?

In this study we found significant differences between the communities to which the teachers and supervisors are committed. The teachers regard themselves as being committed, first and foremost, to the local community—that is, to their students. The students, their beliefs, and their attitude towards Jewish sources are factors that influence the teachers' decisions both in their instruction and in their sense of mission. The teachers are aware of the students' attitudes towards the study material, and they feel responsible for the nature of the connection that will be created between the students and the Jewish sources.

---

[39] Billig et al., *Ideological Dilemmas*, 45–6.

[40] Strauss and Corbin, 'Grounded Theory', 273–4; Gvaton, 'Field-Grounded Theory' (Heb.), 208–9.   [41] Billig et al., *Ideological Dilemmas*, 34.

Yafah: [Sometimes I see] lack of interest on the part of the children. When it seems to me that there's a lack of interest . . . I have a feeling of—what am I doing here?

The students serve as a yardstick for Yafah's self-evaluation of the educational endeavour.

Ayalah, a Bible teacher, feels personally responsible for creating interest in the material, and for making a positive and stirring connection between the students and the sources. She sees herself as mediating between the Bible and the students. Much of the students' attitude towards the Bible is dependent on her:

Ayalah: To teach ninth-grade kids 'prophecy'—it's also a difficult age, it's an age of transition, and they go on afterwards to matriculation—so to what extent can you give them experiential lessons?

Yehudit, another Bible teacher, feels responsible for the consolidation of the students' identity and world-views. She sees a direct connection between what she says in the classroom and her attitude towards the Bible, and the moulding of her students' world:

Yehudit: I don't want the child to say, heaven forbid, from now on, God is wrong . . . in my class there are at least three students about whom I feel that what I say in class is 'holy' . . . So I'm really careful with what I say.

It is not only the students sitting in the classroom who concern the teachers. The teachers also see the students in the context of their families, their parents, and the neighbourhood in which the school operates. They ask themselves: Which of the messages that are conveyed in class reach the students' homes? Do these messages support the values of the students' families, and the connection of these families with Judaism, or do they undermine the messages of the home, or the lifestyle at home?

Na'amah (a Tali teacher) wants to convey messages to the home via the students. It is important to her that these messages are acceptable at home, too:

Na'amah: I aspire [. . . that] it won't just stay in the classroom, because I also think that Judaism must reach the home, otherwise we've done nothing. Because even [for] a child who thinks that it's detached from the home, it'll alienate him all over again and give him an even worse feeling, because what he's told at home and what he's told at school is completely confusing. If the connections are there then there will always be links, even in the smallest things.

Yehudit (a Bible teacher) wants extra caution to be exercised with regard to the messages that are conveyed in the classroom, since they have echoes at home:

Yehudit: Once a kid came and said to me, 'Our Bible teacher at [my previous] school said . . . that all the stories that are written in the Torah—none of it happened, and it's all fairy tales.' I'm sure she didn't say exactly that, but this child went home and said that. Oh, and he said, 'My mother said that the Bible teacher obviously never studied, and she [herself] tells fairy tales.' . . . And this was a child who came from a religious home . . . so we also have to be careful.

What Is the Collective to which the Supervisors Are Committed?

Despite differences in their personal ideologies and, as a result, in their attitudes towards the Jewish content of the teaching, the supervisors shared a clearly manifest and absolute commitment to the ideologies and systems on behalf of which they had been sent to the schools. The supervisors for Bible studies held a profound commitment to the superintendent of Bible studies and to the curriculum of the ministry of education, with its principles and messages. The supervisor representing Tali was committed to what she defined as the 'spirit of Tali', expressed in the Tali Foundation's world-view and educational programmes. The supervisor for Jewish thought was committed to 'the subject matter'—Jewish thought as he perceived its principles, its spirit, and its uniqueness.

The supervisors' sense of ideological commitment and enthusiasm towards these systems serves as a sort of inner guide and obligation.

Sigal, supervisor for Bible studies: The national superintendent for Bible studies is a pioneer! She has vision! Her vision and my vision are very similar, and her vision was actually my reality as a teacher, and my reality also as supervisor . . . It is really well suited to my way of teaching and to my perception of teaching.

Galit, supervisor at Tali: I am simply inspired by it . . . I feel that there are tangible results . . . When I saw the scope of the Tali school, I felt that I had won the jackpot . . . I felt that [it is] something with which I am in such ideological agreement . . . And therefore everything that is connected to Tali . . . I really believe in it.

All the supervisors who participated in this study believe that they are not only carrying out their mission properly, but also faithfully reflecting the values of the educational system in which they are active, and educating the teachers to internalize its values and to teach in its spirit. Perceptions that are different from those acceptable to the system are seen as unsuitable. Each of the supervisors regards him- or herself as part of a greater entity, as an emissary of which he or she appears before the teachers. It is within this framework that the supervisors relate to the teaching profession and express sensitivity to the status and image of the profession in the eyes of the teachers and the students.

Differences in Ideologies between Supervisors and Teachers: The Role of Commitment to the Collective

The supervisors are committed to the ideologies of the educational systems that they represent. The system serves the supervisors as justification for the choice of ideology that they express. In this way the wider community is represented in the professional discourse via the requirements and standards that are set in the curriculum and by the supervisory body.

Sigal, supervisor for Bible studies: There is a discrepancy between the requirement for critical positions in state education and the traditional positions of the teachers.

All four supervisors took the view that they must guide the teacher to present the subject 'correctly', and thereby to represent the ideology of the system:

Amnon, supervisor for Jewish thought: What can happen is that, for example, he [the teacher] forgets for a moment that he is supposed to be representing Jewish thought, not [general] philosophy. And there are differences between the manner in which it is necessary or proper to teach philosophy within Jewish thought.

I cannot dictate that to him; he's the teacher, and he's in control. He will do whatever he pleases in the classroom. But I want to give some sort of counterweight so that something of what I am trying to say will penetrate and eventually find its way to the students.

This loyalty on the part of the supervisors sometimes causes tension in supervisory encounters. Tension arises when the teachers do not agree with the ideological world-view that is represented by the supervisors, and when teachers have a sense that the supervisors are not sensitive to the local school community:

Na'amah, Tali teacher: I have the feeling that Galit [the supervisor] still hasn't connected with the spirit of the school—that we aren't really in the religious spirit; she's very religious, and she brings it in her own style . . . She shouldn't come with what she has to give, but rather with what we want to receive.

Yafah, teacher of Jewish thought: Let each [teacher] teach what he really believes in and loves, and find the personal path; the supervision should help you to allow yourself to choose the materials that are suited precisely to you.

According to the teachers, the supervisory process must allow them to define their own personal approaches to teaching their subjects. Thus, lack of recognition on the part of the supervisors of the influence of teachers' ideologies on teaching may obstruct the supervisory process.

Conclusions

The Presence of Ideology in Supervisory Conferences

Our findings show that the ideology of each participant in the process—teachers and supervisors alike—is an active presence in supervisory conferences. These ideologies influence the ways in which the supervisors promote certain instructional materials, as well as the ways in which they interpret them.[42] Dominant among the ideological motivations that are present in the encounter is a concept of 'community'. We found that the attitudes of teachers and supervisors alike towards a certain collective—whether personal or organizational—influences their ideological worldview and determines the yardsticks by which they mould and judge their educational work.

Teachers' and Supervisors' Different Ideological Commitments

Commitment to 'community' is part of the ideology of both teachers and supervisors. However, we found that the two parties are ideologically committed to different communities. We may make use of the terms *Gemeinschaft* and *Gesellschaft* to describe the differences between the communities which the teachers and supervisors respectively have in mind.

The supervisors identify with the ideology of the systems they represent in their work with schools, and express this ideology in the supervisory

---

[42] Muszkat-Barkan, 'Ideological Encounters' (Heb.), 31–4.

process, out of a sense of identification and mission. They expect the teachers to be loyal to the Jewish educational ideology of this external system within the framework of their classroom teaching. This expectation may be viewed as emanating from the values of *Gesellschaft*, that is, commitment to a framework that is external to the school in the structuring of the study curriculum and the desired materials for instruction in Jewish studies. According to this perception, every school, every teacher, and every class is obliged to implement in full the ideology that is dictated from above.

The teachers, in contrast, relate to the local community within the framework of *Gemeinschaft* values. They look at their students and feel responsibility towards them. The teachers express commitment to the moulding of the students' world-view, and to the creation of continuity between the students' homes and the school, including the Jewish content that is studied there. The teachers are involved in the messages that they are conveying to the students and to the students' families, and try to protect the students from ideological elements which, to the teachers' minds, would be difficult for the students and their families to accept.

Despite the teachers' sensitivity and their commitment to the local community, the dialogue they engage in with parents around instruction of Jewish content does not necessarily take place directly, face to face. Sometimes the teachers receive indirect messages from the students concerning their parents' reactions to the material being studied and respond to what the parents seem to consider important, even if this is not stated explicitly. Thus the ideological choices of the teachers are influenced by their diagnosis of the attitudes of students and their families to the Jewish content, as well as by their commitment to these students and their parents.

The Unacknowledged Ideological Commitment of Supervisors

Our findings show that, in general, the supervisors do not acknowledge the influence of their own ideologies, or the ideological influence of the educational system, on the supervisory process. This is perhaps because they perceive the ideology of the system as part of the mandatory study curriculum. The personal ideology of the supervisors with regard to the Jewish content taught, and their approach to the study of the sources, are likewise perceived by them as elements of a 'professional' approach. It would be interesting to consider how the ideological identification of the supervisors with their systems comes about, since most supervisors have themselves had many years' experience as teachers. Did these supervisors gravitate towards systems with which they identified ideologically, or did this identification come about over the course of their educational work? This question is worthy of a study in its own right—one that examines both how the educational systems select their representatives and how those who become supervisors come to join a body with a clear Jewish cultural ideology.

How Supervisors' and Teachers' Ideological Commitments Influence Supervisory Processes

Teacher supervision creates an ideological encounter between the local community of the school and the broader society. Supervisors, whether they represent the ministry of education or another body, bring with them a system of values and ideas that are translated into practical educational curricula. The teachers, in general, are required to implement these curricula to the best of their ability.

This situation creates an encounter between the teachers' loyalty to the local community and the supervisors' loyalty to the system that sends them to the schools. It is important to examine the degree to which the teachers and school principals are aware of the tension that may exist between that which grows from within the local community and that which is imported from outside and imposed on it.

Our findings raise the possibility that the strong commitment of the supervisors to inculcating the ideologies of the bodies they represent may make it difficult for them to be sensitive to the world of the teachers, to invite dialogue based on the teachers' experiences in the classroom, and to nurture reflective ability.

Ignoring the element of the local community in teacher supervision conveys a message that appears to seize ownership of the Jewish sources and their understanding, removing it from the teachers in order to preserve it in a place that is external to the school, with the 'experts'. Such a message contradicts the professional aspiration to empower the teachers and the school community in their relationship towards Jewish culture.

Ideologies and Supervision: From Community to Range of Communities

Even our use of the term 'school community' does an injustice to the wide range of lifestyles, ideologies, and culturally and religiously based characteristics that exist among teachers as well as among students and their parents. The term 'community', which serves to describe the influence of the environment on educational processes, may be perceived as embodying—from a linguistic, substantive point of view—the assumption that the environment exerts a unified moral and cultural influence on the educational process. In practice, as we have demonstrated, the environment includes an ideological spectrum that is represented in the educational process. Recognition that the school environment, and indeed every educational process, is influenced by a range of communal circles, including *inter alia* opposing communal influences, will be of assistance in exposing the ideological motives of the partners in the supervisory processes—teachers and super-visors alike.

Bibliography

Alpert, B., 'Concepts and Ideas in the Study of Curricula as Key Texts' (Heb.), in A. Hofman and I. Schnell (eds.), *Values and Goals in Israeli School Curricula* [Arakhim umatarot betokhniot halimudim beyisra'el] (Beit Berl College, Kfar Sabba, 2002), 9–29.

Althusser, L., *On Ideology* [Al haidiologia], trans. Azulai Ariela (Tel Aviv, 2003).

Apple, M., *Ideology and Curriculum* (London, 1990).

Billig, M., S. Cordal, D. Edwards, M. Gane, and D. Middleton, *Ideological Dilemmas: A Social Psychology of Everyday Thinking* (London, 1988).

Bowers, C. A., and D. J. Flinders, *Culturally Responsive Teaching and Supervision: A Handbook for Staff Development* (New York, 1991).

Britzman, D. B., 'Cultural Myths in the Making of a Teacher: Biography and Social Structure in Teacher Education', *Harvard Educational Review*, 56/4 (1986), 442–54.

Clark, D., *Schools as Learning Communities: Transforming Education* (London, 1996).

Cochran-Smith, M., 'Editorial: Teacher Education, Ideology, and Napoleon', *Journal of Teacher Education*, 53/1 (2002), 3–5.

Cohen, J., 'Jewish Thought for the Sake of Education: Can Jewish Tradition be "Translated"?' (Heb.), in Z. Lamm (ed.), *Moulding and Rehabilitation: Collected Papers in Memory of Professor Akiva Ernst Simon and Professor Carl Finkelstein* [Itsuv veshikum: asufat ma'amarim lezikhram shel profesor akivah ernst simon uprofesor karl finkelshteyn] (Jerusalem, 1996), 164–82.

—— 'Proposals for the Arrangement of Teaching Jewish Thought in Israeli Education: Survey and Analysis' (Heb.), *Studies in Jewish Education*, 6 (Jerusalem, 1992), 51–79.

—— and A. Shkedi, *The Intent to Kill: An Issue in Jewish Law* (Jerusalem, 1985).

Connelly, M., foreword to Miriam Ben-Peretz, *Learning from Experience: Memory and the Teacher's Account of Teaching* (Albany, NY, 1995).

Elbaz Lubish, F., 'Narrative-Biographical Research in Education and Instruction' (Heb.), in Naama Tsabar Ben-Yehoshua (ed.), *Traditions and Trends in Qualitative Research* [Masorot uzeramim bemehkar ha'eikhutani] (Devir, 2002), 141–65.

Fox, S., 'The Art of Translation', in S. Fox, I. Scheffler, and D. Marom (eds.), *Visions of Jewish Education* (Cambridge, Mass., 2003), 253–95.

Geertz, C., *The Interpretation of Cultures* [Parshanut shel tarbut] (Jerusalem, 1990).

Glickman, C. D., *Supervision of Instruction* (Boston, 1993).

Goren, D. (ed.), 'People and the World: Jewish Culture in a Changing World. Recommendations of the Committee to Examine Jewish Studies in State Schools' (Heb.), Israeli Ministry of Education, Culture and Sports (Jerusalem, 1994).

Grundy, S., and E. J. Hatton, 'Teacher Educators' Ideological Discourses', *Journal of Education for Teaching*, 21/1 (1995), 7–24.

Gudmundsdottir, S., 'Values in Pedagogical Content Knowledge', *Journal of Teacher Education*, 41/3 (1990), 44–52.

Gvaton, D., 'Field-Grounded Theory: Significance of the Process of Data Analysis and Theory Construction in Qualitative Research' (Heb.), in N. Tsabar Ben-Yehoshua (ed.), *Traditions and Trends in Qualitative Research* [Masorot uzeramim bemeḥkar ha'eikhutani] (Devir, 2002), 195–228.

Hansen, D. T., *The Call to Teach* (New York, 1995).

Hillocks, G., *Ways of Thinking, Ways of Teaching* (New York, 1998).

Jackson, P. W., 'Conceptions of Curriculum and Curriculum Specialists', in id. (ed.), *Handbook of Research on Curriculum* (New York, 1992).

Lamm, Z., 'The Ideological Bases of Jewish Studies in Israeli Education' (Heb.), *Haḥinukh hameshutaf*, no. 130 (1988), 57–76.

—— *In the Turbulence of Ideologies: The Bases of Education in the Twentieth Century* [Bemarbolet ha'ideologiyot, yesodot haḥinukh bame'ah ha'esrim] (Jerusalem, 2002).

Merz, C., and G. Furman, *Community and Schools* (New York, 1997).

Ministry of Education (Israel), Director-General's Circular 9(A), 29 Nisan 5763/1 May 2003.

—— Regulations of the Director-General, Permanent Regulations/5760/7(b), Adar I 5760/Mar. 2000.

Muszkat-Barkan, M., 'Ideological Encounters: Case Studies of Teacher Supervision in Jewish Studies' (Heb.), Ph.D. diss., Hebrew University of Jerusalem, 2005.

—— 'Standards for Evaluating Judaica Learning Materials in the Israeli General School System' (Heb.), in B. A. Bakon and D. Zissenwein (eds.), *Studies in Jewish Education* [Meḥkarim beḥinukh yehudi] (Ramat Aviv, 1999).

Nisan, M., *'Educational Identity' as a Major Factor in the Development of Educational Leadership* (Jerusalem, 2007).

Oliva, P., and G. Pawlas, *Supervision for Today's Schools* (New York, 1984).

Rubinstein, Y., *The Supervisor as a Professional: The Perspective of Teachers in Supervisory Roles—Research Findings* [Hamadrikh keprofesional: zavit shel morim betafkid hadrakhah—mimtsa'ei meḥkar] (Jerusalem, 1999).

Schremer, O., *Education between Radicalism and Tolerance* [Hachinuch bein radicaliut lesovlanut] (Jerusalem, 1999).

Schwab, J., 'Translating Scholarship into Curriculum', in S. Fox and G. Rosenfield (eds.), *From the Scholar to the Classroom: Translating Jewish Tradition into Curriculum* (New York, 1977), 1–29.

Sergiovanni, T. J., *Building Community in Schools* (San Francisco, 1994).

Shkedi, A., 'Scholars' Theories about Teaching vs. Teachers' Theories about their Teaching: The Case of Teaching Bible' (Heb.), in M. Frankel and H. Deitcher (eds.), *Understanding the Bible in our Times: Implications for Education, Studies in Jewish Education*, 9 (Jerusalem, 2003), 263–82.

—— *Words of Meaning: Qualitative Research—Theory and Practice* [Milim hamenasot laga'at: mechkar eichutani teoria veyisum] (Tel Aviv, 2003).

Shkedi, A., and M. Nisan, 'Teachers' Cultural Ideology: Patterns of Curriculum and Teaching Culturally Valued Texts', *Teachers College Record*, 108/4 (2006), 687–725.

Strauss, A., and J. Corbin, 'Grounded Theory Methodology', in N. K. Denzin and Y. S. Lincoln (eds.), *Handbook of Qualitative Research* (Thousand Oaks, Calif., 1994), 273–85.

Toennies, F., *Community and Society* (New York, 1957); first published as *Gemeinschaft und Gesellschaft (1887)*.

Townsend, T., *Effective Schooling for the Community: Core-Plus Education* (London, 1994).

Tsabar ben-Yehoshua, N., *Qualitative Research in Teaching and Learning* [Hameḥkar ha'eikhutani behora'ah uvelemida] (Tel Aviv, 1997).

SIXTEEN

Schooling for Change in the Religious World

An Educational Experiment in a Religious Junior High School in Israel

ELANA MARYLES SZTOKMAN

SCHOOLS SHAPE COMMUNITIES as much as communities shape schools. As bell hooks writes, as we work at transforming educational institutions, we are ultimately transforming society 'so that the way we live, teach, and work can reflect our joy in cultural diversity, our passion for justice, and our love of freedom'.[1] Thus schools are places that reflect the values of a society, while holding the potential to transform the injustices in society and deconstruct social hierarchies.

Race and Class in Religious Schools in Israel

Although compulsory state schooling in Israel, enacted in 1949, was intended to provide equal educational opportunities to all the country's citizens, ethnic and class differentiation gradually became entrenched in the system. The educational historian Chaim Adler describes how, from Israel's inception, certain state policies of 'absorption' had a discriminatory effect on immigrants from Middle Eastern countries—oriental Jews, Sephardis, or *mizraḥim*. 'The disadvantaged socio-economic position of Middle Easterners stemmed *inter alia* from the differential treatment by the official agencies during the initial period of "being absorbed".'[2] Moreover, since the 1950s in Israel was a period in which 'Israeliness' was being moulded, the school system reflected that political goal, in which images of 'Israeli' generally meant Ashkenazi, or European. The sociologist Shlomo Swirski argues that 'the entire cultural world represented in the Israeli curriculum was and still is almost exclusively the world of European Jewry'.[3]

I wish to thank the following people for ongoing support and assistance in this work: Dr Beverly Gribetz, Professor Tamar El-Or, Professor Tamar Rapoport, and Dr Ariella Zeller.

[1] hooks, *Teaching to Transgress*, 34.
[2] Adler, 'School Integration', 23.

[3] Swirski, *Politics and Education*, 167.

Formal structures in the school system matched this cultural hierarchy from the earliest days of the state, when Ashkenazi and Sephardi Jews were given different educations. The ethnographer Arnold Lewis writes that schools were divided into two sections, one composed of 'small classes of veterans and new immigrant children from Eastern Europe who pro-gressed along the path towards academic high school' and another which 'stressed reading, writing and other basic skills, [and] was opened and filled mostly by children of North African and Near Eastern immigrants', who, upon completing this programme, 'were prepared to enter a trade as the level of education did not meet the standards for admission into academic high schools'.[4] This practice of ethnically divided school groups remained formally in place through the 1960s.

Discriminatory practices were also in evidence in screening policies. In the late 1950s, of all the immigrant students who passed the entry test for high school, only 38 per cent of Sephardi Jews enrolled in standard (acade-mic) high schools, while 52 per cent of Ashkenazi Jews did.[5] In 1961, median total school attendance for those over 14 years old was 5.9 years for African and Asian immigrants, and 9.1 years for European immigrants.

A vicious cycle was created in which educational backwardness bred social and economic retardation and these in their turn generated a new cycle of educational, social and economic retardation resulting in an educationally, socially and economically disadvantaged status. The vicious circle deprived a large part of the second generation of Asian and African immigrants of the opportunity to rise substantially above their parents' socio-economic status.[6]

In 1968, in order to address the need for equality, the ministry of education put forward a bill for educational reform that called for the creation of junior high schools and for ethnic 'integration'—that is, having Middle Easterners and Europeans attending the same schools. The 'Reforma', as it was called, was meant to establish integrated post-primary schools, de-marcate enrolment districts that would create mixed ethnic groups, build heterogeneous home-rooms (main class groups), introduce pupil tracking by subject, and establish comprehensive (joint academic and vocational) schools, including remedial care for low-achieving students.[7] Although the rationale for the Reforma was to bring about greater social equality by

[4] Lewis, *Power, Poverty and Education*, 92.
[5] Gaziel, *Politics and Policy Making*, 38. [6] Ibid. 44. [7] Ibid. 67.

enabling more Middle Eastern Jews to complete high school, it was prevented from achieving this end following parental pressure on the legislators. 'Western parents whose children were to be "integrated" received assurances by the ministry of education that their school's curriculum would not change and that "standards" would not be lowered.'[8] In response to pressure from parent groups, the state law on integration included a compromise position—that integration would be implemented along with internal tracking, or homogeneous grouping. This policy of what Resh and Dar call 'segregation within integration' effectively retained internally the ethnic hierarchies that it symbolically dismantled externally.[9]

Thus, even in schools where integration policies were adopted, inequality remained, perpetuated by informal cultural and social practices. As Sharan and Rich argue, integration is not a 'cure' for social ills, but an opportunity to change the way education is done. 'It seems clear that positive effects are more likely to be achieved when desegregation is accompanied by educational adaptations within the classroom, which aim to improve both minority-pupils' achievement and inter-ethnic relations . . . Unfortunately . . . the same teaching–learning conditions characterizing the ethnically and socially homogeneous class have been transplanted to the mixed class with only nominal alternations.'[10] Indeed, studies conducted in the late 1970s on integration showed that junior high schools promoted educational continuity and more years of schooling on average, and also promoted *social* integration—but not *academic* improvement for disadvantaged students. Moreover, the Knesset Committee on Integration found in 1981 that integration had been applied fully in only 46 localities, partially in 28, and not at all in 75, and that there still existed a substantial disparity in the quality of teaching staff between advantaged and disadvantaged regions.[11] As Swirski notes, the reform 'signaled the passage from a unitary and universal curriculum to curriculae adapted to the "individual capacities of different pupils," meaning particularly a differentiation between European and Middle Eastern pupils'.[12] In 1984 the Knesset Education Committee recommended a moratorium on new junior high schools because they were not achieving integration.[13]

---

[8] Halper et al., 'Communities, Schools and Integration', 49.
[9] Resh and Dar, 'Segregation within Integration'.
[10] Sharan and Rich, 'Field Experiments', 190.   [11] Gaziel, *Politics and Policy Making*, 68.
[12] Swirski, *Politics and Education*, 11.   [13] Gaziel, *Politics and Policy Making*, 69.

While the formal educational structures that had begun with ethnic hierarchies attempted and then rejected change, more subtle forms of ethnic differentiation took hold in the language of educational policy-making, with sometimes troubling references to essentialist notions of difference. The term te'unei tipuaḥ—students in need of 'special nurturing'—was introduced in the 1960s as a formal classification of ethnic groupings. 'The operational definition . . . was, until 1994, overtly ethnic. The creation of this term was originally meant to create different materials for different tracks, but since that was too hard a task for policy makers, the te'unei tipuaḥ programs simply used smaller amounts of the mainstream materials.'[14] Underlying this policy was the ubiquitous understanding that te'unei tipuaḥ are Middle Eastern students. As Professor Ernst Simon of the Hebrew University, one of the architects of the integration policy, said blatantly in 1964, Middle Eastern children often 'burn with strong egoism, like all of us . . . If this program . . . succeeds, those egocentric ambitions will be regulated and directed towards individual advancement and assimilation into those who have made it.'[15] In other words, Middle Eastern children are 'almost normal', like 'us'. For 'them' the egoism as it stands is problematic, whereas for 'us' it is a wonderful tool for personal advancement. The assumption among many policy-makers was that Middle Eastern students were slow, incapable, immature, emotionally undeveloped, and simple.

By 1977, 37 per cent of all junior high school students were defined as te'unei tipuaḥ, all of them Middle Eastern students.[16] In an educational system in which 50–60 per cent of the population are Middle Eastern, not only was te'unei tipuaḥ by definition mizraḥi, but most mizraḥi students were labelled te'unei tipuaḥ, defined as 'functionally incapable of coping with the regular study programs'.[17]

Ethnic and socio-economic discrimination in Israeli schools takes some particularly striking twists within state religious schooling, where religious hierarchies overlap with ethnic ones. Significantly, when Israel introduced integration in the 1970s, fewer state religious schools than state secular schools adopted integration, and those that did implemented it only minimally in practice. One reason why state religious schools resisted integration is possibly that integration also meant religious pluralism, introducing different customs and religious cultures, and religious educational ideolo-

---

[14] Swirski, *Politics and Education*, 179.   [15] Education Council, quoted ibid. 186.
[16] Swirski, *Politics and Education*, 176.   [17] Ibid. 180.

gies resist these phenomena.[18] Chen, Levy, and Adler suggest that segregation is more prominent in religious schools because these schools like to segregate 'talented' students for more intense religious instruction.[19] Underlying these trends is a tight interlacing of social structures. As Schwarzwald argues, 'Within the religious public schools, the Middle Eastern tradition was disparaged . . . suggest[ing] a variety of negative socio-educational effects for the disadvantaged Middle Eastern students.'[20] In other words, in religious schools socio-economic and ethnic segregation are bound up with religious hierarchies.

Tracking or streaming, as opposed to integration, suits religious ideology since the language of the classic colonial 'intellectual–emotional' dichotomy dominated religious educational thinking for many years.[21] The trend of creating religiously elitist *torani* schools (lit. 'of Torah', implying 'more religious') became a convenient avenue for ethnic discrimination embedded in constructs of 'stricter adherence'. These schools, which are by definition anti-integration, seek out perceived 'religious excellence'—that is, more strict religious adherence according to their own definitions, which effectively means Ashkenazi only. The flight of upper-class Ashkenazi students to these schools parallels the 'white flight' in the American public system that accompanied desegregation. Here, though, the ethnic/socio-economic trend overlaps with a religious one,[22] constructing an Ashkenazi upper-class religious and ethnic elitism.

Although these practices have become an intractable part of religious schooling, they have not been explored or studied in any real systematic way. Analyses have just barely begun to rear their heads in public, as stories of Sephardi girls being rejected or expelled from girls' religious schools begin to surface.[23] The subtle forms of discrimination embedded in everyday life in religious schools are often even more heavily masked than the formal ones, and correspondingly harder to unravel.

This study focuses on the dynamics of ethnic and socio-economic hierarchies in a religious junior high school in Israel. The research exposes the often subtle ways in which the dynamics of everyday life participate in the process of constructing ethnic and socio-economic structures, and the ways

[18] Gaziel, *Politics and Policy Making*, 83.　[19] Chen et al., *Process and Product*.
[20] Schwarzwald, 'Integration as a Situational Contingent', 106.
[21] Swirski, *Politics and Education*, 190.　[22] Gaziel, *Politics and Policy Making*, 86.
[23] Sela, 'Discrimination from the First Grade'; Rotem, 'Sorry, Rejected'.

in which staff and students navigate these structures. The case study raises issues about the role of religious schooling in the transformation of society and in bridging ethnic and socio-economic gaps, while bringing to public awareness processes of marginalization within religious schooling.

The Focus of the Research: The Levy Girls' Religious School

This chapter is part of an ethnographic case study of a state religious junior high school, the Levy Girls' Religious School, in Israel.[24] It is based on three years of qualitative research at the school, from 1999 to 2002, during a period in which it was undergoing an experiment in social and ethnic transformation. The research as a whole includes dozens of interviews with students, staff, parents, and other interested parties, as well as observations of all aspects of school life, including classes, meetings, field trips, assemblies, and countless daily interactions in corridors, courtyards, and corners of the school. This chapter focuses on the school's principal, Dr Sylvia Cohen, and is based on ten open-ended interviews and dozens of observations during the course of the research.

The Levy School, a 140-year-old landmark institution that until recently comprised a primary and a secondary school, was first opened in the nineteenth century as a private initiative by a European Jewish organization. At the time it was considered revolutionary, both as one of the first Jewish schools in Palestine, and for introducing non-religious subjects and promoting the idea that religious girls should be productive members of the new society. Interestingly, from the first years of the school Sephardi girls were in the majority, since the Sephardi leadership of the Jewish community in Palestine at this time was in favour of secular learning for their young women. The highest proportion of Ashkenazi pupils in the late nineteenth century was 25 per cent in 1882, but the numbers went down after that.[25]

However, the establishment of the State of Israel in 1948 eroded the distinctiveness of the school. When free public education was implemented, the local municipality and the ministry of education gradually took over

---

[24] All names and identifying details have been disguised to protect the informants.
[25] Mannenberg, 'Evolution of Jewish Educational Practices in the Sancak', 25.

responsibility for the school, a move that transformed the Sephardi student body into masses of inferior 'other', faceless to the governing bureaucracy. By the 1960s and 1970s the unique character of this pioneering school had become a matter of historical anecdote, having been replaced by that bland, neglected poverty typical of many other public, Sephardi-dominated schools in Israel. Extra-curricular activities were dropped, matriculation rates remained low, and the city bureaucracy lost interest in the school for decades. In short, the once vibrant institution became stagnant, impoverished, and a site of prejudice.

In 1996 the city municipality restructured the school system with a new policy of *ḥituv* (the creation of middle schools) that aimed at alleviating some discrimination by, at the very least, keeping all students in school longer. The body overseeing education in the municipality employed a new principal, Dr Sylvia Cohen, a modern Orthodox, feminist, American immigrant, to build the junior high school, consolidating grades 7, 8, and 9 into a separate entity.

Although people at the municipality warned Dr Cohen that it would be difficult to recruit students, she took this as a challenge and a mission. She set out to recruit girls from all over the city, from all ethnic and socio-economic backgrounds, and to transform the reputation of the school. By the second year of the school's operation, seventy-two sixth-grade girls turned up for the entrance exam—more than for any other religious school in the city. By the third year there were four classes in each grade and a waiting list. An influx of middle- and upper-class families, bringing throngs of English-speaking students, forced the opening of extra classes and turned the Levy School into a meeting ground for girls from widely diverse ethnic and socio-economic backgrounds. With these developments opened a new chapter in the annals of the Levy School.

This particular school is thus of special interest, both because of its widely diverse student population and because of its new principal, a reformer and innovator for whom the school became an experiment in rebuilding culture and effecting social change. Approximately one-third of the girls at the school during the research period came from families on welfare, most of them from families that had emigrated from Arab countries. Another third are Ashkenazi of Israeli background, while the remaining third come from families of Euro-American or 'Anglo-Saxon' backgrounds,[26] some from the highest socio-economic sectors in the city. Most 'American' girls, as they were dubbed, are Ashkenazi. The Levy School is a place where the cultural structure is explicit, transparent, and intentional. The school constitutes a cultural junction where different paths of religiousness, gender, ethnicity, and socio-economic class meet and cross.

An Experiment in School Change

Cohen spent over a year developing a plan and a vision before opening the doors of the new school. Her goal was initially to instil certain religious values in line with her own American-style, modern liberal, religious Judaism. But she soon encountered a different reality that changed her mind:

I am not sure I was prepared for what hit me when I opened the new junior high . . . I thought that the challenge they were giving me was to bring my own brand of Orthodox pluralism to run a school that was starting from the ground up . . . I spent close to a year thinking about religious issues, how we would deal with them . . . And it took me less than a week, after I had thought about this for a year, to realize that the religious issue was not the issue . . . but that the major issue would be the ethnic issue, the issue of the different ethnic groups that exist together in the state religious system.

Cohen came into contact with people from cultures unfamiliar to her, some of whom may have regarded her religious vision as irrelevant. Liberal Orthodox New York feminism acquired its own distinct identity in the school, among many other diverse identities bouncing around.

Cohen described to me her personal transformation, in which awareness of her privileged status became the dominant impetus in reforming her central goals:

What I am talking about is the feminism of the non-elites and empowerment of the non-elites . . . And it is in fact about listening to other voices and voices that I, having grown up in the world of New York modern Orthodoxy . . . wasn't aware of . . . I had absolutely no idea what it meant to build a heterogeneous society and what this meant for girls' education in particular within the modern religious world in this city.

---

[26] 'Anglo-Saxon', 'Anglo', and 'American' are all interchangeably used terms. They have come to refer to families who immigrated from English-speaking or west European countries. Although a misnomer, it is a popular term used widely in the press, in the community, and, by default, in the school.

Rather than focusing on the *religious* identities of the girls, Cohen began to focus on their *socio-economic* and *ethnic* identities. She came to see herself as almost an outsider in the context of the school social fabric, and began her work of studying culture before imposing her own.

To her tremendous credit, Cohen quickly learned her way around the local scene, and changed course according to her appreciation of some of the social injustices that 'plague Israeli society'. She set out to promote a wider educational and social agenda aimed at closing socio-economic and ethnic gaps through education or, in her words,

to create a new society that does not have ethnic divisions within it, because the ethnic divisions that plague Israeli society right now are very, very serious . . . Basically it is an issue of Ashkenazis and Sephardis. The Levy High School . . . over the last twenty years has been 95 per cent Middle Eastern origin. Because it [has been] 95 per cent *mizrahi*, it has [had] limited funding. It has a look that is minimalist and not maximalist. It looks like it is a society in distress and we somehow have to figure out a way to overcome this.

Cohen came to see the distress of the school as reflective of the distress of *mizrahim* in general, and to see the socio-economic divide as resulting from systematic ethnic discrimination, as evidenced by disparities in educational funding.

In developing her 'new' social agenda her first step was getting to know the lives and experiences of girls from *mizrahi* families; and her initial focus was on socio-economics, not ethnicity.

We have now, under the new administration, very wealthy families and very poor families . . . I can never see Jewish poverty the way I saw it first at the school when I went to visit one of the girls, who unfortunately had lost her father and I went to see her sitting *shivah* [observing the seven-day mourning period]. The family lived in a very poor neighbourhood. They had five children in one bedroom. Their refrigerator was the type of refrigerator that I took to a dorm room in college, you know, a little refrigerator that you stick under the counter. I quickly realized that this was close to 50 per cent of my student body.

The realization that dire poverty existed in the school was a shock. Cohen's identity of privilege was quickly challenged and deconstructed by an encounter with the life of a particular family. This created in her a new mission: to ensure that at least economically, if not ethnically, girls in her school would gain equal access to education. She said, 'If we don't do this we will not create the new society that I really believe now is necessary if we are to save Israel. And I know it sounds a little pretentious, but I have become very much on a mission.'

Academic Achievement and Social Class

Cohen initially translated this 'mission' of socio-economic transformation into plans around 'academic achievement':

I wanted to meet the challenge that [the municipality] set me, which is raise the *bagrut* [matriculation exams]. Right now the average *bagrut* for the whole country of the state religious people who finish twelfth grade with a complete *bagrut* is less than 40 per cent . . . But [this school] is one of these low ones. Fewer than 70 per cent of the girls finish with a full *bagrut*. It is better than ten years ago . . . But I would like to hope that some day this school will be 100 per cent *bagrut* . . . yes, to get to that if that is a standard by which Israeli schools are measured.

For Cohen, the academic goal of everyone passing *bagrut* does not have an essential value. She has set as her goal the undoing of social inequalities by means of achievement in the *bagrut*.

Cohen understands that an emphasis on *bagrut*, couched in a language of 'achievement' that sometimes uses test scores as instruments for ignoring social injustices and constructing essentialist differences, is problematic in the context of the Levy School:

Obviously I want to know what they know and their values and all of that. But I am not going to turn around and say, 'Oh you know only 80% of the girls passed, but all the others are *ba'alot ḥesed* [kind].' That is fake. You know, I want both.

Cohen is trapped between construction and deconstruction. Although she wants to deconstruct identity as *bagrut*, the only readily apparent alternative construct for adolescent religious girls is the classic feminine *ḥesed*. This is problematic not only because it is female-owned but, more pressingly, because it lacks social capital. Indeed, these two points are interrelated: *ḥesed* is imposed on women and is not valued in real terms in society. Here is where Cohen is trapped: although she is reluctant to promote hegemonic constructs such as the *bagrut*, the only existing alternative will leave her students powerless in society. In order to empower the girls in society today, she has to buy into the existing system of constructs. Stated differently, she sees the opposite of the *bagrut* construction—the girls' 'values'—as 'fake', a superficial means for pacifying those who are denied access to the cultural capital which a *bagrut* certificate offers. Thus, what is perhaps powerful personally—that is, 'values' or interpersonal relationships—is powerless socially, while what is powerless personally—that is, *bagrut*, an almost arbitrarily determined measure of 'self-worth'—is very powerful socially. Thus Cohen recognizes *bagrut* as a necessary tool for changing girls' lives by enabling them to gain access to elite institutions and expensive schooling, a form of cultural capital not to be minimized, and leaves other goals aside for now.

Between Equality and Excellence

Just as Cohen is torn between academic achievement and 'values', she is similarly torn between building an academically elite school and building a school that is fair, equal, and just. Although she prides herself on the fact that there are now as many Ashkenazis as Sephardis in the school (many of the Ashkenazis are Anglo, or immigrants from English-speaking countries), this attitude embodies the maintenance of the ethnic hierarchy: the presence of Ashkenazis is an external validation of the greater 'worthiness' of the school. The increased number of Ashkenazi students in the school is a measure of success—but only within a system that constructs that ethnic hierarchy. Again, Cohen is trapped between building a school which offers underprivileged girls access to privilege and actually challenging the existing hierarchies. Thus, in order to offer underprivileged students access to higher-quality education, Cohen feels she has to work hard to attract Ashkenazi students.

Cohen is aware of the sacrifice, of the tension between helping girls within the existing system and challenging the system. She is also cognizant of her responsibilities towards the students who stay in the school: for, while she hopes that the Ashkenazi students will not go to a rival elite school, she can be sure that the Sephardi girls will not.

Thus the task Cohen has taken on is effectively to offer a privileged education to underprivileged students. Deconstructing the surrounding cultural hierarchy is a goal beyond her reach, a fact that illustrates the paradox involved in working for social change within a racist system: she cannot fight to bring about change on the micro and the macro levels at the same time. She describes the struggle within herself to keep her focus on educating the underprivileged Sephardis, rather than the privileged Ashkenazis. 'I want to remember that I am there for the girls who are poor and who don't have a lot of opportunities', she emphasized.

From *Ḥesed* to Social Justice

Cohen spends a lot of time creating practices within the school to implement her social mission, which is socio-economically and culturally very complicated. For example, when a group of English-speaking women from Hadassah visited the school and asked her if she had a *ḥesed* or social action programme similar to those in Jewish schools around the world, she responded:

We can't have a project like that. Half of the girls can give up their old coats, but the other half of the girls are recipients of the coats. I haven't yet figured out how you teach . . . charity and teach social action to all of them in a society where some of them just have so little, it is next to nothing.

Cohen has changed her view of 'other' as 'recipient' to 'other' as 'student'. Here again she has had to change her own identity as a privileged upper-middle-class New York Jew. In New York, poverty was invisible in that charity was handed out to anonymous people simply called 'The Poor', and the purpose of *ḥesed* was to make the giver a better Jew or a better person. Here, underprivileged people were coming into focus as her *students*—as people who are not necessarily 'different' from her. Implementing change means transforming her own gaze on other members of society.

Now, Cohen believes that helping underprivileged students means understanding that she and they share a society and a community in which poverty should be eliminated. Now, in assuming the responsibility for solving these social problems and easing human suffering, the point was not just 'doing *ḥesed*' but also changing the way of looking at people in society. 'We must be very careful of not having condescension', she explained, 'like "I am going to come into the school with you to 'save the masses'."' We are not saving the masses. We are going to change the society.' In other words, the goal of eliminating poverty has become a very personal duty to society, involving changing her own identity first and seeing the constructs herself.

Cohen described her anger at seeing discrimination that was previously invisible to her.

I had no idea that Jews could live in such poverty. I'm very angry at the State of Israel. I wrote a memo: . . . *mifal hapayis* [the national lottery], with the money of the State of Israel, built an auditorium and a building for labs [in the Sinai private school] that are so fabulous that I've never seen anything like it. I wrote a letter to [the municipality] about this. That I cannot understand how the state can put money like this into a private school, where all the families have money and give nothing to all the girls in the [poor neighbourhoods]. It's scandalous. It's like mocking the poor! I am very, very angry!! If I had money to build one lab auditorium in a state religious school in this town, I would build it for the Levy School. The school has kids from the poor neighbourhoods who can't pay. I wouldn't give it to Sinai which has everything anyway.

In her position as principal of the Levy Junior High School, Cohen has come to see striking injustices in schooling and bureaucracy that urge her on to action.

Indeed, Cohen sees the building of her school as a powerful act towards eliminating the socio-economic gap, and offering equal access to the social capital of *bagrut*. In fact, when asked what she does with her frustration about discriminatory state policies, Cohen replied: 'I run the Levy School!' School practices are her answer to socio-economic gaps. 'I make sure that every girl has a locker. I make sure that there's no financial discrimination in the school and that every girl can go on every outing.' This form of resistance is more private than public, but for Cohen it is vital nonetheless. 'I am not yet trying to stir up the parents or the kids to be *hafganati* [demonstrative/provocative] about it. Maybe when they get to the twelfth grade we'll talk about how they're going to go out now and change the world.' For Cohen, then, practices outside formalized education, curriculum, and exams—such as how to distribute lockers—assume an explicit role within this narrative of closing socio-economic gaps, as significant as verbalized, direct discussion about issues in class.

Cohen also unofficially brings in elements of socialism, in which she tries to 'spread the wealth' within the overall school community in order to close the socio-economic gap. Some wealthier parents, inspired by Cohen, offered to subsidize poorer students:

In Israeli schools in general, there are not lockers for every student like we have in American schools. But what the schools do is they send out a flyer and they say if you want the lockers you pay eighty shekels, one hundred shekels or more. There are girls that carry their books on their backs, and there are girls who use the lockers. I knew that if we put in the lockers and made it optional, what would happen is the rich kids would have them and the poor kids would not have them. And I was not willing to have a situation like that in the school, even if it was accepted in other schools. The first year I just avoided lockers altogether, then the parents came to me and said the girls are breaking their backs, we have to get the lockers. So I met with a group of parents and I said, this is my philosophy of lockers and how my philosophy of lockers fits in with my philosophy of the whole school and that I would not have a situation where one could have it and where one couldn't have it. Thank God there were three parents who said, 'Tell us what the shortfall is going to be, give everybody the lockers, whoever will pay will pay, whoever will not, we will take care of it.'

For Cohen, 'lockers for everyone' became the icon of a social mission, a pragmatic and phenomenological expression of a social and educational ideology.

Privileged Education for All

The story of Miri Abadi is one of Cohen's favourite success stories, in which she provided an underprivileged girl with a privileged educational encounter, that is, an elite, expensive after-school art workshop at the museum:

When we went to the museum to do the [workshop] at the museum, I asked Sylvie the art teacher to give me a list of the most talented kids, and then I invited some of their parents in over the summer just to discuss the possibility. So Miri Abadi was one of the girls who was listed as very talented, but the parents didn't come to the meeting, and at the beginning of the year, she didn't sign up. So I went to her and said, 'Why didn't you sign up? You're so talented, and Sylvie says you like it.' She says, *Ken, zeh lo bediyuk bishvili*. [Yes, it's not exactly for me.] . . .

I had a bad feeling about her saying it's not for me. So I called the mother, and I said, 'Are you aware of the art workshop at the museum?' and she said, 'No, I don't know what you're talking about.' I explained what we're doing and she said, 'Miri doesn't seem to want to.' So I said, 'You know, I have already gotten the scholarship from the city. You're not going to pay the fee.' I heard her on the phone start to cry. Because that was the issue. But I had really already taken care of it, I mean, when Sylvie gave me the list, I already knew who I was going to get scholarships for. And I had already done it.

She started to cry on the phone, and the next day Miri came in ready for the workshop. See, because they don't expect it. But to me, it's clear that Miri Abadi deserves what Leah Goldberg does, but the Goldbergs are going to pay full to get it and the Miris are going to pay twenty per cent to get it.

And then of course, the first time I went to visit them at the museum, she was beaming, she was just beaming, and she was so proud for me to see her there. And the fact is, in that museum thing, most of the kids are the Ashkenazi rich kids of town. She would have never gotten that in any other school. There is no other school that would have given her this opportunity.

This story is a classic illustration of Cohen's educational narrative, perhaps her entire *raison d'être*. It was not about religion or gender, but rather about offering the privileges of a financially backed education to girls whose families could not give them those privileges. This is what she meant when she talked about the 'integration' of poor girls into the world of the privileged. It was not about sharing ethnicities or cultures, but about closing a socio-economic gap that has long existed between groups within the religious school system and which strongly echoes ethnic boundaries. Although 'the poor' for Cohen meant 'poor Sephardi', and privileged meant 'rich Ashkenazi' (or, more likely, 'rich Anglo')—generalizations that remained largely unchallenged—nonetheless she assumed the task of creating a culture around schooling for social change within the setting of religious girls in Israel.

Discussion

The Levy School in the years 1999–2002 resembled the top layer of a *tel*, an archaeological mound made up of complex layers of history. Once the school had represented a revolution in religious education both for girls in general, and for Sephardis in particular, in the new Yishuv; but since its early years those revolutionary characteristics have fallen away one by one through events including the establishment of the state, the marginalization of Sephardis, and the overall bureaucratization of the school system in Israel. For the last quarter of the twentieth century the school was predominantly Sephardi, with a below-average rate of matriculation, thus contributing to the wide socio-economic gaps in society and their overlap with the ethnic division.

Dr Sylvia Cohen, an educated, Ashkenazi, liberal feminist Orthodox woman, was brought in by the bureaucracy to change the school by building a new junior high and high school within the framework of the existing primary and secondary schools. She almost immediately took upon herself the responsibility for narrowing the socio-economic gaps in society, instituted practices intended to promote equal access to education for all sectors of Israeli society, and began working on offering privileged education to all populations, regardless of economic capacity.

Still, Cohen's identity has a very specific meaning within the existing school culture. Moreover, her actions bring their own dilemmas. She was often faced with the choice between helping an individual girl and challenging underlying constructions, highlighting the fundamental difficulty inherent in promoting social change: How does one empower an underprivileged group without seeing that group's culture as inferior? Is it possible to create social mobility for a group whose culture is deemed inferior while deconstructing the larger hierarchies? The Levy School experiment opened up these questions in striking ways.

Indeed, the school reform was ostensibly about offering a high-class education to poor students. That is, it was about making the invisible visible, about reversing the decades-old pattern of viewing *mizrahi* students as *te'unei tipuah* and working, rather, under the assumption that ethnicity is not—or perhaps should not be—a determining factor in academic success. Yet within this noble goal rests a paradox; for change here came from an Anglo, upper-class, Ashkenazi source. This source undoubtedly worked tirelessly for change. Yet it was, unavoidably, a source for whom *mizrahi* was, by definition, other. A significant question that emerges from this study, then, is whether true reform for underprivileged populations can be effected from the outside. It resembles the dilemma raised by Penina Motzafi-Haller, who resents being told, when she writes about *mizrahi* women, that her voice is 'authentic', because it places her as 'other'—even if, at the same time, natives of a cultural group still are probably its best representatives.[27]

This study illustrates that reform from the outside can go a long way in bringing about change and offering opportunities that are otherwise out of reach. Nevertheless, there are perhaps other types of reform that require personal identification and a different element of empathy. Just as feminist educators and health practitioners have long recognized that there are some locations where only women can empower women, so too perhaps—

[27] Motzafi-Haller, 'A Mizrahi Call for a More Democratic Israel'.

Penina Motzafi-Haller's poignant arguments notwithstanding—ethnic empowerment has more legitimacy when effected by a member of that ethnic culture.

Perhaps the most difficult challenge raised here is that of challenging a system while working within it. If indeed the key to socio-economic mobility is getting a *bagrut* certificate and achieving academic success, then this requires working fully within and supporting the existing structures. Thus, if the cultural perspective of the *bagrut*-centred system is an Ashkenazi–male one, a *mizraḥi* girl from a poor neighbourhood does not have the luxury of resisting that system. She needs to adapt to it and even make it her own if she is to change her life. It's a painful irony, one that formed a strong current within this educational experiment, and one that does not have a simple solution.

Despite these inherent difficulties, this story of Sylvia Cohen's reform of the Levy School makes a vital contribution to religious schooling. That is, it provides a living example of an attempt to bring the amelioration of ethnic and socio-economic inequalities into the mission of a school. It provides a model for schooling for social change, and offers, therefore, profound inspiration that the goal of eliminating socio-economic and ethnic gaps can and should become a central component of religious schooling.

Bibliography

Adler, C., 'School Integration in the Context of the Development of Israel's Educational System', in Y. Amir and S. Sharan (eds.), *School Desegregation: Cross-Cultural Perspectives* (Hillsdale, NJ), 21–45.

Chen, M., A. Levy, and C. Adler, *Process and Product in Educational Endeavour: The Contribution of the Junior-High Echelon to the Educational System* [Halikh vetotsa'ah bema'aseh ha ḥinukh: terumatah shel ḥativat habeinayim lema'arekhet] (Jerusalem, 1978).

Gaziel, H., *Politics and Policy Making in Israel's Education System* (Brighton, 1999).

Halper, J., M. Shokeid, and A. Weingrod, 'Communities, Schools and Integration', in Y. Amir and S. Sharan (eds.), *School Desegregation: Cross-Cultural Perspectives* (Hillsdale, NJ, 1984), 47–62.

hooks, b., *Teaching to Transgress: Education as the Practice of Freedom* (New York, 1994).

Lewis, A., *Power, Poverty and Education* (Ramat Gan, 1979).

Mannenberg, E., 'The Evolution of Jewish Educational Practices in the Sancak (Eyalet) of Jerusalem under Ottoman Rule', Ph.D. diss., University of Connecticut, 1976.

Minkovich, A., *Educational Achievement Evaluation in Israeli Primary Schools* [Ha'arakhat hahesegim haḥinukhiyim beveit hasefer hayesodi beyisra'el] (Jerusalem, 1977).

Motzafi-Haller, P., 'A Mizrahi Call for a More Democratic Israel', *Tikkun: A Bimonthly Jewish Critique of Politics, Culture and Society*, special issue on 'Israel at Fifty' (Mar. 1998), 50–3.

Resh, N., and Y. Dar, 'Segregation within Integration in Israeli Junior High Schools', *Israel Social Science Research*, 11/1 (1996), 1–22.

Rotem, T., 'Sorry, Rejected; Your Grandmother's Sephardi', *Ha'aretz*, 5 Aug. 2003, <http://www.haaretz.com/hasen/objects/pages/PrintArticleEn.jhtml?itemNo=325595>.

Schwarzwald, J., 'Integration as a Situational Contingent: Secular versus Religious Public Education', in Y. Amir and S. Sharan (eds.), *School Desegregation: Cross-Cultural Perspectives* (Hillsdale, NJ, 1984), 99–117.

Sela, N., 'Discrimination from the First Grade', Ynet News, 30 Apr. 2007, <http://www.ynetnews.com/articles/0,7340,L-3393620,00.html>.

Sharan, S., and Y. Rich, 'Field Experiments on Ethnic Integration in Israeli Schools', in Y. Amir and S. Sharan (eds.), *School Desegregation: Cross-Cultural Perspectives* (Hillsdale, NJ, 1984), 189–217.

Swirski, S., *Politics and Education in Israel: Comparisons with the United States* (New York, 1999).

Yadlin, A., *The Integration of Exiles: Study Days at the Hebrew University in Jerusalem* (Jerusalem, 1969).

SEVENTEEN

Home-Made Jewish Culture at the Intersection of Family Life and School

ALEX POMSON AND RANDAL F. SCHNOOR

THE INTERACTIONS between parents and schools occur in two loca-tions: at school itself, where parents come into direct contact with school life, and at home, where children literally and figuratively transport school back to their families in their knapsacks. It is clear to those who have stud-ied or sought to cultivate these interactions that their overriding purpose is to support the work of schools with children.[1]

Having completed a four-year study of the relationships between par-ents and their children's Jewish day schools, we are convinced that these interactions also possess no small significance for parents' own lives and for their communities. We will not reproduce the major findings of our study here,[2] but want to pay attention in this chapter to one of our most unexpected discoveries: that what children bring back from school can serve as an important resource for the nurture of Jewish social and cultural capital in the home.

This finding was unexpected because we embarked on our study aware of more than four decades of sociological research demonstrating that schools are generally weak socializing agents when it comes to their impact on children's lives, especially when compared with the influence of fami-lies.[3] At the outset we did not, therefore, expect that what children brought home from school might result in changes to the Jewish lives of their parents. Such an outcome, we will show, calls into question two common-place assumptions that undergird the work of those who study and develop 'school–community connections': first, that there is a generally unidirec-tional sequence of cause and effect (from home to school) in the relation-

---

[1] Epstein, 'Theory to Practice'; Henry, *Parent–School Collaboration*.
[2] Pomson and Schnoor, *Back to School*.
[3] Coleman, *Equality of Educational Opportunity*.

ships between communities/parents and schools;[4] and second, that the primary outcomes of these relationships have greater significance for children than for parents.[5] At the same time, we suggest, these outcomes confirm an emerging strand of thought within the study of contemporary Jewry, one that emphasizes the fluidity of adult Jewish identities, even—if not especially—among those who may not have previously been deeply engaged with aspects of Jewish life.[6]

Background

Our study was conducted between 2002 and 2006 in and around the Downtown Jewish Day School (DJDS), a private, religiously pluralistic Jewish elementary school in Toronto, Canada. A small school, with just under 110 students between kindergarten and grade 6 at the time of the study, DJDS is a pioneering institution committed to a progressive educational mission. It is located in a downtown city neighbourhood that was once home to a major concentration of Jews but today is at some distance from centres of Jewish residence in the city.

The DJDS parent body differs in a number of respects from that of a typical Jewish day school.[7] These differences are worth detailing, given our concern in this chapter with what happens to the Jewish culture of families once their children start to attend an all-day Jewish school.

In terms of their religious behaviour, DJDS parents tend to be nonconformists who are certainly not inclined to do things because they or their own parents have always done them that way. Half of the couples we interviewed were either intermarried or conversionary. In just over a quarter of the family units in our sample, one parent was not Jewish at the time of the research.

This is a highly educated—one might say intellectual—group, many of whom have been attracted to the downtown area because of its proximity to cultural institutions and to a major North American university. For a group of private school parents, they seem relatively lacking in materialism. As one teacher put it: 'For these parents, what is important is more the kinds of kids they have than the things their kids have.'

[4] Gamoran et al., 'The Organizational Context of Teaching and Learning'.
[5] Honig et al., 'School–Community Connections'; Swap, *Developing Home–School Partnerships*.   [6] Horowitz, *Connections and Journeys*; Grant et al., *A Journey of Heart and Mind*.
[7] Pomson, 'Schools for Parents?'.

For most of these parents, living downtown is also an expression of intent to disengage from organized and denominational Jewish life. Only about half of the parents belong to Jewish institutions other than the downtown Jewish community centre where the school itself is located. Conventionally, social scientists view synagogue membership as a primary indicator of Jewish communal connection. Yet, while some 85 per cent of day school parents in Toronto (and 95 per cent in the United States) currently maintain synagogue membership, only 50 per cent do so at DJDS, and a quarter of these are members of what Wertheimer would call a 'progressive niche synagogue', a local fellowship where Jews band together periodically for prayer and other activities.[8] Those parents who do attend services at synagogues tend to prefer the style at a local 'traditional egalitarian' service rather than any of the denominational congregations in the city's midtown neighbourhoods. Others prefer to develop their own rituals either within their own immediate families or with close friends. They 'believe without belonging', to use a phrase coined by one British sociologist in her study of contemporary religious life.[9]

What this means in practice was explained by one DJDS mother during an interview:

We still feel connected to our Judaism but not necessarily in the traditional way; a little more secular. Neither of us like synagogue, we haven't really found a place that we like to go as a family and our kids completely hate it and we don't want to make them go ... So we sometimes do go to Shaarei Chesed[10] [a Conservative synagogue] ... to be with John's father in respect to him ... Otherwise on Rosh Hashanah we like to apple orchard, and to have our own family ceremonies as well. We sit in the orchard and talk about what our new year's resolutions are and we will go around and say what we want to do ... Or on Yom Kippur we go to a ravine and we ask for forgiveness from one another. We do things that are personally meaningful ... Generally, it is the six of us doing it together ... Our neighbour wanted to come with us this year, she is like a surrogate aunt. She is not Jewish but she is a surrogate aunt; so she came with us.

Strikingly, given that parents have selected a parochial Jewish school for their children, none seem interested in living in neighbourhoods where there are many other Jewish families. Their homes are located in areas of

---

[8] Wertheimer, 'The American Synagogue'.   [9] Davie, *Religion in Britain since 1945*.
[10] A pseudonym, like the names of all other institutions and individuals in the chapter other than DJDS.

town that are socio-economically and culturally diverse; in many cases they are the only Jewish family on the street. What brings such families to send their children to a Jewish day school is a mixture of four factors that we explore at length elsewhere.[11] These are: (1) (as an inhibitor) the parents' general ambivalence towards parochial Jewish schools; and, more positively, (2) their search for a quality education for their children, (3) their concern for their children's Jewish future, and (4)—a factor until now overlooked in research on Jewish school choice—their search for an institution that can satisfy some of their own personal and social needs as Jewish adults. It was this last factor (one that surfaced during our first round of interviews with new parents) that alerted us to the need to examine if and how parents' personal and social lives are changed once their children start attending the school.

Methodology

Our data for taking up this question come from two primary sources: parents and children. We interviewed twenty-eight parents twice, first when their children started at the school and again two years later, whether or not the children were still enrolled at DJDS. We interviewed a further sample of twenty-eight 'old-timer' parents whose children were in one of the school's higher grades and who had been associated with the school for at least four years. Separately, we twice interviewed in one-to-one conversations the children of this second group. Over a two-year period, a member of the research team also conducted periodic naturalistic observations of these children at regular intervals in their classrooms, and supplemented these observations by interviewing their teacher.

In order to understand the particularities of DJDS families better, we interviewed six further samples of parents, more than 100 people in total. Two groups had children enrolled in other day schools in Toronto; the other groups had children in one of four day schools in a city in the American Midwest. In all instances, interviews were recorded and transcribed.

Taken together, these data enable us to piece together over time and over triangulated data points an account of what we call 'the school at home': the encounters between parents and their children's school as these are played out within the privacy of their own homes.

[11]   Pomson and Schnoor, *Back to School*, ch. 2.

How School Enters People's Homes

Young children bring school into their homes almost every day. Unlike adolescents, who are notoriously reticent about reporting at home what took place during school hours, younger children often need little prompting to share new knowledge or to involve their parents in celebrating their achievements and in confronting their problems. The 9-year-old pupils we interviewed found no difficulty in providing examples of how they taught their parents things which, they say, their parents had either forgotten or had never known.

Joanne, who in her own words 'always likes to tell [her] mom and dad about all the different things that [she] learn[s]', reports teaching her mother 'how to do fractions' since 'she'd forgotten how to do them', telling her parents about the exciting medieval times unit they're doing, and, she says, teaching her non-Jewish stepfather 'prayers and stuff' since he doesn't know Hebrew.

It's striking that even one of Joanne's classmates, Isaac, has noticed how much Joanne's father has learnt from the school:

Isaac: My friend Joanne, she's very nice. She has a dad that's not Jewish and she has a mom that is Jewish but her dad caught on very quickly to the Jewish religion.

Interviewer: Why do you think he caught on to the Jewish religion?

Isaac: Well, because I guess he saw how they really celebrated a lot and he comes to the school a lot and I guess maybe he had a little bit of experience before he came into the family—it's her stepdad I think.

On the basis of what we hear in interviews with students, it is difficult to know how much of what children 'teach' their parents is unsolicited and how much has been genuinely unknown or forgotten. Conversations with DJDS parents reveal, however, that since most did not experience an intensive Jewish education of their own, they do find themselves learning about Jewish holidays or concepts that they had not previously known. While all parents were familiar with the major Jewish holidays of Rosh Hashanah, Yom Kippur, and Passover, many were surprised to learn from their children about Tu Bishvat (the new year for trees), Shavuot (the summer harvest festival), and other festivals that are not well known outside Israel. As one father who had attended Sunday school until his bar mitzvah put it:

'[My daughter] knows more about some of the holidays than I do. I'm in big trouble . . . because I only know the top three.' Even those who in their own childhoods experienced a more intensive Jewish education report having learned from their children because of the more engaging educational approach employed by the school.

The most vivid and perhaps the most authentic instances of children bringing school into their homes occur less through the instruction of parents by children and more as a result of unexpected and unsolicited outbursts of song and conversation with which children interrupt the regular life of the family. These outbursts, less scripted than the child–parent instruction described above, take various forms. Children launch into blessings, contemporary Hebrew songs, or traditional festival melodies, in the car on the way to and from school, at home when family are visiting, in the supermarket with parents, or on the street and at the beach. Sometimes children surprise their parents with challenging theological questions that are stimulated by discussions at school, such as: 'If God is everywhere, so God is in the air, and I'm swallowing the air, so does that mean that God is in me and I'm God?'

How Parents React

A significant proportion of DJDS parents came to the school feeling ambivalent both about the consequences of parochial education and about their own Jewish identities. As a result, they reacted to interruptions such as these in diverse and often unexpected ways. In broad terms, these reactions can be viewed along a continuum from resistance and rejection, on the one hand, to adoption and adaptation, on the other. The first set of responses expresses an inclination to keep things the way they are and not to make changes in one's Jewish life; the second suggests a readiness to make changes in the home as a result of what children bring back from school.

Resistance/Rejection (Maintaining Equilibrium at Home)

The most extreme strategy available to parents for rejecting what children bring home is to withdraw them from the school altogether. If parents feel uncomfortable with the Jewish concepts and ideas their children encounter at school, they can transfer their children to other schools that will not present them with these problematic ideas and practices.

We assumed that something of this sort was taking place at DJDS when, during one year of our research, as many as eight families transferred their children out of the school. However, through interviews with four of the couples who had withdrawn their children we discovered that none of them attributed their departure to disappointment or discontent with the school's Jewish orientation. Their complaints were focused on other areas, such as the administration's lack of responsiveness to their concerns or social issues involving their children. These four families, at least, were not expressing in their departure a rejection of the Jewish content of what their children brought home.

Nevertheless, it is quite clear that not all parents have reacted positively to the ways their children learn to talk and act in Jewish terms at DJDS. We found that at regular intervals parents came to the principal to complain about their children talking 'too much' about God or about Israel, about their wanting to recite blessings 'all the time', or simply because their children talked about theological matters in ways that made them feel uncomfortable.

An example of just such discomfort was provided by Maytal Hillberg, a secular Israeli who had married a Jewish Torontonian, and who was highly conflicted about not sending her children to the local public school. Maytal expressed profound unease with religious practices in general, and this disquiet came to a head when her daughter started to recite prayers at home that she'd learned at school.

Maytal: In the beginning when all these prayers were new to Liat, she came home and would be singing her prayers . . . She was singing Adon Olam, she was singing a bunch of prayers, like proper prayer, and I was standing here thinking I should write that school. 'What are they sending my kid home with?!'

Mike: I wasn't like that. I thought it was really cute . . .

Maytal: Like this was my initial reaction. It's like why are they teaching her that, and then I'm thinking, 'Oh my God, I'm paying for this!'

And then I came to the realization that it's good. I know all these songs. I know the tunes. I know the way they pray. Like I don't know the prayers. I don't know anything about prayers—I don't know what prayers you would say in the morning and what prayers you say before you eat. I didn't grow up with that. But she will know and it will make her richer and then she can choose. I don't care what she chooses, like it totally does not relate to me, these prayers. But then if she didn't go to this school she wouldn't have even known that they exist.

Interestingly, Maytal seems to have coped with her discomfort as a parent by finding a way to compartmentalize this experience so that it didn't impinge on her own identity. Instead, she held on to a point of balance she'd previously found in terms of her own Jewish identity that didn't require her to adjust her own thinking or practices in this new situation. She recognizes value in what her daughter now knows, but this recognition doesn't require her to change her own value system.

Neither Rejection nor Adaptation but Acceptance (Maintaining Equilibrium at Home)

One kind of parent reaction, articulated by a very small number of interviewees, expressed a similar lack of change in response to what children brought home from school, but for profoundly different reasons. The three families who talked in this way explained that what their children brought home made little difference to the Jewishness of their homes, not because they weren't interested, but either because their children were getting from the school what they, the parents, would otherwise have given them or because it simply complemented the way they led their lives already. Carolyn Weinstein, the child of a non-Orthodox rabbi, and in periods of her life an active synagogue member, elaborated on what this meant:

We are fairly educated for a liberal Jewish family, I would say . . . I know that for a lot of people, what comes home [from school] with the kids is a major part of the Jewish thing that's going on in the house . . . Whereas here, what comes home with Yoni just complements what's here already. I would say it's not more than what is here, it's just that now he gets to understand it more or be more a part of it, you know what I mean?

Talking with great self-awareness, Carolyn explained what this meant in terms of her own inner Jewish life and why 'the school at home' makes little difference to her own sense of Jewishness:

I mean my Jewish identity actually is located in myself, and it may have its outlet in just everything I do. The decisions I make—what to eat, what to do on the holidays—all that revolves around me. My Jewish identity revolves around me, my home, my whatever. And a lot of it has an outlet in a synagogue context because Jews celebrate holidays in a synagogue community. I don't see that changing [because my child attends a Jewish day school].

Adoption/Adaptation (Change at Home)

The kind of stability expressed by parents in these cases (whether because of their engagement or their lack of engagement with Judaism) was actually rare. More often than not, parents indicated that there had been significant change in their Jewish lives since, perhaps because, their child had started at DJDS. Why this is so starts to become apparent as parents talk about the changes in their homes, but we will wait until a later section to spell out what, we suggest, are the motors behind these effects.

While in many instances parents talked vaguely about how 'there would be no Jewishness in our lives if our child wasn't at the school', a small number of interviewees described precisely what this meant and how it happened. Ed and Sharon Manning, for example, are an intermarried couple who only 'checked out' DJDS because of 'the sheer fact that Sharon's family was Jewish'. In our second interview with them, after two years of association with the school, they described what had happened since Adam, their eldest son, joined the school. Ed, the non-Jewish partner in the marriage, takes up the story:

Ed: When we first started [at the school] there was a lot of talk about [us having chosen a Jewish school].

Interviewer: You mean around the family?

Ed: Yeah, and now I mean it's incorporated into our lives pretty easily to the point where it's not really noticed any more. So on a day-to-day basis it's, let's see your Hebrew homework, let's see your regular homework, and we work through it. But then my mother-in-law, the other day, she is almost more surprised as to how it has affected me than Adam where now that he gets a challah [sabbath loaf] every Friday and brings it home there's reason to do the Friday night prayers that we didn't normally do at all before. And while we've got challah and we made a covering for it so there's even more reason to do it. So I start pulling out the wine cup and the candles and my mother-in-law says, 'Ed, you're getting ready for sabbath dinner!!' I said that's what we do now. And so most Fridays we say the prayers and incorporate it into our weekly life. It's something I look forward to but it's not like a special event any more. It's a part of what we do.

The changes in their Jewish lives at home described by other parents frequently have this quality: they are not dramatic and might not have been noticed if another person hadn't remarked on them. They don't necessarily involve taking on practices that were never previously observed by the family, but rather entail doing them more frequently or more consistently as they become part of a routine organized around the rhythm of the school (or to be precise, the Jewish) calendar.

For some parents it isn't even a question of performing practices more frequently but rather one of doing them differently. Things now feel 'different, more important', explains Ian Maybaum, who was himself enrolled in a Jewish day school until grade 8, but thereafter turned away from Jewish life and ritual for several years. He reports that 'Whenever I'm now in a family situation where it's sabbath or a shivah [a mourning house] or something, I'm paying attention more, I'm reading along more. I find that I'm just more involved instead of standing at the back of the room, scratching my head waiting for this to end.'

Ian's wife Carrie talks in more emotional terms about these affects. She helpfully points both to their son's role in this accelerating process and its infusion of more Jewish spirit into the extended family.

I find that for me it's mostly his excitement about it and his interest and what he brings. You know Michael is at the age where everything Daniel [the DJDS student] does he imitates, so he has started to sing along too. He wants to help light the candle. It's the nice feeling you get, in fact it seems warm and fuzzy. And I can see it in my parents' eyes and my aunts and uncles' eyes, when you see them like that . . . They haven't seen it in us since we were children.

The intensification of Jewish life reported in all of these cases does not occur in uniform fashion, with parents taking up some script for Jewish living that their children have learned at school. Instead, parents absorb and adapt what their children bring home within the family's existing culture and style—sometimes in ways that Jewish educators would find surprising if not challenging.

The Lombards, for example, who are among the school's founding parents, describe the interaction between Jewish concepts their children have learned at school and the non-traditional Jewish life of their own family. They describe a fluid process that flows to and from school, fuelled, they indicate, by the children's enthusiasm for their learning, which in turn, we suggest, finds a receptive audience at home.

Interviewer: So, has the school brought a lot of Jewishness to you guys as adults? . . . Has it really been a source of Jewish identity for you?

Estelle: Well, it has for me. Well, [the children] get excited about this stuff and so you can't help but sort of get caught up in it to a certain extent. And also you feel like you should, I mean if they are learning the stuff at school. Like when we went out for Chinese food on a Friday night, remember? And Lara goes, as we were leaving the restaurant . . . 'Isn't it sabbath?!' . . . Or the time when Joshua was in SK [senior kindergarten] and every Friday they either say, or they have the parent write, what their *mitsvah* of the week is. So there we were having our Chinese food, eating, and there wasn't any shrimp left and Lara wanted another one, and Joshua said I could give her mine. Hey that could be my *mitsvah*! I don't think he did write it.

Ray: I thought he did. I think we were talking about what if he did want to write it, would we feel comfortable enough at school . . .

Estelle: You know what's great, like I remember in SK, Joanna, the teacher, asked the kids what their favourite foods are and I think Lara said shrimp, so a note goes up on the board. Like, yeah, I don't know about other Jewish day schools. I don't know how that would have gone over but I think . . . that's the reflection of the school and the families that go to the school.

Ray: And for us not to feel guilty about it. I mean that's how we are living our life.

This case is instructive. At first glance it might be taken to provide an example of parents unmoved by what their children bring home. After all, the family doesn't seem to have taken on any special sabbath or dietary practices as a result of what their children have learned (as some of the families previously described have done). And yet during the course of this conversation it becomes apparent that Ray and Estelle, who themselves received only a limited Jewish education, have absorbed concepts and ideas from their children, albeit on their own terms. Their conversation is peppered with Jewish ideas and words, many of which they have learned from their children. Their social life is more or less built around the Jewish families they met through their children and whom they didn't know before connecting with the school. They have also now joined a synagogue because, as they put it, 'We thought, well, if our kids are going to a Jewish school, it would also be nice if we belonged to a synagogue.' And yet, as they say, they are perfectly comfortable with how they lead their Jewish lives, shrimp and all. In their case, the school has not taken over the home, although it is undoubtedly *in* the home, brought there by their children, where it interacts and is syncretized with a pre-existing family culture.

Why Do Parents React in These Ways?

In order to make sense of these various parental reactions, we take up some sociological categories that have been widely used for analysing the relationships between parents and schools. The categories we have in mind—those of social capital and cultural capital—can help provide a general explanation for the patterns we observed without requiring us to infer the internal motivations of interviewees from their conversations with us.[12]

Social capital, as defined by Putnam, refers to the 'social networks among individuals . . . and the norms of reciprocity and trustworthiness that arise from them'.[13] Cultural capital refers to forms of knowledge, skill, education—any cultural advantages a person has which give them a higher status in society.[14] In the DJDS samples we find that, in almost all cases, those who are most inclined to adopt and adapt the Jewish content of what their children bring home from school are the families with limited Jewish social capital and limited Jewish cultural capital.

Characteristically, when these families enrolled at the school they had few Jewish friends and associates; only about half of them were connected with any other public Jewish institutions, and many of them—recall that half of those we interviewed were conversionary or intermarried couples—possessed few Jewish family connections. These are the characteristics of limited Jewish social capital.

At the same time, there is evidence that our sample also possessed limited Jewish cultural capital. None had attended an all-day Jewish school outside Israel beyond the elementary level, and most had received only a rudimentary Jewish education for between one and three afternoons a week until the age of 12 or 13. Their knowledge of Jewish literature, practice, and culture was limited, and few knew Hebrew well.

It seems that once such families had made the decision to join the school, they took full advantage of opportunities to develop their own Jewish social and cultural capital. Families with the most limited pre-existing Jewish cultural literacy and social life were those most ready to engage with the school at home. In fact, as some made clear in interviews, it was precisely because of their awareness of their own Jewish deficits that they had

---

[12] See Coleman and Hoffer, *Public and Private High Schools*; Fine, '[Ap]parent Involvement'; Lareau, *Home Advantage*; McNeal, 'Parental Involvement as Social Capital'.

[13] Putnam, *Bowling Alone*.   [14] Bourdieu, 'The Forms of Capital'.

chosen the school in the first place. Others may not have enrolled at the school so deliberately but, over time, they also recognized the difference made in their lives both by their children bringing their Jewish learning home from school and by their own participation as adults in the life of the institution.

Two interviewees who seemed well aware of why they first enrolled at the school and what that meant for their family were an intermarried couple, Adele and Dave Wallace. The couple talk with great frankness about originally choosing the school because Adele recognized that unless their son was in a Jewish school he would not develop a meaningful Jewish identity at home. Adele appreciated that Dave was allergic to institutional Jewish life. Having been connected to the school for more than four years, they can now see the difference in their lives at home.

Interviewer: What is your Jewish family life like here, the three of you?

Dave: Well, what are the components of it? We often will light the candles on Friday night and say kiddush and because of Sam being at the school I think this leads us to celebrate the holidays in a more, not rigorous, but I guess more routine way because when holidays come up Sam is involved with them in school all the time. Since Sam was, I don't know how long now—since he was six or something like that, we joined a group, the Danforth Jewish Circle. Have you heard of it?

Interviewer: Yeah.

Dave: And we do go to services on Yom Kippur and Rosh Hashanah. What else, dear?

Adele: I would say that apart from the school . . . you see, we have very little close family. Dave has two cousins in town so they celebrate Jewish holidays. And his mom is 91. His father has passed away. His brother lives in Vancouver, and he isn't Jewish at all, so we have virtually no Jewish support structure . . . We do go to Montreal [where his mother lives] but it's kind of too late. His mom is 91, and in her 80s she didn't want us there for the holidays, it was just too much to handle, so I would say we have virtually no family Jewish culture except for what *we've* brought in since *he* has come to this school. The sorts of things that you mentioned and going to *shul* and so on. You've always *davened* [prayed] on your own on the high holidays even before Sam. But the school was a pivotal decision for us because I kind of said to Dave I'm not prepared to do extra-curricular Judaism, after-school Judaism like an add-on. Like I felt if we were going to introduce him to a Jewish identity it had to be done authentically and in the context of a community because we had no family context for it—virtually none, I couldn't convey much. [emphasis added]

Strikingly, in this case it is Adele, the non-Jewish partner, who was most alert to the Jewish cultural deficit in the home, a phenomenon replicated in Prell's study of intermarried families in Philadelphia.[15] Adele's initiative (an ultimatum, in fact, since she'd threatened to raise the child in her own faith if they didn't register at a day school), combined with Sam's enthusiasm for what he'd learned at school, has stimulated a significant change in the family's Jewish culture. This change has meant not simply adopting what comes home from school but rather adapting it to and integrating it with what the parents themselves bring in. This is confirmed by our conversations with Sam himself, who made the point that although he was Jewish, because his father 'comes from a Jewish family and his mother doesn't', they celebrate Christmas and Easter at home. This is in contrast to some of his schoolmates' families who celebrate only Jewish holidays because in those families 'they're all Jewish'.

In similar fashion, those for whom the social aspect of school life was most meaningful were the individuals and families who came to the school with the most attenuated Jewish social capital. Weak Jewish social capital, it seems, leads to active participation in the religious aspects of school life, whether through participation in school events that mark Jewish festivals or through gathering together with other DJDS families in their own homes to celebrate festivals together.

A single mother, Joyce Silver, provides an account of this dynamic, and of the intimate connection between the workings of social and cultural capital. Although Joyce was born into a traditional Jewish home, she 'went off the rails' following her parents' divorce, dropping out of school and leaving home as early as was legal. Eventually she put herself through college and became a successful businessperson. She maintained very few Jewish friends or family relationships but, in her own words, she 'missed the connection to the tradition, the stories and the songs and the really wonderful memories of my childhood in the religion'. As a result of a chance conversation, she 'kind of fell into the DJDS . . . and it fit, because I felt like in a sense that it was a school for the freaks—the Jewish downtown freak parents. So it was perfect for me.'

---

[15] Prell, 'Jewish Families and Education'.

Retrospectively, this sense of belonging, of connection with a group of like-minded parents, is a large part of what Joyce has taken from the experience.

I got a lot out of the school as a community . . . My family is small. There's Joanne and the dog, myself, the hamsters, and the fish. Joanne doesn't have cousins. I don't have a husband. Her father lives in Halifax, so [the school] really acts as an extension to the family . . . And although I've become a bit concerned about the quality of the education . . . it's the community that holds me there.

As Joyce reflects on what the school has meant to her, it becomes apparent that the school's significance goes beyond its nurturing of her social connection with other Jews. Its importance derives also from what has been made possible in the home where she and her daughter, together, engage in what might be called the sub-atomic work of Jewish cultural construction, or what would be more conventionally referred to as the cultivation of Jewish cultural capital. In many ways, and despite Joyce's self-description, this cultural work looks much less freakish than she imagines:

So you know what, my home life now is very much talking about all the things that I had when I was a kid. We cook the same food and we build the sukkah out here. We don't do it the kosher way but we do it and have fun; and Joanne, I'm thrilled that she knows. Like we lit candles on Friday night and her friend Cheryl was over and they did the long blessing over the wine which I don't know. I mean I can hum along with it but I never really learned it and it gives me great joy that Joanne knows the blessings. That's where she excels. She loves the study of the Torah and loves the prayers, so it's wonderful. I get such joy out of it. We talk a lot about that—about relationships to God. And I believe in God, it's in my own kind of Jewish–Buddhist way, but it's there. So I bring that into our home.

In many ways it is hard to imagine a more effective articulation of this chapter's themes than is provided by this statement. The school-at-home is a source for both Jewish social and Jewish cultural capital. Through their children, and at private, often deeply meaningful moments, parents acquire new Jewish social connections and new Jewish knowledge. But, as we have seen, social and cultural capital is not simply deposited at home by children returning from school. Parents process, adapt, and ultimately syncretize capital with and within an already existing family culture; and, as we have suggested, this can take place in ways that Jewish educators might find challenging or at least idiosyncratic.

Implications

We recognize that there is something counter-intuitive about parents' lives being so much changed as a consequence of what their children bring home from elementary school. As we noted at the outset, sociologists have conventionally assumed that influences between school and home flow in a different direction, from parents to school. It is tempting, therefore to dismiss our data as a freakish consequence of the unusual profile of the parent body at DJDS or the school's relative newness and small size.

In fact, after comparing findings from DJDS with data we collected at six other Jewish day schools, we conclude that the affects we observed at DJDS were unique not in their occurrence but only in their frequency. This, we suggest, is not because of the school's size or age but because its distinctive downtown location and particular educational orientation have brought about a concentration of families with limited Jewish social and cultural capital. It is these families for whom Jewish day schools possess the greatest significance in terms of their Jewish lives.

If this sounds tautologous—that those who gain most from the encounter with day schools are those who have most to gain from it—it is worth emphasizing how much this claim departs from previous assumptions about the relationship between non-Orthodox parents and Jewish day schools. Since the 1970s, a spate of studies has found that less traditional families enrolled their children in day schools *in spite of* the Jewish education they offered.[16] It was assumed that many parents were prepared to tolerate the Jewishness of Jewish day schools as the price for access to the kind of high-quality general education they provided. Even today, this continues to be an assumption widely held by those who market day schools within the religiously non-Orthodox community, where emphasis is placed on the capacity of day schools to produce Ivy League candidates rather than their potential to prepare students with particular Jewish strengths. Our study indicates that a lack of prior Jewish engagement does not necessarily inhibit parents' interest in a school's Jewish content or their responsiveness to their children's Jewish learning; indeed, it may actually fuel their interest and engagement in the school.

[16] Kelman, 'Motivations and Goals'; Zeldin, *Cultural Dissonance in Jewish Education*.

Bibliography

Bourdieu, P., 'The Forms of Capital' (trans. R. Nice), in J. C. Richardson (ed.), *Handbook of Theory and Research for the Sociology of Education* (New York, 1986), 241–58.

Coleman, J. S., *Equality of Educational Opportunity* (Washington, DC, 1966).

—— and T. Hoffer, *Public and Private High Schools: The Impact of Communities* (New York, 1987).

Davie, G., *Religion in Britain since 1945: Believing without Belonging* (Oxford, 1994).

Epstein, J. L., 'Theory to Practice: School and Family Partnerships Lead to School Improvement and Student Success', in B. Schneider and J. S. Coleman (eds.), *Parents, their Children, and Schools* (Boulder, Colo., 1994), 40–52.

Fine, M., '[Ap]parent Involvement: Reflections on Parents, Power, and Urban Public Schools', *Teachers College Record*, 94/4 (1993), 682–729.

Gamoran, A., W. G. Secada, and C. B. Marrett, 'The Organizational Context of Teaching and Learning: Changing Theoretical Perspectives', in Maureen T. Hallinan (ed.), *Handbook of Sociology of Education* (New York, 2000), 37–63.

Grant, L. D., D. Tickton-Schuster, M. Woocher, and S. M. Cohen, *A Journey of Heart and Mind: Transformative Jewish Learning in Adulthood* (New York, 2004).

Henry, M. E., *Parent–School Collaboration: Feminist Organizational Structures and School Leadership* (Albany, NY, 1996).

Honig, M. I., J. Kahne, and M. W. McLaughlin, 'School–Community Connections: Strengthening Opportunity to Learn and Opportunity to Teach', in V. Richardson (ed.), *Handbook of Research on Teaching*, 4th edn. (Washington, DC, 2001), 998–1028.

Horowitz, B., *Connections and Journeys: Assessing Critical Opportunities for Enhancing Jewish Identity* (New York, 2000).

Kelman, S. L., 'Motivations and Goals: Why Parents Send their Children to Non-Orthodox Day Schools', *Jewish Education*, 47/1 (1979), 44–8.

Lareau, A., *Home Advantage: Social Class and Parental Intervention in Elementary Education* (Lanham, Md., 2000).

McNeal, R. B., Jr, 'Parental Involvement as Social Capital: Differential Effectiveness on Science Achievement, Truancy and Dropping Out', *Social Forces*, 78/1 (1999), 117–44.

Pomson, A., 'Schools for Parents? What Parents Want and What They Get from their Children's Jewish Day Schools', in J. Wertheimer (ed.), *Family Matters: Jewish Education in an Age of Choice* (Hanover, NH, 2007), 101–42.

—— and R. F. Schnoor, *Back to School: Jewish Day School in the Lives of Adult Jews* (Detroit, 2008).

Prell, R.-E., 'Jewish Families and Education: How Children's Uniqueness and Parental Choice Will Shape American Judaism in the 21st century', in J. Wertheimer (ed.), *Family Matters: Jewish Education in an Age of Choice* (Hanover, NH, 2007), 3–33.

Putnam, R. D., *Bowling Alone: The Collapse and Revival of American Community* (New York, 2000).

Swap, S. M., *Developing Home–School Partnerships: From Concepts to Practice* (New York, 1993).

Wertheimer, J., 'The American Synagogue: Recent Trends and Issues', *American Jewish Year Book*, 105 (New York, 2005), 3–108.

Zeldin, M., *Cultural Dissonance in Jewish Education: The Case of Reform Day Schools* (Los Angeles, 1988).

EIGHTEEN

Teacher Perspectives on Behaviour Problems

Background Influences on Behavioural Referral Criteria and Definitions of Rebellious Behaviour

SCOTT J. GOLDBERG, BINYAMIN KROHN, AND MICHAEL TURETSKY

S CHOOLS are often faced with two competing goals. They must develop the individual, and in pursuit of that end have a duty to facilitate a child's growing understanding, subjectivity, and responsibility. At the same time, though, schools are training grounds for society's institutions.[1] As a result of this twin purpose there is often a tension between fostering individuality, on the one hand, and nurturing citizenship and communal responsibility, on the other.

While this tension exists in almost all communal settings, in certain circumstances the conflict of roles becomes especially complex. Bronfenbrenner argued that the child's development is based in large part on the support he or she receives and the structure in which he or she is embedded.[2] Figure 18.1 shows that although parents and friends may have the

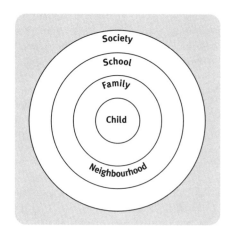

FIGURE 18.1. Bronfenbrenner's Ecological Model of Development. The child is embedded within nested contexts of influence

[1] Olsen, *Psychological Theory and Educational Reform.*
[2] Bronfenbrenner, *The Ecology of Human Development.*

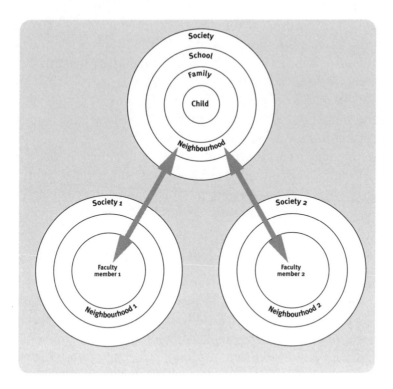

FIGURE 18.2. Reconsidering Bronfenbrenner for a multilingual/multicultural educational setting. Faculty members may come from different neighbourhoods and societies and bring diverse cultures into the school

most direct impact on the child, the child is also part of a neighbourhood and society that have certain values and expectations.

A model of this kind may be adequate to explain the development of a child living in an isolated, unicultural community. However, the circumstances of a multilingual and/or multicultural educational setting provide good reason for re-examining Bronfenbrenner's model, while the special circumstances of a bilingual educational setting, in which teachers and students from different cultures may speak different first languages and practise different religions, pose a powerful challenge to the model. In multicultural and multilingual schools, a child may come from a family whose society and culture differ radically from those not only of one faculty member, but possibly of several. Figure 18.2 highlights the complexity this may add to Bronfenbrenner's model.

Against the backdrop of these issues, two studies are reported here concerning the role community plays in defining appropriate and inappropriate or antisocial behaviour. The first examines office referrals in a multilingual, multicultural school to determine the extent to which community affiliation influences the point at which a behaviour is considered inappropriate and should be referred to the office.[3] The second study builds on the results of the first by asking teachers from a variety of multilingual and multicultural schools to give specific examples of normal, at-risk, and rebellious behaviours. The combined results of these studies shed light on some of the challenges presented by the cultural and linguistic heterogeneity of Jewish schools and suggest positive approaches to managing such issues.

Behaviour and the Cultural Background of Children

The relationships between children and the adults in their lives are affected by the culture in which the children are raised. For example, culture has an impact on the extent to which a child will be independent, or at least given the opportunity to be independent. Zuniga found that Latino children in pre-school may still drink from a (baby) bottle.[4] Similarly, because Asian families are generally more protective of their children, those children are likely to move away from their families at a much later age than many others.[5] Orthodox Jewish families, by contrast, appear to stress autonomy more than either Latino or Asian parents. In Jewish families—especially among the Orthodox, where families tend to be larger—'sibling parenting' occurs, where one of the older children may take the place of the mother at times and play a significant role in the development of the younger children.[6] In addition, it is common for some Orthodox Jews to send their children to boarding school, in which case the parents' role will almost certainly be diminished, regardless of how involved they are in their child's schoolwork.[7]

These childrearing practices are influenced by what a culture considers appropriate behaviour; and this, as Garbarino has noted, varies from one

---

[3] An 'office referral' is a report to a principal or administrator responsible for behaviour in a school, delineating the nature of an infraction, as well as other information relevant to understanding its context, such as the time and place of the occurrence.

[4] Zuniga, 'Families with Latino Roots', 229.   [5] Chan, 'Families with Asian Roots', 302.

[6] Dickstein, 'The Effects of Older Sibling Caretaking'.

[7] Anglin, *Pain, Normality, and the Struggle for Congruence*.

culture to another.[8] In a particular study conducted in the early 1980s, Garbarino asked adolescents in two distinct societies, the Amish in Pennsylvania and the Lebanese in Beirut, what was the worst behaviour they had ever seen. The Amish teens noted that once someone wore a pink handkerchief in his pocket. When pressed, they added that there was an unconfirmed case of a teenager hitching a ride on a tractor. In stark contrast the Lebanese, in the midst of a civil war, discussed killing within one's own clan.[9]

Interactions between adults and children are also governed by cultural norms. At one extreme, Iranian children may be expected not to speak in the presence of adults or touch food without permission.[10] In some Jewish schools the students may all stand up, as a sign of respect, when an adult walks into the classroom; and when a teacher already in the room stands up to address the group, the students may stand up again, as a sign of reverence for the teacher. By contrast, it is common in American society for adults to be introduced to children by their first names and for these names then to be used by the children.

Cultural norms also direct social interactions among children. While many cultures support a healthy amount of interaction between the sexes, Orthodox Jewish boys and girls are expected to avoid physical contact with one another. Shaking hands or even attending the same party may be considered inappropriate. There are even schools that may expel students for speaking to a member of the opposite sex.

Cultural differences also influence how children are disciplined. Some cultures reward in understated ways; others use highly visible means.[11] Some cultures may engage in spanking and other forms of physical punishment, while others may consider this unthinkable.[12]

Cultural diversity, expressed in different social or behavioural expectations and combined with the unreflective use of language, may also strain the relationship between students and teachers.[13] For example, many special education providers come from mainstream culture and will define

---

[8] Garbarino, *Children and Families in the Social Environment.*
[9] Cited in Pelcovitz, *The At-Risk Adolescent in the Orthodox Jewish Community*, 5
[10] Sharifzadeh, 'Families with Middle Eastern Roots'.
[11] Chen, Downing, and Peckham-Hardin, 'Working with Families of Diverse Cultural and Linguistic Backgrounds'.
[12] Harry, *Cultural Diversity, Families, and the Special Education System.*
[13] Chen, Downing, and Peckham-Hardin, 'Working with Families of Diverse Cultural and Linguistic Backgrounds'.

behaviour that deviates from their culture as 'abnormal'. For a particular child, though, it is possible that what the teacher sees as 'abnormal' behaviour is appropriate for the setting in which he lives or has lived.

When assessing and studying student behaviour, then, there is a need to be aware of discrepancies between the observer's and the student's cultural backgrounds. Also, certain measurement tools may be culturally insensitive. Pelcovitz found that people in Sri Lanka would consider it inappropriate to complete a survey of psychological functioning because of their habitual reverence for professionals.[14] The first author of this chapter encountered a similar problem while attempting to study hasidim in Brooklyn. Given the great reverence in this community for school leaders, it was difficult to acquire parental consent for children to participate in a study because parents feared that acquiescing in such a request would amount to an acknowledgement that the school leaders were not in control and incapable of performing their job properly.

Because of all these variations, it is important that service providers understand the unique culture of each individual family with whom they work. Different families retain aspects of their culture to varying degrees, thereby necessitating an intimate knowledge of each family's background.[15] For example, many parents prefer informal meetings with the service provider rather than scheduled formal conferences.[16] It is also important that questions are formulated in a way that makes the family feel comfortable: certain families are intimidated by authority figures and may be hesitant to respond directly to them.[17]

Implications of Cultural Diversity for Understanding Student Behaviour

Each home environment may exhibit different social norms, levels of tolerance for particular behaviours, and responses to inappropriate behaviours. As a result, when children from different backgrounds attend school together, problems can ensue as a result of different expectations. Various researchers and practitioners have recommended solutions to this dilemma.

---

[14] Pers. comm., 6 Feb. 2006.   [15] Chen, Brekken, and Chan, *Project CRAFT.*
[16] Harry, *Cultural Diversity, Families, and the Special Education System.* See also Harry et al., 'Communication versus Compliance'; Sileo and Prater, 'Creating Classroom Environments'.
[17] Ishii-Jordan and Peterson, 'Behaviour Disorders in Culture and Community'. See also Lowenthal, 'Training Early Interventionists'.

In school settings, in which several cultures may be represented, 'culture and language variations should be considered' when making a decision about teaching social skills to children.[18] Furthermore, linguistic differences raise questions concerning the definition of, and specific language for, instruction in and display of behavioural expectations. While all this suggests the importance of always being sensitive to individuals' needs, schools have to balance the needs of the individual (and his or her own cultural background) with those of the institution.[19] Indeed, lack of clarity regarding behavioural norms can lead to both students and teachers not understanding what a school considers to be appropriate behaviour. Deal and Peterson suggest that when a school lacks a shared purpose or is afflicted by a splintered mission, it may become a toxic culture with associated negative outcomes such as low student achievement.[20]

An alternative approach to imposing a singular cultural norm on the group, or attempting to institute multiple simultaneous conceptions of acceptable behaviour, is to deal with the impact of multicultural and multi-linguistic differences on behaviour in a school by forming a common approach to behaviour management. School-wide positive behavioural support (PBS) has been shown to be one such effective system of collaborative behavioural management.[21] A key feature of the system is agreement among the teaching staff on what the institution regards as acceptable and unacceptable behaviours. Teachers and families, regardless of their own backgrounds, focus on student learning and relinquish individual beliefs, in the context of the school, for the sake of institutional beliefs. A positive institutional culture depends on such common beliefs applied to curriculum, instruction, student support, and other important areas of school functioning.[22]

The Case of Jewish School Settings

Many Jewish schools are bilingual if not multilingual, and the impact of a second language in such settings can be substantial. For example, in schools that emphasize communication and study in the Hebrew language,

---

[18] Darch and Kame'enui, *Instructional Classroom Management*, 163.
[19] Olsen, *Psychological Theory and Educational Reform*.
[20] Deal and Peterson, *Shaping School Culture*.
[21] Safran and Oswald, 'Positive Behavior Supports'.
[22] Deal and Peterson, *Shaping School Culture*.

qualified teachers often have to be sought in Israel, from where they bring to the United States different expectations for discipline and communication. Additionally, although religious schools are often characterized as homogeneous, Jewish day schools have a dual mandate to educate children in knowledge, skills, and dispositions of both a religious and a general kind. As a result, cultural differences among the faculty members in Jewish schools assigned to different parts of the curriculum may be even greater than in a typical school. In Jewish schools, the Jewish and secular studies departments often have different goals and outlooks, and these are sometimes at odds with each other. At the same time, different families may emphasize certain subjects at the expense of others, and many parents may not agree entirely with the school's approach towards integrating Judaic and secular studies. Consequently, the Jewish school may face an even greater challenge than others in the task of providing an education to all while also presenting a clear and common message to the students.

The studies described below considered the extent to which such diversity within the Jewish school setting frames teachers' views of student behaviour. The first study explored the relationship between the number of office referrals for student behaviour problems and the cultural background of the teachers in order to determine whether a teacher's personal threshold of acceptable behaviour may be grounded in his or her cultural background. The second study examined teacher definitions of acceptable and unacceptable behaviour in order to see more specifically how cultural background manifests itself in views on behaviour.

Study 1

Method

The data on referrals for poor behaviour in an elementary school (kindergarten to eighth grade) in a suburban setting were collected and analysed over the course of two school years. A staff survey was conducted, the results of which indicated that a high percentage of the school's staff felt it was a matter of the utmost priority to address behavioural concerns in non-classroom settings, but that little had been done practically to improve the situation. These circumstances provided the impetus within the school for learning about and implementing PBS, a school-wide approach to behaviour management involving both students and faculty in clarifying, teaching, and monitoring behaviour. Within the context of this study, such an approach was seen as a way to reduce the effect of differences in the cultural background of teachers and students by promoting institutional behavioural values. PBS was implemented prior to our second year of work with the school.

Of the approximately 300 students in the school, half of the students were of Ashkenazi and half of Sephardi descent. The data included referrals from thirty-two teachers in the school. The Judaic studies staff consisted of both Ashkenazi and Sephardi teachers, some of whom were originally from Israel. The general studies staff were mostly non-Jewish and of English-speaking origin. There was also a French studies staff. A typical programme of study includes classes in English, Hebrew, and French, along with different content taught in each of these languages.

Data came in the form of referrals from the teacher to the principal's office—a commonly used gauge of behaviour in schools.[23] The referral form that accompanies a student sent to the office for misbehaving includes the time of the behaviour, the specific behaviour, its location, and the name of the teacher making the report, as well as other defining information. All identifying information was stripped from these referral forms by the school, and identification numbers assigned to each teacher and student were noted on the forms. Information about the culture and nationality of the teachers and students was provided by the school. The faculty was also surveyed prior to implementation of PBS to determine what teachers considered the most important aspects of behaviour requiring improvement.

This study considered the following question: Is there a relationship between student behaviour and the discrepancy between student/family culture on the one hand and teacher culture on the other in Jewish schools? It was hypothesized that more behavioural referrals would be given by non-Jewish teachers as well as by non-American teachers of Hebrew and French, given the cultural and linguistic differences among the staff and their potential to affect definitions of appropriate and inappropriate behaviour.

Results

Generally, the implementation of PBS was successful at reducing behavioural problems across the entire school. Specifically, after a set of common

---

[23] Colvin et al., 'Reconceptualising Behaviour Management'. See also Jackson and Panyon, *Positive Behavioural Support in the Classroom*.

behavioural guidelines were established, the number of office referrals declined from 531 in 2005 to 157 in 2006 for the same five-month period of the year. Also, not only was there an overall reduction in the number of referrals, but the largest declines were found in classroom behavioural referrals and 'other' (undefined) behaviour issues. This may indicate that PBS was making a difference throughout the school, inside and outside the classroom, by reducing the effect of cultural differences among students and teachers. Of course, further study with a larger sample in multiple settings is needed to determine whether these effects and those presented below are generalizable.

Some of the most intriguing findings related to the location of problem behaviours. When the mean numbers of office referrals were compared for locations in which English, Hebrew, or French was the language/subject of instruction, statistically significant ($p < 0.05$) results showed 25 per cent, 30 per cent, and 45 per cent of referrals from these classes, respectively. That is, there were statistically significant differences between the three groups (English, Hebrew, and French classes) in terms of office referrals. As noted above, the student population consists mainly of children from English-speaking families. Many of these children have been learning Hebrew, and using it in their daily prayers, since they were in kindergarten or even younger, while few have had consistent contact with French. It is, therefore, noteworthy that although common behavioural expectations reduced behavioural referrals generally, as the language of instruction was more foreign to the student, so the number of referrals rose.

When the mean numbers of office referrals by teachers of various nationalities were compared, again there were noteworthy differences. The largest numbers of office referrals were made by teachers whose cultural backgrounds differed from those of the students. One teacher from a different culture and speaking a different native language from the students made twenty times more office referrals than her peers during the same period of time. However, these results were not statistically significant. This is probably because the sample size of teachers was small (thirty-two).[24]

---

[24] Lack of statistically significant differences between nationalities of teachers does not necessarily mean that there is not a difference in office referrals between such nationalities. Rather, such differences are simply not apparent because the power of the statistic is related to sample size.

Discussion

The correlation between differing student and teacher cultures and the higher number of office referrals may be understood through the frame of what are called 'portable' and 'situation-specific' behaviours.[25] If a child behaves consistently in all settings, the behaviours are considered 'portable'. If, on the other hand, the student generally meets behavioural expectations but has problems in a specific setting (in one specific class or one particular time of day) the behaviours can be considered 'situation-specific'. 'Situation-specific' behaviour is attributed in some part to the child but mostly to the context in which the behaviour is occurring.

Epkins has found that, as teachers spend more time with a specific age group, they become more accustomed to the behaviours that are considered appropriate and inappropriate for that grade level.[26] At the same time, Wentzel has found that teachers' measurements of classroom phenomena are relatively accurate and reliable.[27] However, teachers are not always trained to observe problem behaviours and may use different standards depending on the customs and mores with which they are familiar. Also, some teachers may be more assiduous than others about recording children's behaviour, generating different results.[28] Therefore, when looking at accounts of student behaviour, such as office referrals, it is important to keep in mind that the norms of one teacher may be significantly different from those of another, and this may be a consequence of their experience in teaching a specific age group rather than because of their particular culture.

In the present study, in which the language and culture of the teachers are compared with those of the students in relation to behavioural referrals, the norms of these teachers appear to be at odds with one another. Indeed, it appears that each teacher defines the behavioural norms according to his/her own cultural background or according to the norms of the school. However, the data suggest a 'situation-specific' understanding, not because teachers do not have common expectations *defined*, but because of inconsistent implementation of the school-wide PBS plan. That is, even after implementation of PBS, although office referrals generally declined, the discrepancies in numbers of referrals between teachers of a culture different from that of the students and those of similar descent to their students were still apparent. This may indicate that even common expectations may be

[25] Witt et al., *Functional Assessments*.   [26] Epkins, 'Teachers' Ratings'.
[27] Wentzel, 'Social-Motivational Processes'.   [28] Weisz et al., 'A Multimethod Study'.

translated into practice differently by people from different backgrounds at the moment of execution. Alternatively, the issue may well be grounded in differing expectations of behaviour, beyond language and general cultural background. To investigate this possibility further, the next study looked at differences in behavioural norms based not on language or culture-specific differences but on religious background.

Study 2

Method

To understand the differences between societal behavioural norms, teachers from an array of Jewish day schools were surveyed to find out how different communities define prosocial, at-risk, and antisocial behaviour ('rebelliousness'). Respondents were asked to include information about their gender, ancestry, history of religious affiliation, and teaching history, and to state whether they themselves had adolescent offspring and, if so, whether their children would be considered 'rebellious' according to themselves and others. In all, 104 responses were received from 60 males and 44 females. Of this total, 6 of the teachers were from elementary schools, 30 from middle schools, and 68 were high school teachers; 10 were on the faculty of Conservative Jewish day schools, 70 from Modern Orthodox schools, and 24 from yeshiva or hasidic schools (all these affiliations were self-reported).

Each teacher was asked to give examples of three different types of behaviour according to the following definitions. A 'normal' behaviour was categorized as one that might arouse suspicion or worry in the eyes of a parent, although a teacher would recognize it as age-appropriate. 'Yellow flag' or 'emerging problem' behaviours were defined as those that are a legitimate cause for concern but do not necessarily indicate a serious problem. Finally, 'red flag' or 'rebellious' behaviours were defined as those that do indicate a serious problem. The results showed similarities across all of the schools, but interesting differences among them as well.

This study looked into whether there is a difference in how diverse religious groups characterize behaviour. In particular, it was hypothesized that the more religious a school is, the more religious behaviours would be included by the teachers within the school in each category.

Results

Completed forms were sorted according to the school in which the respondent teaches and then according to the three types of behaviour—normal, at-risk, and rebellious. Similarities and differences were grouped on the basis of categories that emerged from the data, such as academic, behavioural, clothing, social, illegal, and sexual. Comparisons between the various religious groups were made.

Teachers in the Conservative schools responded that normal behaviour is characterized by a student who begins spending more time with friends (of both genders) than with family, begins to dress differently, and becomes very interested in one specific area (for example, sports, poetry). However, a student who changes his or her peer group entirely, begins experimenting with cigarettes, begins having difficulty academically, or has difficulty acting appropriately in class, may be demonstrating signs of a problem. Finally, teachers in the Conservative schools agreed on the whole that a student who is involved in sexual activity, drug use, or truancy would be considered rebellious.

The responses from teachers in modern Orthodox day schools differed from the Conservatives' responses in some respects. These teachers also believed that it is normal for an adolescent to want to spend more time with friends, including speaking on the phone or staying out until late at night, especially with those of the opposite gender. Students may normally be argumentative about what should be considered appropriate dress, and may occasionally drink alcohol with their peers. Adolescents may be late to school and may even miss or fail an assignment on occasion. It is normal to have difficulty with acting appropriately in class.

Moving along the continuum, though, teachers in the modern Orthodox schools believed that a student who begins wearing provocative clothing, clothing with sexually explicit messages, or 'gothic' clothing would be showing signs of an emerging problem. Also, if a student were to begin failing classes, missing assignments consistently, skipping school, and not participating in class, this too would be cause for concern. Teachers also mentioned that a student who yells at a teacher, fights in the schoolyard, is found to be going to parties frequently, and is generally chronically disruptive would be considered at risk for an emerging problem. For the modern Orthodox, too, a student who is no longer praying would raise concern of an emerging problem. Here we see the first sign of behaviour change in the religious realm being included by respondents.

Signs of rebellion in the case of the modern Orthodox schools included the typical antisocial behaviours one might expect. Illegal behaviours, such as hazing, drug and alcohol use, and stealing are all cause for serious concern. Constant fighting in school, cutting school without parental knowledge, cursing at teachers, and the like were all noted as other indications of serious rebellion. A student who misses so many assignments that he or she cannot pass his or her classes and makes no attempt to catch up on missed assignments would be considered rebellious, as would one who is openly pursuing sexual activity or is eating *treif* (non-kosher food).

In the hasidic and yeshiva schools, religious behaviour plays an even more prominent role. These teachers noted some of the same 'normal' behaviours for adolescents mentioned by the teachers in Conservative and modern Orthodox schools. However, they mentioned not only social changes, such as spending more time with friends of both genders, and occasional behaviour problems at home and in school, but also lack of interest in learning. These teachers regarded questioning of religious practice as normal for the children's stage of development.

Staying out very late with friends of both genders, changing to a different peer group, experimenting with cigarettes, and having difficulty in school are taken as indications of an emerging problem in the yeshiva and hasidic schools. The teachers also mentioned change in dress, such as wearing a blue shirt (rather than the more traditional and conforming white shirt), not wearing a tie on the sabbath, and change of *yarmulke* as significant 'yellow flags'. In addition, boys not wearing a *yarmulke* or *tsitsiyot*, and girls wearing revealing clothing, raise concerns. Listening to *goyishe* or secular rock music was also noted as a sign of an emerging problem.

A student who is involved in drug use, cutting school, or sexual activity is believed to have a serious problem, according to the hasidic and yeshiva teachers. One who is eating *treif*, stops davening (praying), is not keeping the sabbath, doesn't come to the sabbath table to eat with his or her family, has contact with the opposite sex in social situations, and wears *goyishe*/secular clothing would also be considered rebellious.

Discussion

While certain behaviours were commonly considered normal, at-risk, and rebellious by all teachers, at other times the teachers diverged in their classifications. Teachers in all groups considered it typical for an adolescent to begin spending more time with his or her friends instead of family, and viewed academic difficulty as a sign of an emerging problem. All of them classed drug use and sexual activity as rebellious behaviour. Although it was hypothesized that the behaviours included in each category would be influenced by the religious practices and beliefs of a particular community, none of the respondents included religious behaviours in their examples of normal behaviours.

Change in dress, though considered a sign of emerging or rebellious behaviour for the modern Orthodox and hasidic/yeshiva group, is considered normal by the Conservative teachers. Although all groups consider sexual activity of some degree to be a sign of an emerging problem, actual contact and pursuing such contact were considered rebellious only by the modern Orthodox and hasidic/yeshiva teachers. Also, only the hasidic/yeshiva teachers mentioned listening to secular (*goyishe*) music as a sign of any type of problem. It appears, therefore, that religious beliefs and practices play a significant role in defining at-risk and rebellious behaviour for the Orthodox, while the Conservative community defines its behavioural norms in parallel to the general population, without reference to religious issues.

Decline in religious behaviour appears only minimally as a rebellious behaviour among the modern Orthodox, although it is mentioned. At the same time, this issue is the main focus of the rebellious behaviours identified by hasidic/yeshiva teachers and is mentioned minimally by them as a sign of an emerging problem. Specifically, rebellious behaviour for the hasidic and yeshiva group includes not only the typical, such as drug use and truancy, but also the religious behaviours of eating *treif*, not praying, and not keeping the sabbath. Sexual activity and inappropriate clothing also feature in the list of rebellious behaviours for the hasidic and yeshiva group.

Conclusions

The common thread through the two studies presented here is the subjectivity of behavioural norms. Teachers' perspectives on behaviour problems were explored by investigating the kinds of behaviours by students that result in referrals to the office, and specific definitions/examples of behaviours that are considered rebellious. In each case, the effect of the cultural and linguistic background of the teacher was apparent. No doubt it was logical to hypothesize, on the basis of previous research, that some connection would be found. However, the extent of the differences in referral data for varying cultures in the first study is striking. In particular, it is remarkable that the results were apparent even after an effort was made to develop common behavioural expectations, teach them, and review them throughout the year.

Also striking is the extent to which religious background influences specific examples and definitions of behaviour. In some schools, one might expect behaviour management to be a greater challenge when differences between teachers and students are clear. However, the results of the second study suggest that religious background may have a particular influence on community norms. One would not necessarily expect a continuum of behavioural problems to reflect religious differences in such a striking way, breaking down according to religious affiliation without prompting.

The greater focus on religious behaviour by the teachers within more strictly religious institutions makes it tempting to consider the extent to which such behaviours are assessed within these organizations. Interestingly, the method of office referral, used by many schools to track student behaviour to ensure that students do not pose a risk to themselves or others, rarely seems to be employed for purely religious difficulties or even those with a religious component. Further, particular schools may find that measures commonly used to assess antisocial behaviour lack key religious components and fail to take account of other behaviours influenced by religious values that may be indicative of an emerging or existing problem. Clearly, such values are community-specific.

Thus, taken together, the two studies highlight the need for community-specific assessment tools for early detection and prevention of problem behaviours as defined by each community. Religious schools must recognize the need regularly to consider and track behaviour unbefitting a member of its community on general as well as religious grounds. Such a realization will foster a better understanding of developing children within the context of their own communities. Accordingly, each community will be better equipped to support appropriate development and growth towards citizenship among its young people, and to take the initiative in supporting children when challenges arise in both general and religious domains.

Bibliography

Anglin, J. P., *Pain, Normality, and the Struggle for Congruence: Reinterpreting Residential Care for Children and Youth* (Binghamton, NY, 2002).

Bronfenbrenner, U., *The Ecology of Human Development* (Cambridge, Mass., 1979).

Chan, S., 'Families with Asian Roots', in E. W. Lynch and M. J. Hanson (eds.), *Developing Cross-Cultural Competence: A Guide for Working with Children and their Families* (Baltimore, Md., 1998), 251–354.

Chen, D., L. Brekken, and S. Chan, *Project CRAFT: Culturally Responsive and Family Focused Training* (Baltimore, Md., 1997).

—— J. E. Downing, and K. Peckham-Hardin, 'Working with Families of Diverse Cultural and Linguistic Backgrounds: Considerations for Culturally Responsive Positive Behaviour Support', in J. M. Lucyshyn, G. Dunlap, and R. W. Albin (eds.), *Families and Positive Behaviour Support: Addressing Problem Behaviours in Family Contexts* (Baltimore, Md., 2002), 133–54.

Colvin, G., E. J. Kame'enui, and G. Sugai, 'Reconceptualising Behaviour Management and School-Wide Discipline in General Education', *Education and Treatment of Children*, 16/4 (1994), 361–81.

Darch, C. B., and E. J. Kame'enui, *Instructional Classroom Management: A Proactive Approach to Behaviour Management* (Upper Saddle River, NJ, 2004).

Deal, T. E., and K. D. Peterson, *Shaping School Culture: The Heart of Leadership* (San Francisco, 1999).

Dickstein, M. C., 'The Effects of Older Sibling Caretaking Upon Younger Children's Security of Attachment and Self-Esteem', Ph.D. diss., University of Maryland, 2000.

Epkins, C. C., 'Teachers' Ratings of Inpatient Children's Depression, Anxiety, and Aggression: A Preliminary Comparison between Inpatient-Facility and Community-Based Teachers' Ratings and their Correspondence with Children's Self Reports', *Journal of Clinical and Consulting Psychology*, 24/1 (1995), 63–70.

Garbarino, J., *Children and Families in the Social Environment* (Hawthorne, NY, 1992).

Goldberg, S. J., 'The Relationship between English (L1) and Hebrew (L2) Reading and Externalizing Behaviour amongst Orthodox Jewish Boys', Ph.D. diss., New York University, Steinhardt School of Education, 2004.

Harry, B., *Cultural Diversity, Families, and the Special Education System: Communication and Empowerment* (New York, 1992).

—— N. Allen, and M. McLaughlin, 'Communication versus Compliance: African-American Parents' Involvement in Special Education', *Exceptional Children*, 61/4 (1995), 364–77.

Ishii-Jordan, S., and R. L. Peterson, 'Behaviour Disorders in Culture and Community', in R. L. Peterson and S. Ishii-Jordan (eds.), *Multicultural Issues in the Education of Students with Behavioural Disorders* (Cambridge, Mass., 1994), 251–62.

Jackson, L., and M. V. Panyon, *Positive Behavioural Support in the Classroom: Principles and Practices* (Baltimore, Md., 2002).

Lowenthal, B., 'Training Early Interventionists to Work with Culturally Diverse Families', *Infant–Toddler Intervention*, 6/2 (1996), 145–52.

Olsen, D. R., *Psychological Theory and Educational Reform* (Cambridge, 2003).

Pelcovitz, D., *The At-Risk Adolescent in the Orthodox Jewish Community: Implications and Interventions for Educators* (New York, 2005).

Safran, S. P., and K. Oswald, 'Positive Behavior Supports: Can Schools Reshape Disciplinary Practices?', *Exceptional Children*, 69/3 (2003), 361–73.

Sharifzadeh, V.-S., 'Families with Middle Eastern Roots', in E. W. Lynch and M. J. Hanson (eds.), *Developing Cross-Cultural Competence: A Guide for Working with Children and their Families* (Baltimore, Md., 1998), 441–82.

Sileo, T. W., and M. A. Prater, 'Creating Classroom Environments that Address the Linguistic and Cultural Backgrounds of Students with Disabilities', *Remedial and Special Education*, 19/6 (1998), 323–37.

Weisz, J. R., W. Chaiyasit, B. Weiss, K. L. Eastman, and E. W. Jackson, 'A Multimethod Study of Problem Behaviour among Thai and American Children in School: Teacher Reports versus Direct Observations', *Child Development*, 66/2 (1995), 402–15.

Wentzel, K. R., 'Social-Motivational Processes and Interpersonal Relationships: Implications for Understanding Motivation at School', *Journal of Educational Psychology*, 91/1 (1999), 76–97.

Witt, J. C., E. M. Daly, and G. H. Noell, *Functional Assessments: A Step-by-Step Guide to Solving Academic and Behaviour Problems* (Longmount, Colo., 2000).

Zuniga, M. A., 'Families with Latino Roots', in E. W. Lynch and M. J. Hanson (eds.), *Developing Cross-Cultural Competence: A Guide for Working with Children and their Families* (Baltimore, Md., 1998), 209–50.

NINETEEN

Shabbatonim as Experiential Education in the North American Community Day High School

JEFFREY S. KRESS AND JOSEPH REIMER

THE RAPID PROLIFERATION in North America during the past decade of new communal and Conservative Jewish day high schools has caught many by surprise. For years nearly all Jewish day high schools were run under Orthodox auspices. However, beginning in the 1990s, the demand for Jewish day school education beyond eighth grade expanded among a more liberal constituency. Families pleased with their children's elementary day school education were eager for that education to continue into the high school years. Marvin Schick reports that between 1992 and 2004 the numbers of students in American non-Orthodox day high schools grew from 1,500 to 4,100.[1] In 2007 we know of thirty-four such high schools throughout North America.

These schools all provide a formal Jewish education through academic classes in Jewish subjects; now many have created 'experiential' opportunities for their students 'to live their Judaism'. The focus of this chapter is on the most common intensive experiential opportunity the schools offer, the Shabbaton, a retreat focusing on the communal celebration of the sabbath. These Shabbatonim are a distinctive form of experiential Jewish education;[2] yet despite their widespread implementation and the growth of experiential educational efforts in day schools, they have been given little attention in the educational literature. To address this lack, we draw on our experiences in training school-based experiential educators in order to discuss the educational goals of these Shabbaton programmes, the principles of running a successful programme, and the challenges faced by the experi-

The authors express their gratitude to the AVI CHAI Foundation for its generous support of their work.

[1] Schick, *A Census of Jewish Day Schools*.
[2] Chazan, 'The Philosophy of Informal Jewish Education'; Reimer and Bryfman, 'What We Know about Experiential Jewish Education'; Reisman, *The Jewish Experiential Book*.

ential educators who are charged with planning and implementing these programmes.

Background

In North America, the non-Orthodox Jewish day high school came of age during the decade between 1995 and 2004. These years saw existing schools grow and new schools created in communities throughout the continent. Of the current thirty-four such high schools in North America, twenty-eight identify themselves as communal and six as Conservative. Officially, communal or community schools are open to Jewish students across a broad spectrum of Jewish backgrounds and do not follow the teachings of a single religious denomination; the Conservative schools follow the teachings of their movement. However, the realities on the ground are more varied than official policy would suggest. Since there is no official body that systematically gathers information about these schools—their policies or curricula—we have been unsystematically gathering such information. This information suggests that these schools are primarily the creation of local Jewish cultures and that their policies and practices are shaped by the dynamics of those local cultures. Thus they follow the well-known North American pattern of Jewish education being primarily a local affair.[3]

We have also found in the course of our information-gathering that the following generalities characterize the fourteen community and two Conservative schools we have come to know:

1. The students are Jewish (though definitions of 'Jewish' can vary); the schools are committed to teaching Jewish subjects (though the proportions of the curriculum dedicated to Jewish studies vary) and promote a positive Jewish identity.

2. All schools offer a full general academic programme with the assumption that all students are bound for university. The schools are responsible for preparing the students for acceptance into the appropriate universities of their choice.

3. The schools also offer a wide range of extracurricular activities such as athletics, arts activities, clubs, and trips.

---

[3] Wertheimer, *Linking the Silos.*

4. These are private schools that charge tuition fees and raise funds from private and Jewish communal sources to sustain themselves financially. They do offer scholarships; in most cases, however, families spend substantial sums to educate their children in these schools.[4]

The families who patronize private Jewish day schools are notoriously ambitious for their children, and these schools feel the pressure to be academically productive. A school whose graduating students were not accepted into the appropriate universities would probably cease to be viable. The heads of school and teachers know this and guard their academic priorities zealously. The question they face is how, given that priority, they are to balance their programmes so that they are both well-rounded and Jewishly effective.

Life might be simpler if gaining greater Jewish knowledge automatically resulted in taking one's Jewish commitments seriously. But in an adolescent population that is not always the case, and both parents and school heads recognize this. Since these schools inevitably attract students from a variety of religious backgrounds and their families practise their Judaism in quite diverse ways, the schools cannot assume common personal standards of Jewish practice (such as *kashrut* and sabbath observance). If, during these pivotal years, adolescents are to develop serious personal Jewish commitments, that development has to happen in part via the school experience. Realizing this, some schools had by the mid-1990s begun to explore introducing more experiential Jewish learning through programmes like Shabbatonim and trips to Israel.

At this point the AVI CHAI Foundation became involved. The leaders of this influential foundation have very publicly declared their support for Jewish day school education and view its expansion to accommodate a growing number of young Jews as a key strategy for the survival of Judaism in North America. Given this stance, they could be expected to favour the growth of schools such as these that attract a Jewishly diverse student body, and indeed the Foundation's staff were eager to support experiential programmes that they viewed as likely to foster the Jewish identities of students. Accordingly, in 1997 the Foundation began offering financial support to schools that would initiate Shabbaton programmes. Between that year and 2003, they offered this support to as many as ten schools.[5]

---

[4] Schick and Dauber, *The Financing of Jewish Day Schools*.   [5] Warshaviak, memo.

Yet as time passed it seemed to the Foundation's staff that this support was not leading to any consistent enhancement of these Shabbatonim. There was little consistency in who staffed the programmes and what the available staff knew about running them. The venture remained somewhat haphazard, with much potential but lacking a common direction. The question the Foundation faced was how to harness that potential and spread best practices from a few schools to the many others.[6]

In 2004 the AVI CHAI staff approached the newly formed association of these high schools, the North American Association of Jewish High Schools (NAAJHS), to ask if it would take this Shabbaton programme in hand. An agreement was reached and NAAJHS appointed two of the most talented school-based experiential educators to give direction to this initiative. It wanted to expand the number of schools that would participate in the programme and to develop common norms among the schools for what constituted a 'successful Shabbaton programme'.

The NAAJHS also agreed to initiate a professional development seminar for the experiential educators from these schools, turning to one of us (Reimer) to plan and implement these seminars, and to the other (Kress) to evaluate that effort. Our goal was to work with these educators to identify both the features of a 'successful high school Shabbaton' and the educational skills that an experiential Jewish educator would need to run such a Shabbaton programme successfully.

Shabbatonim in Community Day High Schools

Of the sixteen high schools accepted onto the AVI CHAI experiential education programme during the autumn of 2004, about half already had a Shabbaton programme in place and the others were just beginning to construct one. Of the sixteen experiential educators involved, some were veterans with a couple of years' experience in running Shabbatonim, while the others were new to this kind of programme (though they had other informal educational experience). All the schools received grants to subsidize the costs of their programmes, and their experiential educators were required to attend a twice-yearly professional development seminar—designed by the Institute for Informal Jewish Education (IJE) at Brandeis

---

[6] Warshaviak, memo.

University—to enhance their skills in and perspectives on running quality programmes.

We now turn to a description of what we have learned about the nature of the Shabbatonim in these sixteen schools. All of this information was gathered from the reports that the school educators submitted as part of their participation in the experiential education programme between 2004 and 2006.

The Variety of Shabbatonim

There is no Bible for experiential Jewish education that prescribes what a Shabbaton at a Jewish high school should be. Clearly, such a programme involves the communal celebration/observance of the sabbath. But what that celebration/observance should entail, where the programme should take place, who should be involved as staff and participants, and what should be the goals were questions that had been left up to each school to decide. Some of the key areas of variation are the following:

1. *Religious observance.* While the common element is the communal celebration of sabbath, the rules defining that celebration differ. In some schools, observance is defined by Orthodox halakhah; in the Conservative schools, it is defined by Conservative halakhah. In schools that aspire to pluralism there are common norms for public behaviour, but more tolerance of diversity in private behaviour. Those pluralistic schools also sponsor a variety of prayer options that range from *meḥitsah* to egalitarian *minyanim* as well as alternative spiritual expressions such as meditation and nature walks.

2. *Participation, location, and timing.* A Shabbaton may be for the whole student body, a particular grade, or a particular interest group. Attendance at a Shabbaton may be required or voluntary for those who are eligible. The programme may take place at a camp, a retreat site, a local synagogue, or at the school itself. The duration and cost of the programme will vary by location, but costs are generally subsidized.

3. *Adult leadership.* Every programme is planned and supervised by adults. Who those adults are varies. There is always, in these schools, an experiential educator in charge. Other faculty and administrative staff are usually invited, but their attendance and role vary depending on their level of

Jewish knowledge. Jewish youth workers from other contexts may be invited to enhance the Jewish staff presence.

4. *Student roles.* Some schools prepare student leaders—often both juniors and seniors, but usually chosen from among those who have been at the school some time—to help plan and implement the programme. They may take an active role in an all-school programme or a programme for younger grades. The degree to which all students are invited to take active roles in running activities varies by school and grade.

5. *Educational programme.* Some schools specialize in creating a special *ruaḥ shabat* with intense singing and dancing, while others offer a wider range of experiential activities within their sabbath norms. Some offer an organized educational theme that runs through the programme while others create a highly informal atmosphere with more time for hanging out and 'schmoozing'.

The Goals of the Shabbatonim

For all this variety in practice, we learned that the Shabbaton programmes shared broadly similar declared goals. Reviewing the goal statements prepared by the experiential educators, we found that the goals for their Shabbatonim clustered into three areas:

1. *Celebrating sabbath together.* Since there is no presumption that most students come from sabbath-observant homes, the primary goal of the schools' Shabbaton programme is to provide a communal celebration of the sabbath that students will enjoy. The goal is to enable students to experience a complete cycle of sabbath observance that will be both enjoyable and spiritually meaningful.

2. *Developing student leadership and ritual skills.* A Shabbaton is an opportunity for students to exercise leadership in diverse areas. These include the sabbath rituals that students may lead as well as the other aspects of the informal programme that students can help in leading. In undertaking leadership roles, students work more closely with educators. That allows educators to help students develop their skills both in leadership and in Jewish ritual.

3. *Building a cohesive community.* Jewish high schools are busy places, and opportunities are rare for students and teachers to experience being in

company with one another as members of a cohesive community. The Shabbaton provides that very opportunity. In the slowed-down, informal atmosphere of celebrating sabbath, students get to know one another and to interact more informally with their educators. As noted above, schools vary in terms of who attends these Shabbatonim; but whichever educators do attend, a stated goal is for them to get to know the students more intimately and help build a more cohesive community in their school.

In each of these three areas there are also challenges which the educators identified as foci for improvement over the course of the two years of the professional development project.

Describing and Achieving Quality Shabbatonim

To execute and evaluate a programme to enhance Shabbatonim and to support the efforts of those who plan them required that we develop an understanding of the notion of 'quality' in these contexts. To achieve this we needed to consider:

1. What are the components of a quality Shabbaton?

2. What do educators need to know, or to be able to do, to achieve these outcomes?

Moreover, both of these questions are predicated on the answer to a broader set of questions, namely: What impact, if any, do Shabbatonim have—particularly in the long term—on participants; and, if Shabbatonim do have an impact, what elements of the experience are most central in achieving this impact? Thus, while pragmatically we chose to focus on the two questions set out above, we recognize that questions of 'best practice' cannot be completely addressed without a thorough analysis of Shabbatonim.

Our efforts to answer these questions proceeded in step with our work with the AVI CHAI experiential education programme. At this point norms or best practices had not been established or articulated. The experiential educators did not bring to bear explicit theories of how to run a successful Shabbaton programme. Rather, like many informal educators, they operated on the basis of their past experiences working with teenagers and adapted their field-based knowledge to the particulars of a day high school environment. The process of describing quality Shabbatonim involved viewing the work done by the educators through a lens of developmental and community psychology theories. Observing Shabbatonim and listening to the educators as they spoke about their work helped in shaping a rubric of those components that seem to embody a quality Shabbaton. Because outcome markers were lacking (that is, there was no way, in this project, to assess 'success' in terms of outcomes for students), 'quality' was seen as the intersection of those implicit theories held by the educators (made explicit through their work and discussions) and theoretical guidelines derived from the literature. As such, the description of quality components is grounded both in theory and in the work done by the educators.

Theoretical Underpinnings

We were familiar with Barry Chazan's theoretical papers on informal Jewish education and found them very helpful.[7] We also turned to guiding principles drawn from several theories that fall under the broad heading of community psychology. Such approaches are rooted in ecological developmental theories, which emphasize the reciprocal interaction of person and environment.[8]

Psychologists have increasingly turned their attention not only to the developing individual, but to the nature of the settings in which he or she participates. For example, 'positive developmental assets' are defined as 'concrete, common sense, positive experiences and qualities essential to raising successful young people',[9] and include both internal qualities (such as social competency and commitment to learning) and external factors that, when part of a youth's experience, will help promote positive outcomes. For example, positive developmental environments provide, among other things, supportive and caring relationships, opportunities for meaningful participation and input into the workings of the environment (particularly for adolescents), and clear boundaries.

The field of social and emotional learning (SEL) also contributed to the theoretical basis of these components. SEL, with its focus on bringing together the cognitive, affective, and behavioural/social aspects of the edu-

---

[7] Chazan, 'The Philosophy of Informal Jewish Education'.
[8] e.g. Bronfenbrenner, 'Ecological Systems Theory'.
[9] Lerner and Benson, *Developmental Assets*.

cational experience, is particularly relevant to the experiential nature of Shabbaton programming. SEL emerged in part from the work of Daniel Goleman, who focused on those internal social and emotional competencies that provide individuals with the tools needed to face life challenges—skills such as emotional awareness, self-control, and problem-solving.[10] More recent work has focused on those conditions that best facilitate the development of such skills and indeed foster learning in general. SEL theory stresses the importance of relationships as providing the basis of the educational endeavour, and the understanding of emotional aspects of the learning environment.[11] Again, the focus of SEL, like that of developmental assets theory, is not only on the skills and competencies of the individual, but also on the opportunities afforded by the environment to develop these skills and competencies.

These theoretical lenses led us to view the high school Shabbaton as a particular instance of educators creating a special environment within which to foster the development of several of their students' competencies. To work well, a Shabbaton needs to create a sabbath atmosphere that promotes both a shared positive experience of traditional Jewish observances and a set of relationships that students experience as personally enjoyable and offering growth.

In considering components of quality Shabbatonim, we draw on these theories and others to consider Shabbatonim as developmental-educational settings. The key points of application of these theories can be distilled into the following five guiding ideas that influenced our thinking about the nature of quality Shabbatonim.

Guiding Idea One: **Positive developmental-educational settings are marked by safety, personal respect, and clear boundaries** On Shabbatonim, students and teachers leave the set of structures within which they usually interact. At the very least, educators should not assume that students will be able to transfer and translate school rules to the Shabbaton setting. Moreover, the intense demands of communal living put additional demands on the creation of communal behavioural expectations. Therefore it is important to consider logistics, transitions between activities, and the handling of glitches and crises. Finally, it is particularly important for Shabbatonim in

---

[10] Goleman, *Emotional Intelligence.*
[11] National Center for Innovation and Education, *Lessons for Life.*

pluralistic settings that clear expectations are established with regard to religious practice and that a respectful process for handling and negotiating
these issues is developed.

Guiding Idea Two: **Positive developmental-educational settings are marked
by warm, caring, relationships among all members of the community** At a
Shabbaton there is the opportunity to change and enhance a variety of relationships. One cannot assume this will happen naturally. Opportunities
should be planned, for example, for staff and students to interact in ways
that differ from their interactions in school. Shabbatonim also present the
opportunity to deepen relationships among students, but care must be
taken to mix established groups and to create opportunities for students to
share in both learning and playing with one another.

Guiding Idea Three: **Young people, particularly adolescents, benefit most
from settings that they can help substantially to shape, and in which they
can fill meaningful roles** While student leadership roles vary widely from
school to school, in all cases there are meaningful roles for students to play
in a Shabbaton beyond that of simply attending. Students can become
active participants in aspects of *tefilah*, song leadership, or even organizing
the football game during a break. In our view all such active student participation enhances their experience of the Shabbaton.

Guiding Idea Four: **Multiple entry points into ritual practice and the study of
texts facilitate students' engagement with the tradition** This principle can
be encapsulated as 'pluralistic communities meets multiple intelligences'.
There are many ways 'into' a text, as exemplified by the emergence of 'modern *midrash*'—the use of art and drama in textual understanding. The informal nature of the Shabbaton makes it an ideal setting for diverse expression
if the educators are open to and aware of the need to accommodate this
diversity in their midst. We suggest the operative question in communal
practice ought not to be simply: 'Is everyone comfortable?' but: 'Is there a
variety of ways in which one can engage with text and ritual here?'

Guiding Idea Five: **Quality developmental-educational settings are marked
by forethought and attention to the affective experiences of the participants
and the deep integration of 'learning' and 'feeling'** This guideline encompasses the other four, each of which has emotional ramifications, either in
its adherence or its breach. Do participants feel safe and focused, or unsafe

and confused? Accepted and bonded to peers, or rejected and lonely? Empowered and involved, or passed over and talked down to? Engaged or bored? The balance will depend on how the previous four guidelines are followed; a negative emotional experience will often point to departure from a particular guideline. A focus on affect often takes form on a Shabbaton under the heading of *ruah* or 'spirited engagement'. *Ruah* presents one entry point into the emotional experience of Shabbaton participants, when ordinary experiences—meals, *tefilot*, even bus rides—are enhanced by the intensity of singing and dancing. Throughout the programme, participating educators described and demonstrated a variety of ways to achieve a desired *ruah*, for example by telling stories, providing reflections, and leading certain types of songs. *Ruah* is discussed in more detail below.

Six Component Areas of Quality Shabbatonim

These five guiding principles provide a structure for the consideration of those elements that comprise a quality Shabbaton. In order to make the connection between these ideas and the concrete skills needed by educators to run quality Shabbatonim, we needed to translate these principles into specific recommendations applicable to these unique settings. Toward this end, one of the authors (Kress), with significant input from the programme co-ordinators, the programme participants, and representatives of the funding body, and having attended Shabbatonim as a participant observer, developed a rubric of six component areas of quality Shabbatonim. These are broad descriptions of areas of competence that the educators we worked with found helpful for capturing the complex tasks they need to master in running a quality Shabbaton.

These components help to organize not only our understanding of the Shabbaton experience, but also the skills an educator would need to make these happen. The six categories are: logistics, relationships, ritual, *ruah*, student leadership, and educational/programme content. The components have been used in ways both anticipated (including as a framework for observation of Shabbatonim and as a vehicle for educators to reflect on their work) and unanticipated (for example, by educators who have used them in training student *madrikhim* who assist in Shabbaton planning).

The components are seen as a work in progress. In particular, empirical investigation is needed to link them to outcomes for students. At present they are intended as pointers for future research and validation; only thereafter can they be considered 'prescriptive'. Also, it should be noted that one challenge in the development of the components was the diversity of settings involved in the programme. While efforts were made to frame the components broadly enough to apply to a variety of communities, the relative emphasis on, and expression of, these components will vary across specific school settings. Thus all these components must be considered in the context of the school in which the Shabbaton is being implemented.

We now turn to an overview of each of the six component areas.

1. *Logistics.* Achieving the educational and developmental aspects of a Shabbaton depends first of all on the practicalities of making it happen. Running a quality Shabbaton demands that educators master a host of logistical arrangements whose smooth operation is key to the success of the programme. However impressive one's teaching skills may be, if the buses are late in getting back to school an educator is in big trouble. Further, educators can link the schedule and rules to the educational goals for the Shabbaton. For example, an educator might handle an infraction of sabbath observance policy in a way that enables the student to understand the reasoning behind the rule that was set in place, how that relates to the meaning of the sabbath, and so on.

2. *Relationships.* Students attend Shabbatonim to enhance their relationships with their peers. But it is a special bonus when their relationships with educators are also enhanced. Shabbatonim can provide unique opportunities for this, as students and educators have the opportunity to interact in novel ways such as informal discussion, participation in sabbath afternoon games or sports, and singing and celebrating. Rules are less stringent; interactions are less structured but, because of the nature of communal living, can be very intense. Students can also have the opportunity to interact with each other in new ways, the intensity of the experience providing a bridge between those who might ordinarily be separated by class assignment or clique. These relationship components do not happen automatically. Without proactive attempts to build community, clique groups might be solidly maintained even on the Shabbaton. Educators must be sensitive to issues of boundaries with students, while at the same time being able to stretch their usual repertoire of behaviour in school beyond that of formal educator.

3. *Ritual.* All sabbath celebration entails enacting multiple rituals. On a successful Shabbaton, students experience these rituals as enhancing and educational and not boring. A particular challenge in these settings has to do with the diversity of student practice (discussed further below). It cannot be assumed that students come to the Shabbaton with a set of agreed-upon norms for sabbath observance, nor that in a communal setting all would be satisfied following the most stringent ritual practices. It falls to the educator to address the diversity of the group within the framework of the ritual observance that may be mandated by the school. A leader needs to make sure not only that rituals take place, but also that they are carried out in a way that engages and involves students from a range of backgrounds. As such, *hidur mitsvah* (the enhancement of the beauty of ritual) is a theme in the 'Ritual' section of the components guidelines, as is student participation in ritual. It takes a lot of planning and skilful implementation to ensure that everything from preparing for sabbath to eating the special meals to closing with *havdalah* is done in ways that both include different customs and enhance students' experience of the sabbath.

4. *Ruah.* This category is perhaps the most difficult to translate and describe; it can be said to be among those things that 'one knows when one sees them'. However, in order to use this category to guide programming and assessment, we define this term to mean a positive energy or a spirited engagement. *Ruah* can be seen as the ambient mood, the expression of the bridging of emotion and experience. *Ruah* is not synonymous with 'raucousness', though it can take that form. Rather, it is seen as situationally determined: a boisterous spirit may be appropriate for certain occasions (say, dancing during sabbath lunch, or celebrating a *simha*), but inappropriate for others (for example, *se'udah shlishit*). *Ruah* is often marked by its spontaneous appearance, and in consequence it may seem counterintuitive to think of this as an element of Shabbatonim that can be planned. However, our perspective is that there are factors that can be put in place to make it more likely that *ruah* will occur. These may include preparing students to participate by teaching basic *nigunim* and designating students as 'ruah leaders' who start the action. Educators also need to attend to the logistics of *ruah* by making sure that space is provided for dancing, and that acoustics are accounted for in choosing spaces for *tefilot* and meals.

5. *Student leadership.* Educators who learn how to sponsor more effective student leadership tend to feel that the success of the Shabbaton rests on many other shoulders as well as their own. Student leadership is also a way to empower students to become engaged in the Shabbaton. Learning how to get more students involved, we find, takes time and effort, but seems to pay off in the long run as the student leaders develop a greater investment in the success of the Shabbaton and enhance their own leadership skills. They will also recruit other students to come and encourage them to take seriously the community-building and ritual aspects of the experience. Students can have roles preparing for the Shabbaton (for example, marketing and recruitment; programme planning) and during the Shabbaton itself (for example, running *tefilot* or educational/social programmes). Importantly, student leadership needs the scaffolding provided by quality educators. Students may have limited formal opportunities for leadership and may need training, guidance, and supervision in their work. Further, educators need to be ready to step in appropriately when a student-run activity is faltering. A strong educator would be able to support the activity while still preserving the dignity and sense of leadership of the student organizer(s).

6. *Educational/programme content.* Every aspect of the Shabbaton has educational value if the educators know how to infuse it. We have seen sabbath afternoon programmes that are as full of fun as they are of learning. Often that learning is informal and implicit, but is still palpable and powerful. Because of the wide array of learning opportunities available at a Shabbaton, and the broad range, in these schools, of student knowledge and background, diversity and multiple entrance points are prominent educational themes. Educators who can learn the magic of teaching through informal interactions often emerge as the strongest leaders of quality Shabbaton experiences. These educators can successfully plan some programmes that can be accessed in different ways, or from different starting points of background knowledge. They can also offer opportunities for students who desire more, or more formal, learning opportunities. Many educators work to relate various educational experiences on a Shabbaton to a central theme (for example, the importance of community, or *tikun olam*). Education on a Shabbaton may be informal; it need not be unplanned and unstructured.

Challenges and Future Directions

Our work has led us to appreciate some of the challenges facing experiential educators in community high schools, and we close our chapter with a look at three key issues which have become of particular concern to us and to the programme participants.

The Challenges of Pluralism

All the schools we studied, even those with a denominational affiliation, are attended by students with a broad range of Jewish backgrounds and ritual observance. 'Community' schools in particular often address this diversity by offering multiple acceptable options for ritual participation. For example, at these schools it is a common practice to offer, in parallel with morning *tefilah*, options that include 'alternative *tefilah*' (perhaps including singing and/or meditation) or discussion sessions. This diversity, which of course can present wonderful opportunities for those with different practices to learn from one another, also poses unique challenges when applied to the communal setting of a Shabbaton, particularly in terms of creating a unified sabbath experience in which all can genuinely participate. How can that be accomplished? How can different prayer regimes be accommodated? How can different levels of sabbath observance be harmonized?

It may be complicated to make space, for example, for students who want to mark the sabbath by listening to a guided meditation CD alongside students who cherish a technology-free experience of the sabbath. Further, the more ritual options are available, the fewer students can attend any one of them. A non-egalitarian *tefilah* option, for example, would have low attendance (perhaps not even drawing a *minyan*) if other participants opted to attend the concurrent egalitarian *minyan*, mediation session, nature walk, and so on. Finally, and more subtly, the proliferation of options for ritual observance can complicate the experience of a cohesive community, itself a component of Shabbatonim.

Educators have responded creatively to this dilemma by enhancing those communal ritual times in which differences in practice can be de-emphasized in the name of community-building. *Havdalah*, *oneg*, and 'pre-*kabalat shabat*' are times when the community can participate together. By giving these common times greater emphasis, educators have found ways to respect religious differences while also responding to a felt need to celebrate together as a whole community.

The Place of Experiential Education in the Community High School

Schools vary in the degree to which Shabbatonim are connected to the remainder of the school experience. By and large, the Shabbaton is seen as a 'stand alone' event, planned specifically to remove students from the ordinary range of experiences in order to build an intensive, though temporary, community, thereby showing them 'what could be' in terms of sabbath observance. However, there are various potential points of connection. It is possible, for example, to link the educational content of the Shabbaton with the school curriculum. Classes focusing on the sabbath, or on the centrality of community in Judaism, can spring to life on a Shabbaton. Songs or tunes for prayers learned on a Shabbaton can be sung at school, and vice versa.

However, educators participating in our study did not all agree with the idea of strengthening connections between Shabbaton and school. To paraphrase one educator, 'these kids go to competitive schools and are involved in a lot of extra-curricular activities, so their time is really tight already. The last thing they need is a sixth day of school at the Shabbaton.' They viewed the Shabbaton specifically as a safe haven, and saw this as the best way to foster students' appreciation of the restfulness that the sabbath can bring.

Similar concerns were expressed about building student leadership of, and faculty participation in, Shabbatonim. Students are busy fulfilling their usual academic and extracurricular responsibilities. How can time be found also to involve them in planning and implementing a Shabbaton? How much responsibility can the students take on? How can they assume enough authority to lead their fellow students? How can teachers be recruited to give up free time to attend a Shabbaton? Which teachers are appropriate for that role? How can the experiential educator speak effectively for the importance of the Shabbatonim so that the faculty and administration will support this programme as a school priority?

We have found that the answers to these questions have both skill-based and structural components. That is, experiential educators can gain skills in marketing themselves and their programmes to their peers and supervisors and can become more adept at recruiting help or seeking resources. However, these efforts are often constrained by the marginalized position of the experiential educator. Participating educators, almost all of whom have responsibilities beyond experiential education, struggled with the difficulty of adapting school schedules, getting staff to participate, or obtaining sufficient funding. These educators report lacking the institutional support to ask teachers, for example, not to schedule an important exam on the Monday following a Shabbaton weekend. Changing this situation will involve extending efforts beyond the educator to work with school leaders so that Shabbatonim, and experiential education more generally, are incorporated more fully into their programmes.

Beyond Shabbatonim: Extending the Reach

One disadvantage of viewing the Shabbaton as 'an experience apart' is that activities that occur in isolation tend to have isolated effects. Students may have wonderful sabbath experiences and experience a range of emotions during *tefilah* and other rituals. They may leave the Shabbaton welcoming the opportunity to repeat the experience. However, services at their home synagogues and back at school look, sound, and feel nothing like those of the Shabbaton. Students who 'bonded' at the Shabbaton return to the school and are once again members of different cliques, taking different classes on different schedules, and living in different towns.

Those interested in affecting the life-courses of young people have come to appreciate the difficulty of the task, and the multiple, often contradictory, influences on their development. Yes, it is possible that a Shabbaton participant, several years down the road and now a college student, might recall a fantastic sabbath experience and choose to explore the options at Hillel. However, this scenario is dependent on the handful of excellent Shabbaton experiences outweighing the many potentially mediocre or negative sabbath experiences, and also on the availability of a community and a service at the college that would approximate the Shabbaton experience.

Clearly, educators need to 'stack the deck' in order to make desired outcomes more likely. It is here that larger, more systemic interventions may be needed. How might the prayer experience in school come to look and feel more like a Shabbaton experience? How might Shabbaton participants be encouraged to attend other intensive Jewish communal experiences such as a youth group convention, a residential summer camp, and/or a Jewish travel experience? How might opportunity be provided for discussions, or projects, started on a Shabbaton to continue within the course of a school schedule? Might adolescents be helped to reflect on the Shabbaton experience and what it meant to them, and be engaged in a continuing conversation about how the experience relates to what they want as Jews and how and where this can be achieved? These questions suggest a role for experiential education that is far bigger than the Shabbaton, and goes beyond the usual scope of the work of an individual experiential educator. However, this is a challenge that must be pursued. How can formal and informal experiences be more tightly interwoven? How can educators reach beyond the boundaries of their individual settings in order to co-ordinate the developmental experiences of youth?

This discussion points to a further challenge, perhaps the most complex of all. That is, we talk about the importance of Shabbatonim, how to enhance them, and how to bolster their impact; but the actual impact of the Shabbaton experience on the participants remains unknown. There is certainly reason to believe in the potential of Shabbatonim, and there is no doubt that participating in a Shabbaton, even as an observer, can be an exciting, emotional, educational experience. We do not know, however, what remains of this experience the next week, month, year, or beyond. A Shabbaton is a complex, multifaceted experience, but it is only a piece of a larger puzzle. Those responsible for planning and funding Shabbatonim must ask themselves: What are the key outcomes we want for the young Jews for whom we plan Shabbatonim? How do we see the Shabbaton as fostering movement towards these outcomes? What else—what other experiences— might help to achieve these outcomes? How will we be able to track progress towards these outcomes?

Conclusions

The early stages of research growing from our work with Shabbatonim in community day high schools and the experiential educators who run them has allowed us to describe Shabbatonim as experiential educational settings in order to provide a springboard for further research and practice. We have come to appreciate the diversity of forms and formats that Shabbatonim take. Researchers and practitioners (for example, those training experiential educators) must account for this diversity in their work. The former, for example, may explore the differential impact of different 'types' of Shabbatonim, and/or the relative contribution of these variant factors to the overall Shabbaton experience. The latter may need to shape professional development efforts to fit the unique demands faced by educators in their specific settings.

While diversity is a hallmark of the range of Shabbatonim offered, the goals for Shabbatonim converge on three themes: celebrating sabbath together, developing student leadership and ritual skills, and building a cohesive community. The articulation of these themes can help experiential educators to engage better in 'backwards planning' in crafting Shabbatonim to meet these goals, by asking questions such as: 'If fostering student leadership is a key goal for my school, how can I best craft a Shabbaton experience to reach that goal? Researchers and evaluators, in turn, can use these three goals or themes as organizing principles in analysing the impact of Shabbatonim.

Our work has also led us to develop an understanding of those components that, as key contributors to 'quality' Shabbatonim, can be seen as a set of hypotheses as to what constitutes 'best practice'. Further research is needed to validate these components by testing them against outcomes for students. While it is too early to suggest that these components can serve as a standard for the field, the positive response from the participating experiential educators was notable. These educators overwhelmingly felt that the framework, even in its speculative, emergent form, might help them better focus their own work and, importantly, communicate with peers and superiors in their schools about the work they do.

Experiential educators in Jewish day high schools face challenges as they try to do work that is 'informal', without exams and mandates, in a 'formal' context. The academic focus of these schools puts the work of these educators at risk of perception, by themselves, their peers, and their superiors, as secondary or less important. The absence of a structured understanding of the types of experiences these educators create and the work they must do to create these only feeds this perception. The participating educators felt that in providing a detailed framework for their work, the components gave them guidance and validation. If these schools are indeed to expand their experiential offerings, it is important that those involved do not conflate 'informal education' with 'unstructured education'. In beginning to map out the terrain of experiential education in day high schools, we have shown the complexity of the issues involved in building programmes that have great potential to enhance both Jewish community and Jewish identity.

Bibliography

AVI CHAI Foundation, *The Jewish Investment Portfolio* (New York, 1999).

Bronfenbrenner, U., 'Ecological Systems Theory', in R. Vasta (ed.), *Six Theories of Child Development: Revised Formulations and Current Issues* (London, 1992), 187–249.

Chazan, B., 'The Philosophy of Informal Jewish Education', paper presented at a seminar for the Department for Zionist Jewish Education, The Jewish Agency for Israel, June 2002, <http://www.jafi.org.il/education/moriya/newpdf/Chazan.pdf>.

Goleman, D., *Emotional Intelligence: Why It Can Matter More than IQ* (New York, 1995).

Lerner, R. M., and P. L. Benson (eds.), *Developmental Assets and Asset-Building Communities: Implications for Research, Policy, and Practice* (New York, 2003).

National Center for Innovation and Education, *Lessons for Life: How Smart Schools Boost Academic, Social, and Emotional Intelligence* (Bloomington, Ind., 1999).

Reimer, J., and D. Bryfman, 'What We Know about Experiential Jewish Education', in P. Flexner and R. Goodman (eds.), *What We Know about Jewish Education*, 2nd edn. (Los Angeles, 2008).

Reisman, B., *The Jewish Experiential Book* (New York, 1979).

Schick, M., *A Census of Jewish Day Schools in the United States 2003–04* (New York, 2005).

—— and J. Dauber, *The Financing of Jewish Day Schools* (New York, 1997).

Warshaviak, M. (AVI CHAI Israel Programme Officer), memo, 14 Nov. 2005.

Wertheimer, J., *Linking the Silos: How to Accelerate the Momentum in Jewish Education Today* (New York, 2005).

TWENTY

Teaching Leadership through Town Meeting

JAY DEWEY

IN 2003 Schechter Regional High School opened with the specific aims of developing individual accomplishment, Jewish commitment, and community leadership. Co-heads of school were appointed, one from Jewish education, the other from an independent, non-sectarian school. Both were particularly interested in developing leaders with strong collaborative skills.

The leadership team, known as the LT, consisting of the two co-heads, posited that leadership opportunities would come to Schechter Regional graduates even if the school did nothing to promote this; society looks towards well-educated adults to fill its many leadership needs. The real challenge was to develop effective and ethical leaders capable of meeting these needs. Thus Schechter Regional became a leadership lab with Town Meeting at the centre.

The leadership team chose as its guidebook James M. Kouzes and Barry Z. Posner's *The Leadership Challenge* because it was so widely used in college and corporate leadership programmes. Kouzes and Posner questioned over 75,000 individuals worldwide on which qualities they most sought and admired in their leaders. Their research identified four foundational qualities for leadership credibility: honesty, looking forward, competence, and inspiration.[1] By studying credible leaders Kouzes and Posner explored the 'dynamic process of leadership' and identified five practices of exemplary leadership: modelling the way, inspiring a shared vision, challenging the process, enabling others to act, and encouraging the heart.[2] Since Kouzes and Posner's research subjects were adults, the leadership team was faced with selecting and nurturing those precursory teenage behaviours and habits of mind that would most likely mature, in post-collegiate adulthood, into Kouzes–Posner leadership traits.

[1] Kouzes and Posner, *The Leadership Challenge*, 23–39.

[2] Ibid. 22.

Anecdotally, when the team asked adult leaders to identify who in high school most significantly 'trained' them for leadership, most identified their sports team coaches. These coaches had encouraged them, in their teens, to extend their training into everyday life; examine their and the opposition's game strategies; practise repetitive core skills; develop habits of initiative and independent thinking; reflect deeply on past performance to prepare for the future; inspire team spirit and good sportsmanship; play to win but learn how to lose well; intuit the full field; and practise, practise, then practise some more. The Schechter team designed its leadership programme on this coaching model.

Extending Leadership Training beyond the Classroom

Every aspect of school became a leadership teaching opportunity. The curriculum catalogue listed classes in basic leadership skills, liturgy leading, and leadership theory. Community service was required. Student leaders had personal mentors. Internships brought together students and community activists.

From 8 a.m. to as late as 10 p.m., Schechter Regional vibrated with students, teachers, office staff, and administrators. What affected one affected all; the responsibility for the community's well-being was everyone's responsibility. This was the 'Town'. At the weekly Town Meeting, each member had a single vote and equal freedom to discuss community issues. While the leadership team retained authority over academics, employment, budgeting, and discipline, and the board oversaw funding, major policies, and long-range planning, students and faculty were regularly invited into authentic discussions at all levels. Town Meeting decisions were real; the Town was entrusted with real power and real responsibility—and the real ability to make mistakes.

Though parental reaction was at first guarded—'Sounds like the inmates might be running the asylum'—their trust in the leadership team permitted the new programme design to take effect. Teachers were trained in the process during the faculty training week prior to the first week of school, and new students learned the ropes at the opening school retreat. Though the leadership team maintained the right of veto, in three years of Town Meetings it never had to exercise this power. Teenagers often have wisdom that they hide from dismissive adults.

Examining Game Strategies

Typically, an ad hoc committee studies an issue first. Each committee's faculty adviser, appointed by the leadership team, sets the process in motion by calling the first meeting, asking the group to choose a moderator and a secretary, and then asking the question: 'What are the immutable underlying principles?' From here the committee moves to the 'mutables'—that which the Town can change, providing that the changes meet and enhance the immutables. Note the strategy: state the question; identify the basic principles (the immutables); trust the group process; and then find answers that meet and enhance these principles.

Henry's Story

Ninth-grade Henry liked everything spelled out.[3] During the opening retreat's first Town Meeting, he challenged the ambiguity of the school's dress code; it stated only basic principles like modesty, neatness, cleanliness, and that clothing and adornments not distract from the purpose of being in school. The leadership team had hoped that a student would address the absence of mandates. Henry did, much to the consternation of his classmates, who feared stiffer guidelines.

LT: Some things are immutable . . .

Students (backs bristle; faces redden): But, but, but . . .

LT: The principles are immutable. Clothing must be modest, conducive to learning, not provocative or expressive of illegal or immoral behaviours . . .

Henry (jumping up): What a sham . . .

LT: Within these general standards, how would you write the dress code?

Students (jaws drop): We can do that?

LT: The rest is . . . *(searching for right word)* . . . well . . . mutable.

The Town chose a committee with Henry as the chair. By the end of the retreat, basic dress rules had been established by majority vote, this time based on the students' own, rather sophisticated, awareness of what would be appropriate. Since both students and adults had

---

[3] The stories in this chapter derive from two sources. As part of leadership training, students learned to take minutes. Though these are not set down verbatim, the Town Meeting minute book provided a strong factual reference source. In addition, the author referred to his own journal entries for dialogue and on-the-spot observations. Sometimes these also included notes from his mentoring sessions with the student Town moderators. Some of the Town Meetings were videotaped, though this was neither a regular practice nor a primary source for this chapter. No real names are used in the chapter.

a voice and a vote, no one objected that the rules were unfair or arbitrary. Students learned to address issues directly, and turn complainers into leaders.

It was abundantly clear, even in the school's first few months when it had only twenty students, that Town Meeting was not always efficient, sometimes not even productive. Discussions took time, testing the attention spans of even the adults. The moderator, still one of the leadership team, assumed the right to appoint smaller ad hoc committees to explore issues and bring thoughtful suggestions back to the Town. This process assumed trust by the leadership team; student seriousness; and active but not overriding teacher participation. Each committee chose its own chair and secretary; the adviser called the first meeting, helped articulate the immutables, and further institutionalized the habit that the committee chair sought advice on the immutables from the leadership team, thus confounding the possibility of a veto.

All Town members requesting Meeting time wrote their topic and name on a large post-it sheet positioned in a public place. The moderator determined the agenda's order, ran the meeting, and, for the weightier issues, appointed ad hoc working committees. The assistant moderator kept track of all these committees and shepherded their tasks to completion. Most committees met during the lunch break or after school. The Town secretary kept minutes; the treasurer watched over Town funds—income from the school's vending machines and occasional fundraisers; the leadership team felt strongly that the Town could be independent only if it had its own sources of income. Though any member of the Town, student or faculty, could hold office, at the time of writing only students have run for office.

A shofar blast announced the start of Town Meeting. Minutes from the previous meeting were approved. Order was maintained and votes were taken according to a modified version of Robert's Rules of Order.[4]

Skills

Students interested in leadership learned basic skills: keeping a minute-book; developing a budget; speaking in public; following Robert's Rules of Order; making proposals; power brokering; preparing for a meeting; and

---

[4] These parliamentary procedures for running meetings have become fairly standard for organizations in the United States. We used Zimmerman, *Robert's Rules in Plain English*.

campaigning for office. An elective course in basic leadership skills covered these topics.

Habits of Initiative

Concerned that students should not be subject to expectations inappropriate to their ages, the leadership team turned to the work of Erik Erikson, who noted that before reaching adolescence youngsters develop the 'virtues' of hope, will, purpose, and competence.[5] Adolescents have the capacity to hope that their wishes and goals are attainable, to will their own behaviours, to direct their energies purposefully, and to exercise their own skills and competences. Because Schechter Regional students were well educated and came from supportive homes, most approached high school with Erikson's four virtues well established.

Lev Vygotsky's 'zone of proximal development' is the difference between current ability and what can be achieved.[6] No stretch, no growth; stretch too far, failure. An appropriate zone not only increases ability but also becomes the staging platform for the next achievement. When a baby cries, he is fed. Crying solves a problem: it brings food and cuddling on the sofa. Cooing brings another reaction; sneezing another. One simple tool, making a sound, soon becomes far more sophisticated; the infant learns to signal his needs and call for caretakers. A simple tool that develops in one zone opens up many new possibilities, each new zone requiring more sophisticated instruments. Vygotsky attributed the evolution of learning to the human ability to develop or modify 'tools' in order to make bridges to new zones of proximal development. By high school, each person has a highly individuated leadership skill set. Thus a leadership programme aimed at this age group has to take advantage of each student's personal risk limits, desires, and levels of confidence (already battered by puberty and the middle school years).

The leadership team had its own immutable principles regarding teenage leadership development: adolescents are regularly capable of great wisdom when supported with trust; building a community requires everyone's participation; teenagers will put aside the me-first attitude so predominant in the American ideal of the solitary, self-reliant individual; most opportunities spring up informally; and the backbone of firm values is best

---

[5] Erikson, *Erik Erikson Reader*, 188–98.   [6] Vygotsky, *Thought and Language*.

learned through community action rather than through preaching. The Town system created both formal offices and informal opportunities for leadership practice as well as the need to make value judgements. Students were urged and cajoled to show initiative; while some jumped forward, others needed gentle nudging.

Rich's Story

At the end of a November Town Meeting, Rich's sprawling freshman body barely shifted; he listened draped over three chairs, luxuriating in his suddenly acquired height—except this time he lingered a bit longer than usual. His normally winsome grin was quizzical, even a bit rebellious. Before long he was up, matching his stride to the director's, their shoulders almost touching as he leaned in with his just-between-us voice whispering, 'Why can't we run Town Meeting?' He was wrestling the old man for power by flexing his charm. The 'we' here meant students, and specifically it meant Rich.

Director (playing dumb): Do you think you could do it?

Rich: You know I can. I ran that meeting while you were at a conference.

Director: True. I heard you did a good job—even finished before the end of the period.

(Rich smiles with self-confidence)

Director *(peppering Rich with questions)*: How would the new moderator be chosen? Would there be guidelines? Terms? Officers? Would students accept another student's authority?

Rich: You mean we need a constitution?

Director: At least a set of by-laws.

After three arduous months, meeting after school twice a week, Rich's committee brought a proposed draft of by-laws to Town Meeting. Informal conversation in the corridor had kept most of the students informed. The Town debated, made revisions, and after two meetings voted in the Town's first by-laws. Elections were held. Rich was indeed elected moderator. The new officers pledged to uphold the by-laws and to model the Honour Pledge.[7] The 'old man' smiled as he stepped down from the podium for the last time.

The Town by-laws created offices, job descriptions, the committee process, an election procedure, and guidelines for Town Meetings. New officers were sworn in; their names were recorded on a plaque. The teaching

---

[7] The *derekh erets* (honourable conduct) pledge, 'As a member of the Schechter Regional High School *kehilla* [community], I set as my goals individual accomplishment, Jewish commitment, and community leadership. I promise to live my life with *derekh erets*—as a responsible person, whose word is my bond, whose work is my own, and around whom the dignity of others is honoured and the property of others is safe.'

faculty provided an adviser to the executive committee and a personal mentor for each officer. While the adults provided support, feedback, and the opportunity for reflection, the officers themselves owned the task of leading the Town.

Through his ability to hope for something bigger, his will to make it happen, his envisaging a new outcome, and his confidence in his own competence, Rich took some real social and institutional risks and profited from his mis-steps even more than from his successes. He learned to read the mood of the Town, and steer through emotional swamps to reach legislation. He demonstrated that 'even' a 15-year-old could plan for the future, inspire a shared vision, and demonstrate affective peer power.

Reflection

Teenagers shape their identities by seeking occupations worthy of their time. Adolescents are 'devoted to individual leaders and to teams, to strenuous activities, and to difficult techniques; at the same time they show a sharp and intolerant readiness to discard and disavow people'.[8] Adolescence is a paradoxical time of empowerment and disempowerment, supreme confidence and complete bewilderment, devotion to the fixed and to the variable. What results is the ability to sustain loyalties that have been freely selected—what Erikson refers to as 'fidelity'. Adolescents are very much interested in community but are far less trusting or patient about process. Town Meeting stretches their process tolerance: important decisions take time; wisdom takes listening; and community discussion takes planning and structure. Student leaders model the way.

Aryeh's Story

As faculty co-ordinator of Jewish life, Aryeh was eager for students to attend a pro-Israel rally at Rutgers University. The teachers and the leadership team realized that here was a prime leadership opportunity. The students were eager for the excitement of a university rally laced with the joy of missing classes. At the next Town Meeting, teacher after teacher raised an objection or introduced a new problem as the faculty deliberately set up issues to stretch students' zones of proximal development: Was this rally really important? What would it accomplish? What about tests scheduled for that day? What were the rally's expected outcomes? Would the Town merely be political pawns of the school administration? Would the rally only produce more ill-will towards Jews, or towards Israel?

[8] Erikson, *Erik Erikson Reader*, 288.

The moderator patiently appointed student/teacher committees to research and report back to the Town. At the next Town Meeting, just as all the philosophical questions were resolved, a teacher asked about transportation, the availability of water and kosher food, and permissions slips. Students who only six months earlier had been accustomed to having adults (parents and teachers) work out all these details for them were suddenly thrust into the very practical world of having to handle logistics themselves. They called bus companies to find the best price, drafted permission slips, and found water and food solutions.

Some of the students were in shock. That a Jewish school, institutionally supportive of Israel, could ever question the value of such a trip seemed absurd. This was the leadership lab at work. Students took initiative, envisaged what they wanted, and planned accordingly. They were empowered to take on adult responsibilities. This event was a watershed: Town became relevant and real; there were so many subsequent requests for agenda time that the Town passed an ordinance limiting discussion to those items posted in advance.

Dr H's Story

Dr H was a passionate recycler. Midway through one of the meetings, she rose to announce her latest project. The gutsy student moderator politely informed her that since she had not listed her topic, her issue would have to wait until a future meeting. Dr H was flabbergasted; she assumed that Town rules applied only to students. Unwittingly and unhappily, she modelled the inclusivity of Town authority.

Jackie's Story

Schechter Regional's curriculum was academically intensive. Jackie was especially conscientious about her studies and felt truly pressed by the homework load. She requested Town time to complain about a specific teacher. When the moderator met with her to prepare for the meeting, he pointed out that targeting an individual teacher was contrary to the school's *derekh erets* pledge.

Jackie faced a dilemma: how to address a topic affecting the Town without violating the immutable standard of protecting others' dignity (*derekh erets*). Her solution was to generalize, talking about how much total time she spent on homework, especially given that the school had no private study areas. When she introduced the topic at Town Meeting, the moderator first advised the faculty to review its policies on homework. He then appointed an ad hoc committee (including students and teachers) to review the schedule and suggest improvements. The faculty listened to and adopted many of the committee's recommendations.

Thus the right of the Town to advise the faculty was established. Issue by issue, the Town and its student members moved beyond wishing and complaining to the much higher moral plane of attending to the welfare of the community.

Constructivism argues that learning occurs when humans actively construct and reconstruct their knowledge by confronting the constraints of their environment.[9] For adolescents these environments are overwhelmingly social. Greene quotes the anthropologist Clifford Geertz about the importance of 'regarding the community as the shop in which thoughts are constructed and deconstructed' and about how cognition, perception, imagination, and memory are conceived 'as themselves, and directly, social affairs'.[10]

Leadership techniques are learned by constructing answers to real issues and dilemmas. Schechter Regional students 'do' leadership; they practise the real thing. Lambert proposes that 'Leadership inhabits [the] spaces, fields, or zones among [people] in a . . . community. Leadership like energy is not finite, not restricted by formal authority and power; it permeates a healthy school culture and is undertaken by whoever sees a need or an opportunity.'[11] Leadership inhabits the social world of interactions, and only a fraction of these occur in the formal classroom. What happens between activities is especially important. Power is gleaned from conversations in the corridor, lunchtime clusters, and whispers in classrooms, as well as through relationships outside school. Since students at Schechter have real power, real lobbying occurs, real alliances are built, and real collaborative thinking takes place. The teachers and leadership team serve as advisers and mentors, supporting students as they form strategies, applauding them when they succeed, and dusting them off when they stumble and fall.

Team Spirit

Thomas J. Sergiovanni, writing on moral leadership, insists that the first and most important task of school leaders is to be community builders, supporting the bond that holds a community together.[12] He urges schools to build covenantal communities around a common belief system. The

---

[9] Walker in Lambert et al., *Constructivist Leader* (introduction (p. xv) and ch. 1 (pp. 1–33)) presents a fine introduction to constructivist thinkers including Dewey, Piaget, Vygotsky, Bruner, and Kegan.   [10] Walker, introduction to Lambert et al., *Constructivist Leader*, p. viii.
[11] Lambert, ibid. 43.   [12] Sergiovanni, *Moral Leadership*.

smaller the distance between values declared and values practised, the stronger the bond will be. The more authority a person or group has, the more important—and, correspondingly, the more difficult—it is to maintain credibility. How school leaders nurture this bond defines how well the organization models the way, shares the vision, challenges the status quo, recruits others, and appeals to their hearts.[13] 'Youth selectively offers its loyalties and energies to the conservation of that which feels true to them and to the correction or destruction of that which has lost is regenerative significance.'[14]

While the parents sign a financial contract before their child is enrolled, students sign a value contract, the *derekh erets* pledge. New officers pledge not only to follow the principles of *derekh erets* personally, but to dedicate themselves to the welfare of the whole Town. Underlying the very essence of the pledge is a mutual covenant of trust.

As a living metaphor, when the leadership team opened the school it forbade locks on lockers, thus hoping to force students to develop bonds of trust with each other and to rely on the Town to sort out disputes.

Levana's Story

Levana (in the leadership team's office): My father says I have to have a lock on my locker. He paid too much for the graphing calculator to have it stolen.

LT: Please tell your dad that we are developing a community of trust and that it is important for students to trust each other.

Levana's friends helped her watch her locker even as they were careful not to interfere with anyone else's locker. By necessity a community of trust was developing.

When a local synagogue began to use the school's worship space every weekend, Levana grew more alarmed. Because the lock rule was set by the leadership team, it was beyond the authority of the Town, except to discuss and advise.

Levana (at Town Meeting): Things have changed. (*Turning to the LT*) You were right, we can trust the students and our teachers, but who are these new people? Do they use our halls? Could they get into our lockers?

Student A: We are responsible for our things; how can we be responsible when we are not here and the building is not locked?

LT: This requires some time, let's discuss it at the next meeting.

[13] Kouzes and Posner, *The Leadership Challenge*, 13.
[14] Erikson, *Erik Erikson Reader*.

Students (whispering): Sounds like a cop-out. They are not listening to us. No way!

The leadership team felt challenged; even attacked. The student argument was sound, but backing down now seemed like defeat and a loss of face.

Moderator (at the next Town Meeting): Unfinished business: the question of the locks. Is the leadership team ready to speak to this?

LT: Two weeks ago the no lock rule seemed very important. We do not personally believe in locks, but in the interest of Town security we yield our authority and will abide by the decision of the Town.

Students (whispering among themselves): Huh? Since when do adults listen to kids? They're kidding. What?

(LT delivers an impassioned speech about trust)

Levana: Over the weekend, the teachers lock their cubbies in the faculty room and the leadership team locks its office doors; shouldn't we be allowed to do the same?

Moderator calls a vote, and announces: The Town has voted in favour of locks. (*Turning to the leadership team*) Is that OK?

Students are silent for a moment.

LT: Mr Moderator, thank you for asking. Yes, we stand by what we said: the Town decision prevails.

Despite their newly won right, very few students chose to use locks. Each student owned his or her own decision. Each was an empowered participant in the covenantal community of trust.

Playing for Real

Levana took a risk by challenging the process. Would the adults be angry? Would they dislike her? Would they speak to her parents? How would her peers respond? What if she lost the vote? Students take real social risks just by speaking up. Besides the worry about what others will think, they also risk losing face by being voted down. Leadership requires tremendous ego investment.

Playing the Full Field

Fine soccer players sense movement, not just around the ball but all over the field. They grasp the unfolding strategies of the whole field and then choose among a variety of turns, kicks, and headers within a dynamic interplay. They see the big picture and make decisions based on a bird's-eye perspective. Ron Heifetz, in his book on adaptive leadership, describes the leader's need to climb up 'to the balcony' in order to get a wider perspective of what is happening on the main floor.[15] Seeing the big picture enables a leader to think politically and orchestrate responses.

Tom's Story

The founding year was so busy, who had time to collect pictures? By year two, parents and teachers feared that history was being lost. A yearbook seemed crazy until there was a graduating class, and there was no interest on the part of the students who were too busy living the history of pioneering a school.

During the June exam week, Tom and a few of his freshmen friends wandered into the director's office wondering if they could start a yearbook. During the summer, the director followed up with Tom to meet for a 'business lunch'; encouraging student initiative was a basic premise of the leadership lab. Though Tom had never put a yearbook together, he reasoned that the mechanics could be learned. What did concern him were the politics in getting this off the ground: evidence that the school's leadership lab was working for him.

Tom wondered if the juniors would allow a rising sophomore to put together a yearbook committee. He had time during the summer and did not want to wait until the Town next met in September. He was filled with questions: How could he bring together a small, dedicated group of planners without seeming to undermine the Town's new officers? Where would he get the money? Did he need the Town's permission? Did he need its help to raise funds? This was a strategy meeting—it truly was a business lunch. Tom raised questions, argued points, made notes.

Even before school began, rumours were flying. 'He never talked the project over with us', groaned one of the Town's officers. 'Only his friends will be on the yearbook, and I wanted to help', said a freshman. 'Tom is only doing this for his own glory', said a jealous classmate.

The social pressures on Tom were tremendous. Though he was a young man of strong convictions, he liked to please others; he knew he had to learn some new interpersonal skills, quickly. Tom asked a teacher to mentor him. He tried different approaches and reported back limited success. This was very tough territory, sorting out major issues from minor messes. Feelings were running high, and he began to imagine ill-will even where none existed.

Tom's mentor took him up to Heifetz's balcony, so that he could look down and see how to separate the important from the trivial. Together they talked about what was going on, and Tom created his action plan. With his mentor's help, he practised adaptive leadership. After a

---

[15] Heifetz and Linsky, *Leadership on the Line.*

few months Tom was able to retreat to the balcony himself. What finally won the day was Tom's openness to including others as long as they were real workers and interested in the yearbook. What he appealed to was their devotion—their fidelity. By the time Tom took the yearbook project to the Town for approval, it passed easily.

Practice . . .

Schechter Regional High's leadership lab was designed:

1. to model directly values-driven and collaborative authority;

2. to open up real opportunities for students to assume leadership;

3. to support student leaders through a system of advisers and mentors;

4. to encourage and financially support student-initiated projects;

5. to uphold a strong moral code, grounded in Jewish tradition and articulated in the *derekh erets* pledge;

6. to provide direct instruction in leadership knowledge, skills, and techniques; and

7. to work within students' zones of proximal development to encourage them to leap forward.

The Town Meeting and the *derekh erets* pledge are the lab's most obvious features. Both depend on adult faith in the wisdom of young people and in the capacity of their best judgement to prevail. Both enforce a covenant of mutual belief. While the adults serve as guides, the adolescents bear the burden of real practice. The Town Meeting, with its corridor politics and various committees, is a classroom, perhaps an unconventional one, where students not only construct their knowledge of what leadership is all about but also, more importantly, test out these leadership skills in real situations with real consequences.

High School Leadership: The Challenge

Little attention has been paid in the literature to the assertion that upbringing and pre-collegiate education prepares leaders for their future roles. Was the Battle of Waterloo really won on the playing fields of Eton, as the Duke of Wellington is supposed to have claimed? If secondary education can have that kind of impact, it is well worth studying.

Did Eton provide all the right social connections, or did it provide a certain training that was important? Are the skill sets, connections, and habits of mind necessary to support the leaders of today different from those that equipped past leaders, and, by implication, different from those that will be needed by leaders of the future? Can we predict what curriculum is best? Is the distance between high school graduation and adult success too wide for specific comparative research?

Schechter Regional built a school on well-educated hunches. This school's jury goes into deliberation with the first graduating class in 2007; the verdict will be long delayed by the intervening years towards adulthood.

Can Schechter Regional's principles and practices be applied by other school founders? Can these methods exist outside a faith-based school? Outside this faith? Which of these practices can profit an existing school? Will this programme even remain viable beyond the founding years? What types of evidence should be gathered along the way? (Videos? Journals? Outside observers? Personal testimony?) How will the school's programme evolve as the school grows?

The story of this school, and the stories of Henry, Rich, Jackie, Levana, Aryeh, and Tom raise interesting questions. How their stories end will be better known over time. Youth organizations as well as more and more high schools have developed well-articulated leadership programmes. Their stories also need to be told. Adolescent leadership and its preparation for adult roles is a field ripe for research.

Bibliography

Erikson, E., *The Erik Erikson Reader*, ed. R. Coles (New York, 2000).
Heifetz, R. A., and M. Linsky, *Leadership on the Line: Staying Alive through the Dangers of Leading* (Boston, 2002).
Kouzes, J. M., and B. Z. Posner, *The Leadership Challenge* (San Francisco, 2002).
Lambert, L., D. Walker, D. P. Zimmerman, J. E. Cooper, M. D. Lambert, M. E. Gardner, and P. J. Ford Slack, *The Constructivist Leader* (New York, 1995).
Sergiovanni, T. J., *Moral Leadership: Getting to the Heart of School Improvement* (San Francisco, 1992).
Vygotsky, L. S., *Mind in Society: The Development of Higher Psychological Processes* (Cambridge, Mass., 1978).
—— *Thought and Language* (Cambridge, Mass., 2000).
Zimmerman, D. P., *Robert's Rules in Plain English*, 2nd edn (New York, 2005).

Building Community in a Pluralist High School

SUSAN L. SHEVITZ AND RAHEL WASSERFALL

Context and Questions

The religious practice at an intentionally pluralistic Jewish high school in the United States that we are calling 'Tikhon' entails prayer services in the morning and, for those who are interested, in the afternoon as well. In order to provide services that are appropriate to the full range of its students, Tikhon organizes dozens of options in the morning, ranging from traditional services, in which males and females sit separately and men assume the leading liturgical roles, to discussions and yoga with meditation. Students choose the service that is of interest to them and—to some extent, since these are adolescents—with which their families are comfortable. By doing this, Tikhon legitimates the range of approaches to Judaism that Tikhon families hold and makes a statement about its understanding of pluralism.

Despite this effort to respect and support the multiplicity of approaches to prayer, conflicts that challenge students sometimes arise. Reflecting on her experience of pluralism during her first year, a girl who believes that females should not be counted in a *minyan* and who goes with her friends to the *meḥitsah minyan* recalls a morning when the *meḥitsah minyan* did not have the ten men needed for a participant to say Kaddish (the prayer to remember a deceased relative):[1]

This research was supported by a generous grant from the Mandel Center for Studies in Jewish Education at Brandeis University.

[1] *Minyan* technically refers to the quorum of ten needed for the group to include several of the prayers; more generally, the term refers to the entire prayer group. In the *meḥitsah minyan*, males and females sit separately and only males are allowed to lead the prayers, read from Torah and assume other liturgical responsibilities. The *egalitarian* ('egal') *minyan* gives equal opportunity for males and females to participate in and lead the services and allows them to sit together during the services.

I remember [what happened] earlier in the year, [with] my friends who couldn't say Kaddish because there wasn't a *minyan*. So one girl from the [*meḥitsah minyan*] was actually willing to go to the egal *minyan* so that they could have a *minyan* [because a boy from the egal *minyan* came into the *meḥitsah* one and preserved the quorum] . . . so that the person in *meḥitsah* could say Kaddish. I don't know how you categorize that, like what's that called? But [the girl who left the *meḥitsah minyan* and went to the egalitarian one] honestly believed that she should not be counted in a *minyan*, but she went anyway for the sake of someone who had to say Kaddish. And that was just—people do make sacrifices.[2]

A boy who identifies himself as a Reform Jew quickly concurs: 'You can keep your own beliefs, but at the same time help other people, acknowledge, accept and respect their beliefs.'

Tikhon aspires to a form of pluralism that respects and develops students' religious differences. The head of school's message on the school's website explains:

Jewish pluralism is a hallmark of our school. Our students represent a broad spectrum of religious, educational and cultural beliefs. Tikhon is a place where Conservative, Orthodox, Reconstructionist, Reform and secular Jews can come together as a caring community in which to learn and to grow. Here we celebrate the values we have in common as we explore the important ideological differences that make us distinct. The pluralism we preach is one of engagement through which we challenge each other in the process of understanding each other.

The tension between, in this statement's words, 'the values we have in common' and 'the important ideological differences that make us distinct' are visible in the discussion above of the *minyan* decision. The student's ideological position is clear. Committed to the *meḥitsah minyan*, she neither dismisses nor denigrates the other *minyanim*. Despite her commitment, she faces a dilemma. If she sticks with her beliefs and stays in her own *minyan*, another person is unable to say Kaddish, something this student agrees is important. This tension reveals a second key commitment: being part of a wider community. The student expresses her resolution as a 'sacrifice', neither taken lightly nor regretted.

This case uncovers the complex questions that are the focus of this chapter. They are always below the surface at Tikhon and in other settings that value diversity: when is loyalty to one's own ideas and actions paramount,

---

[2] These and all following quotations from student and faculty are from written or recorded field notes.

and when are the needs of others in the community taken into account when religious belief is at stake? How does Tikhon's emphasis on diversity affect its efforts to build a cohesive school community? With its focus on the differences among people, pluralism can be seen as a centrifugal force that helps individuals and sub-groups develop their unique viewpoints. The concept of community, on the other hand, is a centripetal force that brings people closer to a shared core. If supporting individuals' diverse positions is essential to Tikhon's form of pluralism, what does it do to harness centripetal, community-building forces?

This chapter investigates how Tikhon deals with these questions in its educational practice, and analyses what the practices reveal about its understanding of pluralism. It argues that two dynamics are fundamental to Tikhon's efforts: first, the need to create an environment in which participants can risk the differentiation, debate, discussion, and openness to co-operation and change that are at the heart of Tikhon's understanding of community; and second, the need to create a psychological sense of community in which 'difference' is central to the conception of community.

Our enquiry is part of a larger project to study how pluralism is enacted and understood at Tikhon. During the 2005/6 school year the authors of this chapter followed the incoming class to see how they were being socialized into the school's conception of pluralism. This observation took place in classes, at school events, and in committee meetings; in detailed interviews with thirty administrators and teachers; in focus groups with students; and through analyses of student work, curricula, school papers and magazines, the website, and other relevant materials. We believe that the approach and methods we found at Tikhon can be applied to other settings where the tension between the individual and the group is central to the educational approach.

Community, Diversity, and Pluralism at Tikhon

Founded in 1997, Tikhon draws students from a large metropolitan area. Students in the 2005/6 ninth-grade class that was followed come from families in thirty-five towns; 37 per cent of these families receive scholarships from the school that enable their children to attend. As an intentionally pluralist school, Tikhon works hard to recruit students from across the spectrum of Jewish practice and beliefs, from secular at one end to Orthodox at the other, as well as students who are all—in the phrase heard frequently in the school—'serious about their Jewish lives'. While all high schools face the problem of forging a disparate group of ninth-graders into a functioning class that follows the school's preferred values and norms, the problem of socializing new students in this school has an additional complication: the school's commitment to a particular type of pluralism.

Our analysis of pluralism is framed by the work of Walzer, who distinguishes between 'tolerating' (the attitude) and 'tolerance' (the practice),[3] and of Seligman, who claims that a modern conception of tolerance means the acceptance of difference,[4] not merely the 'ability to suffer and endure what was unacceptable but could not . . . be eradicated'.[5] In the postmodern world this must happen on both the personal and the political level.[6] Tikhon's form of pluralism reflects these ideas as well as those developed by Stone, who defines pluralism as

coexistence with difference that is born out of an appreciation for diversity, multiplicity and particularity; and a recognition that distinct traditions and opinions are nonetheless interdependent—that they share certain goals and common projects and therefore that social collaboration and legal interaction are both possible and necessary even between groups or individuals otherwise holding mutually exclusive, conflicting viewpoints, each deemed by the other to be in error.[7]

A senior student at Tikhon expressed this idea directly:

During my time at Tikhon I have learned the importance and necessity for tolerance. It is a message ingrained in the very idea of Tikhon—a pluralistic day school tolerant of all forms of Jewish religious practice.

One way in which the types of pluralism enacted in Jewish educational settings may be distinguished is to see these efforts on a continuum of engagement with difference on which three points are identified: (1) demographic, (2) co-existence, and (3) generative pluralism. Tikhon goes beyond demographic and co-existence pluralism. While it actively seeks demo-

[3] Walzer, *On Toleration*, pp. xi–xiii.
[4] Seligman, *Modest Claims*, p. xx.   [5] Seligman, 'Introduction', 10–12.
[6] Walzer, *On Toleration*, 90–1. There is a long political and philosophical discourse on the concept of pluralism which, in the work of Isaiah Berlin and others, goes 'beyond acceptance of plurality to a radical acceptance of the existence of many truths'. See Hardy, 'Taking Pluralism Seriously'.   [7] Stone, 'Tolerance versus Pluralism', 107.

graphic diversity, and assumes that individuals and groups will learn to tolerate each other and co-exist with the different ideas and ideologies represented, it strives for 'generative pluralism' as its ideal model. The school's visionaries define pluralism as 'the ability to understand, hold, and grapple with multiple, even contradictory interpretations and perspectives'.[8] They expect that students will learn to articulate their own ideas, engage with others' ideas, and think deeply, all towards the goals of strengthening their own positions, possibly changing their own positions, or together generating new approaches. Diversity of opinion does not necessarily exist only between different groups; it may also exist within any particular group, as it does among Tikhon students. In such cases, the challenge is that people who hold very different versions of a shared tradition and culture have to 'tolerate, appreciate and *work with* others' interpretations'.[9] Generating new ideas together with people who have different beliefs is the distinguishing characteristic of this type of pluralism. A Tikhon senior gives thoughtful voice to this idea:

The Jews are a wandering people, both geographically itinerant and spiritually roving. A Jew can never stay in one state of mind for too long. We debate; we change our minds; we amend. Everything I've learned at Tikhon has bolstered this view . . . Tikhon allowed me to change my opinions and alter my beliefs in an environment where I can gracefully cede even my strongest certainties to new ideas.

An administrator at Tikhon illustrates one aspect of generative pluralism by relating how a very traditional student from the *meḥitsah minyan* challenged a young woman from the traditional but egalitarian *minyan* to explore why she was not putting on *tefilin* (phylacteries) even though she was wearing a *talit* (prayer shawl) and leading the service. She says that Tikhon asks people the question: 'Within the context of your own Jewish construct, how can you be a stronger Jew?' We also see Tikhon's pluralism in the way in which it crafted a new way to chant the opening section of *birkat hamazon* (grace after meals) that was acceptable to all students, from the most liberal to the most traditional.[10] Diversity at Tikhon, especially around significant Jewish ideas and practices, is the grist for the intellectual

---

[8] Tikhon, 'Self-Study', 47. See also Wasserfall and Shevitz, 'The Language of Pluralism', for further discussion of how Tikhon understands this.

[9] Walzer, *On Toleration*, 65 (emphasis added).

[10] The more traditional students do not accept the legitimacy of a female leading the prayer, while other students believe that an egalitarian approach is the proper way.

and religious mill associated with generative pluralism. It is a precondition for exploring and expanding beliefs and actions.

This stance is similar to the approach advocated by Diana Eck, one of the leading scholars of religious pluralism. Eck asserts that in contemporary American society, which is characterized by a religious diversity going far beyond the three monotheistic faiths that dominated just fifty years ago—Protestantism, Catholicism, and Judaism—pluralism entails 'engagement, involvement and participation. It is the language of traffic, exchange, dialog and debate . . . [that must be] claimed anew' as the context changes.[11]

Tikhon's pluralism focuses on the pluralism within the Jewish community. It relies heavily on cognitive approaches, which it promotes through its formal and informal curricula by both implicit norms and explicit instruction. It wants to enrol, in words heard repeatedly, 'serious Jews' who will engage with ideas and texts. Teachers do not want 'wishy-washy students' but enjoy encountering adolescents who can 'push back'. They claim this is not an 'anything goes' approach but one that wants students to justify positions with information and textual references. As one teacher sees it, 'You need to understand that your interpretations come from your religious beliefs and you must be willing to interpret your rules . . .' Revealing assumptions and recognizing principles on which one will not compromise are part of the Tikhon experience. The same teacher who emphasizes that people must 'do things for the sake of the community' recognizes that 'sometimes you have to keep your own principles'.

Enacting Pluralism at School

Tikhon asks its students to take a risk; they are to relinquish certainty as they engage with people holding different ideas. Its commitment to this is nowhere more apparent than its 'de-bate *midrash*'. The phrase itself is a play on the Hebrew words *beit midrash*—the traditional term for the 'house of study' which, in Tikhon's vocabulary, is also the large room in which the school community gathers for special events. The process leading to a 'de-bate *midrash*'—as well as the event itself—demonstrates Tikhon's commitment to individuals' perspectives and group needs. One example follows.

Several male students complained that Tikhon was becoming, in their words, 'less Jewish'. Administrators suggested that they bring their com-

---

[11] Eck, *A New Religious America*, 69.

plaints and suggestions to the rabbis' committee that consists of the school's varied rabbis: Reform, Conservative, traditional, Orthodox, and those who choose no denominational label. As the students entered the committee meeting, it was clear they were accustomed to speaking their minds. One charge followed another, infused with the emotion of aggrieved adolescents. Finally, some rabbis intervened, asking the complainants what they wanted to do about the situation. The students rattled off several ideas: the ninth graders should have more mandatory prayer; Tikhon should limit the number of students coming from public (state) schools; and males should have to wear *kipot* when they study the Judaic subjects. A 'de-bate *midrash*' was called on the topic: 'Should boys be required to wear *kipot* for *limudei kodesh* [study of Jewish texts]?'

As the 'de-bate *midrash*' began a teacher stood in front of the large assembly, between the gathered students and academic staff members. Groups were arranged in a U shape. People taking the 'pro' position stood on one side of the room, those arguing 'con' stood on the other, and the undecideds formed the base of the U. As speakers made their points, individuals among both students and faculty moved from one side to another, with undecided audience members joining the fray as they formed opinions. Any individual might change his or her mind and cross the room multiple times. The governing rules for the 'de-bate *midrash*' were that people take turns in speaking and use respectful but strong language—they were not allowed to use 'mushy' words. Below is an outline and paraphrase of the debate.

Teacher 1 (pro): In the entire world you take your hat off as a sign of respect. For a Jew everybody needs to have their head covered: this is a sign of respect.

Boy 1 (con; reads from a text he brought and says): It is only a custom, not a halakhah [rabbinic law].

(*Boy 2, pro, wearing a* kipah, *gets up and looks for a gemara [Talmud text] to refute this argument*)

Girl 1 (pro): It is a *minhag* [custom], but a symbol of learning and we should respect the learning.

Boy 1 (con): It has become a symbol of observance; it is all about division, not about learning. I do not feel differently when I study and I should not be obliged to wear a *kipah*.

Teacher 2 (con): It bothers me emotionally to see somebody without a *kipah* learning but I am against making it a required practice because I see it as a very powerful symbolic act that somebody can study without a *kipah*. It means that the most secular person can have a claim on these texts. *Kipah* can also be divisive, *kipah serugah* [a knitted *kipah*, generally seen as a sign that the wearer is a modern Orthodox or right-wing Conservative Jew], where you wear it on your head . . . or if you wear a hat . . ., *kipah* defines and divides Jews.

At that moment Teacher 1 stands and moves to the con side with Teacher 2.

Many things are going on in this vignette. Students are comfortable airing their complaints to administrators and teachers who take them seriously and are willing to devote a precious resource, time, to exploring the topic through a 'de-bate *midrash*'. Students and teachers are expected, in the school's words, to be 'engaged' with the issue and each other. They develop arguments, citing texts and precedent, but they also speak personally, as did the boy who describes how he feels when he wears a *kipah*. A teacher changes his position even while acknowledging that he is not necessarily comfortable with the outcome—'it bothers me emotionally'— having been convinced that not requiring the *kipah* is the better option. The 'de-bate *midrash*' is a public display, not only of individuals' positions, but also of two other factors: how well a position can be argued and whether a participant will allow him- or herself to be persuaded enough to change positions. Participants change position only when they feel safe enough to risk publicly disclosing their ideas and changing their minds without fear of ostracism or ridicule.[12] Focusing on individuals' positions while maintaining the sense of safety are preconditions to the school's form of pluralism. They are also components of its community-building efforts.

The seriousness with which Tikhon takes the individual's perspectives—at least about religious matters—can be seen in many aspects of school life. To give one example, there are thirty-seven different prayer experiences available over the course of a week, ranging from *meḥitsah* and traditional egalitarian *minyanim* to yoga or art and prayer, and from Reform to neo-hasidic formats. And should a student not find one that meets her needs, she can approach an administrator to create another, as did the student who was 'angry at God' and didn't think any *minyan* addressed this

---

[12] The only time the researchers saw any ridicule was at the Purim celebration, where students poked fun at administrators, teachers, and a few other students. Although Purim is a topsy-turvy day, the faculty was aghast when a student was ridiculed.

adequately. Another student, believing that society's racial and ethnic diversity were not adequately acknowledged in the school, was empowered to find ways to address this in a study group.

An additional element of Tikhon's pluralism is that the issues must really matter to the students.[13] When this happens, they become a centripetal force that unites the students and teachers. Like the *kipah* question, issues often emerge from the students. At other times Tikhon tries to stimulate enquiry around issues students might care about but rarely explore: beliefs about God, Judaism, religious practice, as well as social and political positions.[14] It creates programmes that challenge students' self-understanding, such as showing a documentary, *Mixed Blessings*, about how four intermarried families deal with their religious differences. Involving both students from intermarried families and others from families firmly committed to endogamy, the discussion about the film evoked deeply personal responses. In a small group debriefing, one student told of her father's boycott of his niece's marriage to a non-Jew. Another girl in the same session described how she feels pulled between her intermarried parents, one a fundamentalist Christian, the other an Orthodox Jew. In the administration's words, the purpose of these encounters is for students 'to take [the presenting issue] seriously' and apply the ideas to their own lives. This process is fraught with risk, especially for adolescents, who are exquisitely sensitive to their place in the group even as they explore new behaviours and try on new ideas.

Balancing Risk and Safety: Tikhon as a 'Safe Enough Place'

Because Tikhon expects that students and teachers will risk self-disclosure and argument as well as openness to change, it needs to provide an environment in which all feel sufficiently safe to do this. Adapting Winnicott's well-

[13] Sociologist of religion Robert Wuthnow asserts that many manifestations of pluralism in America are shallow and avoid the hard questions about difference, pluralism, and society. He advocates a more 'intentional' approach or what he calls 'reflective pluralism', which acknowledges 'how and why people are different (and the same)'. See Wuthnow, *America and the Challenges of Religious Diversity*, 286–95. See also Shields, 'Learning from Educators', on multiculturalism in the classroom.

[14] A weekly all-school assembly, called *limud kelali*, is one forum where a wide range of speakers come to introduce students to interesting, sometimes controversial, ideas.

known concept of the 'good enough mother',[15] we see Tikhon as trying to be a 'safe enough' environment that stimulates differentiation and debate while also providing support and acceptance. Many teachers and administrators define the school and its pluralism as a safe place. Some mean by this that the school is a haven from the harsh divisiveness of Jewish life, while others describe how the school tries to create a safe environment for students to take the risks that are central components of Tikhon's brand of pluralism. The community does not shy away from controversy, even controversy that may be related to students' identities. Precisely because such controversies are relevant to students' lives, Tikhon believes that it is important to engage adolescents with them.

Tikhon tries to structure a 'safe enough' environment in several ways. It works hard to develop personal trust and understanding among and between students and faculty. On the most obvious level, it has incorporated many established approaches to building a school community. The process starts with the orientation, where all the new students, from their different communities and backgrounds, interact with one another. Small advisory groups serve as places where concerns can be raised. There are dozens of informal learning programmes outside the classroom that allow students and faculty to experience different facets of each other. The office of the director of student life is a hub of the concerns that the students bring. There are grade-wide and school-wide Shabbatonim, and weekly *limud kelali* assemblies that teach the entire school about interesting ideas, people, and projects. All these community-building activities run alongside a plethora of standard extracurricular activities, including many sports teams and clubs. The assumption is that individual connections build the necessary goodwill and trust among students with differing views that will serve as 'money in the bank' when conflict, inevitably, occurs.

Vulnerable Student Groups

Even with these measures in place to help build a supportive community, teachers and administrators still identify three groups of students they believe to be vulnerable: students with less Jewish knowledge than most, students with special educational needs, and those whose religious practices are more liberal or more traditional than the perceived norm.

---

[15] Winnicott, *The Child, the Family*.

Tikhon's largest single group of students comes from Conservative day schools, many of whom also attend Jewish camps and youth groups. They are described by some teachers as being on an 'axis' of Jewish engagement.[16] These students are deeply involved in Jewish practices at school: they sing *zemirot* (special sabbath songs) at Shabbatonim, organize prayer services, and so on. Some teachers think that many students without this background are 'at the periphery' and wonder whether they can be prepared really to engage in the way the school expects. With Tikhon's strong emphasis on rabbinics, Tanakh (the Hebrew Bible), and Hebrew, as well as argument and debate, these students are at a disadvantage that is reinforced by how the school tracks the levels of students in Hebrew and other classes. Special needs students are also identified as vulnerable, since they have to work hard just to keep up with Tikhon's challenging curriculum. They are often at a disadvantage in an environment that stresses verbal and analytical skills, as are students whose strengths lie in other areas.

In addition, students who perceive their religious beliefs to be outside the centre ground are sometimes concerned that their views will be minimized or, if an especially contentious issue is being discussed, in the words of a teacher, 'bashed'.[17] Tikhon challenges students who hold more and also less traditional beliefs. As we saw in the vignette about saying Kaddish, both liberal and traditional students sometimes consider compromising a principle in order to support others in their community. At other times, students feel pressure to fit in—if not at school, then at events outside school. This might be in a setting as simple as a group gathered in a student's house on sabbath afternoon or as exotic as somewhere in Europe with school-mates deciding what to have for dinner. Traditional students are also aware they learn less of the classical rabbinic texts than do students at Orthodox schools, and that, as seniors, they will study the documentary hypothesis

[16]　The pattern of feeder schools in part explains the predominance of Conservative affiliated students. In Tikhon's region there are five K–8 (kindergarten to eighth grade) Conservative or community schools and a sixth, also K–8, is pluralist. There is also one Reform day school and a modern Orthodox K–12 school whose high school programme was considered weak when Tikhon was founded. Many observers claim that Tikhon's opening motivated educational improvements there so that fewer of its students now want to leave after the eighth grade. The Reform presence, though small, is growing, and most of the Orthodox who have enrolled came from the pluralist school or schools that are further away.

[17]　We saw some good-natured teasing but no instances of 'bashing' or belittling others for their religious beliefs, although if this does happen it might take place outside the purview of researchers.

regarding the authorship of the Bible. They face particular dilemmas around dress and behaviour. In the words of a teacher, 'It takes a special kind of Orthodox family to enrol their children here', and the teachers are aware that these students sometimes feel under assault by the majority's more liberal thinking. Even so, some students proudly identify as Orthodox and deeply appreciate being in this environment, and there are students who experiment with and embrace Orthodoxy as a result of Tikhon's pluralism.

Students from more liberal backgrounds likewise feel that they are asked to compromise, in their case to meet the needs of the more stringently observant students. They complain that the ideological seriousness of the liberal position is not always recognized. Students in Tikhon's wide middle range also face these issues, though not as acutely; their beliefs and customs vary too, and they too are tugged by different commitments. Thus all Tikhon's students confront the question: When do I compromise, hold on to, or change my beliefs? Tikhon wants to make these questions discussable; it sees this as a characteristic of engaged, cognitive pluralism. And this can happen only when its students, especially those who are vulnerable, feel safe.

Teachers' Role in Enhancing Safety

Tikhon relies heavily on its faculty to create a 'safe enough' environment in several ways. It assumes that the presence of teachers with diverse viewpoints and lifestyles is itself a powerful message. The range of faculty in terms of Jewish religious belief is immediately visible to anyone literate in the costumes of contemporary Jewry: men who wear hats alongside men who wear knitted, cloth, or no *kipot*; women whose heads are covered alongside others wearing jeans and sweaters. The rabbis' committee, composed of faculty and administrators from across the full spectrum of Jewish life, examine the school's religious and spiritual dimension. There are openly gay/lesbian teachers and non-Jewish faculty and staff. Students recognize this diversity, and some value the opportunity to study with someone whose religious views differ from their own. In interviews, several students mentioned an Orthodox teacher who is popular even though she presents content that seems strange to the less observant students. The stated reasons for her popularity mirror the school's values of privileging cognition and community. The teacher was described as 'brilliant', 'knows as much as any man or rabbi', 'really cares' about the subject, and is 'authentic'. At the same time, Tikhon makes certain that students have access to role models who are more similar to their familiar ways of being Jewish.

Tikhon deliberately arranges for teachers with different points of view to work together, especially when exploring contentious topics such as intermarriage, attitudes towards the Muslim world, or sexuality. The mandatory 'pluralism lab', taken by each ninth-grader for one term, is co-taught by two rabbis who represent different religious ideologies. Students see two authority figures respectfully disagree with each other and use information to bolster their positions. They model relationships based on respect and enquiry.

Not merely passive observers, teachers also stay actively alert to student discomfort. One teacher summarized the position of the teachers who make up the faculty's pluralism committee: 'The school is obligated to make sure—once you're in this school you're protected, you're safe, you're respected. And you shouldn't feel pain. You shouldn't feel insecurity. There should be adult voices who can speak up, "No, I think this is a legitimate position."'

Many teachers take this responsibility seriously. After the documentary and debriefing about intermarriage, for example, several teachers sought out individual students who were upset. One boy felt marginalized because he is from an intermarried family; another was upset, a teacher recalled, 'that the school would show a movie like that, that seemed to be non-judgmental about intermarriage'. Before the ninth-grade Shabbaton, the teacher in charge of the new students instructed colleagues to 'be very aware of kids at the fringes', and a secular Israeli teacher made a point of connecting with students who were not part of the 'axis' of the more actively Jewish students. Several administrators and teachers described their offices as places where students who have concerns come to talk.

In particular, Tikhon works hard to maintain the Orthodox segment of its enrolment; it is widely believed that if it loses its Orthodox population, its community will be seriously compromised. Teachers—especially those teachers who are themselves Orthodox—go out of their way to support traditional students. Noting the liberal tendencies of most of the student body, they believe that when complex, controversial issues such as responses to homosexuality are brought up, 'the real challenge [is] not to the liberal position but to tradition. Would the traditional voice speak up?' One traditional teacher talks about how careful he is to present a 'nuanced view' that might otherwise be lacking. A graduate reported the importance of this teacher's efforts: 'I dreaded going to the [whole school] meeting. It was going to be heavy and there would be tradition-bashing. I am struggling . . . to hold on to my faith. That [the teacher, an Orthodox rabbi] took that position made it OK.' Another graduate wrote that as a student he saw things 'as black or white' and that an Orthodox teacher 'reminded me, by using texts, [that] there are complexities. Not black and white. There can be texts that say homosexuality is wrong but others about how we have to treat people humanely.'

While students from Reform backgrounds might seem to fit Tikhon's ethos more easily, we saw occasions when students or teachers had to remind people that 'Reform is not less, it is other.' There is the constant need at Tikhon to counter the Jewish community's hierarchical assumptions that Orthodox means most religious and Reform means least.

Relying on teachers' sensitivities to weave a safety net for students who may not feel comfortable is an ad hoc approach, and as the school grows it becomes harder for all teachers to be aware of the specific issues individual students face. Students might easily slip through the net, especially if the perception of one teacher who feels that the less Jewishly knowledgeable students are 'disenfranchised' is correct. It remains to be seen whether Tikhon will be able to rely on this close-knit support system as it grows.

An additional, but contested, way in which Tikhon attempts to make the school safe is by avoiding use of the standard denominational labels. Some teachers and administrators want students to work out their approaches to Jewish life on the basis of the principles and beliefs they hold, rather than by clinging to the names that indicate affiliation with a denomination or movement. These people argue that the key point is not loyalty to a movement, but determining one's own beliefs and being able to engage meaningfully with those who disagree. Other teachers and administrators are less comfortable with this approach, asserting that denominations and movements are the students' frames of reference; why pretend they are not there? The disagreement itself expresses Tikhon's pluralism, and since there is no need for a single policy or resolution, the *maḥaloket*—legitimate difference of opinion—can be experienced as either confusing or empowering. It certainly reinforces the sense that different approaches, based in reasoned opinions, can co-exist in the school, and this helps students grow and work together productively.[18]

Characteristics of the Tikhon Community

We have seen how Tikhon creates its pluralism by maintaining a diverse student body and managing the risks involved in self-disclosure and argument with its 'safe enough' environment. At the same time, Tikhon cultivates a sense of community, without which its pluralism would collapse into disconnected sub-groups doing 'parallel play', so to speak. Simply enrolling a heterogeneous student body without helping it explore its diversity would produce mere demographic pluralism rather than the engaged, generative pluralism that Tikhon seeks. What, then, draws the students of different types together? What provides the centripetal force that fosters community? How does commitment to the community develop alongside Tikhon's efforts to support its diversity?

In thinking about how Tikhon creates community, we may usefully turn to Ronald Arnett's definition of community as a group built on shared memories and aspirations.[19] What is the history Tikhon's constituents share, as a people and as a school, and to what can they all aspire?

Part of the reason why this focus on community is so central is that Tikhon is a *Jewish* school. Judaism is a religion that is built on community experience and identity. A core assumption is that Jews are a people who share a common destiny; hence the requirement for praying in a *minyan*, the first-person-plural formulation of many prayers, and other manifestations of the prominence of the group. Valuing the group in this way is not easily compatible with the modern Western focus on the individual, and the tension between the needs of the individual and those of the group lies at the heart of many of Tikhon's dilemmas. As the mission statement says, Tikhon aspires to be 'a sacred community within the Jewish people' and to form 'a diverse and pluralistic community'. It continues: 'Our diversity is a strength. An atmosphere of mutual respect provides a welcome forum for grappling with fundamental religious questions and individual Jewish identities.' The mission statement goes on to assert that the 'school

---

[18] This analysis is based on Sarason, *The Psychological Sense of Community*, and Sergiovanni, *Building Community in Schools*.   [19] Arnett, *Communication and Community*.

nurtures a Jewish community characterized by a shared tradition, a common dedication to social justice and a love of learning'.

In visiting Tikhon, one feels the palpable sense of community. Students interact easily with faculty, administrators, and each other in and out of the classroom. They seem at home in their space, using it respectfully yet fully. There are many informal areas where small groups of students catch up with each other, do schoolwork, or just hang out. Even during large events like school assemblies and fire drills, there is a sense of purpose, order, and belonging. Teachers often joke about Tikhon being their home, demanding as much of their time as it does of the students'. Seniors' statements in the graduation booklet often refer to 'community'—a term they associate with wonderful group experiences, deep friendships, relationships with teachers, and other heartfelt memories that would be expected of high school seniors. But community holds other meanings as well. Typical statements include: 'I have gained an understanding of how important it is for people to support each other.' 'Everybody has a different point of view . . . I think our class is especially strong because we created a community in sincerity and honesty.' 'The community has been hungry for questions and open to different beliefs, and I have had the opportunity to observe both my own and peers' and my evolving sense of curiosity.' And within such an environment, another writes, '[I] learned patience and understanding of different people's ideas and views . . . while still being able to solidify my own beliefs and opinion.'

Many of the ways Tikhon builds a sense of safety simultaneously foster commitment to the community: informal, experiential learning; close student–teacher relationships; opportunities for involvement; and being taken seriously. In addition, teachers and administrators openly describe how they do things differently 'for the sake of' the Tikhon community—or, to use the formulation of the first student quoted in this chapter, how they 'sacrifice' for the good of the whole. A Reform teacher, for example, explains to her classes how she adhered to a more stringent form of *kashrut* for the school barbecue than she would apply in her own home. An Orthodox teacher participates in Shabbatonim though he knows that many participants do things that he believes are prohibited on the sabbath and that he would not want his children (who accompany him) to do. Sensitivity to the needs of others shapes faculty decisions. Students not only hear this; they see the debates and compromises in action and hear about the anxieties and satisfactions that this approach brings.

Stories repeated at Tikhon about occasions in the school's past convey these ideas. Sometimes they celebrate flexibility—as, for example, when the headmaster changed his mind on a highly charged issue about the ways in which the school could support students' struggles with their sexual identities. Another example relates to issues of Jewish identity: a student who is Jewish by patrilineal descent complained that he was not counted in the minyanim—so Tikhon quickly added a liberal minyan in which he would be counted. This is consistent with the oft-repeated principle that if Tikhon admits students who are Jews by patrilineal descent and requires them to pray, it is obliged to provide a real prayer option for them if it is to remain true to its pluralist mission. As a community, Tikhon must make space for all its members.

Other school stories reinforce the responsibility of the group to devise solutions to community dilemmas. We repeatedly heard from students, faculty, and administrators about how, in its first year, Tikhon prepared for its very first Shabbaton. To paraphrase these accounts, 'It was three hours before sabbath and they still didn't know how they would handle sabbath observance and prayer. The headmaster put everyone in a room and said that they couldn't leave before they figured it out.' Another story is told about prayer. Tikhon usually conducts multiple services so that everyone's ritual practices can be honoured. After an emotional tour of Auschwitz, however, the students asked to pray together. Teachers recount with pride how students 'grappled' with the issues and found a way that worked for traditional as well as non-traditional students, although one student chose to pray on her own rather than in the non-egalitarian minyan. The story epitomizes Tikhon's faith that its students will be sensitive to context and will leave room to manœuvre where they can. These events, now part of the school's mythology, demonstrate that Tikhon 'trusts the process', to borrow a term from social work. Sometimes it provides structured settings, such as the 'de-bate midrash', to help its members decide what to do. At other times the arrangement is ad hoc. In both cases, Tikhon confers authority on the group to inform and sometimes make the decision, even though the group is working within a known framework, such as the expectation that there will be prayer or the need to respect sabbath observance. The process assumes that through deliberation the group will successfully craft an approach that meets everyone's needs.

When the process sidesteps the students, as with the occasional issues that are resolved at board level, the students react with chagrin, as the line from the student-written Purim *shpiel* (spoof) shows: 'Pluralism rules, subject to changes based on our whims.' This line captures two of Tikhon's beliefs: pluralism, with its appreciation for differences, does rule at Tikhon; and policies and practices do change, in fact rarely by whim, more often through a process bounded by values and expectations. It also suggests that it is not always clear who, in the end, actually decides what will happen. While the tacit assumption is that the final decision rests with the school head, himself an articulate and passionate advocate of pluralism, the process of determining what to do is often far more complex and nuanced than that.

Dealing with diversity in a community is not a challenge unique to Tikhon. Most other aspects of society, from government to families, confront the same task. Postmodern ideas about community suggest that under conditions of diversity communities must have two components: 'acceptance of otherness and cooperation within difference'.[20] Rather than imposing, however gently, the views of the dominant group and downplaying the needs of the others, people in the community are expected to cooperate with each other and find harmonious ways to deal with difference.[21] In this sense pluralism is 'active engagement with plurality'.[22] Tikhon is intentionally pluralist; it is organized in a way that supports—even favours—this kind of engagement. It tries to be an environment in which students, faculty, and non-teaching staff explore their differences while feeling part of the collective. It aspires to be a community in which people are united by being different, by learning to respect others' positions, and by working with all sorts of Jews. Perhaps this is what is meant by the phrase so often heard at Tikhon: 'We are serious Jews here.' As long as students agree with this claim on some level, they belong at Tikhon, and Tikhon can expect them to explore what this means to themselves and others. The developmental need of adolescents to work out who they are while they try on

[20] Furman, 'Postmodernism and Community', 57.
[21] See Beck, 'Complexity and Coherence', and Furman, 'Postmodernism and Community', for a full discussion of postmodern conceptions of community and their implications for education.
[22] Eck, 'The Challenge of Pluralism'.

identities and distinguish themselves by being distinctive is well served by Tikhon's brand of pluralism. The paradox is that diversity, often a centrifugal force, becomes the centripetal force. Diversity in Tikhon's pluralist environment unifies Tikhon's students, teachers, and administrators in a shared quest for self-definition, acceptance, challenge, debate, and generativity.

Bibliography

Arnett, R. C., *Communication and Community: Implications of Martin Buber's Dialogue* (Carbondale, Ill., 1986).

Beck, L. G., 'The Complexity and Coherence of Educational Communities: An Analysis of the Images that Reflect and Influence Scholarship and Practice', in G. C. Furman (ed.), *School as Community: From Promise to Practice* (Albany, NY, 2002), 23–49.

Eck, D. L., 'The Challenge of Pluralism', *Nieman Reports*, 47/2 (1993), <http://www.pluralism.org/research/articles/cop.php?from=articles_index>.

—— *A New Religious America: How a 'Christian Country' Has Become the World's Most Religiously Diverse Nation* (San Francisco, 2002).

Furman, G. C., 'Postmodernism and Community in Schools: Unraveling the Paradox', in G. C. Furman (ed.), *School as Community: From Promise to Practice* (Albany, NY, 2002), 51–75.

Hardy, H., 'Taking Pluralism Seriously', *Henry Hardy on Isaiah Berlin* (Oxford, 2003), <http://berlin.wolf.ox.ac.uk/writings_on_ib/hhonib/taking_pluralism_seriously.html>.

Sarason, S. B., *The Psychological Sense of Community* (San Francisco, 1974).

Seligman, A. B., 'Introduction', *Journal of Human Rights*, 2/1 (2003), 5–15.

—— *Modest Claims: Dialogues and Essays on Tolerance and Tradition* (South Bend, Ind., 2004).

Sergiovanni, T. J., *Building Community in Schools* (San Francisco, 1994).

Shevitz, S. L., *Protocol for Investigating the Culture of Jewish Day Schools*, pilot draft (Boston, 2005).

Shields, C. M., 'Learning from Educators', in G. C. Furman (ed.), *School as Community: From Promise to Practice* (Albany, NY, 2002).

Sizer, T. R., *Horace's Hope: What Works for the American High School* (New York, 1996).

Stone, S., 'Tolerance versus Pluralism in Judaism', *Journal of Human Rights*, 2/1 (2003), 105–19.

Tikhon, 'Self-Study', unpublished document prepared for school accreditation process (2005).

Walzer, M., *On Toleration* (New Haven, 1997).

Wasserfall, R., and S. L. Shevitz, 'The Language of Pluralism in a Jewish Day High School' working paper, Brandeis University, Waltham, Mass. (Sept. 2006).

Winnicott, D. W., *The Child, the Family and the Outside World* (Reading, Mass., 1987).

Wuthnow, R., *America and the Challenges of Religious Diversity* (Princeton, 2005).

Contributors

AMI BOUGANIM is an educator involved in research, planning, and professional development. He received his Ph.D. from the Hebrew University of Jerusalem and for the past seven years has served as director of the Research and Development Unit of the Department for Jewish Zionist Education of the Jewish Agency for Israel. He is active in the academic community exploring the nature of Jewish spirituality. He has recently published two books: *Jewish Peoplehood in an Arena of Globalization* (Heb., 2007) and *Walter Benjamin, le rêve de vivre* (2007).

ERIK H. COHEN is senior lecturer at the School of Education, Bar-Ilan University, Israel. His research interests include philosophy, cross-cultural studies, tourism, adolescence, educational evaluation, and data analysis. He has published four books and more than 100 scientific articles and reports. Two new books, *Identity, Values and Social Pursuits: Israeli Youth in the Year 2000* and *Youth Tourism to Israel: Educational Experiences of the Diaspora*, are to appear in 2008.

IRA DASHEVSKY has been at the forefront of dozens of national and international Jewish education programmes for Russian immigrants to Israel over the past 20 years. She currently works as chief trainer of teachers in the Israeli Ministry of Education's FSU Jewish Heritage school programmes and as a researcher in the field of Jewish education and conversion.

HOWARD DEITCHER currently serves as the director of the Melton Centre for Jewish Education at the Hebrew University of Jerusalem. Since 1981 he has been teaching courses at the Melton Centre in the following areas: the child's understanding of the biblical story, philosophy for children, and models of educational leadership. He continues to lecture on these topics around the world, and has also published several articles and edited two books.

JAY DEWEY, a founding headmaster of Schechter Regional High School, has pioneered leadership education for adolescents and is an active member of the Association for Leadership Education and the International Leadership Association.

JOSHUA ELKIN is the executive director of the Partnership for Excellence in Jewish Education (PEJE), Boston. Prior to the founding of PEJE he was head of the Solomon Schechter Day School of Greater Boston for twenty years. Rabbi Elkin was ordained at the Jewish Theological Seminary of America and went on to complete a doctorate at Columbia Teachers College in the field of curriculum and teaching.

YOEL FINKELMAN teaches Talmud and Jewish thought at Midreshet Lindenbaum, a women's *beit midrash* in Jerusalem, and is Co-ordinator of Research and Projects at ATID, a foundation that provides training and resources for Jewish educational leadership. He received his Ph.D. from the Department of Jewish Thought at the Hebrew University of Jerusalem.

ZVI GITELMAN is professor of political science and Tisch Professor of Judaic studies at the University of Michigan. He is the author or editor of fourteen books and many articles. His current research is on Jewish identities in Russia and Ukraine and on the Holocaust in the Soviet Union.

SCOTT J. GOLDBERG is director of the Institute for Educational Partnership and Applied Research and director of the Fanya Gottesfeld Heller Division of Doctoral Studies at Yeshiva University's Azrieli Graduate School. He holds a Ph.D. in applied psychology from New York University and an M.S.Ed. in special education from Bank Street College of Education.

ELLEN B. GOLDRING is a professor of education policy and leadership at Peabody College of Vanderbilt University. She received her Ph.D. from the University of Chicago. Before coming to Vanderbilt, Professor Goldring was chair of the Department of Educational Administration at Tel Aviv University, Israel. Her areas of expertise and research focus on improving schools, with particular attention to educational leadership, community, access, and equity in schools of choice.

YOSSI J. GOLDSTEIN is head of the long-term training and professional development academic unit in the Department of Jewish Zionist Education at the Jewish Agency, and a lecturer at the Melton Centre for Jewish Education, Hebrew University of Jerusalem. He gained his Ph.D. in contemporary Jewry from the Hebrew University of Jerusalem. His research concerns South American Jewry, Jewish communities in a globalized world, and Holocaust studies and Jewish education. He is co-editor of *Judaica Latinoamericana*, a research periodical focused on Latin American Jewry.

ELI KOHN is director of curriculum development projects at the Lookstein Center of Jewish Education in the Diaspora at Bar-Ilan University. In this role he specializes in the development of curriculum in Jewish studies for Diaspora Jewish day schools and has lectured to teachers in numerous countries. In 2007 he was appointed educational director of the Jewish Curriculum Partnership in the UK, a joint project of the United Synagogue and the UJIA.

JEFFREY S. KRESS is assistant professor and chair of the Department of Jewish Education at the Jewish Theological Seminary of America. Dr Kress received his doctorate in clinical psychology from Rutgers University and previously worked as a programme development specialist at the University of Medicine and Dentistry of New Jersey–Community Mental Health Center's Social Decision Making/Social Problem Solving programme.

BINYAMIN KROHN is a graduate of Yeshiva College and a rabbinical student at Yeshiva University's Rabbi Isaac Elchanan Theological Seminary (RIETS).

JON A. LEVISOHN is assistant professor of Jewish Education and assistant director of the Mandel Center for Studies in Jewish Education at Brandeis University. His research in philosophy of education and philosophy of Jewish education focuses on the teaching and learning of historical and sacred texts, and he directs a project that promotes research on the teaching of classical Jewish studies.

DEBORAH MEIER began her career as a kindergarten teacher in 1963. Subsequently she founded a network of public elementary and secondary schools in East Harlem and Boston. She was the recipient of the MacArthur Award for innovative practice in 1987. She is the author of many books, including *The Power of their Ideas*, and a board member and writer for *Dissent* and *The Nation* magazines. She is currently a senior scholar at New York University's Steinhardt School of Education.

HELENA MILLER is Director of Research and Evaluation at the UJIA, London. Previously she was Director of Education and Professional Development at Leo Baeck College, London. Her doctorate is in Jewish education and she has written widely on aspects of Jewish education in the UK.

CHRISTINE MÜLLER studied education at the University of Hamburg and Harvard University, with particular emphasis on history and religion. Her doctoral thesis, published in 2007, was concerned with the relevance of religion to Jewish pupils in Germany. Additional research areas are the scientific study of religion, empirical research, and inter-religious and intercultural education.

MICHAL MUSZKAT-BARKAN is the head of the Department of Education and Professional Development at Hebrew Union College, Jerusalem, and heads a specialization in pluralistic Jewish education as part of a joint MA programme of the Melton Centre for Jewish Education of the Hebrew University of Jerusalem. Her areas of research are mentoring, in-service teacher education, curriculum development, and ideologies in education.

ALEX POMSON is a senior lecturer at the Melton Centre for Jewish Education at the Hebrew University of Jerusalem. Formerly chair of the Network for Research in Jewish Education, he received his Ph.D. in religious education from the University of London. He is co-author with Randal Schnoor of *Back to School: Jewish Day School in the Lives of Adult Jews*.

JOSEPH REIMER is director of the Institute for Informal Jewish Education at Brandeis University, where he also serves as a professor in the Hornstein Program in Jewish Communal Service. He received his Ph.D. in developmental psychology from Harvard University and has worked in the field of Jewish education for more than twenty years. In 1997 his book *Succeeding at Jewish Education* was awarded the National Jewish Book Award for Jewish education.

RANDAL F. SCHNOOR is a sociologist specializing in contemporary Jewish life in North America. He teaches at York University in Toronto and has published on a wide range of subjects, including Jewish schools, hasidic Jews, and gay Jewish identity. He currently serves as president of the Association for Canadian Jewish Studies.

SUSAN L. SHEVITZ is an associate professor at Brandeis University, where she directed the Hornstein Program for Jewish Communal Service and is associated with the Mandel Center for Studies in Jewish Education. Her current work focuses on pluralism in Jewish education, organizational culture and change in Jewish schools and congregations, and educational and rabbinic leadership. She holds an Ed.D. from Harvard University in administration, planning, and social policy.

ASHER SHKEDI is head of the Teacher Education Department in the School of Education, and a faculty member of the Melton Centre for Jewish Education, at the Hebrew University of Jerusalem. His areas of specialist interest are teacher education, curriculum development, and qualitative research.

CLAIRE SMREKAR is associate professor of Public Policy and Education at Vanderbilt University and an investigator with the National Center on School Choice. She received her doctorate in educational administration and policy analysis from Stanford University in 1991. She conducts qualitative research studies related to the social context of education and public policy.

ELANA MARYLES SZTOKMAN lectures in education, gender, and society at the Schechter Institute for Jewish Studies and at the Efrata Teacher Training College for Religious Women, Jerusalem. She has taught and written widely on these subjects in Israel, Melbourne, and New York. Her doctorate examines the identity development of adolescent religious girls.

URIEL TA'IR is an expert on the development of school curricula and educational materials. He has a Ph.D. in the sociology of Judaism and education from the Melton Centre for Jewish Education at the Hebrew University of Jerusalem. He consults and provides in-service training and professional development seminars for educators in Israel and the former Soviet Union.

MICHAEL TURETSKY is a graduate of Yeshiva College and a rabbinical student at Yeshiva University's Rabbi Isaac Elchanan Theological Seminary (RIETS).

RAHEL WASSERFALL is senior research associate at Education Matters Inc. and scholar in residence with the Women's Studies Research Center at Brandeis University. She received her Ph.D. in anthropology from the Hebrew University of Jerusalem. Her work has focused on gender and ethnic studies in Israel and in the Jewish world, fields in which she has published widely.

Index